STUDENT ATLAS OF

World Politics

Ninth Edition

John L. Allen
University of Wyoming

Christopher J. Sutton
Western Illinois University

Connect
Learn
Succeed™

STUDENT ATLAS OF WORLD POLITICS, NINTH EDITION

Published by McGraw-Hill, a business unit of The McGraw-Hill Companies, Inc., 1221 Avenue of the Americas, New York, NY 10020. Copyright © 2011 by The McGraw-Hill Companies, Inc. All rights reserved. Previous edition(s) 2008, 2006, 2004. No part of this publication may be reproduced or distributed in any form or by any means, or stored in a database or retrieval system, without the prior written consent of The McGraw-Hill Companies, Inc., including, but not limited to, in any network or other electronic storage or transmission, or broadcast for distance learning.

Some ancillaries, including electronic and print components, may not be available to customers outside the United States.

Student Atlas® is a registered trademark of the McGraw-Hill Companies, Inc.
Student Atlas is published by the **Contemporary Learning Series** group within the McGraw-Hill Higher Education division.

This book is printed on acid-free paper.

1 2 3 4 5 6 7 8 9 0 WDQ/WDQ 1 0 9 8 7 6 5 4 3 2 1 0

MHID 0-07-340148-X
ISBN 978-0-07-340148-5
ISSN 1524-4556

Managing Editor: *Larry Loeppke*
Director, Specialized Production: *Faye Schilling*
Developmental Editor: *Debra A. Henricks*
Editorial Coordinator: *Mary Foust*
Editorial Assistant: *Cindy Hedley*
Production Service Assistant: *Rita Hingtgen*
Permissions Coordinator: *Shirley Lanners*
Senior Marketing Manager: *Julie Keck*
Senior Marketing Communications Specialist: *Mary Klein*
Marketing Coordinator: *Alice Link*
Senior Project Manager: *Jane Mohr*
Design Coordinator: *Brenda Rolwes*
Cover Designer: *Rick D. Noel*

Compositor: *Lachina Publishing Services*
Cartography: *Electronic Publishing Services Inc.*
Cover Image: © *Official White House Photo by Lawrence Jackson*

We would like to thank Digital Wisdom Incorporated for allowing us to use their Mountain High Maps cartography software. This software was used to create maps 139 and 140.

Library in Congress Cataloging-in-Publication Data
I. World politics—1991—Atlases. II. International relations—Atlases.
909.82

www.mhhe.com

A Note to the Student

International politics is a drama played out on a world stage. If the events of and subsequent to September 11, 2001—the worldwide "war on terrorism," the specific regional military actions in Afghanistan and Iraq, the resulting civil war in Iraq, the transit bombings in London and Madrid, the Hezbollah-Israeli conflict in Lebanon—have taught us anything, it is that the drama is very real and the stage is indeed a worldwide one. We are not isolated from events that transpire in other parts of the world; our boundaries do not make us secure; and we ignore the conditions of political, economic, cultural, and physical geography outside those boundaries at our great peril. The maps in this atlas serve as the stage settings for the various scenes in this drama; the data are the building materials from which the settings are created. Just as the stage setting helps bring to life and give meaning to the actions and words of a play, so can these maps and data enhance your understanding of the vast and complex drama of global politics, including the emergence of global terrorism as a political instrument. Use this atlas in conjunction with your text on international politics or international affairs. It will help you become more knowledgeable about this international stage as well as the actors.

The maps in the *Student Atlas of World Politics*, ninth edition, are designed to introduce you to the importance of the connections between geography and world politics. In many instances, the data has been used to produce the patterns that you see on the maps. But where the data may represent absolute values (at least as reported by individual countries), the maps are generalizations based on the data. The maps are not perfect representations of reality—no maps ever are—but they do represent "models," or approximations of the real world, that should aid in your understanding of the world drama. The profiles of the world's countries and dependencies provide a "snapshot" of key demographic, cultural and economic characteristics. Use these in concert with the maps to gain a better understanding of our world.

You will find your study of this atlas more productive in relation to your study of international politics if you examine the maps on the following pages in the context of five distinct analytical themes:

1. Location: Where Is It? This involves a focus on the precise location of places in both absolute terms (the latitude and longitude of a place) and in relative terms (the location of a place in relation to the location of other places). When you think of location, you should automatically think of both forms. Knowing something about absolute location will help you to understand a variety of features of physical geography, since such key elements are often so closely related to their position on the earth. But it is equally important to think of location in relative terms. The location of places in relation to other places is often more important in influencing social, economic, and cultural characteristics than are the factors of physical geography. The exchange of goods and services occurs between large cities at much different levels if those cities are near to each other than if they are thousands of miles apart.

2. Place: What Is It Like? This encompasses the political, economic, cultural, environmental, and other characteristics that give a place its identity. You should seek to understand the similarities and differences of places by exploring their basic characteristics. Why are some places with similar environmental characteristics so very different in economic, cultural, social, and political ways? Why are other places with such different environmental characteristics so seemingly alike in terms of their institutions, their economies, and their cultures? The place characteristics of parts of the world American students have known little about (like Afghanistan and Iraq) have now emerged as vital components of our necessary understanding of the implementation of military and political strategies.

3. Human/Environment Interactions: How Is the Landscape Shaped? This theme focuses on the ways in which people respond to and modify their environments. On the world stage, humans are not the only part of the action. The environment also plays a role in the drama of international politics. But the characteristics of the environment do not exert a controlling influence over human activities; they only provide a set of alternatives from which different cultures, in different times, make their choices. Observe the relationship between the basic elements of physical geography such as climate and terrain and the host of ways in which humans have used the land surfaces of the world. To know something of the relationship between people and the environment in the arid parts of the Old World is to begin to understand the nature of political, economic, and even religious conflicts between the inhabitants of those regions and others. The ongoing unrest in the Darfur region of Sudan or military conflict in the Congo Basin are at least partly attributable to the interaction between people and their environment.

4. Movement: How Do People Stay in Touch? This examines the transportation and communication systems that link people and places. Movement or "spatial interaction" is the chief mechanism for the spread of ideas and innovations from one place to another. It is spatial interaction that validates the old cliché, "the world is getting smaller." We find McDonald's restaurants in Tokyo and Honda automobiles in New York City because of spatial interaction. And the spread of global terrorism is, first and foremost, a process of spatial interaction. Advanced transportation and communication systems have transformed the

world into which your parents were born. And the world that greets your children will be very different from your world. None of this would happen without the force of movement or spatial interaction.

5. Regions: Worlds Within a World. This theme, perhaps the most important for this atlas, helps to organize knowledge about the land and its people. The world consists of a mosaic of "regions" or areas that are somehow different and distinctive from other areas. The region of Anglo-America (the United States and Canada) is, for example, different enough from the region of Western Europe that geographers clearly identify them as two unique and separate areas. Yet despite their differences, Anglo-Americans and Europeans share a number of similarities: common cultural backgrounds, comparable economic patterns, shared religious traditions, and even some shared physical environmental characteristics. Conversely, although the regions of Anglo-America and Southwestern Asia (the "Middle East") are also easily distinguished as distinctive units of the Earth's surface with some shared physical environmental characteristics, the inhabitants of these two regions have fewer similarities and more differences between them than is the case with Anglo-America and Western Europe: different cultural traditions, different institutions, different linguistic and religious patterns. An understanding of both the differences and similarities between regions like Anglo-America and Europe on the one hand, or Anglo-America and Southwest Asia on the other, will help you to understand much that has happened in the human past or that is currently transpiring in the world around you. At the very least, an understanding of regional similarities and differences will help you to interpret what you read on the front page of your daily newspaper or view on the evening news report on your television set.

Not all of these themes will be immediately apparent on each of the 140 maps in this atlas. But if you study the contents of *Student Atlas of World Politics*, ninth edition, along with the reading of your text and think about the five themes, maps and data and text will complement one another and improve your understanding of global politics. As Shakespeare said, "All the world's a stage." Your challenge is now to understand both the stage and the drama being played on it.

A Word about Data Sources

At the very outset of your study of this atlas, you should be aware of some limitations of the maps. In some instances, a map may have missing data. This may be the result of the failure of a country to report information to a central international body (like the United Nations or the World Bank). Alternatively, it may reflect shifts in political boundaries, internal or external conflicts, or changes in responsibility for reporting data have caused certain countries (for example, those countries that made up the former Yugoslavia) to delay their reports. Some reporting bodies include data for overseas dependencies of countries such as French Guiana (France), Greenland (Denmark) and the Falkland Islands (United Kingdom). Not all do, however, and in such situations, the maps include data for the governing country. It is always our wish to be as up-to-date as is possible; earlier editions of this atlas were lacking more data than this one and subsequent versions will have still more data, particularly on the southeastern European countries or on African and Asian nations that are just beginning to reach a point in their economic and political development where they can consistently report reliable information. In the meantime, as events continue to restructure our world, it's an exciting time to be a student of international events!

John L. Allen
University of Wyoming

Christopher J. Sutton
Western Illinois University

What's New in This Edition

The Student Atlas of World Politics, ninth edition, reflects current political, economic, demographic, and environmental change in every part of the world. This edition is the most comprehensive version yet of a book that has long been a standard in the field. Here, in one volume, are 126 thematic maps, and 14 reference maps rich in details of physical and political geography. A number of new thematic maps highlight the impact of demographic stresses on political stability at a global scale. New maps have also been added in the political, economic, demographic, and environmental sections of the atlas. The section on current hotspots or "flashpoints" includes a number of up-to-date areas of actual or potential conflict.

New to this edition are profiles of the world's countries and dependencies. The profiles contain key political, cultural, urban, and economic statistics.

This unique combination of maps and data makes the atlas an invaluable pedagogical tool. It also serves to introduce students to the five basic themes of spatial analysis:

- Location: Where is it?
- Place: What is it like?
- Human-Environment Interaction: How is the landscape shaped?
- Movement: How do people stay in touch?
- Regions: How is the surface of the world arranged and organized?

To further enhance the learning process, an introductory section on "How to Read an Atlas" helps students evaluate and interpret map data more easily.

Concise and affordable, this up-to-date *Student Atlas of World Politics,* ninth edition is suitable for any course dealing in current world affairs.

About the Authors

John L. Allen is emeritus professor of geography at both the University of Connecticut and the University of Wyoming. He taught at the University of Connecticut from 1967 to 2000, when he moved to the University of Wyoming as professor and chair of the Department of Geography. He retired from service at the University of Wyoming in 2007. He is a native of Wyoming and received his bachelor's degree (1963) in International Studies and his master's degree (1964) in Political Science from the University of Wyoming. In 1969 he received his Ph.D. in Geography from Clark University. His areas of special interest include human attitudes toward environmental systems, the impact of contemporary human activities on landscapes, and the historical geography of human-environment interactions. Dr. Allen is the author and editor of many scholarly books and articles as well as several other student atlases, including the best-selling *Student Atlas of World Geography*.

Christopher J. Sutton is professor of geography at Western Illinois University. Born in Virginia and raised in Illinois, he received his bachelor's degree (1988) and master's degree (1991) in Geography from Western Illinois University. In 1995 he earned his Ph.D. in Geography from the University of Denver. He is the author of numerous research articles and educational materials. A broadly trained geographer, his areas of interest include cartographic design, cultural geography, and urban transportation. After teaching at Northwestern State University of Louisiana for three years, Dr. Sutton returned to Western Illinois University in 1998, serving as chair of the Department of Geography from 2002 to 2007. Additionally, Dr. Sutton has served as president of the Illinois Geographical Society.

Acknowledgments

Robert Bednarz
Texas A & M University

Gerald E. Beller
West Virginia State College

Kenneth L. Conca
University of Maryland

Femi Ferreira
Hutchinson Community College

Paul B. Frederic
University of Maine at Farmington

James F. Fryman
University of Northern Iowa

Michael Gold-Biss
St. Cloud State University

Herbert E. Gooch III
California Lutheran University

Lloyd E. Hudman
Brigham Young University

Edward L. Jackiewicz
Miami University of Ohio

Artimus Keiffer
Indiana University–Purdue University at Indianapolis

Richard L. Krol
Kean College of New Jersey

Jeffrey S. Lantis
The College of Wooster

Robert Larson
Indiana State University

Mark Lowry II
United States Military Academy at West Point

Max Lu
Kansas State University

Taylor E. Mack
Mississippi State University

Kenneth C. Martis
West Virginia University

Calvin O. Masilela
West Virginia University

Patrick McGreevy
Clarion University

Tyrel G. Moore
University of North Carolina at Charlotte

David J. Nemeth
The University of Toledo

Emmett Panzella
Point Park College

Daniel S. Papp
University System of Georgia

Lance Robinson
United States Air Force Academy

Jefferson S. Rogers
University of Tennessee at Martin

Barbara J. Rusnak
United States Air Force Academy

Mark Simpson
University of Tennessee at Martin

Jutta Weldes
Kent State University

Table of Contents

A Note to the Student   iii
What's New in This Edition   v
About the Authors   vi
Acknowledgments   vi
Introduction: How to Read an Atlas   xi

Unit I   The Contemporary World   1

Map 1   World Political Boundaries   2
Map 2   World Climate Regions   4
Map 3   Vegetation Types   5
Map 4   Soil Orders   6
Map 5   World Topography   7
Map 6   Plate Tectonics   8
Map 7   World Ecological Regions   9
Map 8   World Natural Hazards   10
Map 9   Land Use Patterns of the World   11
Map 10   Urbanization   12
Map 11   Transportation Patterns   13
Map 12   World Population Density   14
Map 13   World Religions   15
Map 14   World Languages   16
Map 15   World External Migrations in Modern Times   17

Unit II   States: The Geography of Politics and Political Systems   19

Map 16   Political Boundary Types   20
Map 17   Political Systems   22
Map 18   The Emergence of the State   23
Map 19   Organized States and Chiefdoms, A.D. 1500   24
Map 20   European Colonialism, 1500–2000   25
Map 21   Federal and Unitary States   26
Map 22   Sovereign States: Duration of Independence   27
Map 23   The United Nations   28
Map 24   United Nations Regions and Sub-Regions   29
Map 25   Political Realms: Regional Changes, 1945–2003   30
Map 26   European Boundaries, 1914–1949   31
Map 27   An Age of Bipolarity: The Cold War ca. 1970   33
Map 28   Europe: Political Changes, 1989–2009   34
Map 29   The European Union, 2009   35
Map 30   The Geopolitical World at the Beginning of the Twenty-First Century   36
Map 31   Democracy on the Rise   37
Map 32   The Middle East: Territorial Changes, 1918–Present   38
Map 33   Africa: Colonialism to Independence   39
Map 34   South Africa: Black Homelands and Post-Apartheid Provinces   40
Map 35   Asia: Colonialism to Independence, 1930–2007   41
Map 36   Global Distribution of Minority Groups   42
Map 37   Linguistic Diversity   43

Map 38   International Conflicts in the Post–World War II World   44
Map 39   World Refugees: Country of Origin, 2009   46
Map 40   World Refugees: Host Country, 2009   47
Map 41   Internally Displaced Persons, 2009   48
Map 42   Post–Cold War International Alliances   49
Map 43   Flashpoints, 2009   50
Map 44   International Terrorist Incidents, 2000–2006   68
Map 45   The Political Geography of a Global Religion: The Islamic World   70
Map 46   Countries with Nuclear Weapons   71
Map 47   Size of Armed Forces   72
Map 48   Military Expenditures as a Percentage of Gross National Product   73
Map 49   Abuse of Public Trust   74
Map 50   The Perception of Corruption   75
Map 51   Political and Civil Liberties   76
Map 52   Human Rights Abuse   77
Map 53   Women's Rights   78
Map 54   Capital Punishment   79

Unit III   Population, Health, and Human Development   81

Map 55   Population Growth Rates   82
Map 56   Infant Mortality Rate   83
Map 57   Average Life Expectancy at Birth   84
Map 58   Population by Age Group   85
Map 59   International Migrant Populations   86
Map 60   Urban Population   87
Map 61   Illiteracy Rates   88
Map 62   Primary School Education   89
Map 63   The Gender Gap: Inequalities in Education and Employment   90
Map 64   The Global Security Threat of Infectious Diseases   91
Map 65   Global Scourges: Major Infectious Diseases   93
Map 66   Adult Incidence of HIV/AIDS, 2007   94
Map 67   Undernourished Populations   95
Map 68   The Index of Human Development   96
Map 69   Demographic Stress: The Youth Bulge   97
Map 70   Demographic Stress: Rapid Urban Growth   98
Map 71   Demographic Stress: Competition for Cropland   99
Map 72   Demographic Stress: Competition for Fresh Water   100
Map 73   Demographic Stress: Death in the Prime of Life   101
Map 74   Demographic Stress: Interactions of Demographic Stress Factors   102

Unit IV   The Global Economy   103

Map 75   Membership in the World Trade Organization   104
Map 76   Regional Trade Organizations   105
Map 77   Relative Wealth of Nations: Purchasing Power Parity   106
Map 78   Inequality of Income and Consumption   107
Map 79   The World's Poorest   108
Map 80   Economic Output Per Sector   109
Map 81   Employment by Economic Activity   110
Map 82   Unemployment by Economic Activity   111

Map 83   Central Government Expenditures Per Capita   112
Map 84   The Indebtedness of States   113
Map 85   Global Flows of Investment Capital   114
Map 86   Inflation Rates   115
Map 87   Dependence on Trade   116
Map 88   Trade with Neighboring Countries   117
Map 89   Aiding Economic Development   118
Map 90   The Cost of Consumption, 2008   119
Map 91   A Wired World: Internet Users   120
Map 92   The Rise of the Personal Computer   121
Map 93   Traditional Links: The Telephone   122

Unit V   Food and Energy   123

Map 94   The Value of Agriculture   124
Map 95   Average Daily Per Capita Supply of Calories (Kilocalories)   125
Map 96   Food Supply from Marine and Freshwater Systems   126
Map 97   Cropland Per Capita: Changes, 1996–2007   127
Map 98   World Pastureland, 2005   128
Map 99   Fertilizer Use, 2007   129
Map 100   Energy Production Per Capita   130
Map 101   Energy Consumption Per Capita   131
Map 102   Energy Dependency   132
Map 103   Flows of Oil   133

Unit VI   Environmental Conditions   135

Map 104   Deforestation and Desertification   136
Map 105   Forest Loss and Gain, 1990–2005   137
Map 106   Soil Degradation   138
Map 107   Global Air Pollution: Sources and Wind Currents   139
Map 108   The Acid Deposition Problem: Air, Water, Soil   140
Map 109   Pollution of the Oceans   141
Map 110   Water Resources: Availability of Renewable Water Per Capita   142
Map 111   Water Resources: Annual Withdrawal Per Capita   143
Map 112   Water Stress: Shortage, Abundance, and Population Density   144
Map 113   Carbon Dioxide Emissions   145
Map 114   Potential Global Temperature Change   146
Map 115   The Loss of Biodiversity: Globally Threatened Animal Species   147
Map 116   The Loss of Biodiversity: Globally Threatened Plant Species   148
Map 117   Global Hotspots of Biodiversity   149
Map 118   Degree of Human Disturbance   150
Map 119   The Green and Not-So-Green World   151

Unit VII   Regions of the World   153

Map 120   North America: Physical Features   154
Map 121   North America: Political Divisions   155
Map 122   North American Land Use   156
Map 123   South America: Physical Features   157
Map 124   South America: Political Divisions   158

Map 125   South American Land Use   159
Map 126   Europe: Physical Features   160
Map 127   Europe: Political Divisions   161
Map 128   European Land Use   162
Map 129   Asia: Physical Features   163
Map 130   Asia: Political Divisions   164
Map 131   Asian Land Use   165
Map 132   Africa: Physical Features   166
Map 133   Africa: Political Divisions   167
Map 134   African Land Use   168
Map 135   Australia and Oceania: Physical Features   169
Map 136   Australia and Oceania: Political Divisions   170
Map 137   Australia and Oceania: Land Use   171
Map 138   The World Ocean   172
Map 139   The Arctic   173
Map 140   Antarctica   173

Unit VIII   Country and Dependency Profiles   175

Unit IX   Geographic Index   203

Sources   221

Introduction: How to Read an Atlas

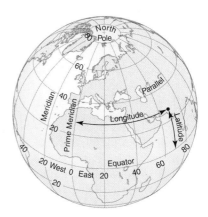

The Coordinate System

An atlas is a book containing maps which are "models" of the real world. By the term "model" we mean exactly what you think of when you think of a model: a representation of reality that is generalized, usually considerably smaller than the original, and with certain features emphasized, depending on the purpose of the model. A model of a car does not contain all of the parts of the original, but it may contain enough parts that it is recognizable as a car and can be used to study principles of automotive design or maintenance. A car model designed for racing, on the other hand, may contain fewer parts but would have the mobility of a real automobile. Car models come in a wide variety of types containing almost anything you can think of relative to automobiles that doesn't require the presence of a full-size car. Since geographers deal with the real world, virtually all of the printed or published studies of that world require models. Unlike a mechanic in an automotive shop, we can't roll our study subject into the shop, take it apart, and put it back together. We must use models. In other words, we must generalize our subject, and the way we do that is by using maps. Some maps are designed to show specific geographic phenomena, such as the climates of the world or the relative rates of population growth for the world's countries. We call these maps "thematic maps," and Units I through VI of this atlas contain maps of this type. Other maps are designed to show the geographic location of towns and cities and rivers and lakes and mountain ranges and so on. These are called "reference maps" and they make up many of the maps in Unit VII. All of these maps, whether thematic or reference, are models of the real world that selectively emphasize the features that we want to show on the map.

In order to read maps effectively—in other words, in order to understand the models of the world presented in the following pages—it is important for you to know certain things about maps: how they are made using what are called *projections;* how the level of mathematical proportion of the map or what geographers call *scale* affects what you see; and how geographers use *generalization* techniques such as simplification and symbols where it would be impossible to draw a small version of the real world feature. In this brief introduction, then, we'll explain to you three of the most important elements of map interpretation: projection, scale, and generalization.

Map Projections

Perhaps the most basic problem in *cartography,* or the art and science of map-making, is the fact that the subject of maps—the earth's surface—is what is called by mathematicians "a non-developable surface." Since the world is a sphere (or nearly so—it's actually slightly flattened at the poles and bulges a tiny bit at the equator), it is impossible to flatten out the world or any part of its curved surface without producing some kind of distortion. This "near sphere" is represented by a geographic grid or coordinate system of lines of latitude or *parallels* that run east and west and are used to measure distance north and south on the globe, and lines of longitude or *meridians* that run north and south and are used to measure distance east and west. All the lines of longitude are half circles of equal length and they all converge at the poles. These meridians are numbered from 0 degrees (Prime or Greenwich Meridian) east and west to 180 degrees. The meridian of 0 degrees and the meridian of 180 degrees are

halves of the same "great circle" or line representing a plane that bisects the globe into two equal hemispheres. All lines of longitude are halves of great circles. All the lines of latitude are complete circles that are parallel to one another and are spaced equidistant on the meridians. The circumference of these circles lessens as you move north or south from the equator. Parallels of latitude are numbered from 0 degrees at the equator north and south to 90 degrees at the North and South poles. The only line of latitude that is a great circle is the equator, which equally divides the world into a northern and southern hemisphere. In the real world, all these grid lines of latitude and longitude intersect at right angles. The problem for cartographers is to convert this spherical or curved grid into a geometrical shape that is "developable"; that is, it can be flattened (such as a cylinder or cone) or is already flat (a plane). The reason the results of the conversion process are called "projections" is that we imagine a world globe (or some part of it) that is made up of wires running north-south and east-west to represent the grid lines of latitude and longitude and other wires or even solid curved plates to represent the coastlines of continents or the continents themselves. We then imagine a light source at some location inside or outside the wire globe that can "project" or cast shadows of the wires representing grid lines onto a developable surface. Sometimes the basic geometric principles of projection may be modified by other mathematical principles to yield projections that are not truly geometric but have certain desirable features. We call these types of projections "arbitrary." The three most basic types of projections are named according to the type of developable surface: cylindrical, conic, or azimuthal (plane). Each type has certain characteristic features: they may be *equal area* projections in which the size of each area on the map is a direct proportional representation of that same area in the real world but shapes are distorted; they may be *conformal* projections in which area may be distorted but shapes are shown correctly; or they may be *compromise* projections in which both shape and area are distorted but the overall picture presented is fairly close to reality. It is important to remember that all maps distort the geographic grid and continental outlines in characteristic ways. The only representation of the world that does not distort either shape or area is a globe. You can see why we must use projections—can you imagine an atlas that you would have to carry back and forth across campus that would be made up entirely of globes?

Cylindrical Projections

Cylindrical projections are drawn as if the geographic grid were projected onto a cylinder. Cylindrical projections have the advantage of having all lines of latitude as true parallels or straight lines. This makes these projections quite useful for showing geographic relationships in which latitude or distance north-south is important (many physical features, such as climate, are influenced by latitude). Unfortunately, most cylindrical-type projections distort area significantly. One of the most famous is the Mercator projection. This projection makes areas disproportionately large as you move toward the pole, making Greenland, which is actually about one-seventh the size of South America, appear to be as large as the southern continent. But the Mercator projection has the quality of conformality: landmasses on the map are true in shape and thus all coastlines on the map intersect lines of latitude and longitude at the proper angles. This makes the Mercator projection, named after its inventor, a sixteenth-century Dutch cartographer, ideal for its original purpose as a tool for navigation—but not a good projection for attempting to show some geographical feature in which areal relationship is important. Unfortunately, the Mercator projection has often been used for wall maps for schoolrooms and the consequence is that generations of American school children have been "tricked" into thinking that Greenland is actually larger than South America. Much better cylindrical-type projections are those like the Robinson projection used in this atlas that is neither equal area nor conformal but a compromise that portrays the real world much as it actually looks, enough so that we can use it for areal comparisons.

Conic Projections

Conic projections are those that are imagined as being projected onto a cone that is tangent to the globe along a standard parallel, or a series of cones tangent along several parallels or even intersecting the globe. Conic projections usually show latitude as curved lines and longitude as straight lines. They are good projections for areas with north-south extent, like the map of Europe to the right, and may be either conformal, equal area, or compromise, depending on how they are constructed. Many of the regional maps in the last map section of this atlas are conic projections.

Conic Projection of Europe

Azimuthal Projections

Azimuthal projections are those that are imagined as being projected onto a plane or flat surface. They are named for one of their essential properties. An "azimuth" is a line of compass bearing, and azimuthal projections have the property of yielding true compass directions from the center of the map. This makes azimuthal maps useful for navigation purposes, particularly air navigation. But, because they distort area and shape so greatly, they are seldom used for maps designed to show geographic relationships. When they are used as illustrative rather than navigation maps, it is often in the "polar case" projection shown here where the plane has been made tangent to the globe at the North Pole.

The Mercator Projection

The Robinson Projection

 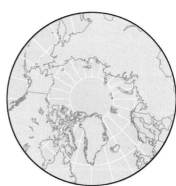

Azimuthal Projection of the North Polar Region

Map Scale

Since maps are models of the real world, it follows that they are not the same size as the real world or any portion of it. Every map, then, is subject to generalization, which is another way of saying that maps are drawn to certain scales. The term *scale* refers to the mathematical quality of *proportional representation,* and is expressed as a ratio between an area of the real world or the distance between places on the real world and the same area or distance on the map. We show map scale on maps in three different ways. Sometimes we simply use the proportion and write what is called a *natural scale* or representative fraction: for example, we might show on a map the mathematical proportion of 1:62,500. A map at this scale is one that is one sixty-two thousand five-hundredth the size of the same area in the real world. Other times we convert the proportion to a written description that approximates the relationship between distance on the map and distance in the real world. Since there are nearly 62,500 inches in a mile, we would refer to a map having a natural scale of 1:62,500 as having an "inch-mile" scale of "1 inch represents 1 mile." If we draw a line one inch long on this map, that line represents a distance of approximately one mile in the real world. Finally, we usually use a graphic or linear scale: a bar or line, often graduated into miles or kilometers, that shows graphically the proportional representation. A graphic scale for our 1:62,500 map might be about five inches long, divided into five equal units clearly labeled as "1 mile," "2 miles," and so on. Our examples here show all three kinds of scales.

The most important thing to keep in mind about scale, and the reason why knowing map scale is important to being able to read a map correctly, is the relationship between proportional representation and generalization. A map that fills a page but shows the whole world is much more highly generalized than a map that fills a page but shows a single city. On the world map, the city may appear as a dot. On the city map, streets and other features may be clearly seen. We call the first map, the world map, a *small-scale* map because the proportional representation is a small number. A page-size map showing the whole world may be drawn at a scale of 1:150,000,000. That is a very small number indeed—hence the term *small-scale* map even though the area shown is large. Conversely, the second map, a city map, may be drawn at a scale of 1:250,000. That is still a very small number but it is a great deal larger than 1:150,000,000! And so we'd refer to the city map as a *large scale* map, even though it shows only a small area. On our world map, geographical features are generalized greatly and many features can't even be shown at all. On the city map, much less generalization occurs—we can show specific features that we couldn't on the world map—but generalization still takes place. The general rule is that the smaller the map scale, the greater the degree of generalization; the larger the map scale, the less the degree of generalization. The only map that would not generalize would be a map at a scale of 1:1 and that map wouldn't be very handy to use. Examine the relationship between scale and generalization in the four maps on this page.

Map 1 Small Scale Map of the United States

Map 2 Map of the Northeast

Map 3 Map of Southeastern New England

Map 4 Large Scale Map of Boston, MA

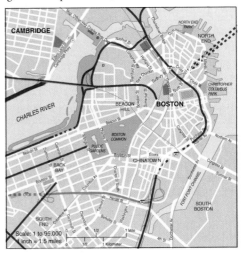

Generalization on Maps

A review of the four maps should give you some indication of how cartographers generalize on maps. One thing that you should have noticed is that the first map, that of the United States, is much simpler than the other three and that the level of *simplification* decreases with each map. When a cartographer simplifies map data, information that is not important for the purposes of the map is just left off. For example, on the first map the objective may have been to show cities over 1 million in population. To do that clearly and effectively, it is not necessary to show and label rivers and lakes. The map has been simplified by leaving those items out. The final map, on the other hand, is more complex and shows and labels geographic features that are important to the character of the city of Boston; therefore, the Charles River is clearly indicated on the map.

Another type of generalization is *classification*. Map 1 on the previous page shows cities over 1 million in population. Map 2 shows cities of several different sizes and a different symbol is used for each size classification or category. Many of the thematic maps used in this atlas rely on classification to show data. A thematic map showing population growth rates (see Map 55) will use different colors to show growth rates in different classification levels or what are sometimes called *class intervals*. Thus, there will be one color applied to all countries with population growth rates between 1.0 percent and 1.4 percent, another color applied to all countries with population growth rates between 1.5 percent and 2.1 percent, and so on. Classification is necessary because it is impossible to find enough symbols or colors to represent precise values. Classification may also be used for qualitative data, such as the national or regional origin of migrating populations. Cartographers show both quantitative and qualitative classification levels or class intervals in important sections of maps called *legends*. These legends, as in the samples that follow, make it possible for the reader of the map to interpret the patterns shown.

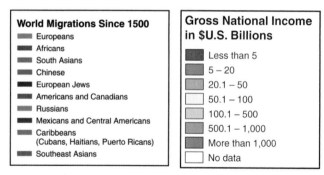

Map Legends

A third technique of generalization is *symbolization* and we've already noted several different kinds of symbols: those used to represent cities on the preceding maps, or the colors used to indicate population growth levels on Map 55. One general category of map symbols is quantitative in nature, and this category can further be divided into a number of different types. For example, the symbols showing city size on Maps 1 and 2 on the preceding page can be categorized as *ordinal* in that they show relative differences in quantities (the size of cities). A cartographer might also use lines of different widths to express the quantities of movement of people or goods between two or more points.

The color symbols used to show rates of population growth can be categorized as *interval* in that they express certain levels of a mathematical quantity (the percentage of population growth). Interval symbols are often used to show physical geographic characteristics such as inches of precipitation, degrees of temperature, or elevation above sea level. The following sample, for example, shows precipitation.

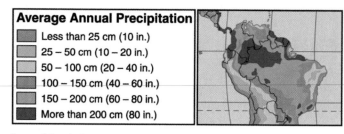

Interval Symbols

Still another type of mathematical symbolization is the *ratio* in which sets of mathematical quantities are compared: the number of persons per square mile (population density) or the growth in gross national product per capita (per person). The following map shows GDP change per capita.

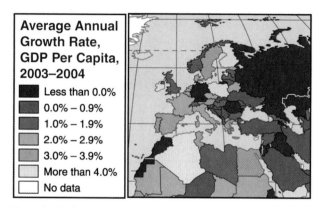

Ratio Symbols

Finally, there are a vast number of cartographic symbols that are not mathematical but show differences in the kind of information being portrayed. These symbols are called *nominal* and they range from the simplest differences such as land and water to more complex differences such as those between different types of vegetation. Shapes or patterns or colors or iconographic drawings may all be used as nominal symbols on maps.

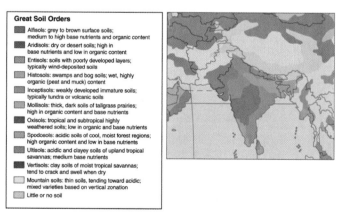

Nominal Symbols

The final technique of generalization is what cartographers refer to as *interpolation*. Here, the maker of a map may actually show more information on the map than is actually supplied by the original data. In understanding the process of interpolation it is necessary for you to visualize the quantitative data shown on maps as being three dimensional: *x* values provide geographic location along a north-south axis of the map; *y* values provide geographic location along the east-west axis of the map; and *z* values are those values of whatever data (for example, temperature) that are being shown on the map at specific points. We all can imagine a real three-dimensional surface in which the *x* and *y* values are directions and the *z* values are the heights of mountains and the depths of valleys. On a topographic map showing a real three-dimensional surface, contour lines are used to connect points of equal elevation above sea level. These contour lines are not measured directly; they are estimated by interpolation on the basis of the elevation points that are provided.

It is harder to imagine the statistical surface of a temperature map in which the *x* and *y* values are directions and the *z* values represent degrees of temperature at precise points. But that is just what cartographers do. And to obtain the values between two or more specific points where *z* values exist, they interpolate based on a class interval they have decided is appropriate and use *isolines* (which are statistical equivalents of a contour line) to show increases or decreases in value. The following diagram shows an example of an interpolation process. Occasionally interpolation is referred to as *induction*. By whatever name, it is one of the most difficult parts of the cartographic process.

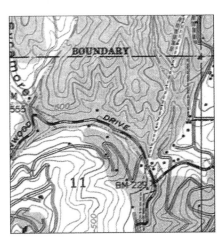

Interpolation

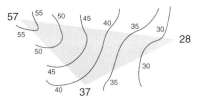

Degrees of Temperature (Celsius)
Interval = 5 degrees

And you thought all you had to do to read an atlas was look at the maps! You've now learned that it is a bit more involved than that. As you read and study this atlas, keep in mind the principles of projection and scale and generalization (including simplification, classification, symbolization, and interpolation) and you'll do just fine. Good luck and enjoy your study of the world of maps as well as maps of the world!

Unit I

The Contemporary World

Map 1   World Political Boundaries
Map 2   World Climate Regions
Map 3   Vegetation Types
Map 4   Soil Orders
Map 5   World Topography
Map 6   Plate Tectonics
Map 7   World Ecological Regions
Map 8   World Natural Hazards
Map 9   Land Use Patterns of the World
Map 10   Urbanization
Map 11   Transportation Patterns
Map 12   World Population Density
Map 13   World Religions
Map 14   World Languages
Map 15   World External Migrations in Modern Times

Map 1   World Political Boundaries

Scale: 1 to 125,000,000

Note: All world maps are Robinson projection.

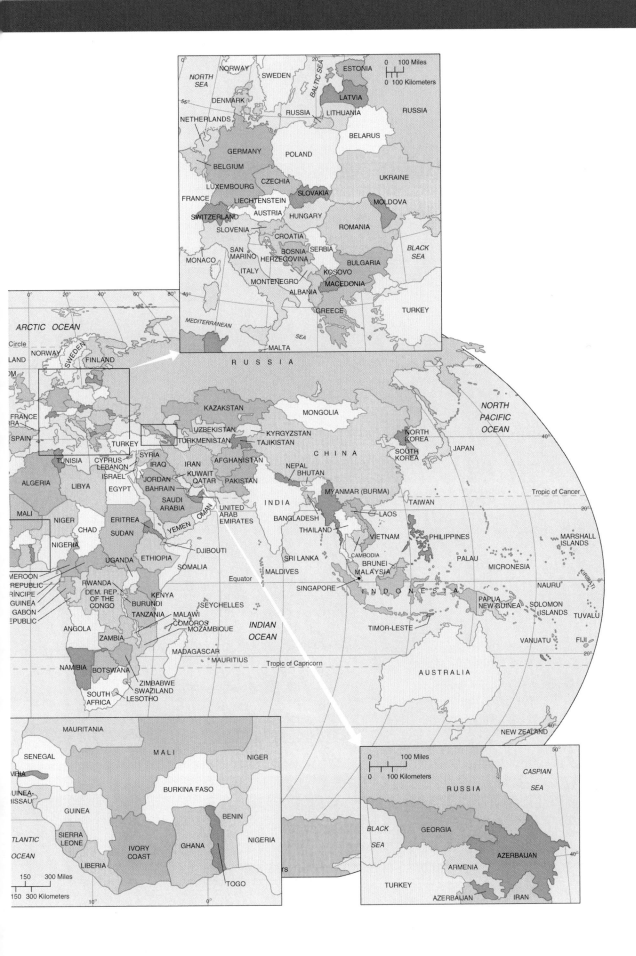

Map 2 World Climate Regions

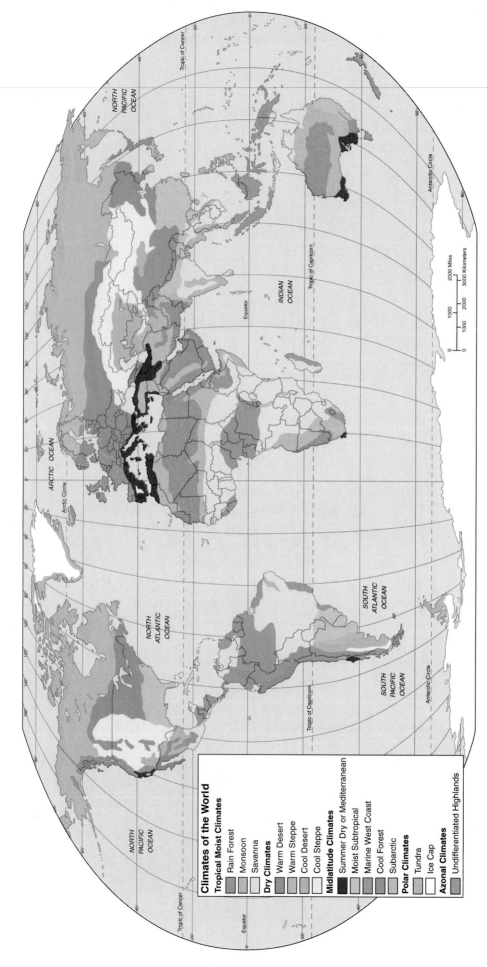

Climates of the World

Tropical Moist Climates
- Rain Forest
- Monsoon
- Savanna

Dry Climates
- Warm Desert
- Warm Steppe
- Cool Desert
- Cool Steppe

Midlatitude Climates
- Summer Dry or Mediterranean
- Moist Subtropical
- Marine West Coast
- Cool Forest
- Subarctic

Polar Climates
- Tundra
- Ice Cap

Azonal Climates
- Undifferentiated Highlands

Of the world's many physical geographic features, climate (the long-term average of such weather conditions as temperature and precipitation) is the most important. It is climate that conditions the types of natural vegetation patterns and the types of soil that will exist in an area. It is also climate that determines the availability of our most precious resource: water. From an economic standpoint, the world's most important activity is agriculture; no other element of physical geography is more important for agriculture than climate.

Map 3 Vegetation Types

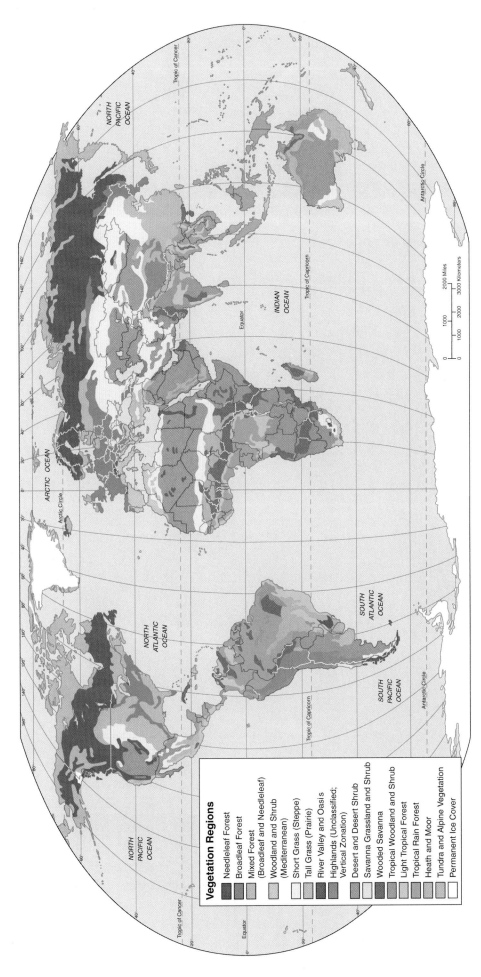

Vegetation Regions

- Needleleaf Forest
- Broadleaf Forest
- Mixed Forest (Broadleaf and Needleleaf)
- Woodland and Shrub (Mediterranean)
- Short Grass (Steppe)
- Tall Grass (Prairie)
- River Valley and Oasis
- Highlands (Unclassified; Vertical Zonation)
- Desert and Desert Shrub
- Savanna Grassland and Shrub
- Wooded Savanna
- Tropical Woodland and Shrub
- Light Tropical Forest
- Tropical Rain Forest
- Heath and Moor
- Tundra and Alpine Vegetation
- Permanent Ice Cover

Vegetation is the most visible consequence of the distribution of temperature and precipitation. The global pattern of vegetative types or "habitat classes" and the global pattern of climate are closely related and make up one of the great global spatial correlations. But not all vegetation types are the consequence of temperature and precipitation or other climatic variables. Many types of vegetation in many areas of the world are the consequence of human activities, particularly the grazing of domesticated livestock, burning, and forest clearance. This map shows the pattern of natural or "potential" vegetation, or vegetation as it might be expected to exist without significant human influences, rather than the actual vegetation that results from a combination of environmental and human factors.

Map 4   Soil Orders

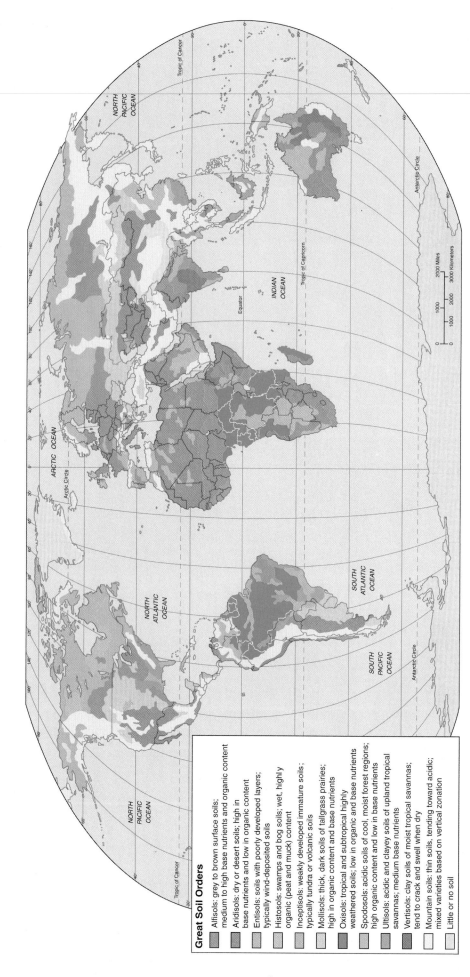

Great Soil Orders

- Alfisols: grey to brown surface soils; medium to high base nutrients and organic content
- Aridisols: dry or desert soils; high in base nutrients and low in organic content
- Entisols: soils with poorly developed layers; typically wind-deposited soils
- Histosols: swamps and bog soils; wet, highly organic (peat and muck) content
- Inceptisols: weakly developed immature soils; typically tundra or volcanic soils
- Mollisols: thick, dark soils of tallgrass prairies; high in organic content and base nutrients
- Oxisols: tropical and subtropical highly weathered soils; low in organic and base nutrients
- Spodosols: acidic soils of cool, moist forest regions; high organic content and low in base nutrients
- Ultisols: acidic and clayey soils of upland tropical savannas; medium base nutrients
- Vertisols: clay soils of moist tropical savannas; tend to crack and swell when dry
- Mountain soils: thin soils, tending toward acidic; mixed varieties based on vertical zonation
- Little or no soil

The characteristics of soil are one of the three primary physical geographic factors, along with climate and vegetation, that determine the habitability of regions for humans. In particular, soils influence the kinds of agricultural uses to which land is put. Since soils support the plants that are the primary producers of all food in the terrestrial food chain, their characteristics are crucial to the health and stability of ecosystems. Two types of soil are shown on this map: zonal soils, the characteristics of which are based on climatic patterns; and azonal soils, such as alluvial (water-deposited) or aeolian (wind-deposited) soils, the characteristics of which are derived from forces other than climate. However, many of the azonal soils, particularly those dependent upon drainage conditions, appear over areas too small to be readily shown on a map of this scale. Thus, almost none of the world's swamp or bog soils appear on this map.

Map 5 World Topography

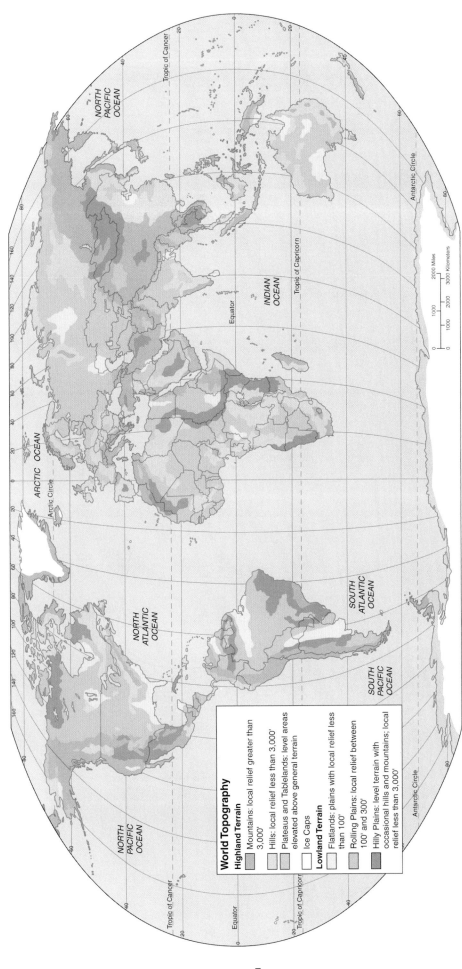

World Topography

Highland Terrain

- Mountains: local relief greater than 3,000'
- Hills: local relief less than 3,000'
- Plateaus and Tablelands: level areas elevated above general terrain
- Ice Caps

Lowland Terrain

- Flatlands: plains with local relief less than 100'
- Rolling Plains: local relief between 100' and 300'
- Hilly Plains: level terrain with occasional hills and mountains; local relief less than 3,000'

Second only to climate as a conditioner of human activity—particularly in agriculture and in the location of cities and industry—is topography or terrain. It is what we often call *landforms*. A comparison of this map with the map of land use (Map 9) will show that most of the world's productive agricultural zones are located in lowland regions. Where large regions of agricultural productivity are found, we tend to find urban concentrations and, with cities, industry. There is also a good spatial correlation between the map of landforms and the map showing the distribution and density of the human population (Map 12). Normally, the world's landforms shown on this map are the result of extremely gradual primary geologic activity, such as the long-term movement of crustal plates (sometimes called continental drift). This activity occurs over hundreds of millions of years. Also important is the more rapid (but still slow by human standards) geomorphological or erosional activity of water, wind, and glacial ice, and waves, tides, and currents. Some landforms may be produced by abrupt or cataclysmic events, such as a major volcanic eruption or a meteor strike, but these are relatively rare and their effects are usually too minor to show up on a map of this scale.

Map 6 Plate Tectonics

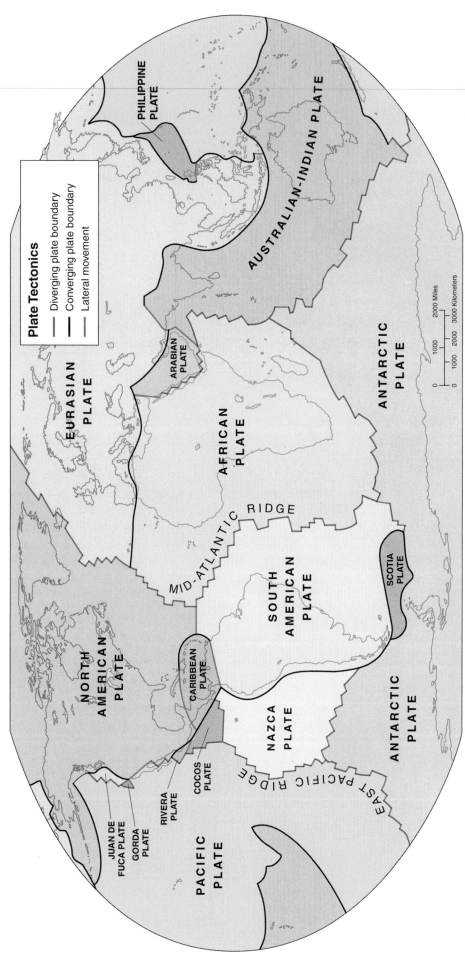

Plate Tectonics

— Diverging plate boundary
— Converging plate boundary
— Lateral movement

PHILIPPINE PLATE

AUSTRALIAN-INDIAN PLATE

EURASIAN PLATE

ARABIAN PLATE

AFRICAN PLATE

ANTARCTIC PLATE

MID-ATLANTIC RIDGE

NORTH AMERICAN PLATE

CARIBBEAN PLATE

SOUTH AMERICAN PLATE

SCOTIA PLATE

COCOS PLATE

JUAN DE FUCA PLATE

GORDA PLATE

RIVERA PLATE

NAZCA PLATE

ANTARCTIC PLATE

EAST PACIFIC RIDGE

PACIFIC PLATE

0   1000   2000 Miles
0   1000   2000   3000 Kilometers

An understanding of the forces that shape the primary features of the earth's surface—the continents and ocean basins—requires a view of the earth's crust as fragments or "lithospheric plates" that shift position relative to one another. There are three dominant types of plate movement: *convergence,* in which plates move together, compressing former ocean floor or continental rocks together to produce mountain ranges, or producing mountain ranges through volcanic activity if one plate slides beneath another; *divergence,* in which the plates move away from one another, producing rifts in the earth's crust through which molten material wells up to produce new sea floors and mid-oceanic ridges; and *lateral shift,* in which plates move horizontally relative to one another, causing significant earthquake activity. All the major forms of these types of shifts are extremely slow and take place over long periods of geologic time. The movement of crustal plates, or what is known as "plate tectonics," is responsible for the present shape and location of the continents but is also the driving force behind some much shorter-term earth phenomena like earthquakes and volcanoes.

Map 7 World Ecological Regions

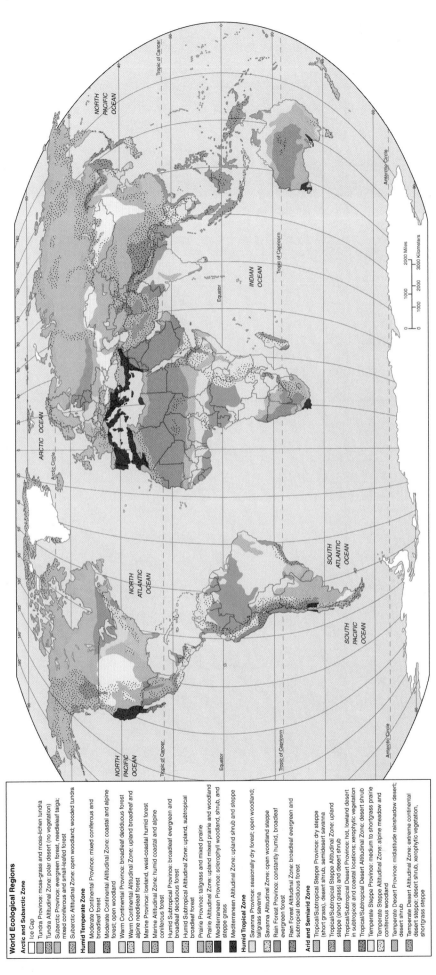

Ecology is the study of the relationships between living organisms and their environmental surroundings. Ecological regions are distinctive areas within which unique sets of organisms and environments are found. Within each ecological region, a particular combination of vegetation, wildlife, soil, water, climate, and terrain defines that region's habitability, or ability to support life, including human life. Like climate and landforms, ecological relationships are crucial to the existence of agriculture, the most basic of our economic activities, and important for many other kinds of economic activity as well.

Map 8 World Natural Hazards

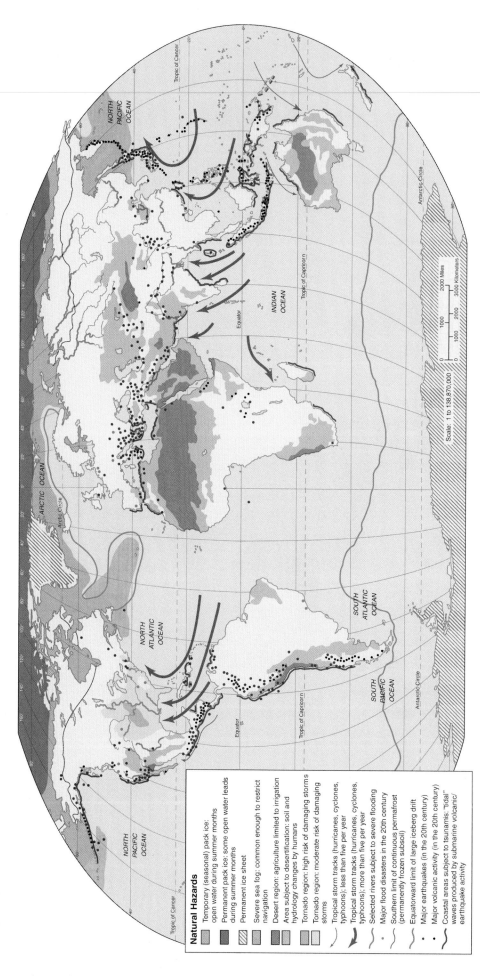

Natural Hazards

Temporary (seasonal) pack ice: open water during summer months

Permanent pack ice: some open water leads during summer months

Permanent ice sheet

Severe sea fog: common enough to restrict navigation

Desert region: agriculture limited to irrigation

Area subject to desertification: soil and hydrology changes by humans

Tornado region: high risk of damaging storms

Tornado region: moderate risk of damaging storms

Tropical storm tracks (hurricanes, cyclones, typhoons); less than five per year

Tropical storm tracks (hurricanes, cyclones, typhoons); more than five per year

Selected rivers subject to severe flooding

Major flood disasters in the 20th century

Southern limit of continuous permafrost (permanently frozen subsoil)

Equatorward limit of large iceberg drift

Major earthquakes (in the 20th century)

Major volcanic activity (in the 20th century)

Coastal areas subject to tsunamis: "tidal" waves produced by submarine volcanic/earthquake activity

Scale: 1 to 138,870,000

Unlike other elements of physical geography, natural hazards are unpredictable. There are certain regions, however, where the probability of the occurrence of a particular natural hazard is high. This map shows regions affected by major natural hazards at rates that are higher than the global norm. Persistent natural hazards may undermine the utility of an area for economic purposes. Some scholars suggest that regions of environmental instability may be regions of political instability as well.

-10-

Map **9** Land Use Patterns of the World

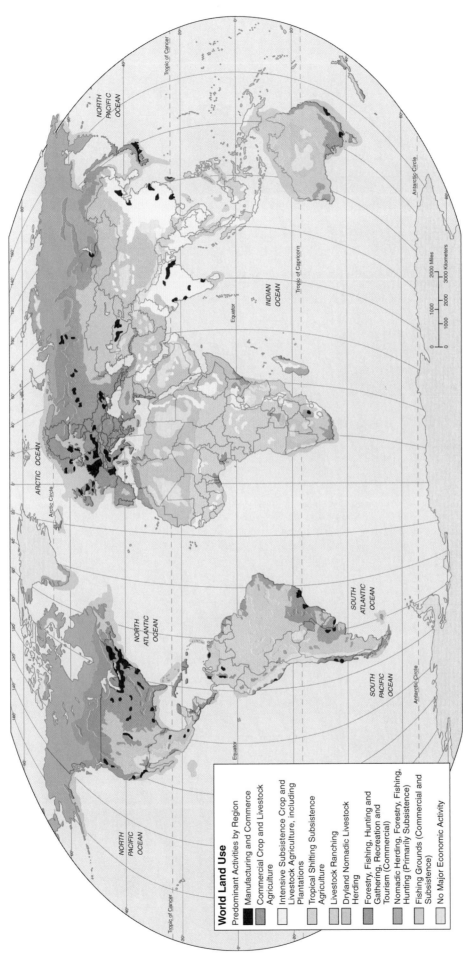

World Land Use

Predominant Activities by Region

- Manufacturing and Commerce
- Commercial Crop and Livestock Agriculture
- Intensive Subsistence Crop and Livestock Agriculture, including Plantations
- Tropical Shifting Subsistence Agriculture
- Livestock Ranching
- Dryland Nomadic Livestock Herding
- Forestry, Fishing, Hunting and Gathering, Recreation and Tourism (Commercial)
- Nomadic Herding, Forestry, Fishing, Hunting (Primarily Subsistence)
- Fishing Grounds (Commercial and Subsistence)
- No Major Economic Activity

Many of the major land use patterns of the world (such as urbanization, industry, and transportation) are relatively small in area and are not easily seen on maps, but the most important uses people make of the earth's surface have more far-reaching effects. This map illustrates, in particular, the variations in primary land uses (such as agriculture) for the entire world. Note the differences between land use patterns in the more developed countries of the middle latitude zones and the less developed countries of the tropics.

Map 10 Urbanization

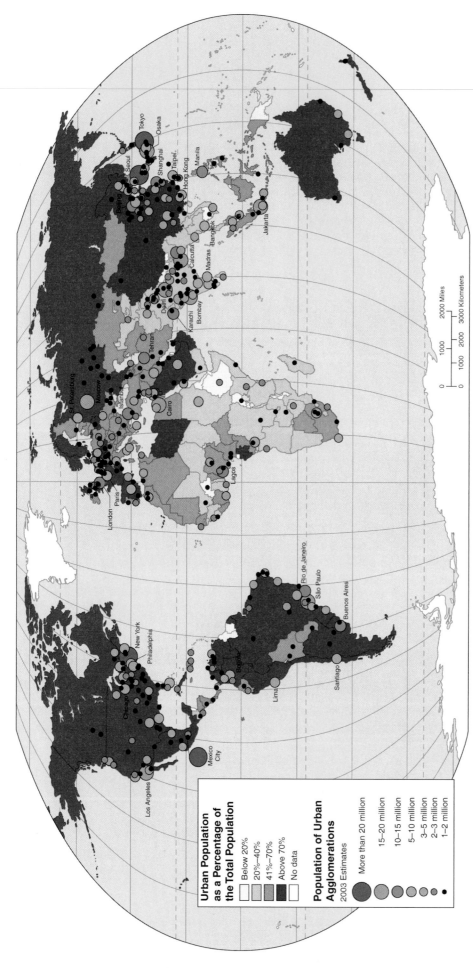

**Urban Population
as a Percentage of
the Total Population**

- Below 20%
- 20%–40%
- 41%–70%
- Above 70%
- No data

**Population of Urban
Agglomerations**

2003 Estimates

- More than 20 million
- 15–20 million
- 10–15 million
- 5–10 million
- 3–5 million
- 2–3 million
- 1–2 million

The degree to which a region's population is concentrated in urban areas is a major indicator of a number of things: the potential for environmental impact, the level of economic development, and the problems associated with human concentrations. Urban dwellers are rapidly becoming the norm among the world's people, and rates of urbanization are increasing worldwide, with the greatest increases in urbanization taking place in developing regions. Whether in developed or developing countries, those who live in cities exert an influence on the environment, politics, economics, and social systems that goes far beyond the confines of the city itself. Acting as the focal points for the flow of goods and

ideas, cities draw resources and people not just from their immediate hinterland but from the entire world. This process creates far-reaching impacts as resources are extracted, converted through industrial processes, and transported over great distances to metropolitan regions, and as ideas spread or *diffuse* along with the movements of people to cities and the flow of communication from them. The significance of urbanization can be most clearly seen, perhaps, in North America where, in spite of vast areas of relatively unpopulated land, well over 90 percent of the population lives in urban areas.

Map 11 Transportation Patterns

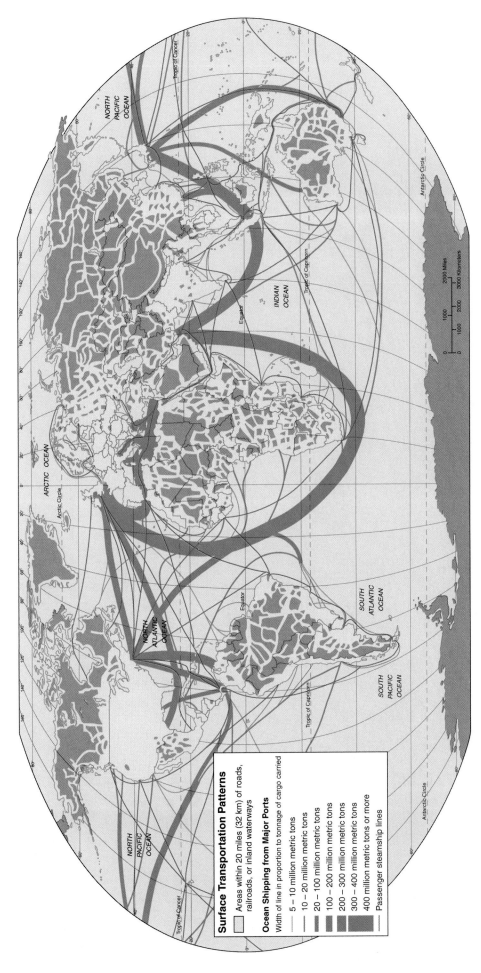

Surface Transportation Patterns

	Areas within 20 miles (32 km) of roads, railroads, or inland waterways

Ocean Shipping from Major Ports

Width of line in proportion to tonnage of cargo carried

5 – 10 million metric tons
10 – 20 million metric tons
20 – 100 million metric tons
100 – 200 million metric tons
200 – 300 million metric tons
300 – 400 million metric tons
400 million metric tons or more
Passenger steamship lines

As a form of land use, transportation is second only to agriculture in its coverage of the earth's surface and is one of the clearest examples in the human world of a *network*, a linked system of lines allowing flows from one place to another. The global transportation network and its related communication web are responsible for most of the *spatial interaction*, or movement of goods, people, and ideas between places. As the chief mechanism of spatial interaction, transportation is linked firmly with the concept of a shrinking world and the development of a global community and economy. Because transportation sys-

tems require significant modification of the earth's surface, transportation is also responsible for massive alterations in the quantity and quality of water, for major soil degradations and erosion, and (indirectly) for the air pollution that emanates from vehicles utilizing the transportation system. In addition, as improved transportation technology draws together places on the earth that were formerly remote, it allows people to impact environments a great distance away from where they live.

-13-

Map 12 World Population Density

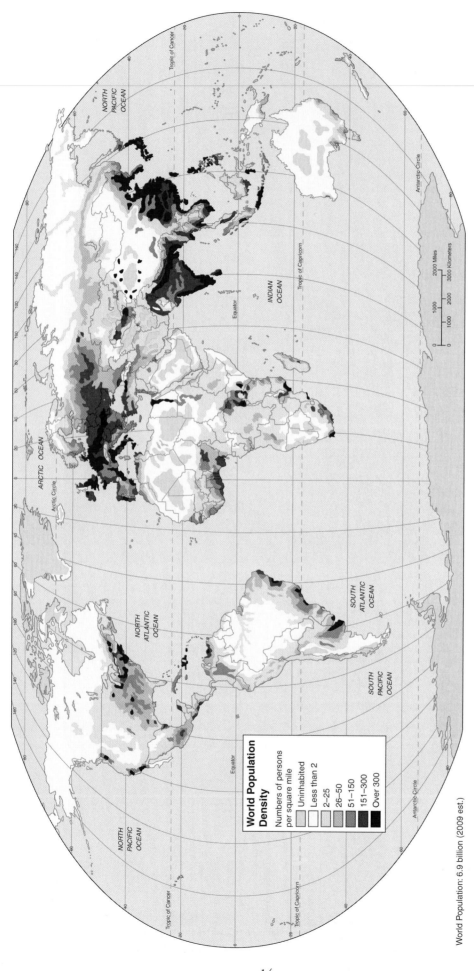

World Population: 6.9 billion (2009 est.)

World Population Density

Numbers of persons per square mile

- Uninhabited
- Less than 2
- 2–25
- 26–50
- 51–150
- 151–300
- Over 300

No feature of human activity is more reflective of environmental conditions than where people live. In the areas of densest populations, a mixture of natural and human factors has combined to allow maximum food production, maximum urbanization, and maximum centralization of economic activities. Three great concentrations of human population appear on the map—East Asia, South Asia, and Europe—with a fourth, lesser concentration in eastern North America. One of these great population clusters—South Asia—is still growing rapidly and is expected to become even more densely populated during the twenty-first century. The other concentrations are likely to remain about as they now appear. In Europe and North America, this is the result of economic development that has caused population growth to level off during the last century. In East Asia, population has also begun to grow more slowly. In the case of Japan and the Koreas, this is the consequence of economic development; in the case of China, it is the consequence of government intervention in the form of strict family planning. The areas of future high density (in addition to those already existing) are likely to be in Middle and South America and Africa, where population growth rates are well above the world average.

-14-

Map 13 World Religions

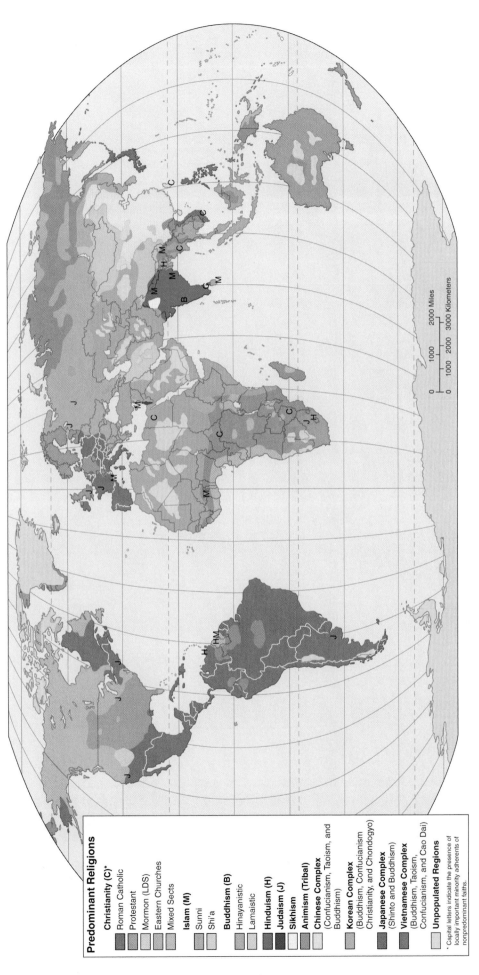

Predominant Religions

Christianity (C)*
- Roman Catholic
- Protestant
- Mormon (LDS)
- Eastern Churches
- Mixed Sects

Islam (M)
- Sunni
- Shi'a

Buddhism (B)
- Hinayanistic
- Lamaistic

Hinduism (H)

Judaism (J)

Sikhism

Animism (Tribal)

Chinese Complex
(Confucianism, Taoism, and Buddhism)

Korean Complex
(Buddhism, Confucianism Christianity, and Chondogyo)

Japanese Complex
(Shinto and Buddhism)

Vietnamese Complex
(Buddhism, Taoism, Confucianism, and Cao Dai)

Unpopulated Regions

* Capital letters indicate the presence of locally important minority adherents of nonpredominant faiths.

1000   2000 Miles

0   1000   2000   3000 Kilometers

Religious adherence is one of the fundamental defining characteristics of culture. A depiction of the spatial distribution of religions is, therefore, as close as we can come to a map of cultural patterns. More than just a set of behavioral patterns having to do with worship and ceremony, religion is an important conditioner of how people treat one another and the environments that they occupy. In many areas of the world, the ways in which people make a living, the patterns of occupation that they create on the land, and the impacts that they make on ecosystems are the direct consequence of their adherence to a religious faith.

-15-

Map 14 World Languages

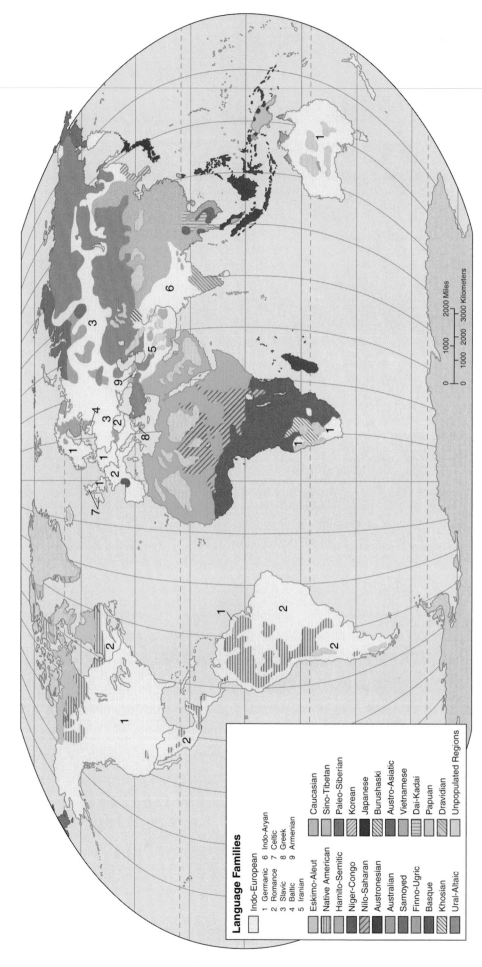

Language Families

☐ Indo-European	
1 Germanic	6 Indo-Aryan
2 Romance	7 Celtic
3 Slavic	8 Greek
4 Baltic	9 Armenian
5 Iranian	

Eskimo-Aleut	Caucasian
Native American	Sino-Tibetan
Hamito-Semitic	Paleo-Siberian
Niger-Congo	Korean
Nilo-Saharan	Japanese
Austronesian	Burushaski
Australian	Austro-Asiatic
Samoyed	Vietnamese
Finno-Ugric	Dai-Kadai
Basque	Papuan
Khosian	Dravidian
Ural-Altaic	Unpopulated Regions

0 1000 2000 Miles
0 1000 2000 3000 Kilometers

Like religion, language is an important defining characteristic of culture. It is perhaps the most durable of all cultural traits. Even after centuries of exposure to other languages or of conquest by speakers of other languages, the speakers of a specific tongue will often retain their own linguistic identity. As a geographic element, language helps us to locate areas of potential conflict, particularly in regions where two or more languages overlap.

Many, if not most, of the world's conflict zones are areas of linguistic diversity. Language also provides clues that enable us to chart the course of human migrations, as shown in the distribution of Indo-European languages. And it helps us to understand some of the reasons behind important historical events; linguistic identity differences played an important part in the disintegration of the Soviet Union.

Map 15 World External Migrations in Modern Times

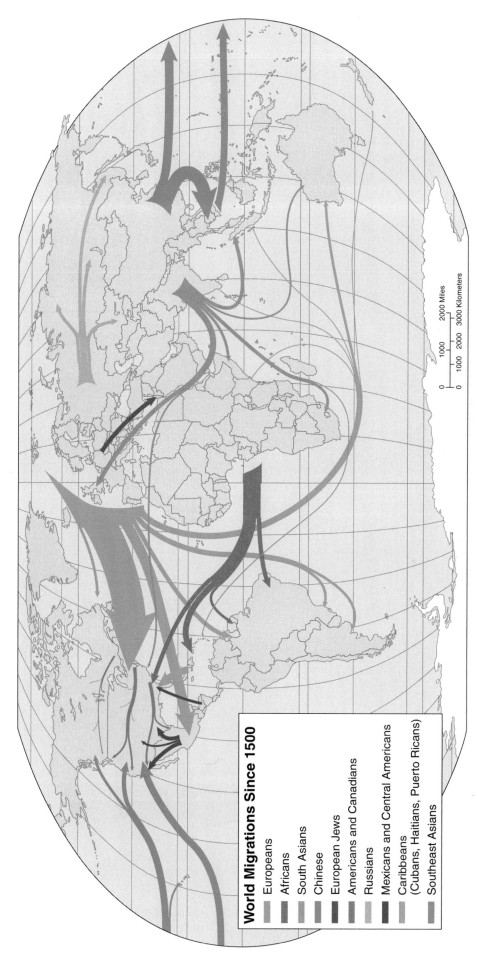

World Migrations Since 1500

- Europeans
- Africans
- South Asians
- Chinese
- European Jews
- Americans and Canadians
- Russians
- Mexicans and Central Americans
- Caribbeans (Cubans, Haitians, Puerto Ricans)
- Southeast Asians

0   1000   2000 Miles
0   1000   2000   3000 Kilometers

Migration has had a significant effect on world geography, contributing to cultural change and development, to the diffusion of ideas and innovations, and to the complex mixture of people and cultures found in the world today. Internal migration occurs within the boundaries of a country; external migration is movement from one country or region to another. Over the last 50 years, the most important migrations in the world have been internal, largely the rural-to-urban migration that has been responsible for the recent rise of global urbanization. Prior to the mid-twentieth century, three types of external migrations were most important: voluntary, most often in search of better eco-

nomic conditions and opportunities; involuntary or forced, involving people who have been driven from their homelands by war, political unrest, or environmental disasters, or who have been transported as slaves or prisoners; and imposed, not entirely forced but which conditions make highly advisable. Human migrations in recorded history have been responsible for major changes in the patterns of languages, religions, ethnic composition, and economies. Particularly during the last 500 years, migrations of both the voluntary and involuntary or forced type have literally reshaped the human face of the earth.

Unit II

States: The Geography of Politics and Political Systems

Map 16	Political Boundary Types
Map 17	Political Systems
Map 18	The Emergence of the State
Map 19	Organized States and Chiefdoms, A.D. 1500
Map 20	European Colonialism, 1500–2000
Map 21	Federal and Unitary States
Map 22	Sovereign States: Duration of Independence
Map 23	The United Nations
Map 24	United Nations Regions and Sub-Regions
Map 25	Political Realms: Regional Changes, 1945–2003
Map 26	European Boundaries, 1914–1949
Map 27	An Age of Bipolarity: The Cold War ca. 1970
Map 28	Europe: Political Changes, 1989–2009
Map 29	The European Union, 2009
Map 30	The Geopolitical World at the Beginning of the Twenty-First Century
Map 31	Democracy on the Rise
Map 32	The Middle East: Territorial Changes, 1918–Present
Map 33	Africa: Colonialism to Independence
Map 34	South Africa: Black Homelands and Post-Apartheid Provinces
Map 35	Asia: Colonialism to Independence, 1930–2007
Map 36	Global Distribution of Minority Groups
Map 37	Linguistic Diversity
Map 38	International Conflicts in the Post-World War II World
Map 39	World Refugees: Country of Origin, 2009
Map 40	World Refugees: Host Country, 2009
Map 41	Internally Displaced Persons, 2009
Map 42	Post-Cold War International Alliances
Map 43	Flashpoints, 2009
Map 44	International Terrorist Incidents, 2000–2006
Map 45	The Political Geography of a Global Religion: The Islamic World
Map 46	Countries with Nuclear Weapons
Map 47	Size of Armed Forces
Map 48	Military Expenditures as a Percentage of Gross National Product
Map 49	Abuse of Public Trust
Map 50	The Perception of Corruption
Map 51	Political and Civil Liberties
Map 52	Human Rights Abuse
Map 53	Women's Rights
Map 54	Capital Punishment

Map 16   Political Boundary Types

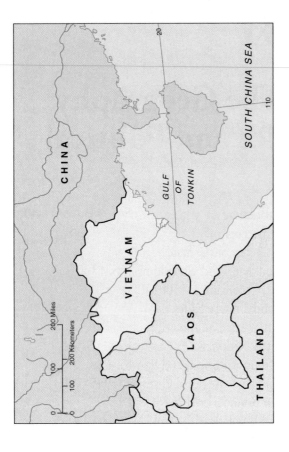

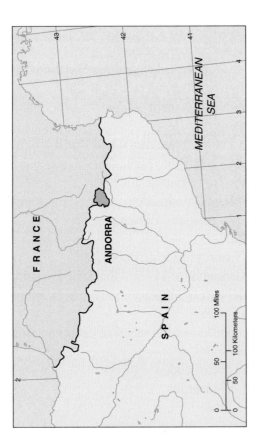

Antecedent: Antecedent boundaries are those that existed as part of the cultural landscape before the establishment of political territories. The boundary between Spain and France is the crest of the Pyrenees Mountains, long a cultural and linguistic barrier and a region of sparse population that is reflected on population density maps even at the world scale.

Subsequent: Subsequent boundaries are those that develop along with the cultural landscape of a region, part of a continuing evolution of political territory to match cultural region. The border region between Vietnam and China has developed over thousands of years of adjustment of territory between the two different cultural realms. Following the end of the Vietnam War, a lengthy border conflict between Vietnam and China suggests that the process is not yet completed.

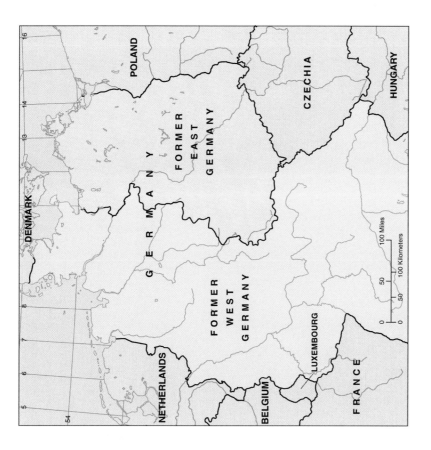

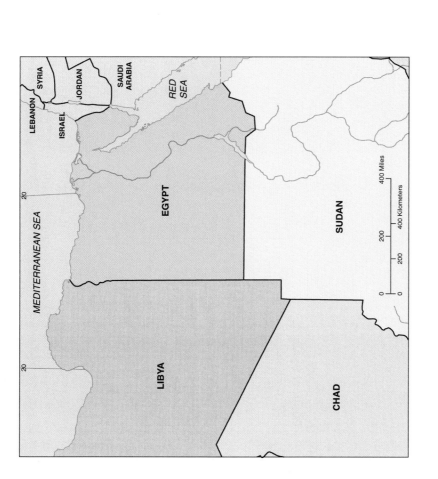

Relict: A relict boundary is like a relict landscape. The boundary between the former North and South Vietnam, along the Ben Hai River, is an example of a relict boundary. So too is the dividing line between the former Federal Republic of Germany (West Germany) and the German Democratic Republic (East Germany). Germany has been unified since 1990, with reintegration of the former Communist East into the West German economy happening progressively and more rapidly than expected. Nevertheless, there are still significant and visible differences between the urban German west and the rural east, between a progressive and modern economic landscape and a deteriorating one.

Superimposed: Superimposed boundaries are drawn arbitrarily across a uniform or homogenous cultural landscape. These boundaries often result from the occupation of territory by an expansive settlement process (see, for example, many of the boundaries of the western states in the United States) or from the process whereby colonial powers divided territory to suit their own needs rather than those of the indigenous population. The borders of Egypt, Libya, and Sudan meet in the center of a uniform cultural and physical region, artificially dividing what from a natural and human perspective is unified.

Map 17 Political Systems

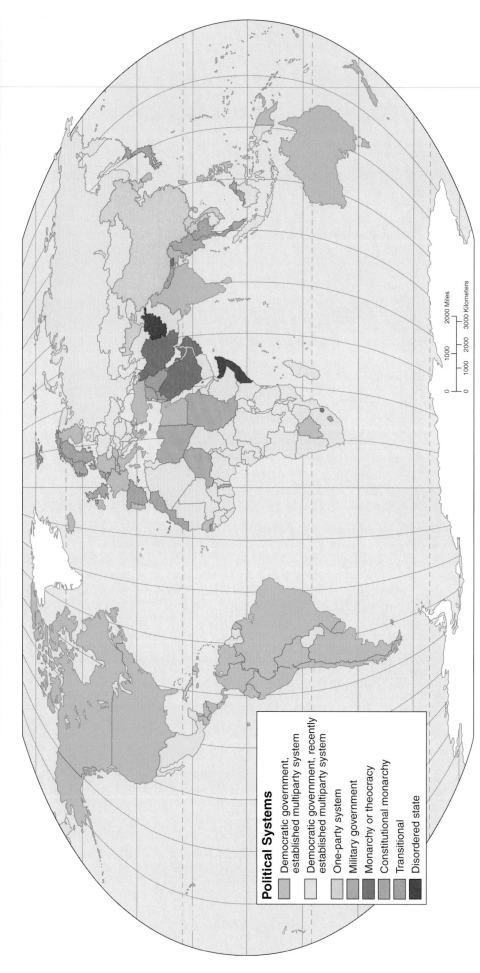

Political Systems

- Democratic government, established multiparty system
- Democratic government, recently established multiparty system
- One-party system
- Military government
- Monarchy or theocracy
- Constitutional monarchy
- Transitional
- Disordered state

0   1000   2000 Miles
0   1000   2000   3000 Kilometers

World political systems have changed dramatically during the last decade and may change even more in the future. The categories of political systems shown on the map are subject to some interpretation: established multiparty democracies are those in which elections by secret ballot with adult suffrage are and have been long-term features of the political landscape; recently established multiparty democracies are those in which the characteristic features of multiparty democracies have only recently emerged. The former Soviet satellites of eastern Europe and the republics that formerly constituted the USSR are in this category; so are states in emerging regions that are beginning to throw off the single-party rule that often followed the violent upheavals of the immediate postcolonial governmental transitions. The other categories are more or less obvious. One-party systems are states where single-

party rule is constitutionally guaranteed or where a one-party regime is a fact of political life. Monarchies are countries with heads of state who are members of a royal family. In a constitutional monarchy, such as the U.K. and the Netherlands, the monarchs are titular heads of state only. Theocracies are countries in which rule is within the hands of a priestly or clerical class; today, this means primarily fundamentalist Islamic countries such as Iran. Military governments are frequently organized around a junta that has seized control of the government from civil authority; such states are often technically transitional, that is, the military claims that it will return the reins of government to civil authority when order is restored. Finally, disordered states are countries so beset by civil war or widespread ethnic conflict that no organized government can be said to exist within them.

-22-

Map 18   The Emergence of the State

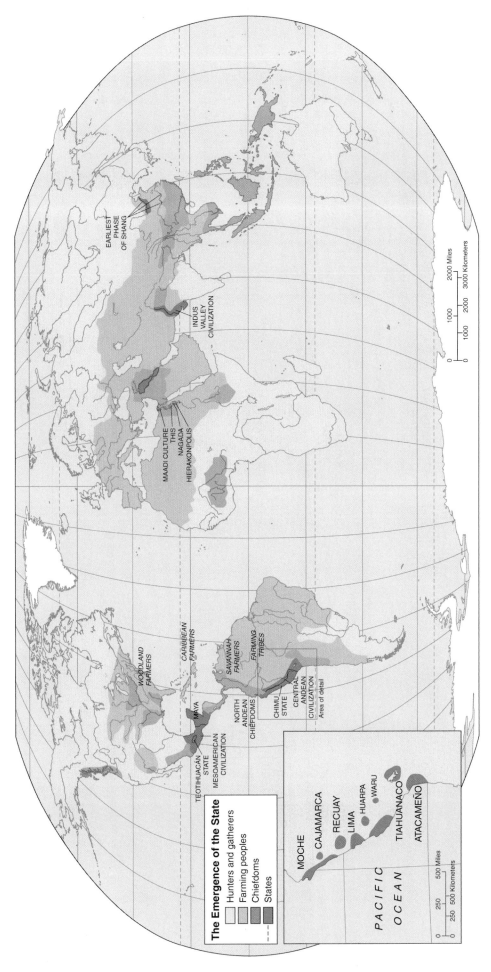

The Emergence of the State

- Hunters and gatherers
- Farming peoples
- Chiefdoms
- States

EARLIEST PHASE OF SHANG

INDUS VALLEY CIVILIZATION

MAADI CULTURE
THIS
NAGADA
HIERAKONPOLIS

WOODLAND FARMERS

CARIBBEAN FARMERS

SAVANNAH FARMERS

FARMING TRIBES

MAYA

TEOTIHUACÁN STATE
MESOAMERICAN CIVILIZATION

NORTH ANDEAN CHIEFDOMS

CHIMU STATE

CENTRAL ANDEAN CIVILIZATION

Area of detail

MOCHE
CAJAMARCA
RECUAY
LIMA
HUARPA
WARU
TIAHUANACO
ATACAMEÑO

PACIFIC OCEAN

0   250   500 Miles
0   250   500 Kilometers

0   1000   2000   2000 Miles
0   1000   2000   3000 Kilometers

Agriculture is the basis of the development of the state, a form of complex political organization. Geographers and anthropologists believe that agriculture allowed for larger concentrations of population. Farmers do not need to be as mobile as hunters and gatherers to make a living, and people living sedentarily can have larger families than those constantly on the move. Ideas about access to land and ownership also change as people develop the social and political hierarchies that come with the transition from a hunting-gathering society to an agricultural one. Social stratification based on wealth and power creates different classes or groups, some of whom no longer work the land. An agricultural surplus supports those who perform other functions for society, such as artisans and craftspeople, soldiers and police, priests and kings. Thus, over time, egalitarian hunters and gatherers shifted to state-level societies in some parts of the world. The first true states are shown in the rust-colored areas of this map.

-23-

Map 19   Organized States and Chiefdoms, A.D. 1500

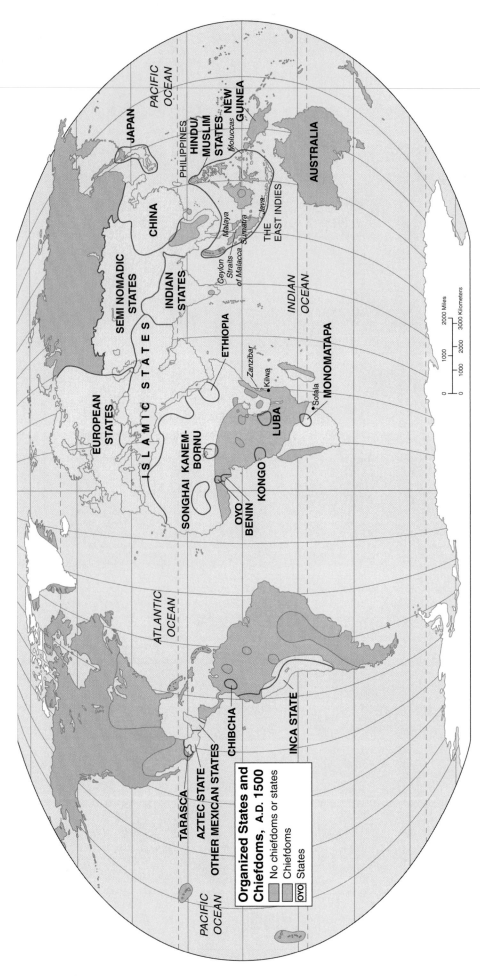

Organized States and Chiefdoms, A.D. 1500

- No chiefdoms or states
- Chiefdoms
- OYO States

As Europeans began to expand outward through exploration and settlement from the late fifteenth to the eighteenth centuries, it was inevitable that they would find the complex political organizations of chiefdoms and states in many different parts of the world. Both chiefdoms and states are large-scale forms of political organization in which some people have privileged access to land, power, wealth, and prestige. Chiefdoms are kin-based societies in which wealth is distributed from upper to lower classes. States are organized on the basis of socioeconomic classes, headed by a centralized government that is led by an elite. States in non-European areas included, just as they did in Europe, full-time bureaucracies and specialized subsystems for such activities as military action, taxation, operation of state religions, and social control. In many of the colonial regions of the world after the fifteenth century, Europeans actually found it easier to gain control of organized states and chiefdoms because those populations were already accustomed to some form of institutionalized central control.

Map 20   European Colonialism, 1500–2000

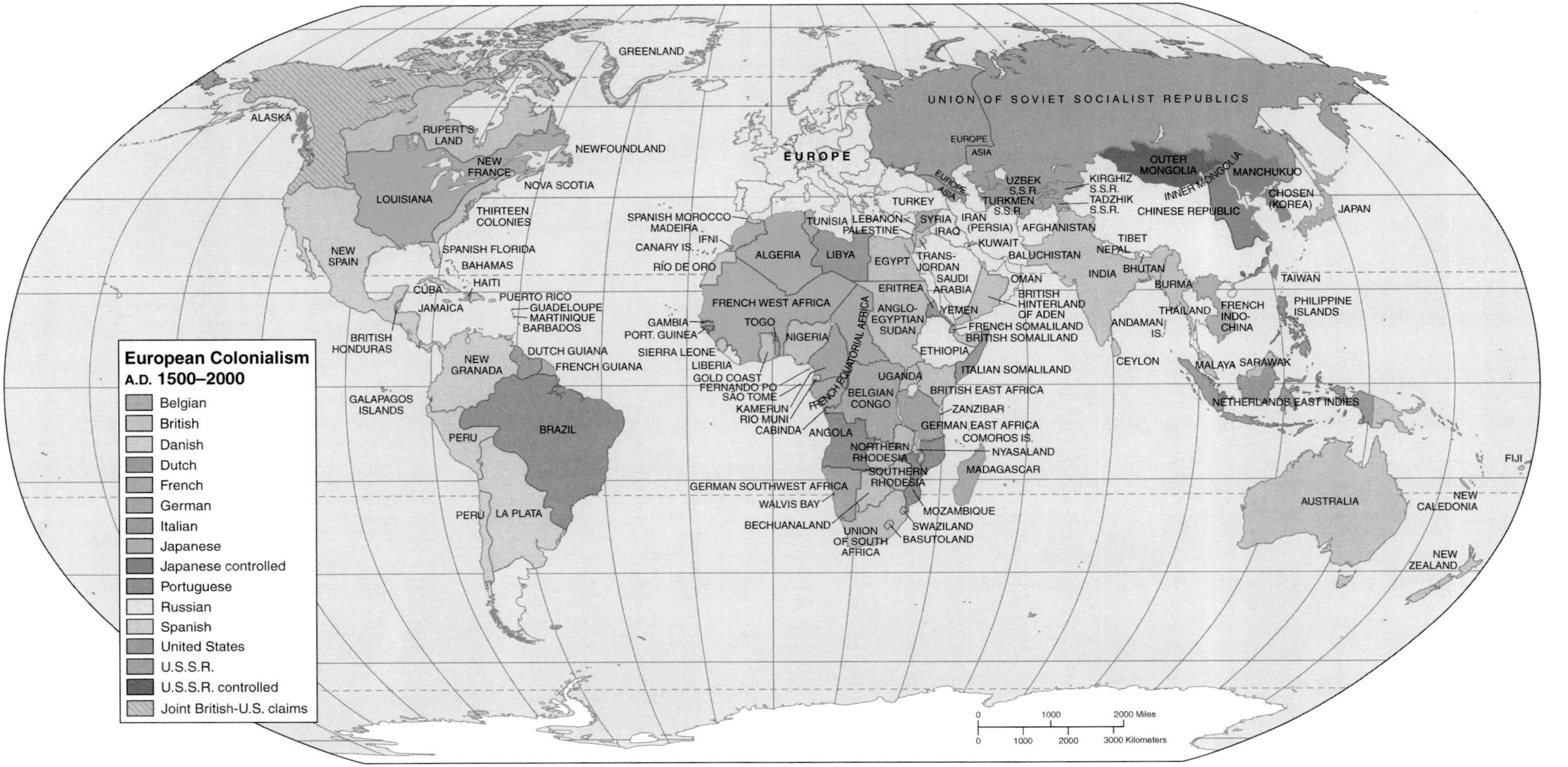

European nations have controlled many parts of the world during the last 500 years. The period of European expansion began when European explorers sailed the oceans in search of new trading routes and ended after World War II when many colonies in Africa and Asia gained independence. The process of colonization was very complex but normally involved the acquisition, extraction, or production of raw materials (including minerals, forest products, products from the sea, agricultural products, and animal furs/pelts) from the areas being controlled by the European colonial power in exchange for

items of European manufacture. The concept of colonial dependency implied an economic structure in which the European country obtained raw materials from the colonial country in exchange for those manufactured items upon which populations in the colonial areas quickly came to depend. The colors on this map represent colonial control at its maximum extent and do not take into account shifting colonial control. In North America, for example, "New France" became British territory and "Louisiana" became Spanish territory after the Seven Years' (French and Indian) War.

European Colonialism A.D. 1500–2000

- Belgian
- British
- Danish
- Dutch
- French
- German
- Italian
- Japanese
- Japanese controlled
- Portuguese
- Russian
- Spanish
- United States
- U.S.S.R.
- U.S.S.R. controlled
- Joint British-U.S. claims

Map 21 Federal and Unitary States

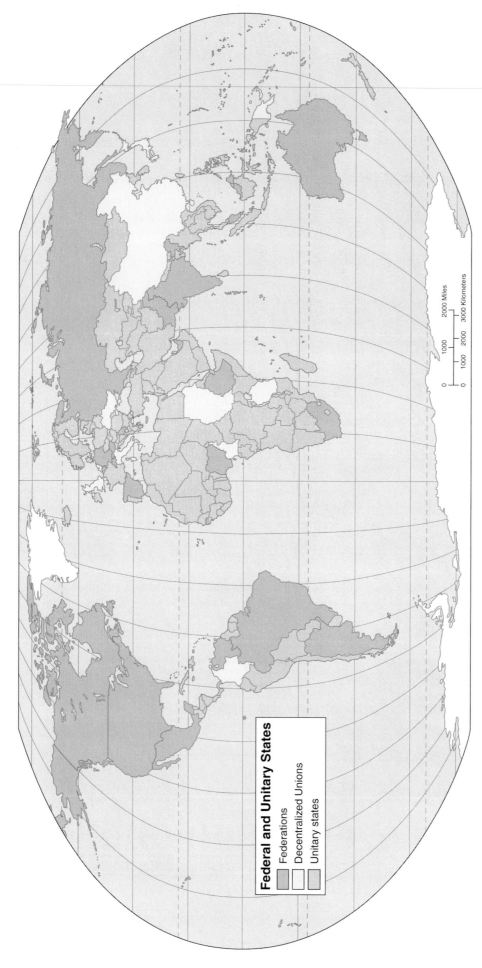

Federal and Unitary States
- Federations
- Decentralized Unions
- Unitary states

0	1000	2000 Miles
0	1000	2000	3000 Kilometers

Countries vary greatly in the degree to which the national government makes all decisions or certain matters are left to governments of subdivisions. In federal states, each subdivision (state, province, and so on) has its own capital, and certain aspects of life are left to the subdivisions to manage. For example, in the United States, motor vehicle and marriage/divorce laws are powers for states rather than the federal government. Federal systems are suited to large countries with a diversity of cultures. They easily accommodate new territorial subdivisions, which can take their places among those already a part of the country. In unitary states, major decisions come from the national capital, and subdivisions administer those decisions. Unitary systems are best suited to small states with relatively homogeneous ethnic and cultural makeup. Some countries, the decentralized unions, have a mix of systems—for example, provinces that follow the dictates of the central government but other subdivisions that have more autonomy.

Map 22   Sovereign States: Duration of Independence

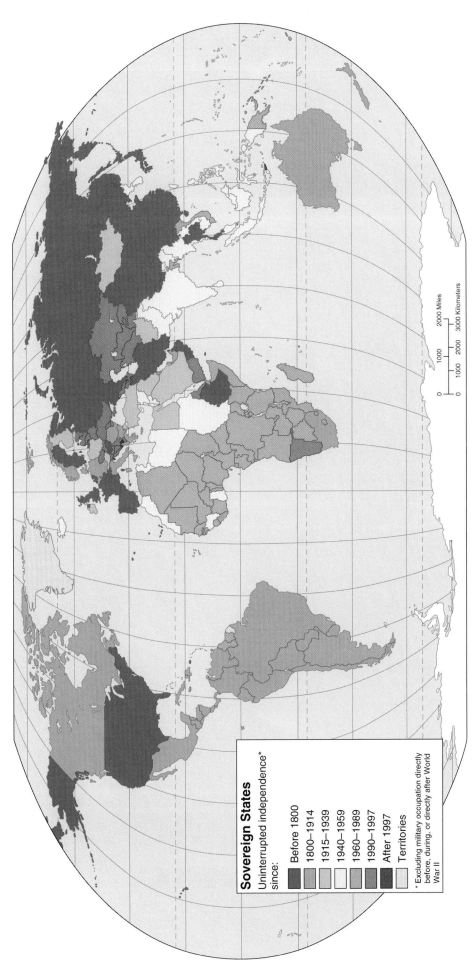

Sovereign States

Uninterrupted independence*
since:

- Before 1800
- 1800–1914
- 1915–1939
- 1940–1959
- 1960–1989
- 1990–1997
- After 1997
- Territories

* Excluding military occupation directly before, during, or directly after World War II

0   1000   2000 Miles
0   1000   2000   3000 Kilometers

Most countries of the modern world, including such major states as Germany and Italy, became independent after the beginning of the nineteenth century. Of the world's current countries, only 27 were independent in 1800. Following 1800, there have been five great periods of national independence. During the first of these (1800–1914), most of the mainland countries of the Americas achieved independence. During the second period (1915–1939), the countries of Eastern Europe emerged as independent entities. The third period (1940–1959) includes World War II and the years that followed, when independence for African and Asian nations that had been under control of colonial powers first began to occur. During the fourth period (1960–1989), independence came to the remainder of the colonial African and Asian nations, as well as to former colonies in the Caribbean and the South Pacific. More than half of the world's countries came into being as independent political entities during this period. During the last decade of the twentieth century, the breakup of the existing states of the Soviet Union, Yugoslavia, and Czechoslovakia created 22 countries where only 3 had existed before. Since 2000, Timor-Leste (East Timor), Montenegro, and Kosovo have joined the ranks of the independent states. While Kosovo's sovereignty has been recognized by the United States, fewer than half of the world's states have followed suit and Kosovo does not have membership in the United Nations.

Map **23** The United Nations

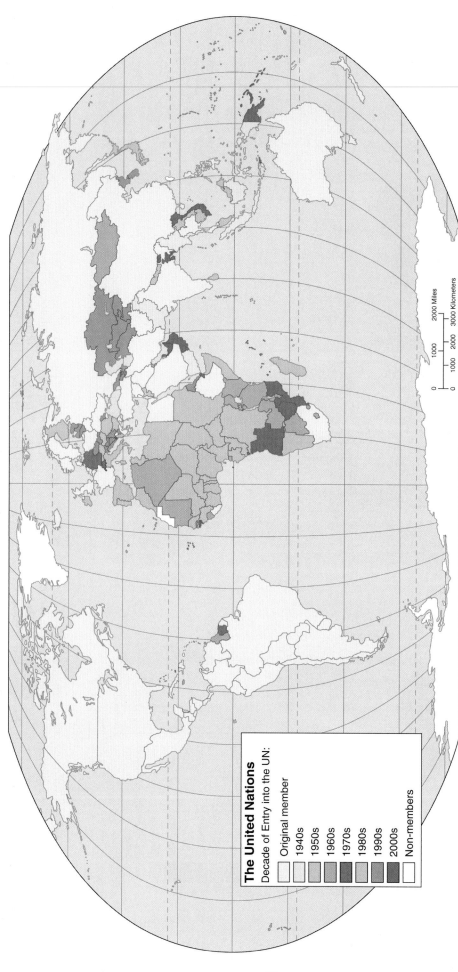

The United Nations

Decade of Entry into the UN:

- Original member
- 1940s
- 1950s
- 1960s
- 1970s
- 1980s
- 1990s
- 2000s
- Non-members

0   1000   2000 Miles
0   1000   2000   3000 Kilometers

The United Nations was formed in 1945 after World War II to maintain international peace and security and to promote cooperation involving economic, social, cultural, and humanitarian problems. Originally consisting of 51 member states, the organization has grown to 192 member states in 2009. Most of the African continent and the smaller Caribbean states entered the UN during the 1960s and 1970s following the end of European colonial rule. The 1990s saw the entry of several countries following the dissolution of the Soviet Union and the breakup of Yugoslavia. Montenegro became the most recent country to join the UN in 2006 following its separation from Serbia.

China was represented by the government of the Republic of China at the creation of the United Nations. Following the Communist victory during Chinese Civil War, the gov-ernment fled to the island of Taiwan. UN representation was maintained by the Republic of China government until 1971 when the government of the People's Republic of China (mainland China) was recognized as the representatives of China to the organization. Western Sahara is not a member of the UN as its sovereignty status is in dispute. Much of the territory of Western Sahara is controlled by Morocco. Kosovo declared its independence in 2008, which was recognized by the United States and 59 other countries. As of 2009, its entry into the UN has been blocked by Russia, which has not recognized its independence from Serbia. The Holy See (Vatican City) and Palestine hold status as observer.

-28-

Map 24 United Nations Regions and Sub-Regions

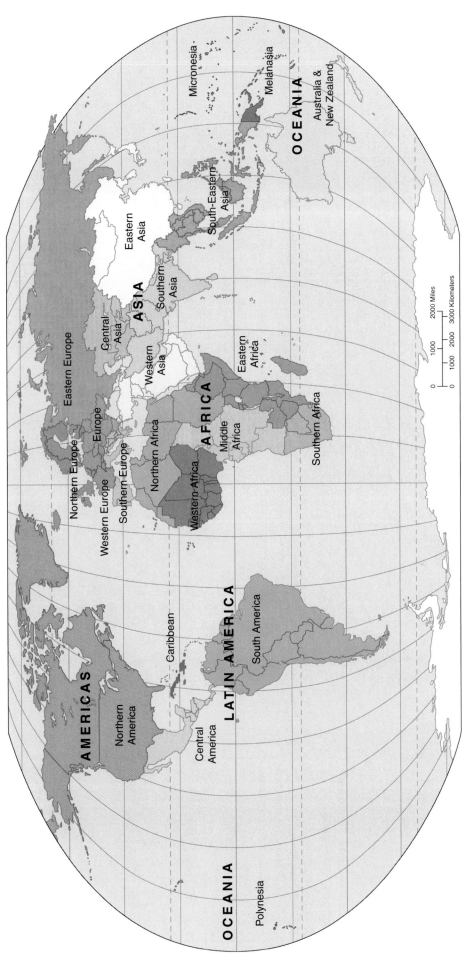

Where in the world is a country? At first, the response to that question seems fairly straightforward: China is in Asia, Angola is in Africa, and so on. The more one learns about the world, however, the more one finds that not everyone groups the world's countries the same way nor do they use standard terminology. For example, is Russia in Europe? Is it in Asia? Is it in both? Some terms commonly used in Western culture tend not to be applicable in a global context. Using "Middle East" to describe the countries of the Arabian Peninsula and the eastern Mediterranean make sense when viewing the world from the United Kingdom, but one would be hard-pressed to characterize these countries as "East" or in the "Middle" of countries to the east if one were in Japan. The map above presents the classification of the world's countries by the United Nations. How well do the names of the regions and sub-regions conform to the names with which you are familiar?

Map 25 Political Realms: Regional Changes, 1945–2003

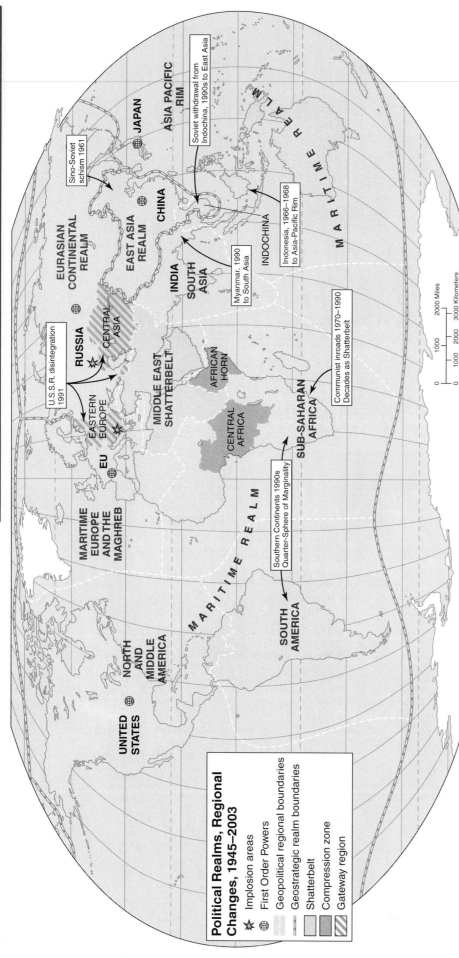

Political Realms, Regional Changes, 1945–2003

- ✪ Implosion areas
- ✺ First Order Powers
- Geopolitical regional boundaries
- Geostrategic realm boundaries
- Shatterbelt
- Compression zone
- Gateway region

U.S.S.R. disintegration 1991

Sino-Soviet schism 1961

EURASIAN CONTINENTAL REALM

RUSSIA

CENTRAL ASIA

EASTERN EUROPE

EU

MARITIME EUROPE AND THE MAGHREB

NORTH AND MIDDLE AMERICA

UNITED STATES

MARITIME REALM

SOUTH AMERICA

Southern Continents 1990s Quarter-Sphere of Marginality

MIDDLE EAST SHATTERBELT

AFRICAN HORN

CENTRAL AFRICA

SUB-SAHARAN AFRICA

Communist inroads 1970–1990 Decades as Shatterbelt

INDIA

SOUTH ASIA

Myanmar, 1990 to South Asia

INDOCHINA

Indonesia, 1966–1968 to Asia-Pacific Rim

EAST ASIA REALM

CHINA

Soviet withdrawal from Indochina, 1990s to East Asia

JAPAN

ASIA PACIFIC RIM

MARITIME REALM

0   1000   2000 Miles
0   1000   2000   3000 Kilometers

The Cold War following World War II shaped the major outlines of today's geopolitical relations. The Cold War included three phases. In the first, from 1945–1956, the Maritime Realm established a ring around the Continental Eurasian Realm in order to prevent its expansion. This phase included the Korean War (1950–1953), the Berlin Blockade (1948), the Truman doctrine and Marshall Plan (1947), and the founding of NATO (1949) and the Warsaw Pact (1955). Most of the world fell within one of the two realms: the Maritime (dominated by the United States) or the Eurasian Continental Realm (dominated by the Soviet Union). The Soviet Union sought to establish a ring of satellite states to protect it from a repeat of the invasions of World War II. The United States and other Maritime Realm states, in turn, sought to establish a ring of allies around the Continental Realm to prevent its expansion. South Asia was politically independent, but under pressure from both realms. During the second phase (1957–1979), Communist forces from the Conti-

nental Eurasian Realm penetrated deeply into the Maritime Realm. The Berlin Wall went up in 1961, Soviet missiles in Cuba ignited a crisis in 1962, and the United States became increasingly involved in the war in Vietnam (late 1960s). The Soviet Union sought increased political and military presence along important waterways including those in the Middle East, Southeast Asia, and the Caribbean. These regions became especially dangerous shatterbelts. The third phase (1980–1989) saw the retreat of Communist power from the Maritime Realm. China, after ten years of radical Communism and chaos of the Cultural Revolution (1966–1976), broke away from the Continental Eurasian Realm to establish a new East Asian realm. Soviet influence declined in the Middle East, Sub-Saharan Africa, and Latin America. In 1989 the Berlin Wall fell, and Eastern Europe began to establish democratic governments. In The 1990's the Soviet Union, Yugoslavia, and Czechoslovakia broke apart into twenty-two independent states.

Map 26 European Boundaries, 1914–1949

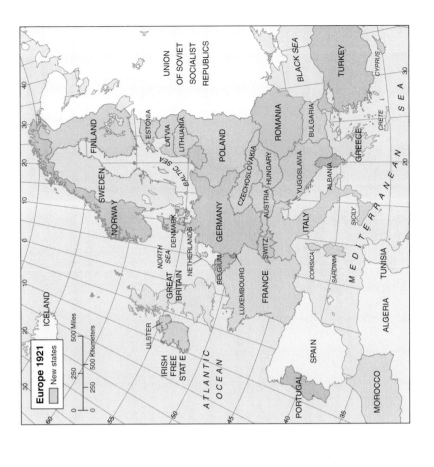

In 1914, on the eve of the First World War, Europe was dominated by the United Kingdom and France in the west, the German Empire and the Austro-Hungarian Empire in central Europe, and the Russian Empire in the east. Battle lines for the conflict that began in 1914 were drawn when the United Kingdom, France, and the Russian Empire joined together as the Triple Entente. In the view of the Germans, this coalition was designed to encircle Germany and its Austrian ally, which, along with Italy, made up the Triple Alliance. The German and Austrian fears were heightened in 1912–14 when a Russian-sponsored "Balkan League" pushed the Ottoman Turkish Empire from Europe, leaving behind the weak and

mutually antagonistic Balkan states Serbia and Montenegro. In August 1914, Germany and Austria-Hungary attacked in several directions and World War I began. Four years later, after massive loss of life and destruction, the central European empires were defeated. The victorious French, English, and Americans (who had entered the war in 1917) restructured the map of Europe in 1919, carving nine new states out of the remains of the German and Austro-Hungarian empires and the westernmost portions of the Russian Empire which, by the end of the war, was deep in the Revolution that deposed the czar and brought the Communists to power in a new Union of Soviet Socialist Republics.

-31-

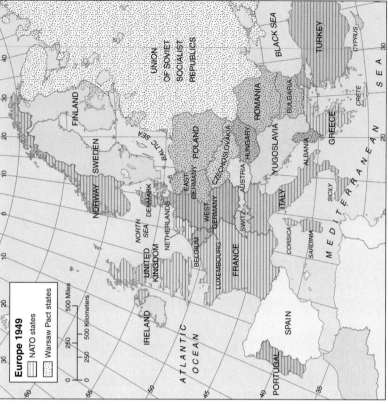

Europe 1949

- NATO states
- Warsaw Pact states

*The Warsaw Pact was not formally established until 1955 but it was a de facto organization prior to that.

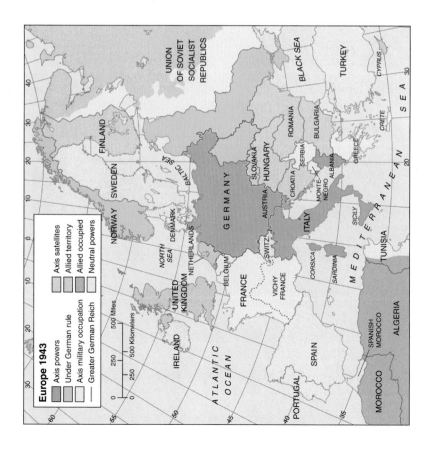

Europe 1943

- Axis powers
- Under German rule
- Axis military occupation
- Greater German Reich
- Axis satellites
- Allied territory
- Allied occupied
- Neutral powers

When the victorious Allies redrew the map of central and eastern Europe in 1919, they caused as many problems as they were trying to solve. The interval between the First and Second World Wars was really just a lull in a long war that halted temporarily in 1918 and erupted once again in 1939. Defeated Germany, resentful of the terms of the 1918 armistice and 1919 Treaty of Versailles and beset by massive inflation and unemployment at home, overthrew the Weimar republican government in 1933 and installed the National Socialist (Nazi) party led by Adolf Hitler in Berlin. Hitler quickly began making good on his promises to create a "thousand year realm" of German influence by annexing Austria and the Czech region of Czechoslovakia and allying Germany with a fellow fascist state in Mussolini's Italy. In September 1939 Germany launched the lightning-quick combined infantry, artillery, and armor attack known as *der Blitzkrieg* and took Poland to the east and, in quick succession, the Netherlands, Belgium, and France to the west. By 1943 the greater German Reich extended from the Russian Plain to the

Atlantic and from the Black Sea to the Baltic. But the Axis powers of Germany and Italy could not withstand the greater resources and manpower of the combined United Kingdom–United States–USSR–led Allies and, in 1945, Allied armies occupied Germany. Once again, the lines of the central and eastern European map were redrawn. This time, a strengthened Soviet Union took back most of the territory the Russian Empire had lost at the end of the First World War. Germany was partitioned into four occupied sectors (English, French, American, and Russian) and later into two independent countries, the Federal Republic of Germany (West Germany) and the German Democratic Republic (East Germany). Although the Soviet Union's territory stopped at the Polish, Hungarian, Czechoslovakian, and Romanian borders, the eastern European countries (Poland, East Germany, Czechoslovakia, Hungary, Romania, Yugoslavia, Albania, and Bulgaria) became Communist between 1945 and 1948 and were separated from the West by the Iron Curtain.

Map 27   An Age of Bipolarity: The Cold War ca. 1970

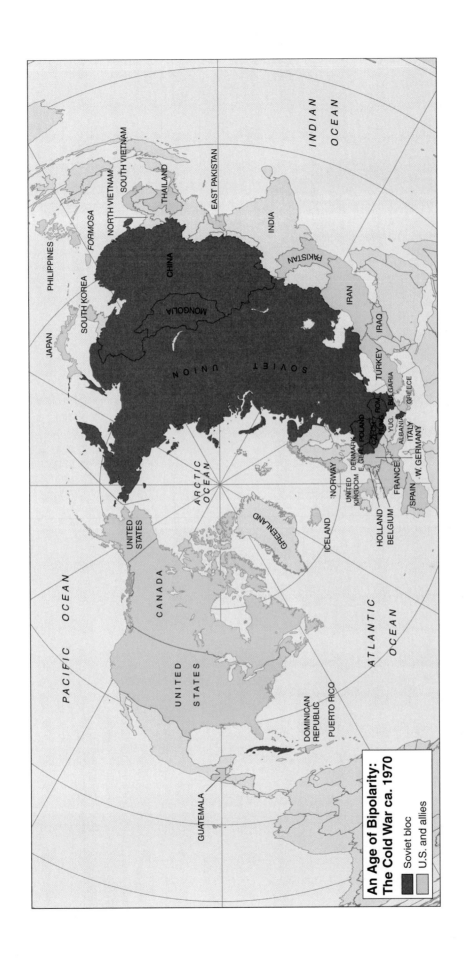

An Age of Bipolarity: The Cold War ca. 1970

- Soviet bloc
- U.S. and allies

Following the Second World War, the world was divided into two armed camps led by the United States and the Soviet Union. The Soviet Union and its allies, the Warsaw Pact countries, feared a U.S.-led takeover of the eastern European countries that became Soviet satellites after the war and the replacing of a socialist political and economic system with a liberal one. The United States and its allies, the NATO (North Atlantic Treaty Organization) countries, equally feared that the USSR would overrun western Europe. Both sides sought to defend themselves by building up massive military arsenals. The United States, adopting an international geopo-litical strategy of containment, sought to ring the Soviet Union with a string of allied countries and military bases that would prevent Soviet expansion in any direction. The levels of spending on military hardware contributed to the devolution of the Soviet Union, and the obsolescence of alliances and military bases in an age of advanced guidance and delivery systems made the U.S. military containment less necessary. Following a peak in the early 1960s, the Cold War gradually became less significant and the age of bipolar international power essentially ended with the dissolution of the USSR in 1991.

-33-

Map 28 Europe: Political Changes, 1989–2009

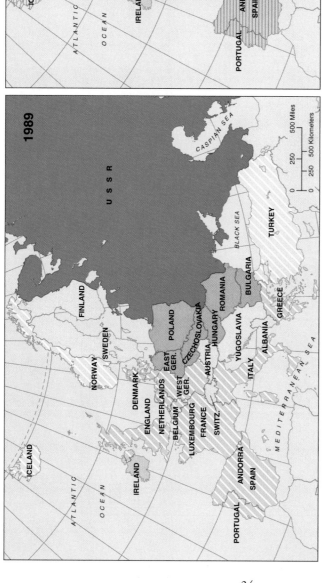

Europe: Political Changes 1989–2009

1989
- Union of Soviet Socialist Republics
- Warsaw Pact Countries (excluding the USSR)
- North Atlantic Treaty Organization Countries
- European Community (formerly the EEC)

2009
- Former Republics of the USSR, now independent countries
- Russian Federation
- NATO Countries 2005
- Associated with NATO / petitioned for entry
- European Union (formerly the EC)

During the last decade of the twentieth century, one of the most remarkable series of political geographic changes of the last 500 years took place. The bipolar East-West structure that had characterized Europe's political geography since the end of the Second World War altered in the space of a very few years. In the mid-1980s, as Soviet influence over eastern and central Europe weakened, those countries began to turn to the capitalist West. Between 1989, when the country of Hungary was the first Soviet satellite to open its borders to travel, and 1991, when the Soviet Union dissolved into 15 independent countries, abrupt change in political systems occurred. The result is a new map of Europe that includes a number of countries not present on the map of 1989. These countries have emerged as the result of reunification, separation, or independence from the former Soviet Union and Yugoslavia. The new political structure has been accompanied by growing economic cooperation.

Map 29   The European Union, 2009

The European Union, 2009

- ■ European Economic Community (EEC) members, 1957
- ▦ EEC/EU members joined 1973–1995
- ▢ EU members joined 2004–2007
- ▨ Candidate countries

After World War II, a number of European leaders became convinced that the only way to secure a lasting peace between their countries was to unite them economically and politically. The first attempts at this were made in 1951, when the European Coal and Steel Community (ECSC) was set up, with six members: Belgium, West Germany, Luxembourg, France, Italy and the Netherlands. The ECSC was such a success that, within a few years, these same six countries decided to go further and integrate other sectors of their economies. In 1957 they signed the Treaties of Rome, creating the European Atomic Energy Community (EURATOM) and the European Economic Community (EEC). The member states set about removing trade barriers between them and forming a "common market." The six original members were joined in the common market of the EEC by Denmark, Ireland, and the United Kingdom in 1973, followed by Greece in 1981, and Spain and Portugal in 1986. In 1992 the 12 countries of the EEC signed the Treaty of Maastricht, which introduced new forms of co-operation between the member state governments—particularly in defense and legal systems—and created the European Union (EU). The original 12 EU members were joined by Austria, Finland and Sweden in 1995. In 2004, 10 new members joined the EU: Cyprus, the Czech Republic, Estonia, Hungary, Latvia, Lithuania, Malta, Poland, Slovakia, and Slovenia; Bulgaria and Romania joined three years later. Croatia and Turkey began membership negotiations in 2005. The EU has worked toward the dropping of trade barriers and labor migration barriers among member countries, along with economic and political cooperation in a number of areas. The adoption of the euro in 2002 as the common currency of the majority of EU countries is expected to aid in the integration of the European economy. A proposed constitution for the EU failed ratification by all member states—France and the Netherlands rejected ratification and several other states postponed indefinitely the ratification vote. The European Council is meeting to attempt the development of a new document. However, the economic components of the EU will remain unchanged.

Map 30   The Geopolitical World at the Beginning of the Twenty-First Century

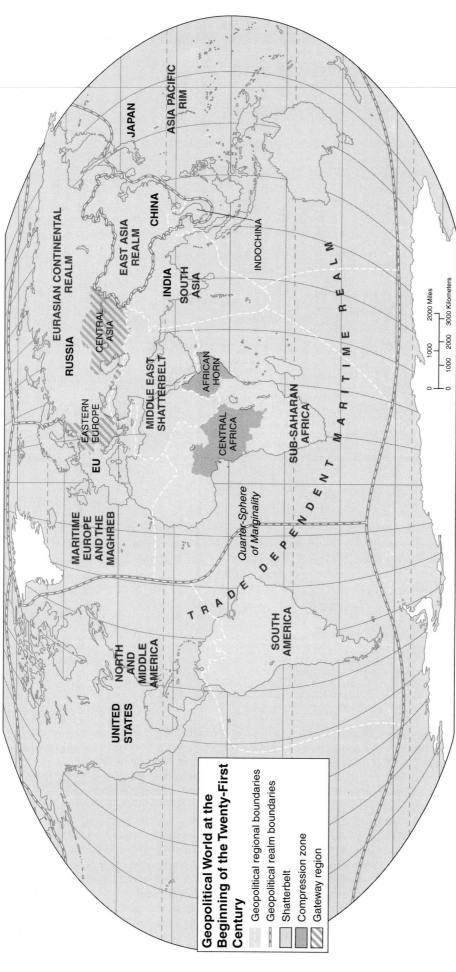

Geopolitical World at the Beginning of the Twenty-First Century

Geopolitical regional boundaries
Geopolitical realm boundaries
Shatterbelt
Compression zone
Gateway region

In the geostrategic structure of the world, the largest territorial units are realms. They are shaped by circulation patterns that link people, goods, and ideas. Realms are shaped by maritime and continental influences. Today's Atlantic and Pacific Trade-Dependent Maritime Realm has been shaped by international exchange over the oceans and their interior seas as mercantilism, capitalism, and industrialization gave rise to maritime-oriented states and to economic and political colonialism. The world's leading trading and economic powers are part of this realm. The Eurasian Continental Realm, centered around Russia, is inner-oriented, less influenced by outside economic or cultural forces, and politically closed, even after the fall of Communism. Expansion of NATO in Europe

has increased its feeling of being "hemmed in." East Asia has mixed Maritime and Continental influences. China has traditionally been continental, but reforms that began in the late 1970s increased the importance of its maritime-oriented southern coasts. Even so, its trade volume is still low, and it maintains a hold on inland areas like Tibet and Xinjiang. Realms are subdivided into regions, some dependent on others, as South America is on North America. Regions located between powerful realms or regions may be shatterbelts (internally divided and caught up in competition between Great Powers) or gateways (facilitating the flow of ideas, goods, and people between regions). Compression zones are areas of conflict, but they are not contested by major powers.

Map 31   Democracy on the Rise

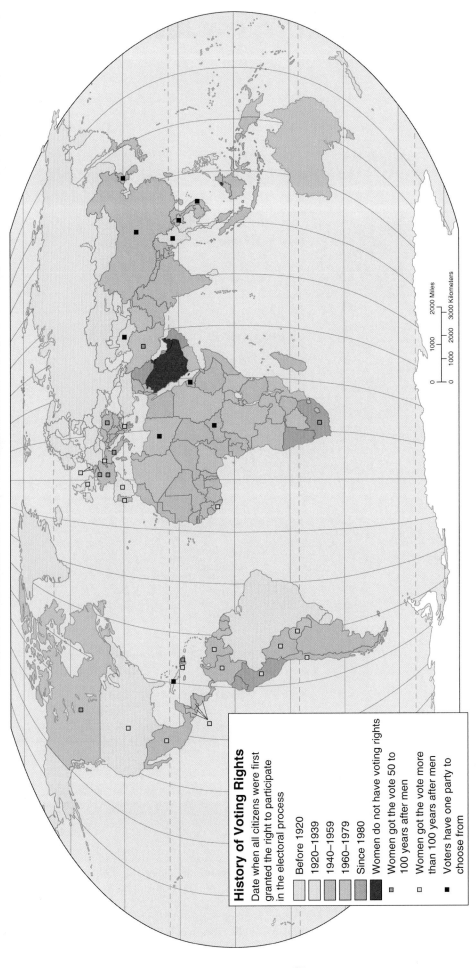

History of Voting Rights

Date when all citizens were first granted the right to participate in the electoral process

- Before 1920
- 1920–1939
- 1940–1959
- 1960–1979
- Since 1980
- Women do not have voting rights

▫ Women got the vote 50 to 100 years after men

▫ Women got the vote more than 100 years after men

■ Voters have one party to choose from

In 1800 most of the world's people were ruled by a monarch—sometimes with a constitution and sometimes with a parliament, but a monarch, nevertheless. Few monarchs remain and where they do, their role is largely that of a figurehead than of an actual ruler. For all the veneration given to, say, Queen Elizabeth II of the United Kingdom, whoever is prime minister in that government has enormously more power—and the prime minister is elected by a constituency. But having elected leaders as opposed to hereditary rulers is not the only criterion for identifying a democracy. Suffrage, or who possesses the right to vote, ought to be universal (it is worth noting that in the United States—one of the world's oldest democracies—black men possessed the right to vote more than a half century before white women). Elections should be competitive: a true democracy can rarely exist without multiple political parties with equal access to the electorate. Elections must also be free from internal or external coercion or corruption. And, in true democracies, there

are a number of other identifying components such as a free press, an advanced legal system in which laws rather than men rule, and a respect for human rights. By these more rigorous standards perhaps only two-thirds of the countries on this map are true, western-style liberal democracies. But that is a great deal better (unless, of course, you are a monarchist) than the situation in 1800. What explains the rise of democratic systems? Most experts point to such things as higher levels of economic development and greater literacy among populations. Even more important, however, is globalization and the shrinking of the world through increased communication systems. People who live in democracies tend to have certain advantages not possessed by those who do not. In a world of low or no barriers to interpersonal and interregional information flows, this fact is hard to hide. Isolatedcountries (North Korea is a case-in-point) are more likely to be autocratic than democratic and the future for truly democratic governance would seem bright.

Map 32   The Middle East: Territorial Changes, 1918–Present

Territorial Changes in the Middle East, World War I to present

- Ottoman Empire to World War I
- British control
- French control
- Kurdish homelands
- International boundaries in 1994

The Middle East, encompassing the northeastern part of Africa and southwestern Asia, has a turbulent history. In the last century alone, many of the region's countries have gone from being ruled by the Turkish Ottoman Empire, to being dependencies of Great Britain or France, to being independent. Having experienced the Crusades and colonial domination by European powers, the region's predominantly Islamic countries are now resentful of interference in the region's affairs by countries with a European and/or Christian heritage. The tension between Israel (settled largely in the late nineteenth and twentieth centuries by Jews of predominantly European background) and its neighbors is a matter of European–Middle Eastern cultural stress as well as a religious conflict between Islamic Arab culture and Judaism.

Map 33   Africa: Colonialism to Independence

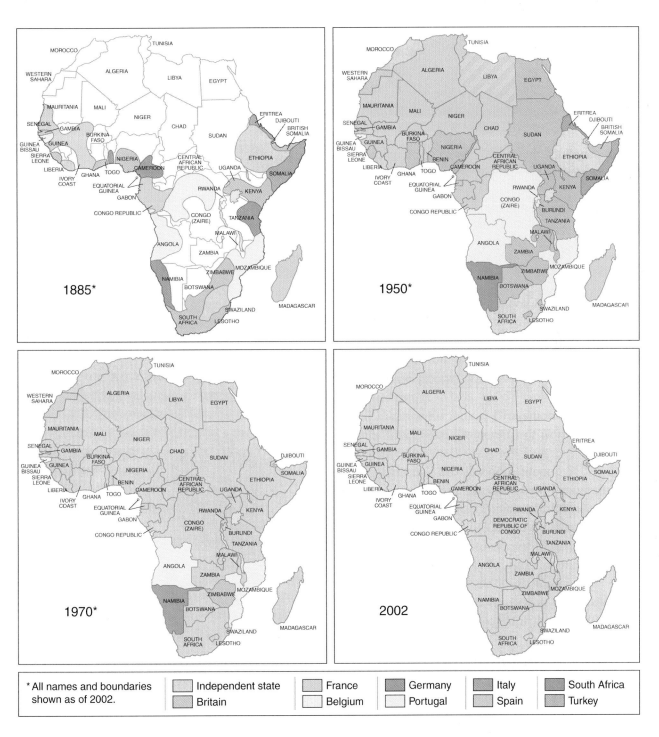

In few parts of the world has the transition from colonialism to independence been as abrupt as on the African continent. Most African states did not become colonies until the nineteenth century and did not become independent until the twentieth, nearly all of them after World War II. Much of the colonial power in Africa is social and economic. The African colony provided the mother country with raw materials in exchange for marginal economic returns, and many African countries still exist in this colonial dependency relationship. An even more important component of the colonial legacy of Europe in Africa is geopolitical. When the world's colonial powers joined at the Conference of Berlin in 1884, they divided up Africa to fit their own needs, drawing boundary lines on maps without regard for terrain or drainage features, or for tribal/ethnic linguistic, cultural, economic, or political borders. Traditional Africa was enormously disrupted by this process. After independence, African countries retained boundaries that are legacies of the colonial past; and African countries today are beset by internal problems related to tribal and ethnic conflicts, the disruption of traditional migration patterns, and inefficient spatial structures of market and supply.

Map 34 South Africa: Black Homelands and Post-Apartheid Provinces

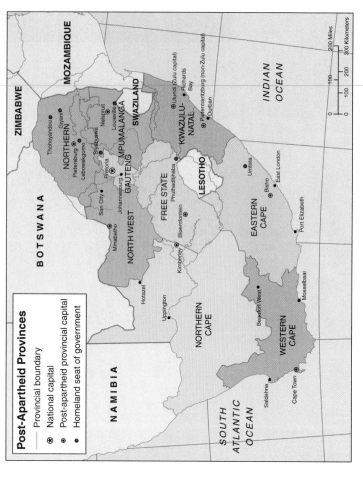

South Africa: Black Homelands

- ▨ Black homeland
- — Provincial boundary
- ⊛ National capital
- • Homeland seat of government

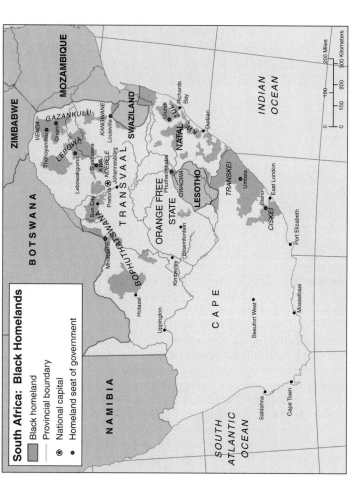

Post-Apartheid Provinces

- — Provincial boundary
- ⊛ National capital
- ◉ Post-apartheid provincial capital
- • Homeland seat of government

After their defeat by the British in the Boer War (1899–1902), the Dutch-descended Afrikaners negotiated with the British for greater powers in South Africa. Eventually, they became the most powerful group and imposed "separate development" or *apartheid* on the country. African (and other minority) populations would live completely separated from white South Africans. Millions were forced to relocate to the ancestral areas, where "homelands" that would be declared "independent" were set up for them. The amounts and quality of the land were completely insufficient to support the populations assigned

to them, and many of the "homelands" were fragmented as well. Thousands of black Africans flocked to the black "townships" around major cities, looking for work. Here, they were foreigners in their own land. After the fall of *apartheid* in 1994, the "homelands" were abolished, and South Africa's political geography was reorganized, with each new province centered around its dominant ethnic group. These provinces now serve as subdivisions within the country without restrictions by race or ethnicity on where people can live. This organization was important in the peaceful transfer to majority rule.

-40-

Map 35 Asia: Colonialism to Independence, 1930–2007

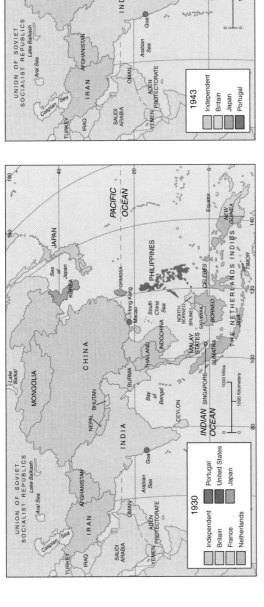

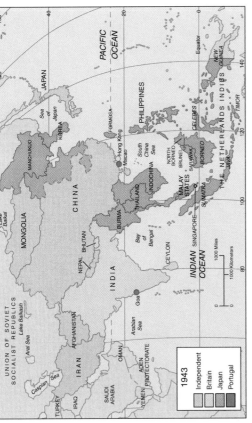

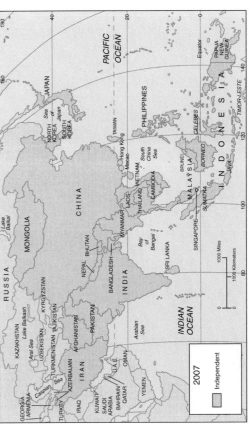

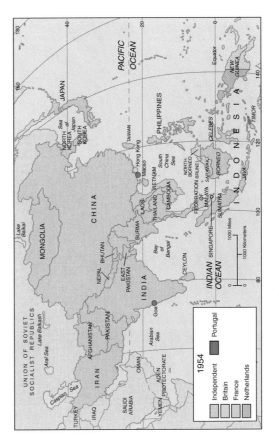

Asian countries, like those in Africa, have recently emerged from a colonial past. With the exception of China, Japan, and Thailand, virtually all Asian nations were until not long ago under the colonial control of Great Britain, France, Spain, the Netherlands, or the United States. For a short period of time between 1930 and 1945, Japan itself was a colonial power with considerable territories on the Asian mainland. The unraveling of colonial control in Asia, particularly in South and Southeast Asia, has precipitated internal conflicts in the newly independent states that make up a significant part of the political geography of the region. The last vestiges of European colonialism in Asia disappeared with the cession of Hong Kong (1997) and Macao (1999) to China.

Map 36 Global Distribution of Minority Groups

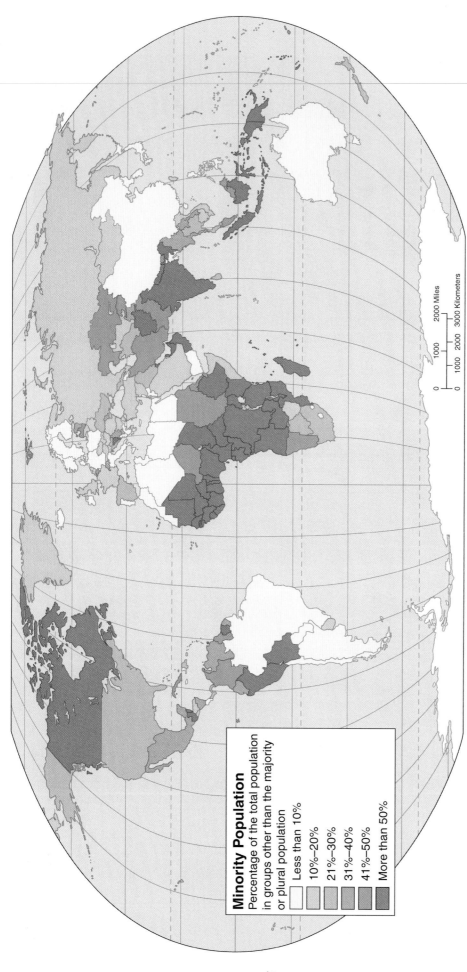

Minority Population
Percentage of the total population in groups other than the majority or plural population

- Less than 10%
- 10%–20%
- 21%–30%
- 31%–40%
- 41%–50%
- More than 50%

0   1000   2000   3000 Kilometers
0   1000   2000 Miles

The presence of minority ethnic, national, or racial groups within a country's population can add a vibrant and dynamic mix to the whole. Plural societies with a high degree of cultural and ethnic diversity should, according to some social theorists, be among the world's most healthy. Unfortunately, the reality of the situation is quite different from theory or expectation. The presence of significant minority populations played an important role in the disintegration of the Soviet Union; the continuing existence of minority populations within the new states formed from former Soviet republics threatens the viability and stability of those young political units. In Africa, national boundaries were drawn by colonial powers without regard for the geographical distribution of ethnic groups, and the continuing tribal conflicts that have resulted hamper both economic and political development. Even in the most highly developed regions of the world, the presence of minority ethnic populations poses significant problems: witness the separatist movement in Canada, driven by the desire of some French-Canadians to be independent of the English majority, and the continuing ethnic conflict between Flemish-speaking and Walloon-speaking Belgians. This map, by arraying states on a scale of homogeneity to heterogeneity, indicates areas of existing and potential social and political strife.

Map 37 Linguistic Diversity

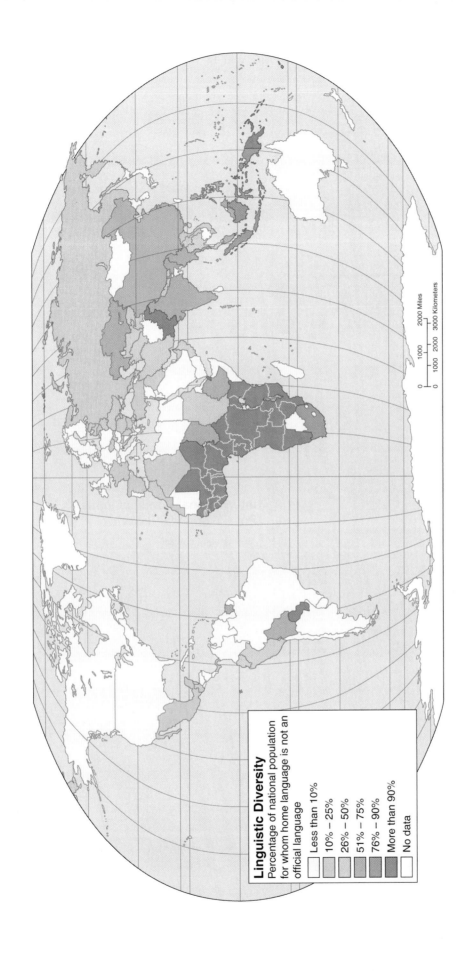

Linguistic Diversity

Percentage of national population for whom home language is not an official language

- Less than 10%
- 10% – 25%
- 26% – 50%
- 51% – 75%
- 76% – 90%
- More than 90%
- No data

Of the world's approximately 5,300 languages, fewer than 100 are official languages, those designated by a country as the language of government, commerce, education, and information. This means that for much of the world's population the language that is spoken in the home is different from the official language of the country of residence. The world's former colonial areas in Middle and South America, Africa, and South and Southeast Asia stand out on the map as regions in which there is significant disparity between home languages and official languages. To complicate matters further, for most of the world's population, the primary international languages of trade and tourism (French and English) are neither home nor official languages.

Map 38   International Conflicts in the Post–World War II World

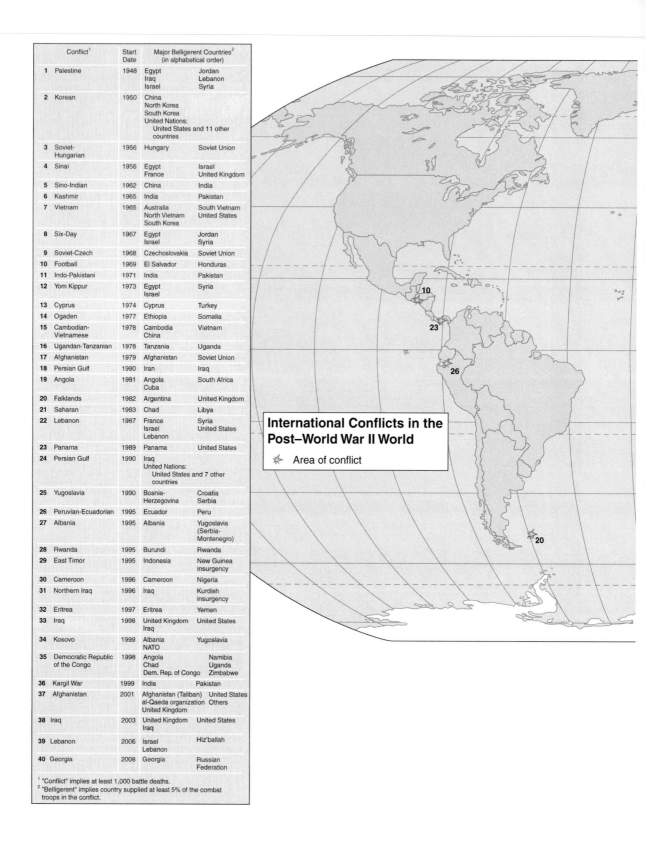

	Conflict[1]	Start Date	Major Belligerent Countries[2] (in alphabetical order)	
1	Palestine	1948	Egypt Iraq Israel	Jordan Lebanon Syria
2	Korean	1950	China North Korea South Korea United Nations: United States and 11 other countries	
3	Soviet-Hungarian	1956	Hungary	Soviet Union
4	Sinai	1956	Egypt France	Israel United Kingdom
5	Sino-Indian	1962	China	India
6	Kashmir	1965	India	Pakistan
7	Vietnam	1965	Australia North Vietnam South Korea	South Vietnam United States
8	Six-Day	1967	Egypt Israel	Jordan Syria
9	Soviet-Czech	1968	Czechoslovakia	Soviet Union
10	Football	1969	El Salvador	Honduras
11	Indo-Pakistani	1971	India	Pakistan
12	Yom Kippur	1973	Egypt Israel	Syria
13	Cyprus	1974	Cyprus	Turkey
14	Ogaden	1977	Ethiopia	Somalia
15	Cambodian-Vietnamese	1978	Cambodia China	Vietnam
16	Ugandan-Tanzanian	1978	Tanzania	Uganda
17	Afghanistan	1979	Afghanistan	Soviet Union
18	Persian Gulf	1980	Iran	Iraq
19	Angola	1981	Angola Cuba	South Africa
20	Falklands	1982	Argentina	United Kingdom
21	Saharan	1983	Chad	Libya
22	Lebanon	1987	France Israel Lebanon	Syria United States
23	Panama	1989	Panama	United States
24	Persian Gulf	1990	Iraq United Nations: United States and 7 other countries	
25	Yugoslavia	1990	Bosnia-Herzegovina	Croatia Serbia
26	Peruvian-Ecuadorian	1995	Ecuador	Peru
27	Albania	1995	Albania	Yugoslavia (Serbia-Montenegro)
28	Rwanda	1995	Burundi	Rwanda
29	East Timor	1995	Indonesia	New Guinea insurgency
30	Cameroon	1996	Cameroon	Nigeria
31	Northern Iraq	1996	Iraq	Kurdish insurgency
32	Eritrea	1997	Eritrea	Yemen
33	Iraq	1998	United Kingdom Iraq	United States
34	Kosovo	1999	Albania NATO	Yugoslavia
35	Democratic Republic of the Congo	1998	Angola Chad Dem. Rep. of Congo	Namibia Uganda Zimbabwe
36	Kargil War	1999	India	Pakistan
37	Afghanistan	2001	Afghanistan (Taliban) al-Qaeda organization United Kingdom	United States Others
38	Iraq	2003	United Kingdom Iraq	United States
39	Lebanon	2006	Israel Lebanon	Hiz'ballah
40	Georgia	2008	Georgia	Russian Federation

[1] "Conflict" implies at least 1,000 battle deaths.
[2] "Belligerent" implies country supplied at least 5% of the combat troops in the conflict.

International Conflicts in the Post–World War II World

⚹ Area of conflict

The Korean War and the Vietnam War dominated the post–World War II period in terms of international military conflict. But numerous smaller conflicts have taken place, with fewer numbers of belligerents and with fewer battle and related casualties. These smaller international conflicts have been mostly territorial conflicts, reflecting the continual readjustment of political boundaries and loyalties brought about by the end of colonial empires, and the dissolution of the Soviet Union. Many of these conflicts were not wars in the more traditional

sense, in which two or more countries formally declare war on one another, severing diplomatic ties and devoting their entire national energies to the war effort. Rather, many of these conflicts were and are undeclared wars, sometimes fought between rival groups within the same country with outside support from other countries. The aftermath of the September 11, 2001, terrorist attacks on the United States indicate the dawn of yet another type of international conflict, namely a "war" fought between traditional nation-states and non-state actors.

Map 39 World Refugees: Country of Origin, 2009

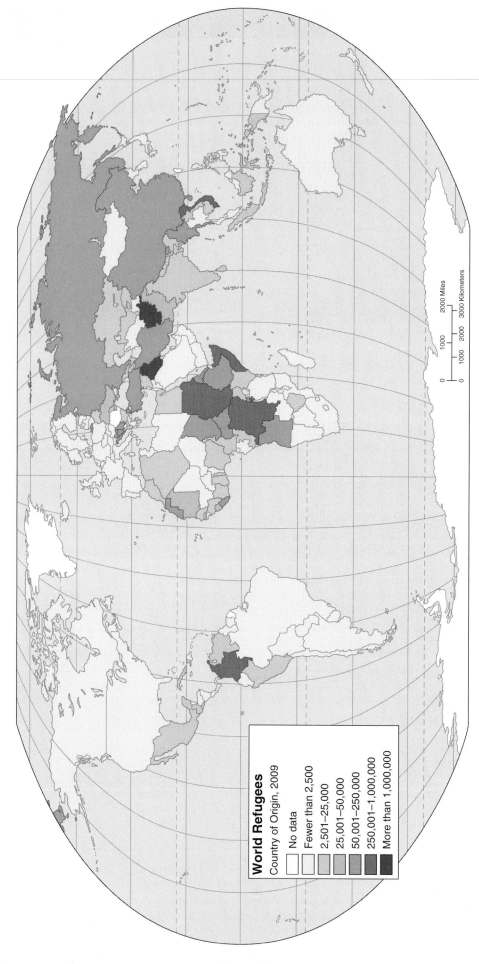

World Refugees
Country of Origin, 2009

- No data
- Fewer than 2,500
- 2,501–25,000
- 25,001–50,000
- 50,001–250,000
- 250,001–1,000,000
- More than 1,000,000

0   1000   2000 Miles
0 1000 2000 3000 Kilometers

Refugees are persons who have been driven from their homes and seek refuge in another country. While there are many reasons why people flee their home country, the vast majority are fleeing armed conflict. In such cases, there may be a mass exodus from the country involving tens or perhaps hundreds of thousands of persons. Most refugees flee into neighboring countries. Because armed conflict is oftentimes short-lived, the number of refugees in the world changes from year to year, sometimes substantially. The refugee population is recognized by international agencies and is monitored by the United Nations High Commissioner for Refugees (UNHCR).

Map 40 World Refugees: Host Country, 2009

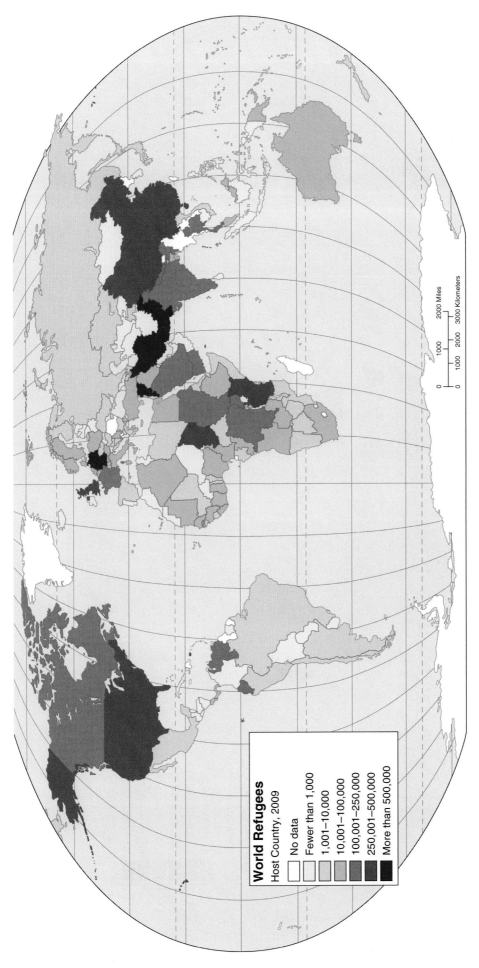

World Refugees
Host Country, 2009

- No data
- Fewer than 1,000
- 1,001–10,000
- 10,001–100,000
- 100,001–250,000
- 250,001–500,000
- More than 500,000

When refugees flee their country, they most commonly flee to a neighboring country, and not every country is equally equipped to handle such an influx of persons. During such times, international agencies often financially reward the countries of refuge for their willingness to take in externally displaced persons. For most of the host countries, the challenge of hosting a large refugee population is a short-term problem. As we have seen in recent decades, the burden of hosting massive numbers refugees can be a destabilizing force for the country of refuge.

Map 41   Internally Displaced Persons, 2009

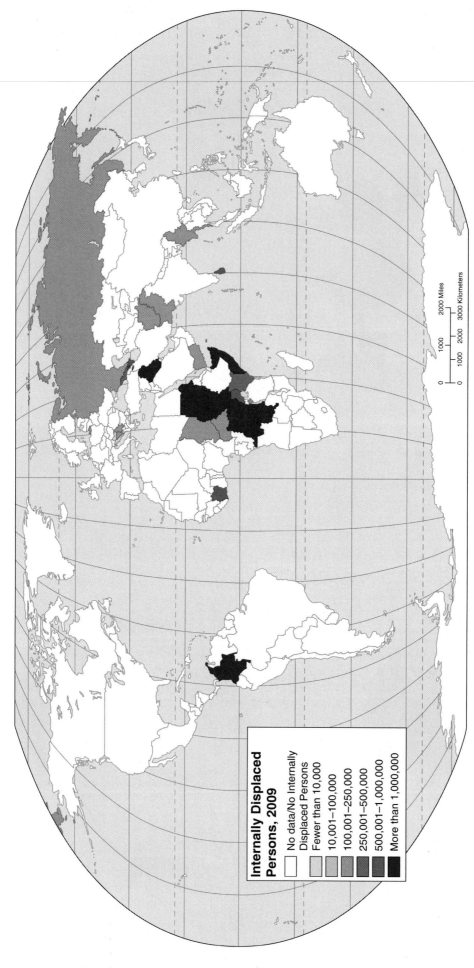

Internally Displaced
Persons, 2009

No data/No Internally
Displaced Persons

Fewer than 10,000

10,001–100,000

100,001–250,000

250,001–500,000

500,001–1,000,000

More than 1,000,000

0   1000   2000 Miles

0   1000   2000   3000 Kilometers

Internally displaced persons (IDPs) are those who flee their homes because of conflict, persecution, or disaster and seek refuge in another location within their country. With the exception of not leaving their country, they are essentially the same as refugees. International organizations offer the same assistance to internally displaced persons as is provided to refugees. The actual number of IDPs is more difficult to assess than refugee data. Not only do IDP populations fluctuate, there likely are a large number of displaced persons who flee to the larger cities in the countries rather than to the camps established by international relief organizations. In early 2009, the countries with the greatest number of IPDs were Colombia, Iraq, Democratic Republic of the Congo, Somalia, and Sudan.

Map 42 Post–Cold War International Alliances

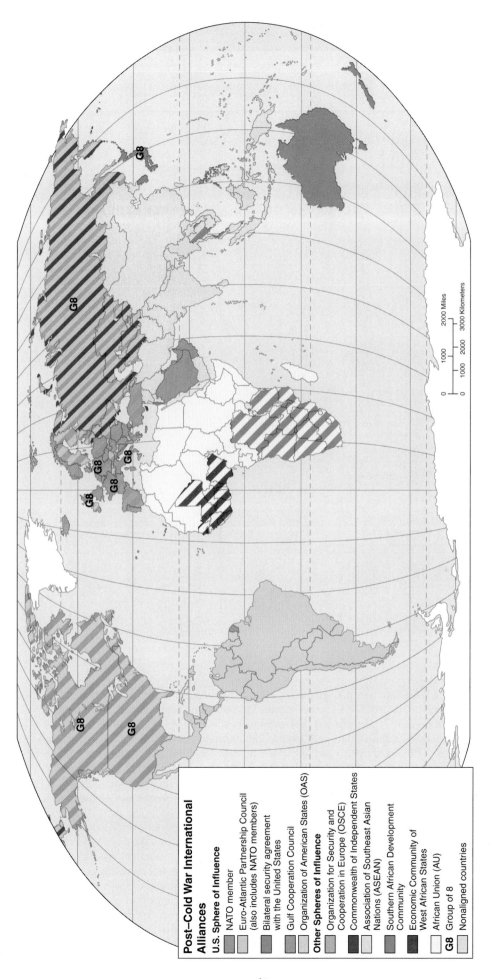

Post–Cold War International Alliances

U.S. Sphere of Influence

- NATO member
- Euro-Atlantic Partnership Council (also includes NATO members)
- Bilateral security agreement with the United States
- Gulf Cooperation Council
- Organization of American States (OAS)

Other Spheres of Influence

- Organization for Security and Cooperation in Europe (OSCE)
- Commonwealth of Independent States
- Association of Southeast Asian Nations (ASEAN)
- Southern African Development Community
- Economic Community of West African States
- African Union (AU)
- **G8** Group of 8
- Nonaligned countries

When the Warsaw Pact dissolved in 1992, the North Atlantic Treaty Organization (NATO) was left as the only major military alliance in the world. Some former Warsaw Pact members (Czechia, Hungary, and Poland) have joined NATO, and others are petitioning for entry. The bipolar division of the world into two major military alliances is over, at least temporarily, leaving the United States alone as the world's dominant political and mili-

tary power. But other international alliances, such as the Commonwealth of Independent States (including most of the former republics of the Soviet Union), will continue to be important. It may well be that during the first few decades of the twenty-first century economic alliances will begin to overshadow military ones in their relevance for the world's peoples.

Map 43   Flashpoints, 2009

Colombia: Colombia was one of three countries (along with Ecuador and Venezuela) that emerged from the collapse of the newly independent country of Gran Colombia in 1830 (the former Spanish Viceroyalty of New Granada). Although possessing a rich natural resource base and agricultural abundance, Colombia has been torn apart internally for more than four decades as the result of conflict between government forces and antigovernment insurgent groups and illegal paramilitary groups. The two largest insurgent groups are the Revolutionary Armed Forces of Colombia (FARC) and the National Liberation Army (ELN). The largest illegal paramilitary group is a semi-organized array of disparate paramilitary forces called the United Self-Defense Groups of Colombia (AUC). Both insurgency and paramilitary organizations are heavily funded by the illegal trade in cocaine, the most important (but untaxed) commodity in the Colombian economy. The insurgents do not have the military or popular support necessary to overthrow the government but continue to engage in attacks against government forces and civilians, and many areas of the country are under the control of guerillas who double as drug traffickers. The insurgency groups, with a more political agenda, and the paramilitary groups, who have a fairly simple agenda of controlling the cocaine trade, not only battle the government forces but also one another. Large swaths of internal Colombia are under the control of either insurgents or paramilitary drug lords. Over the last few years, the Colombian government has increased efforts to regain control of these areas, with some mild success. However, neighboring countries remain concerned about the probability of the violence spilling into their borders. Colombian-organized illegal narcotics, guerrilla, and paramilitary activities penetrate all of its neighbors' borders and have created a serious refugee crisis with over 300,000 persons having fled the country, mostly into neighboring states. In 2006 and 2007 a "fumigation" process sponsored and funded by the United States was implemented to reduce the acres in coca cultivation. This attempt at a reduction in the coca production system has been largely unsuccessful. Although active insurgency movements were somewhat diminished in 2009, the peripheral interior areas of the country remain unstable and are more controlled by political and economic opponents of the central government than they are by the official governing body of the state.

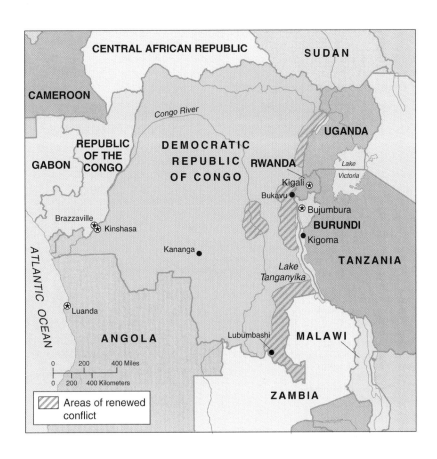

Congo: The war in the Democratic Republic of the Congo (formerly Zaire) has preoccupied the United Nations and African diplomats since 1999. Troops from Zimbabwe, Angola, Sudan, Chad, and Namibia joined with the Congo's President Laurent Kabila against his former allies Rwanda, Burundi, and Uganda, who each backed several separate Congolese rebel groups. The origins of the conflict originally lay in the overthrow of longtime dictator Mobutu Sese Seko by Kabila's army in May 1997 after a year of civil war. Kabila's failure to call elections or stabilize the country's economy led to further rounds of rebellion in the huge but fractious nation—rebellion supported by the economic and military assistance of neighboring Rwanda, Burundi, and Uganda. After Kabila's assassination in 2001 and the succession of his son, Joseph, to the presidency, accord seemed to have been reached, and the various conflicting parties agreed to withdraw troops in 2002. But in early 2003, new fighting flared along the country's eastern border, threatening a new and broadened war and the addition of more deaths to the 3.3 million since 1998. Diplomats called the conflict "Africa's first world war," and fears continue as late as 2008 that the Congo conflict could destabilize the entire southern half of the continent, leading to massive refugee flows and abject poverty. Although the stability of the central government of the Democratic Republic of the Congo seemed to increase in 2006 and 2007 with the successful election of a national assembly and a president, conflict and civil strife in the eastern border regions of the country continued to persist and even intensify in 2008.

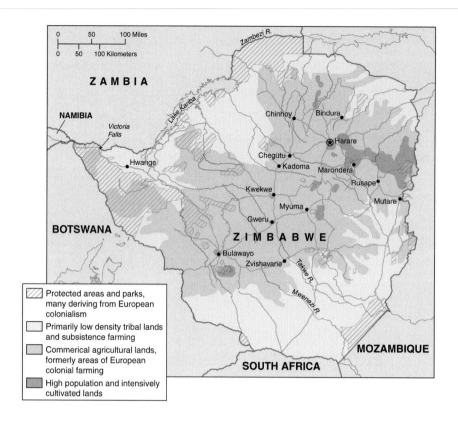

Zimbabwe: Relatively shortly after the former country of Rhodesia obtained its independence from the United Kingdom, it was reconstituted as the country of Zimbabwe in 1980. Its leader was Robert Mugabe, who has remained in power ever since. In 2000, Mugabe instituted an ill-advised land reform program, appropriating white-owned farms and giving them to tribal leaders. A country that had been one of Africa's leaders in agricultural production quickly deteriorated into conditions of abject poverty and famine. Nor does foreign aid do much to alleviate the problem since aid is appropriated and selectively distributed by the Mugabe government. An inflationary rate of nearly 11 million percent has brought the country to the brink of economic collapse. Elections held in March left Mugabe's chief rival, Morgan Tsvangirai, as the leading vote-getter, but he did not receive enough votes to prevent a run-off election. Before that election could be held, Tsvangirai withdrew from the race, claiming (quite probably with some justification) that his supporters had been threatened with beatings, imprisonment, murder, and torture and that he did not wish to subject them to those dangers. In 2009, Tsvangirai was sworn in as Prime Ministare, part of a power-sharing agreement with Mugabe—at least on paper—in which he and Mugabe would combine their forces to try to lead the country out of its economic chaos and medical crisis created by a cholera epidemic. While Zimbabwe does not have the tribal conflicts that beset so many African nations (most Zimbabweans are Shona), the feelings between the supporters of the two rival political factions run deeply enough that, if the power-sharing arrangement does not work and the economy continues to deteriorate, the country could be plunged into a civil war.

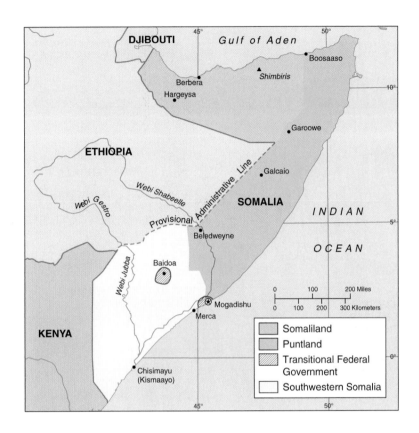

Somalia: With the ouster of the government led by Mohamed Said Barre in January 1991, turmoil, factional fighting, and anarchy have followed in Somalia, with several separate governments arising in different parts of the country. The northern clans declared an independent Republic of Somaliland. Although not recognized by any government, it has maintained a stable existence, aided by the overwhelming dominance of a ruling clan and economic infrastucture left behind by British, Russian, and American military assistance programs. Puntland, the central portion of Somalia, from the Horn of Africa to the coast of the Indian Ocean and the border with Ethiopia, has been a self-governing autonomous state since 1998. The area of Southwestern Somalia is poorly organized and more conflict-ridden than any other part of the country, with much of that conflict centered on attempts to control the nominal Somali capital of Mogadishu and on-going famine. In 2004 a new government, the Transitional Federal Government (TFG), was created for the entire country. The president and parliament of the new government have not yet moved to Mogadishu, and discussions regarding the government's establishment are ongoing in Kenya. Numerous warlords and factions are still fighting for control of the capital city as well as for other southern regions. In 2006 and 2007 a push by central government forces, backed up by units of the Ethiopian regular army, succeeded in driving Islamic extremist forces out of the Mogadishu region. Ethiopian troops pulled out of Somalia in early 2009, but there is still no unification of the country. The lack of a stable government has facilitated Somali piracy in the Indian Ocean, which has been a continued threat to international shipping. By any definition, Somalia is a "disordered" or "failed" state.

Sudan and the Darfur Region: Since achieving political independence in 1956, Sudan has been beset by a series of civil wars. These wars have been rooted in the attempts of northern economic, political, and social interests dominated by Muslims to control territories occupied by non-Muslim, non-Arab southern Sudanese such as the Dinka tribal groups. Since 1983, the war- and famine-related effects have resulted in more than 2 million deaths and over 4 million people displaced. The current ruling regime is a mixture of military elite and an Islamist party that came to power in a 1989 coup. In 2003, fighting broke out in the three Darfur provinces of western Sudan adjacent to the border with Chad and the Central African Republic where pro-government Muslim militias have attacked and killed tens of thousands of non-Muslim tribal peoples. In 2005 and 2006, areas of conflict spilled over the borders of Sudan to involve both Chad and the Central African Republic. The Darfur region is relatively water-rich and forested in a country that is chiefly desert and is therefore desired by Muslim pastoral groups from the north for settlement purposes. International organizations have labeled the conflict in Darfur as "genocide" against the non-Muslim populations, and conflict continues.

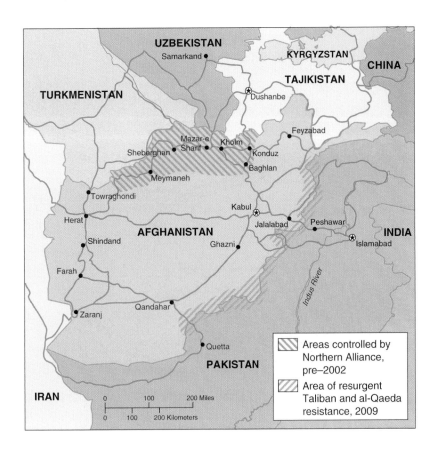

Afghanistan: In the aftermath of the tragic September 11, 2001 terrorist attacks on the World Trade Center and the Pentagon, the United States (backed to varying degrees by its allies) has declared a massive and global "war on terrorism" and any states that may provide "safe harbor" to terrorists. To date, the most prominent target of this U.S. declaration of war has been the Taliban regime of Islamic extremists who controlled about 95 percent of Afghanistan and harbored the al-Qaeda terrorist network of the beleaguered nation of Afghanistan. Beginning with air bombardments and later ground forces, U.S. and British forces, aided by members of the Northern Alliance of Afghan rebels, expelled the Taliban government in 2002. While now under home rule and with a duly elected government, Afghanistan still is plagued by warlords in remote areas of the country who refuse to recognize the legally constituted government. In addition, significant pockets of resistance from remnants of the former Taliban regime and from al-Qaeda forces are engaged in ongoing military conflict with American and Pakistani troops along the Afghanistan-Pakistan border. In 2006 and 2007 a marked resurgence of Taliban military activity occurred along the border between Afghanistan and Pakistan, giving rise to fears that the central government in Kabul—not strong to begin with—was beginning to lose its grasp of the peripheral areas of the country. The Taliban resurgence grew throughout 2008 and into 2009, partly as the result of an ineffective and corrupt central government that, for all practical purposes, controls only the region of the capital city, Kabul. And that control is tenuous. In 2009 President Barack Obama ordered 4,000 extra U.S. military personnel into the country to "disrupt, dismantle and defeat" al-Qaeda.

Chechnya: The area in southern Russia known as the Caucasus Region is home to a large variety of non-Russian ethnic groups; many are Muslim and resent centuries of Russian domination and Soviet-era totalitarianism. After the Soviet Union disintegrated in 1991, several of these ethnic groups began agitating for more autonomy from Moscow or for outright independence. One of the more vocal groups with a history of opposition to Moscow's rule were the Chechens. The Chechens declared themselves a sovereign nation in 1991 and by 1994 relations between the breakaway government in Chechnya and the Russian government had drastically deteriorated. In December of that year, Russian forces attacked Chechnya, beginning the first of two (1994–96 and 1999–present) full-scale military conflicts that have also crept into the neighboring Russian autonomous area of Dagestan, itself largely Muslim. In the mid- and late 1990s Russia experienced several terrorist attacks in cities throughout the nation, which the Russian government attributed to Islamic extremists supporting Chechen independence. As a result, a second round of the conflict began in August 1999 with a full-scale Russian military assault on Dagestan and Chechnya. This assault is ongoing and continues to face intense resistance, with heavy casualties on both sides. In 2003 and 2004 Chechen rebels increased their pressure with urban terrorist activities in Russian cities, including Moscow. Although conflicts between Russian and Chechnyan forces decreased in intensity since 2005, there have been terrorist incidents, including the bombing of a school building that killed numerous children.

Ethnic Pluralities

- Abkhaz
- Adygey
- Ajeri
- Armenian
- Avar
- Azeri
- Balkar
- Chechen
- Dargin
- Georgian
- Ingush
- Kabardin
- Karachay
- Kumyk
- Lak
- Lezghin
- Mingrelian and Svan
- Nogay
- Ossetian
- Russian
- No dominant group

Georgia: Along with Azerbaijan and Armenia, Georgia is one of the trans-Caucasus states attaining its independence after the breakup of the U.S.S.R. Unlike Azerbaijan, which is fairly homogenous in ethnicity and religion (Azerbaijani and Muslim), and Armenia, which is also an ethnically (Armenian) and religiously (Christian) uniform area, Georgia is a crazy quilt of ethnic, linguistic, and religious groups. Such a lack of national uniformity does not bode well for the stability of a political unit, and almost from its independence, Georgia has been beset by internal turmoil. Much of this has been centered in the north, in the province of South Ossetia, and in the west, in the province of Abkhazia. Both provinces have wanted, almost from the creation of Georgian independence, to achieve independence on their own. Matters came to a head in the summer of 2008 when the Russian Federation sent troops to augment already existing "peace-keeping" forces in the breakaway provinces of South Ossetia and Abkhazia. The Russians have no particular religious or ethnic links with populations in either South Ossetia or Abkhazia; the language of neither province is related to Russian and the populations are far from uniformly Russian Orthodox Christians in religion. Indeed, both the South Ossetian and Ahkhazian populations are more similar to the Chechens, a people who have given Russia no end of grief for the last decade and a half. So why did Russia "invade" Georgia? Partly to demonstrate that it could, perhaps, using an ill-advised Georgian military thrust into the breakaway South Ossetian region as an excuse. More important, the increased Russian occupation of areas of the Republic of Georgia signaled to the Georgians that the Russians would not take it kindly if Georgia continued its overtures to the West, particularly to the NATO alliance. In 2009 NATO conducted a series of military exercises near the Georgian capital of Tbilisi, an act that Russian President Medvedev called "an overt provocation." The Russian/Georgian conflict may signal the beginning of a period of increased military tension between the Russian Federation and the United States that some political and military experts are already calling "a new Cold War."

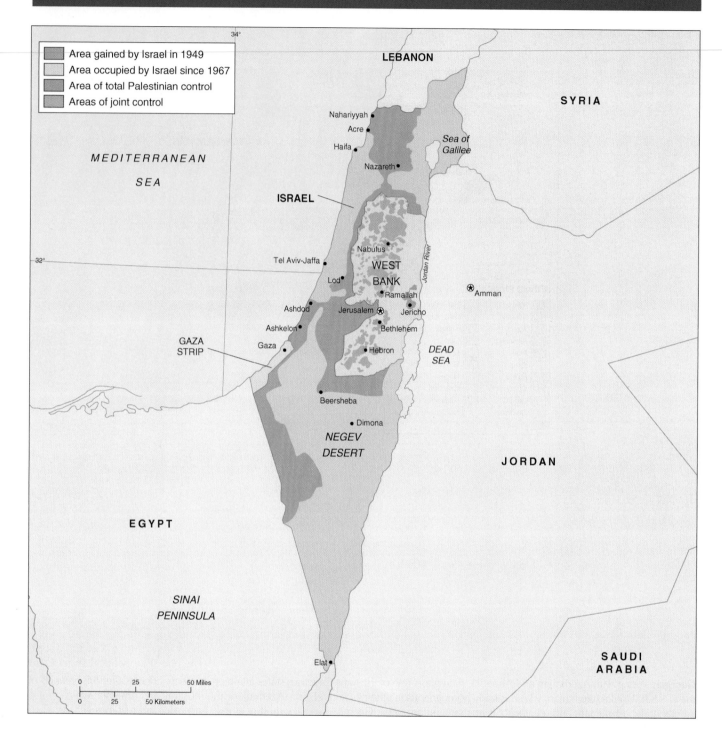

Map Legend:
- Area gained by Israel in 1949
- Area occupied by Israel since 1967
- Area of total Palestinian control
- Areas of joint control

LEBANON

SYRIA

MEDITERRANEAN
SEA

Nahariyyah
Acre
Haifa
Sea of
Galilee
Nazareth

ISRAEL

Nabulus
Tel Aviv-Jaffa
WEST
BANK
Lod
Jordan River
Amman
Ramallah
Ashdod
Jerusalem
Jericho
Ashkelon
Bethlehem
Gaza
GAZA
STRIP
Hebron
DEAD
SEA

Beersheba

Dimona

NEGEV
DESERT

JORDAN

EGYPT

SINAI
PENINSULA

Elat

SAUDI
ARABIA

0   25   50 Miles
0   25   50 Kilometers

Israel and Its Neighbors: The modern state of Israel was created out of the former British Protectorate of Palestine, inhabited primarily by Muslim Arabs, after World War II. Conflict between Arabs and Israeli Jews has been a constant ever since. Much of the present tension revolves around the West Bank area, not part of the original Israeli state but taken from Jordan, an Arab country, in the Six-Day War of 1967. Many Palestinians had settled this part of Jordan after the creation of Israel and remain as a majority population in the West Bank region today. Israel has established many agricultural settlements within the region since 1967, angering Palestinian Arabs. For Israel, the West Bank is the region of ancient Judea and this region, won in battle, will not be ceded back to Palestinian Arabs without protracted or severe military action. The West Bank, inhabited by nearly 400,000 Israeli settlers and 4 million Palestinians, is also the location of most of the suicide bombings carried out by Islamic militant groups from 2001 to 2009. By early 2008, the Gaza Strip had emerged as the most critical flashpoint in the area. The Israeli government and the Palestinian Authority had agreed to resume peace talks with the goal being a peace agreement by the end of the year. But in late 2008 and early 2009, Israeli troops responded to rocket attacks by HAMAS, a leading Palestinian political party, by attacking Gaza in force. By January 2009, over 1000 Palestinians and Israelis had died in this latest conflict.

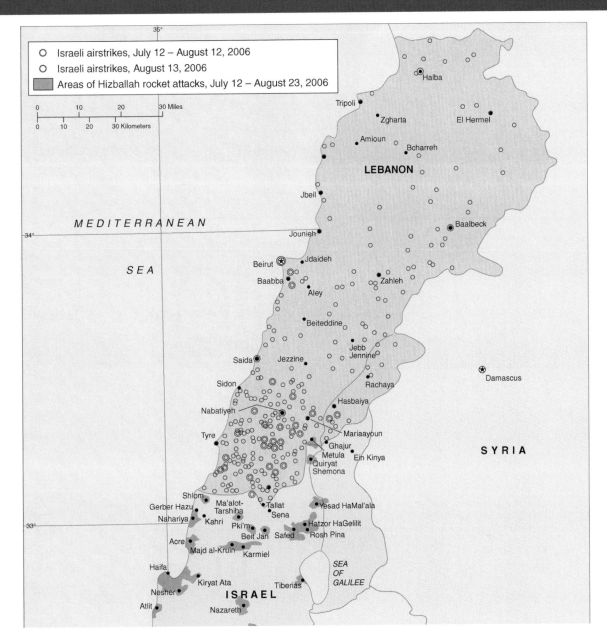

Legend:
- ○ Israeli airstrikes, July 12 – August 12, 2006
- ○ Israeli airstrikes, August 13, 2006
- ▨ Areas of Hizballah rocket attacks, July 12 – August 23, 2006

Lebanon-Israel: Following a devastating 1976–91 civil war between Lebanon's Muslim majority (about 53%) and Christian minority (about 5%), it was agreed to rebuild a political institution in which the Lebanese established a more equitable political system, giving Muslims a greater voice in the political process while institutionalizing sectarian divisions in the government. Lebanon's neighbor, Syria, intruded into Lebanese territory with military forces. In response, Israel occupied a good part of southern Lebanon until 2000 and then withdrew, leaving many areas of Lebanon under Syrian control. The passage of a United Nations resolution in 2004 called for Syria to withdraw from Lebanon and end its interference in Lebanese affairs, encouraging the Lebanese government to oppose Syria's presence. In February 2005, the assassination of a popular former prime minister led to the "Cedar Revolution," massive demonstrations in Beirut against the Syrian presence. In April 2005, Syria withdrew the remainder of its military forces from Lebanon. In spring 2005, Lebanon held its first free legislative elections since the end of the civil war, and the nation began rebuilding its formerly thriving economy. Most militias were disbanded, and the Lebanese Armed Forces extended authority over about two-thirds of the country. But Hizballah, a radical Shi'a organization listed by the U.S. State Department as a Foreign Terrorist Organization, retained its weapons and control over much of southern Lebanon. In July 2006, Hizballah militia kidnapped Israeli soldiers and launched rockets and mortars into northern Israel. Israel retaliated by blockading Lebanese ports and airports and by conducting airstrikes against Hizballah locations throughout Lebanon. Since Hizballah militia were located throughout urban areas, Israeli retaliation resulted in many civilian deaths. Most of the Israelis killed by Hizballah rockets were civilians. Nine hundred thousand Lebanese and three hundred thousand Israelis were displaced by warfare, and normal life was disrupted across all of Lebanon and northern Israel. A UN resolution, approved by both Lebanese and Israeli governments in August 2006, called for the disarming of Hizballah, Israeli withdrawal, and deployment of the Lebanese Army and an enlarged UN peace-keeping force in southern Lebanon. The situation remains tense as Hizballah has not fully disarmed.

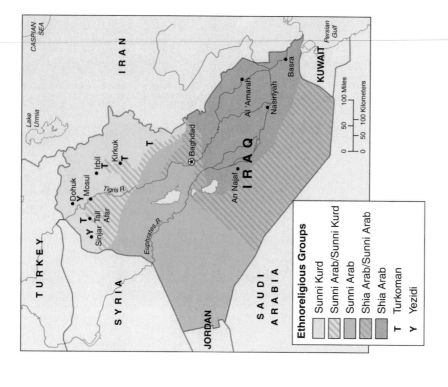

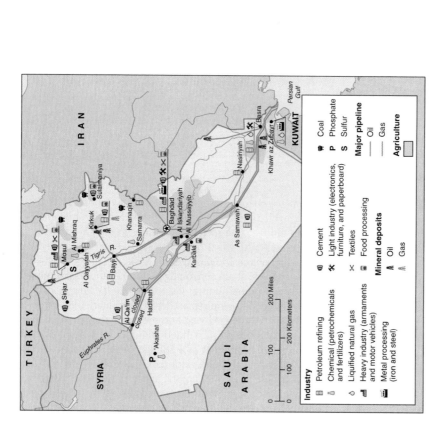

Iraq: Prior to the 1990–91 invasion of Kuwait by Iraq and the subsequent United Nations coalition's military expulsion of Iraq from its neighbor, Iraq was one of the most prosperous countries in the Middle East and the only one with full capacity to feed itself, even without the vast oil revenues generated by the country's immense reserves. Despite the inefficiencies of the Baathist dictatorship of Saddam Hussein, the country had a solid agricultural base and a burgeoning industry. The combination of military adventurism and conflict, in the form of a lengthy war with Iran and the ill-advised invasion of Kuwait, limited further economic development, however. Development was also problematic given the country's internal tensions between Arabic Sunni Muslims and Arabic Shiite Muslims, and between Arabs and Kurds and a few other minority populations in the northern parts of the country.

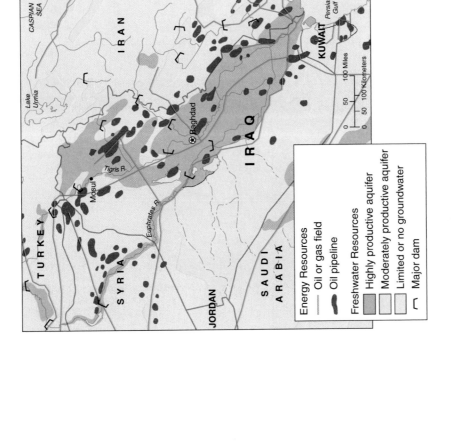

Energy Resources

— Oil or gas field
— Oil pipeline

Freshwater Resources

■ Highly productive aquifer
■ Moderately productive aquifer
■ Limited or no groundwater
⌐ Major dam

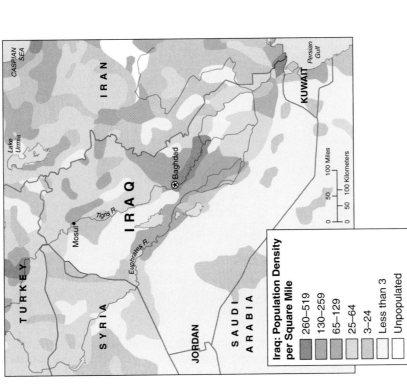

Iraq: Population Density per Square Mile

■ 260–519
■ 130–259
■ 65–129
■ 25–64
■ 3–24
■ Less than 3
□ Unpopulated

The most densely settled areas of Iraq are in the more well-watered portions of the country in the floodplains of the Tigris and Euphrates rivers, the historical center of Mesopotamian civilization since the fifth millennium B.C. To the west of the floodplain region lies the northeastern portions of the great Arabian desert, and population densities here are very low. Most of Iraq's huge oil reserves are located in the areas of greatest population density

and agricultural production, between the rivers and north and east of the Tigris River. The combination of the Middle East's highest potential level of agricultural production and great oil wealth make Iraq unique among states of the region in terms of potential self-sufficiency. That potential is currently being hindered by the ongoing civil conflict between the Shiite majority and the Sunni minority populations.

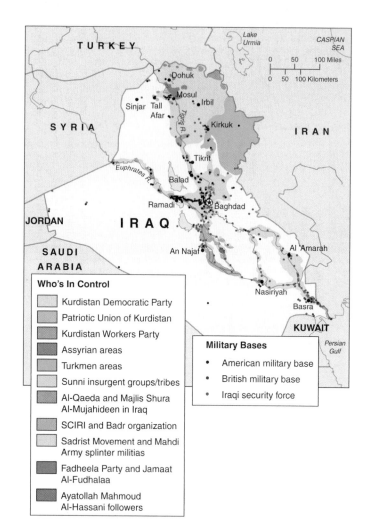

Who's In Control

- Kurdistan Democratic Party
- Patriotic Union of Kurdistan
- Kurdistan Workers Party
- Assyrian areas
- Turkmen areas
- Sunni insurgent groups/tribes
- Al-Qaeda and Majlis Shura Al-Mujahideen in Iraq
- SCIRI and Badr organization
- Sadrist Movement and Mahdi Army splinter militias
- Fadheela Party and Jamaat Al-Fudhalaa
- Ayatollah Mahmoud Al-Hassani followers

Military Bases

- • American military base
- • British military base
- • Iraqi security force

	November 2004	November 2006	November 2008
Iraqi Civilian Deaths From War	2,650	3,475	500
Civilians Displaced, Net Rate (refugees and internally displaced; in thousands)	50	90	0
U.S./Other Foreign Forces (in thousands)	138 / 24	140 / 18	148 / 6
Iraqi Security Forces (in thousands)	114	323	558
Iraqi Security Forces in Top Two Readiness Tiers (in thousands)	5	220	380
U.S. Troop Deaths	137	69	12
Iraqi Security Force Deaths	65	123	27
U.S. Active-Duty Soldiers Having Served Multiple Deployments in Iraq/Afghanistan (percent)	5	20	31
Iraqi Trained Judges	300	1,200	1,180
Number of "Sons of Iraq" (in thousands)	0	5	100
"Sons of Iraq" Paid by Iraqi Government (in thousands)	0	0	54
Electricity Production (average gigawatts; official grid; prewar: 4)	3.2	3.7	5.1
Oil Production (in millions of barrels per day)	2.0 / 1.3	2.1 / 1.4	2.4 / 1.9
Unemployment Rate (percent)	35	33	30
Political Progress Achieved (out of 11 "Iraq index" criteria)	0	0.5	7

More favorable conditions [ ] Less favorable conditions

Nearly 5 years after the U.S.-led invasion, Iraq is still in critical condition, although important strides have been made as the chart comparing 2004 and 2008 shows. Sectarian violence is still rampant, although death tolls have declined, and the price of Operation Iraqi Freedom will likely reach a staggering $3 trillion. As of 2008, the maps above show the state of Iraq nearly 5 years after the end of active military conflict between the Baathist forces of Saddam Hussein and the U.S.-led coalition forces. It is a country fractured by conflicting tribal and religious loyalties, beset by a continuing Sunni insurgency against the Shiite-dominated constitutional government. There are signs of hope, however, and some of the most vocal of the insurgents have toned down their rhetoric. Nevertheless, violence escalated as the U.S. began withdrawing troops in 2009.

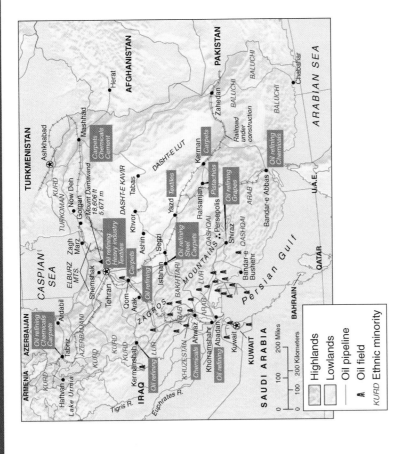

Iran: Iran has been a bone in the throat of the United States and Israel since the overthrow of the pro-Western government of the Shah and the installation of a fundamentalist Islamic republic in 1979. The Iranians took a large number of American hostages following the political revolution and held them for over a year. During an eight-year war between Iran and its nearest neighbor, Iraq, the United States provided military aid to Iraq, further straining the relations between Iran and the West. Iran's promise to continue development of nuclear facilities that could lead to the development of nuclear weapons has heightened distrust of Iran in the West. More likely, however, is that once Iran has developed facilities capable of producing weapons-grade plutonium, Israel will carry out the same type of preemptive strikes it has previously used on Iraq and Syria. Iran is a large and important country, poorly understood by the United States. In 2009, hard-line President Ahmadinejad won re-election in a highly contested and controversial vote. Millions of Iranians took to the street to protest, but Supreme Leader Ayatollah Khamenei endorsed Ahmadinejad as the winner and declared the protests illegal. With an ancient imperial tradition, Iran is the historical core of Shiah Islam (nearly 90% of Iranians are Shiite Muslims) and it possesses enormous reserves of oil and natural gas.

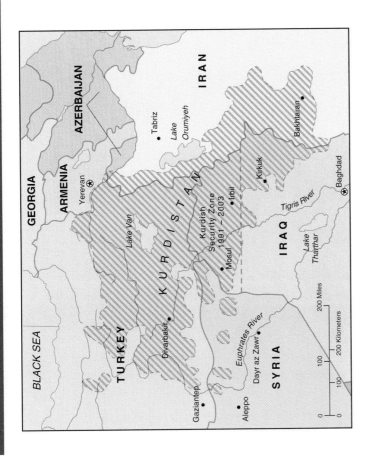

Kurdistan: Where Turkey, Iran, and Iraq meet in the high mountain region of the Tauros and Zagros mountains, a nation of 25 million people exists. This nation is "Kurdistan," but the Kurds, the occupants of this area for over 3,000 years, have no state, and receive much less attention than other stateless nations like the Palestinians. Following the 1991 Gulf War between Iraq and a U.S.-led coalition of European and Arabic states, the United Nations demarcated a Kurdish "security zone" in northern Iraq. From 1991 to 2003 the Security Zone was anything but secure as Iraqi militants from the south and Turks from the north infringed on Kurdish territory, and the internal militant extremist groups, such as the Kurdish Workers' Party, staged periodic attacks on rival villages. During the 2003 U.S.-led invasion of Iraq that eliminated the Baathist regime of Saddam Hussein, the Kurds played an important role in securing the northern portions of Iraq for the U.S.-British coalition and fought alongside American troops in expelling elements of the Iraqi army from cities like Mosul and Kirkuk. Rich in oil and history, Kurdistan will probably remain as a nation without a state, shared by Iraq, Turkey, and Iran—none of which is likely to give up substantial portions of territory for the establishment of a Kurdish state. In 2010, that portion of northern Iraq under Kurdish control was the most stable of that war-torn country.

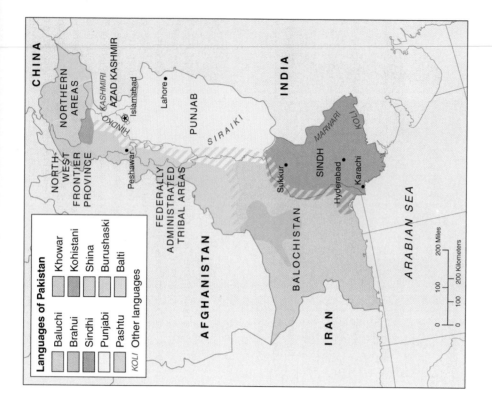

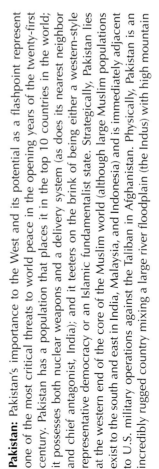

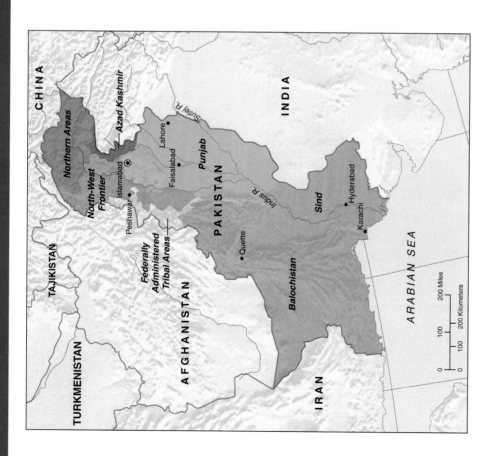

Pakistan: Pakistan's importance to the West and its potential as a flashpoint represent one of the most critical threats to world peace in the opening years of the twenty-first century. Pakistan has a population that places it in the top 10 countries in the world; it possesses both nuclear weapons and a delivery system (as does its nearest neighbor and chief antagonist, India); and it teeters on the brink of being either a western-style representative democracy or an Islamic fundamentalist state. Strategically, Pakistan lies at the western end of the core of the Muslim world (although large Muslim populations exist to the south and east in India, Malaysia, and Indonesia) and is immediately adjacent to U.S. military operations against the Taliban in Afghanistan. Physically, Pakistan is an incredibly rugged country mixing a large river floodplain (the Indus) with high mountain country with peaks in excess of 25,000 feet in elevation in the northwest. Culturally, the country is a mixture of different linguistic and ethnic groups. The government has tried to encourage the use of Urdu as the national language, but less than 10% of Pakistanis speak Urdu as their primary language. About the only source of unity in Pakistan is Sunni Islam, but even here, nearly 20% of the Pakistani population adheres to Shi'a Islam. The long-serving president, Musharraf, who resigned in 2008, was a purported ally of the United States, although his actions indicated otherwise. Asif Ali Zardari, a more West-leaning political figure, was elected president in a landslide but almost immediately was confronted with Islamist militants, mainly Taliban, expanding their control in the North-West Frontier Province toward the capital city of Islamabad.

-64-

Jammu and Kashmir: When Britain withdrew from South Asia in 1947, the former states of British India were asked to decide whether they wanted to become part of a new Hindu India or a Muslim Pakistan. In the state of Jammu and Kashmir, the rulers were Hindu and the majority population was Muslim. The maharajah (prince) of Kashmir opted to join India, but an uprising of the Muslim majority precipitated a war between India and Pakistan over control of this high mountain region. In 1949 a cease-fire line was established by the UN, leaving most of the territory of Jammu and Kashmir in Indian hands. Since then Pakistan and India have waged intermittent skirmishes over the disputed territory that holds the headwaters of the Indus River, a life-giving stream to desert Pakistan. In 1999 extremist Muslim groups demanding independence escalated the periodic battles into a full-fledged, if small, war between two of Asia's major powers—both possessing nuclear weapons. The specter of nuclear exchange caused both Pakistan and India to back down, and while the area remains disputed, military activity has quieted somewhat. There have been some suggestions that the terrorist attack on Mumbai (Bombay) in the summer of 2008 was fueled by tensions over Kashmir. That is less likely than the general simmering feud between Hindu and Muslim that has been part of South Asian politics since independence from Great Britain and partition into separate states in 1947.

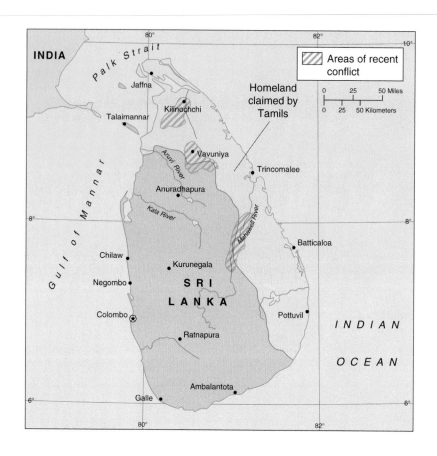

Sri Lanka: The island state of Sri Lanka, historically known as Ceylon, is potentially one of the most agriculturally productive regions of Asia. Unfortunately for plans related to agricultural development, two quite different peoples have occupied the island country: The Buddhist Sinhalese originally from northern India and long the dominant population in Sri Lanka, and the minority Hindu Tamil, a Dravidian people from south India. Since independence from Britain, Sri Lankan governments have sought to "resettle" the Tamil population in south India, actions that finally precipitated an armed rebellion by Tamils against the Sinhalese-dominated government. The Tamils at present are demanding a complete separation of the state into two parts, with a Tamil homeland in the north and along the east coast. A cease-fire between Sinhalese and Tamil fighters was brokered in 2001 but fell apart in late 2003 with the resumption of violence. 2006 and 2007 brought a renewal of terrorist attacks instigated by the Tamil rebels. In 2009, government forces eliminated the last Tamil stronghold, seemingly ending a quarter-century of violence. Time will tell if this is a lasting peace or simply another lull in a protracted conflict.

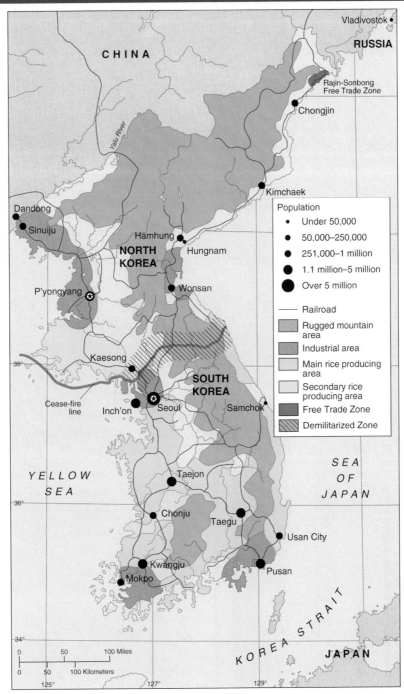

Korean Peninsula: Although active military conflict has not existed since the 1950s, the Korean peninsula remains an important flashpoint. Following the Japanese occupation during World War II, Korea was split into a Communist-dominated north, and an ostensibly republican south, the latter backed by the United States. Between 1950 and 1953 communist North Korea, allied with China, attempted unsuccessfully to reunite the entire peninsula under Communist rule. Since the end of the "Korean War," South Korea has flourished economically. North Korea, on the other hand, adopted a policy of diplomatic and economic "self-reliance," becoming one of the world's most authoritarian and isolated states. North Korea molded its political, economic, and military policies around the core ideological objective of eventual unification of Korea and retains that objective. Yet, North Korea so mismanaged and misallocated its resources that, by the mid-1990s, the country was unable to feed itself. An estimated two million North Koreans have died in the past decade, resulting from severe food shortages. It continues to expend resources to maintain one of the world's largest armies. In 2003, North Korea announced that it would violate a 1994 agreement with the United States to freeze and ultimately dismantle its existing plutonium-based program. It also expelled monitors from the International Atomic Energy Agency (IAEA) and withdrew from the international Non-Proliferation Treaty. By 2006, North Korea announced the development of nuclear weapons and delivery systems designed to "protect" North Korea against American aggression. In 2007, the North Korean government, in exchange for the relaxing of sanctions against it, temporarily agreed to halt its attempt to build a nuclear arsenal. In 2009, North Korea conducted a nuclear test, which was followed by the test firing of several short-range missiles and a long-range rocket. The United Nations imposed sanctions that were supported by North Korean long-time allies China and Russia.

Map **44**   International Terrorist Incidents, 2000–2006

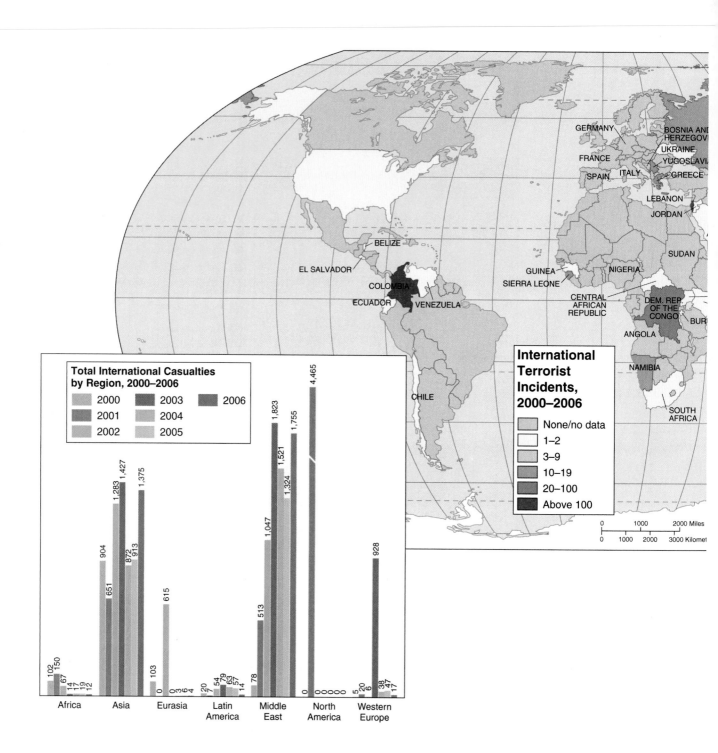

Americans have made a mantra of the saying "the world has changed" as a consequence of the terrorist attacks on the World Trade Center and the Pentagon on September 11, 2001. As the map above and the accompanying graphs of terrorist activities before and after 9/11/01 indicate, however, the world did not change, although the focus of a major terrorist attack shifted from Africa, Asia, and the Middle East to North America. Many other areas of the world have lived with terrorism and terrorist activity for years. In 2000 and 2001, despite the enormous losses in the United States in the 9/11 attacks, more lives were lost in Asia and Africa as a result of terrorism than were lost in North America. The world did not change, but Americans' perception of that world and their place in it has certainly changed. Events subsequent to 9/11 indicate a shift back to more "normal" patterns in North America from 2002 to the present, a time during which terrorist activities have been virtually absent. This is in sharp contrast to other parts of the world where terrorist activities have been on the upswing, the Madrid train bombing that killed nearly 200 people, and the London subway bombing that killed more than 50.

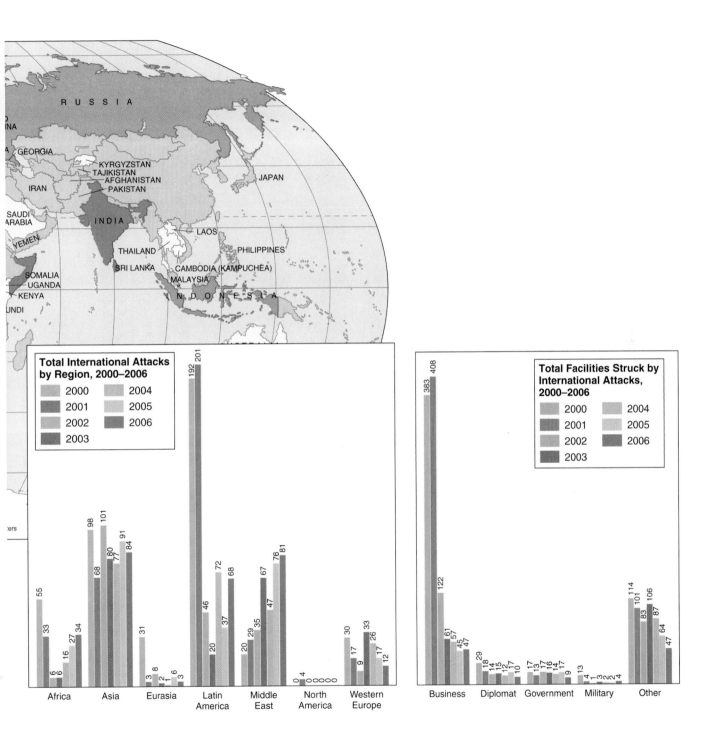

Total International Attacks by Region, 2000–2006

	2000	2001	2002	2003	2004	2005	2006
Africa	55	6	6	16	27	34	
Asia	98	68	101	80	77	91	84
Eurasia	31	3	8	2	1	6	3
Latin America	192	201	46	20	72	37	68
Middle East	20	29	35	67	47	76	81
North America	0	4	0	0	0	0	
Western Europe	30	17	9	33	26	17	12

Total Facilities Struck by International Attacks, 2000–2006

	2000	2001	2002	2003	2004	2005	2006
Business	383	408	122	61	57	45	47
Diplomat	29	18	14	15	12	17	10
Government	17	13	17	16	14	17	9
Military	13	4	1	3	2	2	4
Other	114	101	83	106	87	64	47

Two qualifiers need to be added regarding the data presented: the term "casualties" refers to dead and wounded (the number of the dead represents a relatively small percentage of total casualties by region); the term "terrorist attacks" does not include insurgency events in areas of military conflict or occupation and, therefore, does not include attacks carried out against U.S. forces or others in places like Afghanistan or Iraq where military action continued throughout the time frame of the data. And, as terrible as they are, terrorist attacks do not include the casualties of sectarian violence such as that between Iraqi Shiites and Sunnis or between paramilitary organizations such as Hizballah and the legal state of Israel. In late 2003, the manner of collecting data on terrorist incidents and casualties therefrom changed, as did the definition of what constituted an international terrorist event. Hence, data for 2004 through 2006 are not comparable to data from 2003 and earlier. And reliable data from 2007 on are simply not available, meaning that neither the map nor the chart reflect the deadly terrorist attack on Mumbai, India in late 2008.

Map 45 The Political Geography of a Global Religion: The Islamic World

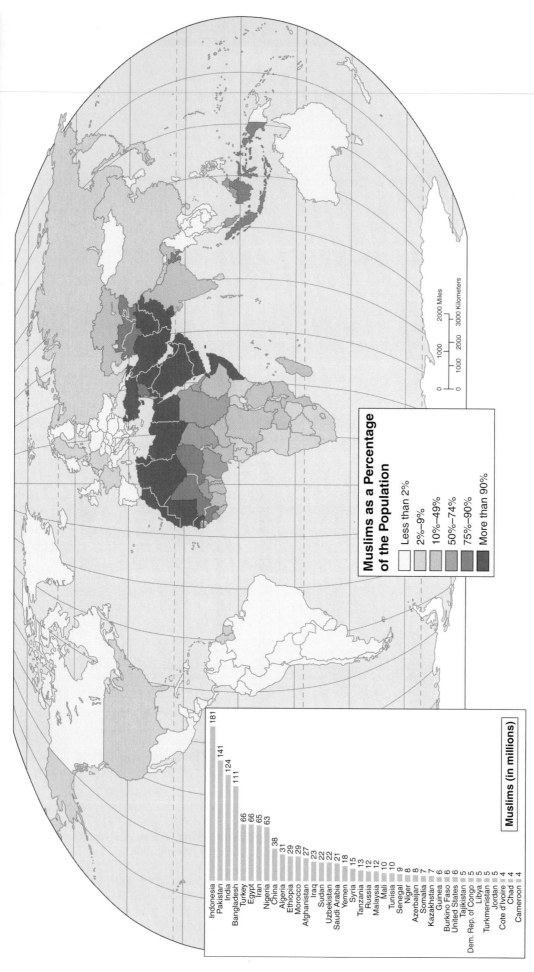

Muslims as a Percentage of the Population

- Less than 2%
- 2%–9%
- 10%–49%
- 50%–74%
- 75%–90%
- More than 90%

0   1000   2000   2000 Miles
0   1000   2000   3000 Kilometers

Muslims (in millions)

Country	Muslims
Indonesia	181
Pakistan	141
India	124
Bangladesh	111
Turkey	66
Egypt	66
Iran	65
Nigeria	63
China	38
Algeria	31
Ethiopia	29
Morocco	29
Afghanistan	27
Iraq	23
Sudan	22
Uzbekistan	22
Saudi Arabia	21
Yemen	18
Syria	15
Tanzania	13
Russia	12
Malaysia	12
Mali	10
Tunisia	10
Senegal	9
Niger	8
Azerbaijan	8
Somalia	7
Kazakhstan	7
Guinea	6
Burkino Faso	6
United States	6
Tajikistan	5
Dem. Rep. of Congo	5
Libya	5
Turkmenistan	5
Jordan	5
Cote d'Ivoire	4
Chad	4
Cameroon	4

Islam, as a religion, does not promote conflict. The term *jihad*, often mistranslated to mean "holy war," in fact refers to the struggle to find God and to promote the faith. In spite of the beneficent nature of Islamic teachings, the tensions between Muslims and adherents of other faiths often flare into warfare. A comparison of this map with the map of international conflict will show a disproportionate number of wars in that portion of the world where Muslims are either majority or significant minority populations. The reasons for this are based more in the nature of government, cultures, and social structure than in the tenets of the faith of Islam. Nevertheless, the spatial correlations cannot be ignored. Similarly, terrorist incidents falling considerably short of open armed warfare are spatially consistent with the distribution of Islam and even more consistent with the presence of Islamic fundamentalism or "Islamism," which tends to be less tolerant and more aggressive than the mainstream of the religion. Terrorism is also consistent with those areas where the legacy of colonialism or the persistent presence of non-Islamic cultures intrudes into the Islamic world.

Map 46 Countries with Nuclear Weapons

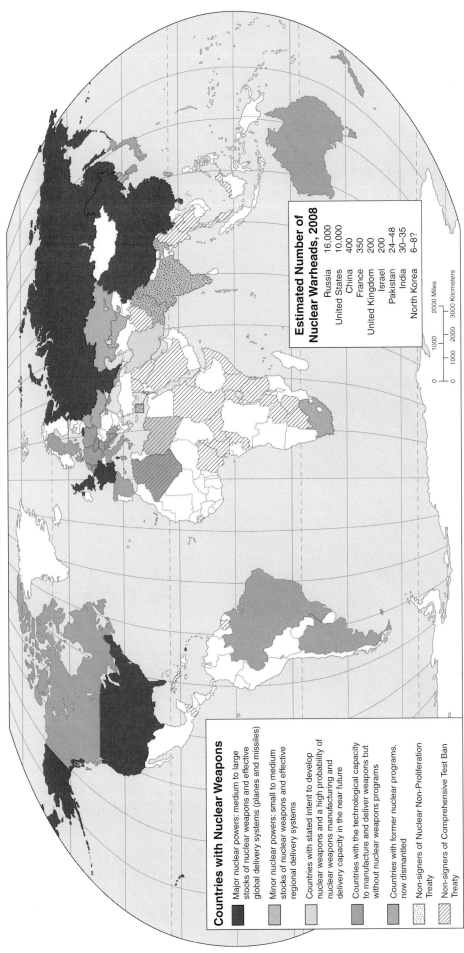

Countries with Nuclear Weapons

- Major nuclear powers: medium to large stocks of nuclear weapons and effective global delivery systems (planes and missiles)
- Minor nuclear powers: small to medium stocks of nuclear weapons and effective regional delivery systems
- Countries with stated intent to develop nuclear weapons and a high probability of nuclear weapons manufacturing and delivery capacity in the near future
- Countries with the technological capacity to manufacture and deliver weapons but without nuclear weapons programs
- Countries with former nuclear programs, now dismantled
- Non-signers of Nuclear Non-Proliferation Treaty
- Non-signers of Comprehensive Test Ban Treaty

Estimated Number of Nuclear Warheads, 2008

Russia	16,000
United States	10,000
China	400
France	350
United Kingdom	200
Israel	200
Pakistan	24–48
India	30–35
North Korea	6–8?

Since 1980, the number of countries possessing the capacity to manufacture and deliver nuclear weapons has grown dramatically, increasing the chances of accidental or intentional nuclear exchanges. In addition to the traditional nuclear powers of the United States, Russia, China, the United Kingdom, and France, must now be added Israel, India, and Pakistan as countries that, without possessing the large stocks of weapons of the major powers, nor the extensive delivery systems of the United States and Russia, still have effective regional (and possibly global) delivery systems and medium stocks of warheads. Countries such as Kazakhstan, Ukraine, Georgia, and Belarus that were created out of what had been the Soviet Union did have some nuclear capacity in the 1991–1995 period but have since had all nuclear weapons removed from their territories. North Korea has recently announced the re-suspension of its nuclear weapons programs, although it may possess a small stock of nuclear warheads along with the capacity to deliver those

weapons regionally. Iran has announced nuclear ambitions and recently tested delivery systems. Until the overthrow of the Baathist regime of Saddam Hussein by a U.S.-led military coalition in 2003, Iraq also had nuclear ambitions. The proliferation of nuclear states threatens global security, and the objective of the Nuclear Non-Proliferation Treaty was to reduce the chances for expanding nuclear arsenals worldwide. This treaty has been partially successful in that a number of countries in the developed world certainly have the capacity to manufacture and deliver nuclear weapons but have chosen not to do so. These countries include Canada, European countries other than the United Kingdom and France, South Korea, Japan, Australia, and New Zealand, and Brazil and Argentina in South America. On the other side of the coin, the still-possible intent of North Korea to emerge as a nuclear power may force countries such as South Korea and Japan to re-think their positions as non-nuclear countries.

Map 47 Size of Armed Forces

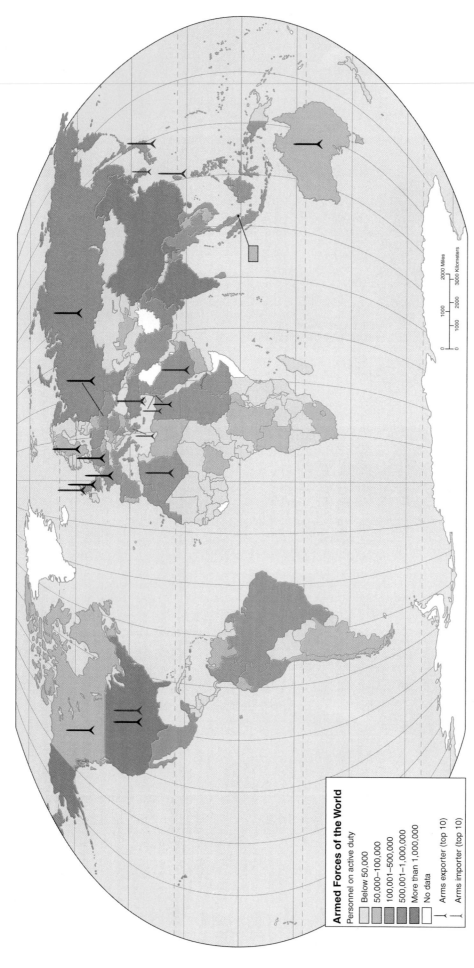

Armed Forces of the World

Personnel on active duty

- Below 50,000
- 50,000–100,000
- 100,001–500,000
- 500,001–1,000,000
- More than 1,000,000
- No data
- Arms exporter (top 10)
- Arms importer (top 10)

While the size of a country's armed forces is still an indicator of national power on the international scene, it is no longer as important as it once was. The increasing high technology of military hardware allows smaller numbers of military personnel to be more effective. There are some countries, such as China, with massive numbers of military personnel but with relatively limited military power because of a lack of modern weaponry. Additionally, the use of rapid transportation allows personnel to be deployed about the globe or any region of it quickly; this also increases the effectiveness of highly trained and well-armed smaller military units. Nevertheless, the world is still a long way from the

predicted "push-button warfare" that many experts have long anticipated. Indeed, the pattern of the last few years has been for most military conflicts to involve ground troops engaged in fairly traditional patterns of operation. Even with its high-tech "unmanned" weaponry, the United States carries out most of its military operations during wartime with ground infantry, with naval and air support using conventional weaponry. Thus, while the size of a country's armed forces may not be as important as it once was, it is still a major factor in measuring the ability of nations to engage successfully in armed conflict.

Map 48 Military Expenditures as a Percentage of Gross National Product

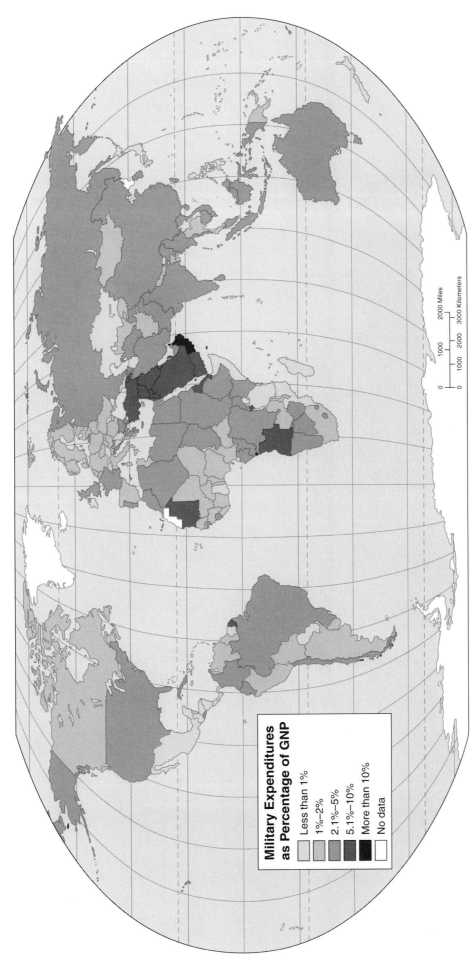

**Military Expenditures
as Percentage of GNP**

- Less than 1%
- 1%–2%
- 2.1%–5%
- 5.1%–10%
- More than 10%
- No data

0   1000   2000 Miles

0 1000 2000 3000 Kilometers

Many countries devote a significant proportion of their total central governmental expenditures to defense: weapons, personnel, and research and development of military hardware. A glance at the map reveals that there are a number of regions in which defense expenditures are particularly high, reflecting the degree of past and present political tension between countries. The clearest example is the Middle East. The steady increase in military expenditures by developing countries is one of the most alarming (and least well-known) worldwide defense issues. Where the end of the cold war has meant a substantial reduction of military expenditures for the countries in North America and Europe and for Russia, in many of the world's developing countries military expenditures have risen between 15 percent and 20 percent per year for the past few years, averaging out to 7.5 percent per year for the past quarter century. Even though many developing countries still spend less than 5 percent of their gross national product on defense, these funds could be put to different uses in such human development areas as housing, land reform, health care, and education.

Map 49 Abuse of Public Trust

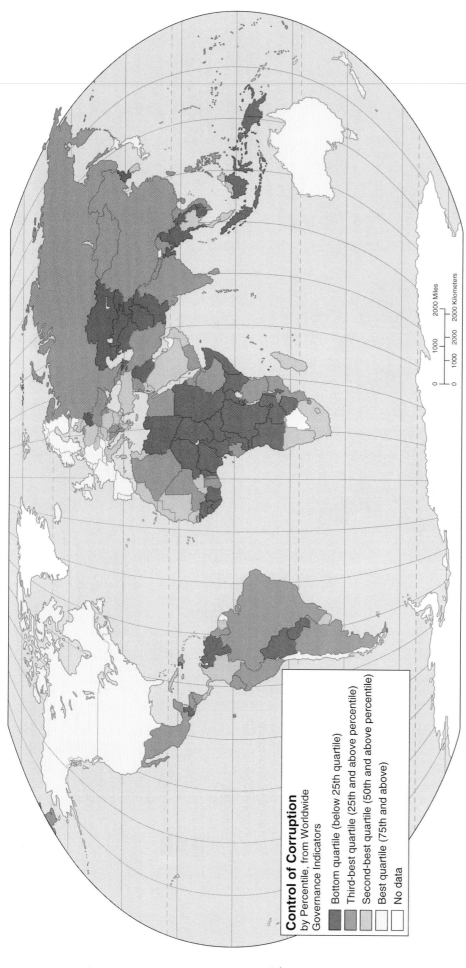

Control of Corruption
by Percentile, from Worldwide
Governance Indicators

- Bottom quartile (below 25th quartile)
- Third-best quartile (25th and above percentile)
- Second-best quartile (50th and above percentile)
- Best quartile (75th and above)
- No data

0   1000   2000   2000 Miles
0   1000   2000   2000 Kilometers

Abusing the public trust is simply another way of saying "corruption in government." In many parts of the world, corruption in the government is not an aberration but a way of life. Normally, although not always, governmental corruption is an indication of a weak and ineffective government, one that negatively affects such public welfare issues as public health, sanitation, education, and the provision of social services. It also tends to impact the cost of doing business and, thereby, drives away the foreign capital so badly needed in many African and Asian countries for economic development. Corruption is not automatic in poor countries, nor are rich countries free from it. But there is a general correlation between abuse of the public trust and lower levels of per capita income—excepting such countries as the Baltic states and Chile that have reached high standards of governance without joining the ranks of the wealthy countries. Studies by the World Bank have shown that countries that address issues of corruption and clean up the operations of their governments increase national incomes as much as four or five times. In those countries striving to attain governments that function according to a rule of law—rather than a rule of abusing the public trust—such important demographic measures as child mortality drop by as much as 75%. Clearly, good government and good business and higher incomes and better living conditions for the general public all go hand-in-hand.

Map 50 The Perception of Corruption

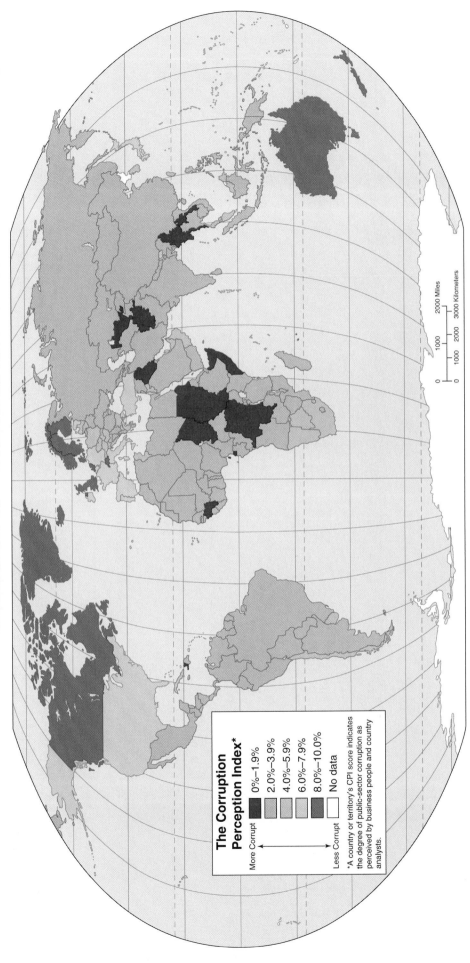

The Corruption Perception Index*

More Corrupt ⟷ Less Corrupt

- 0%–1.9%
- 2.0%–3.9%
- 4.0%–5.9%
- 6.0%–7.9%
- 8.0%–10.0%
- No data

*A country or territory's CPI score indicates the degree of public-sector corruption as perceived by business people and country analysts.

0   1000   2000 Miles

0 1000 2000 3000 Kilometers

A country's Corruption Perception Index is based on analyses by business executives who work with a country's government or whose company does business within the country evaluated; in addition, the CPI is contributed to by analysts from press sources, international organizations, and others whose jobs are involved in the gathering of intelligence on foreign areas. A glance at the map tells us things that we might have easily intuited: Iraq, Afghanistan, Sudan, Somalia, Myanmar, and other disrupted or failed states or military dictatorships fall into the range of "more corrupt." At the same time, northern and western European governments with stable parliamentary democracies and high standards of living are, as we might expect, among the least corrupt. But why should the United States fall into a middle-range category, along with Mediterranean, Central, and Eastern European countries on the CPI scale? Have U.S. governmental actions and/or

business dealings over the last few years reduced our international reputation? It would be tempting to think so. Non-U.S. analysts are not stupid, and when such large percentages of American tax dollars devoted to the Iraq war end up in either American or Iraqi private hands, without discernible benefit, that fact registers with those analysts. The great Scottish poet Robert Burns wrote "Oh, would some Power the gift give us, to see ourselves as others see us" (translated from the Scottish). This may not be a bad plea for American officials to make. It is simply not good enough, in a country that supposedly governs itself by the rule of law, to say, "Well, we're not seen as corrupt as Somalia or Myanmar." It would also be self-defeating to dismiss these perceptions as unimportant. How a country is seen by others is often a very important factor in how that country is dealt with by others.

-75-

Map 51 Political and Civil Liberties

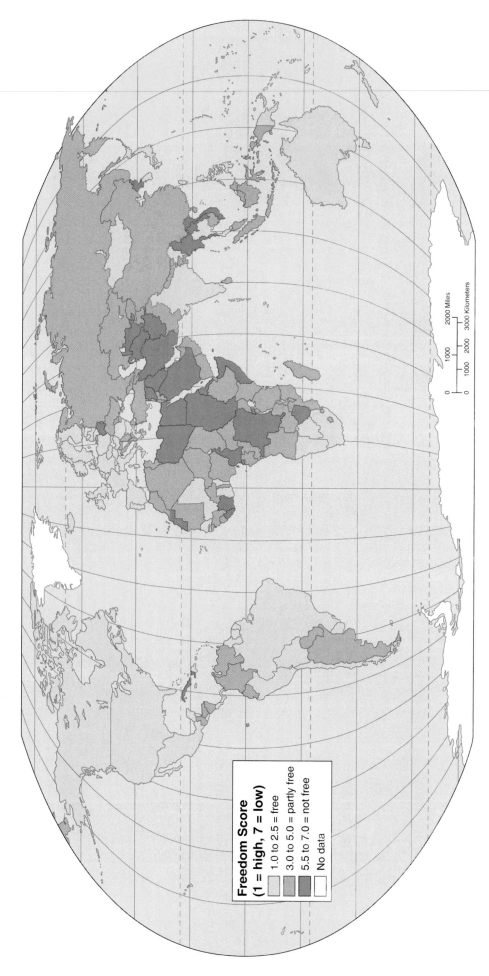

Freedom Score
(1 = high, 7 = low)

- 1.0 to 2.5 = free
- 3.0 to 5.0 = partly free
- 5.5 to 7.0 = not free
- No data

0	1000	2000 Miles
0	1000	2000	3000 Kilometers

Although measures of political and civil liberty are somewhat difficult to obtain and assess, there are some generally accepted standards that can be evaluated: open elections and competitive political parties, the rule of law, freedoms of speech and press, judicial systems separate from other branches of government, and limits on the power of elected or appointed governmental officials. Interestingly, there appear to be correlations between "degrees of freedom" and such other characteristics of a state as per capita wealth, environmental quality, and healthy economic growth—characteristics that may be mutually contradictory. There is no empirical evidence of a causal link between democratic institutions and consumption; on the other hand, there is clear evidence of a positive relationship between wealth and consumption. Therefore, the three variables are closely correlated and should be used in assessing the nature of the state in any part of the world.

Map 52   Human Rights Abuse

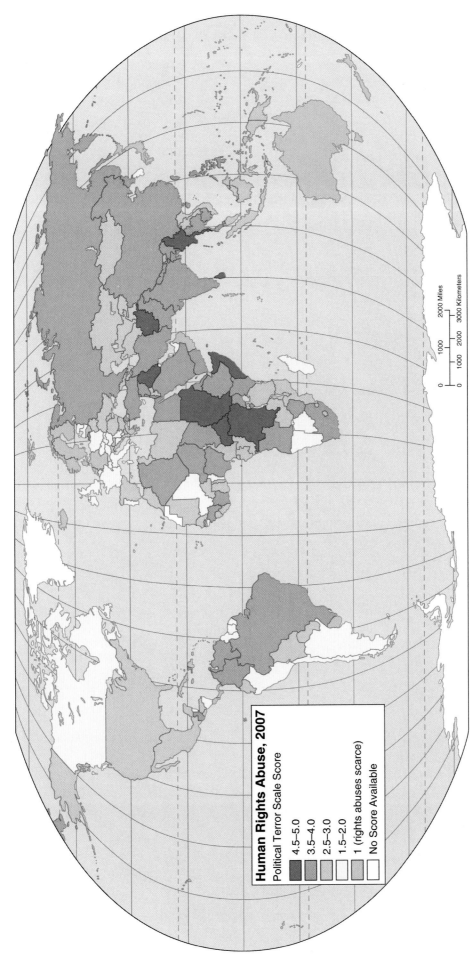

Human Rights Abuse, 2007
Political Terror Scale Score

- 4.5–5.0
- 3.5–4.0
- 2.5–3.0
- 1.5–2.0
- 1 (rights abuses scarce)
- No Score Available

The Political Terror Scale measures levels of political violence and terror that a country experiences in a particular year. The score is calculated using data from the U.S. State Department Country Reports on Human Rights and yearly country reports from Amnesty International. At the lowest end of the scale, torture or political murder are scarce and the rule of law dominates. Higher scores indicate increasing pervasiveness of human rights abuses. At the highest level, a country's entire population is affected by political terror, genocide, or other crimes against humanity. Countries with high scores typically are dic-

tatorships or totalitarian states whose leaders oftentimes carry out political terror through secret police forces or death squads. In many politically unstable countries, the Political Terror Scale may fluctuate from year to year. In the early 2000s countries like Liberia, Colombia, and Rwanda ranked much higher than in 2007. Conversely, Central African Republic, Thailand, and Kenya have seen increases in the score since the early 2000s. Afghanistan, Democratic Republic of the Congo, Somalia, and Iraq have had very high scores since the turn of the century.

Map 53   Women's Rights

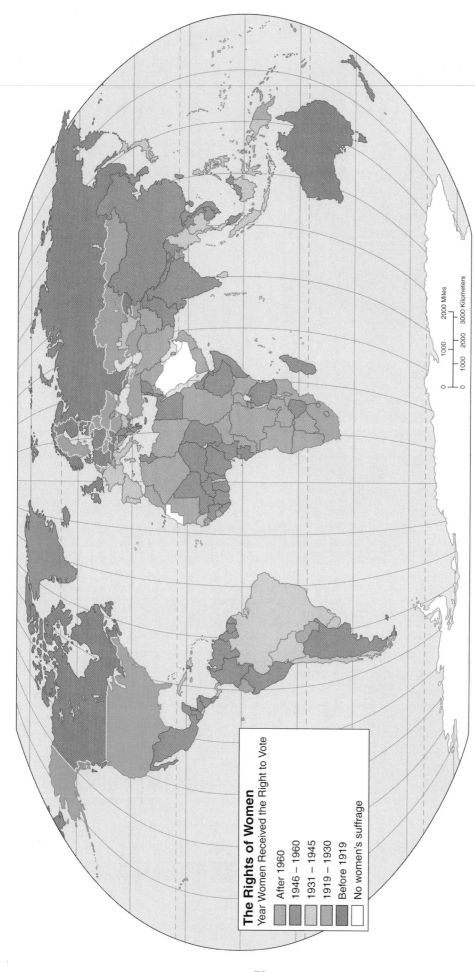

The Rights of Women
Year Women Received the Right to Vote

- After 1960
- 1946 – 1960
- 1931 – 1945
- 1919 – 1930
- Before 1919
- No women's suffrage

0   1000   2000 Miles
0   1000   2000   3000 Kilometers

The "rights" referred to in this map refer primarily to the right to vote. But where women have the right to vote in free elections, the other fundamental rights tend to become available as well: the right to own property, the right to an education, the right to leave a domestic alliance without fear of retribution, or the right to be treated as a human being rather than property. But the time lag between women receiving the right to vote and their attainment of other fundamental human rights does not occur immediately or, in many cases, even relatively quickly. On the map, the most recent countries to grant suffrage to women are in Africa and Southwest Asia. In these regions, women still do not have access to many of the basic rights of what we would consider to be a civilized life. And, of course, there are still areas where women cannot vote: Kuwait, for example. Neither men nor women are allowed to vote in Brunei, Saudi Arabia, United Arab Emirates, or Western Sahara.

Map 54 Capital Punishment

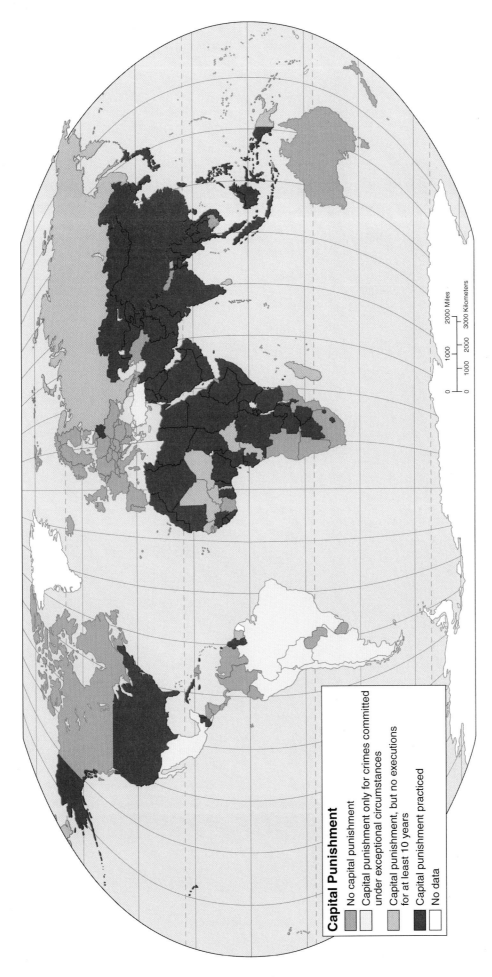

Capital Punishment
- No capital punishment
- Capital punishment only for crimes committed under exceptional circumstances
- Capital punishment, but no executions for at least 10 years
- Capital punishment practiced
- No data

The most basic human right is life itself. More than half the countries of the world have abolished capital punishment by law or in practice. In some of these countries, capital punishment remains on the books, but no one has been executed in so long that in practice, capital punishment can be considered abolished. A few countries retain capital punishment only for crimes committed in extraordinary circumstances, such as military law. About three countries per year have abolished capital punishment in the last decade. Some states in the United States retain capital punishment; in others it has been abolished.

-79-

Unit III

Population, Health, and Human Development

Map 55   Population Growth Rates
Map 56   Infant Mortality Rate
Map 57   Average Life Expectancy at Birth
Map 58   Population by Age Group
Map 59   International Migrant Populations
Map 60   Urban Population
Map 61   Illiteracy Rates
Map 62   Primary School Education
Map 63   The Gender Gap: Inequalities in Education and Employment
Map 64   The Global Security Threat of Infectious Diseases
Map 65   Global Scourges: Major Infectious Diseases
Map 66   Adult Incidence of HIV/AIDS, 2007
Map 67   Undernourished Populations
Map 68   The Index of Human Development
Map 69   Demographic Stress: The Youth Bulge
Map 70   Demographic Stress: Rapid Urban Growth
Map 71   Demographic Stress: Competition for Cropland
Map 72   Demographic Stress: Competition for Fresh Water
Map 73   Demographic Stress: Death in the Prime of Life
Map 74   Demographic Stress: Interactions of Demographic Stress Factors

Map 55 Population Growth Rates

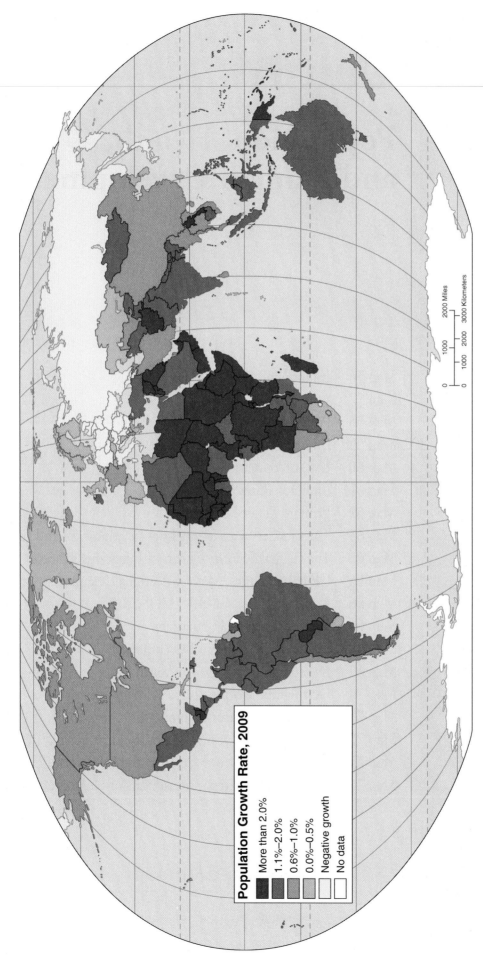

Population Growth Rate, 2009

- More than 2.0%
- 1.1%–2.0%
- 0.6%–1.0%
- 0.0%–0.5%
- Negative growth
- No data

0 1000 2000 Miles

0 1000 2000 3000 Kilometers

Of all the statistical measurements of human population, that of the rate of population growth is the most important. For a specific country, this figure will determine many things about the country's future ability to feed, house, educate, and provide medical services to its citizens. Some of the countries with the largest populations (such as India) also have high growth rates. Since these countries tend to be in developing regions, the combination of high population and high growth rates poses special problems for political stability and continuing economic development; the combination also carries heightened risks for environmental degradation. Many people believe that the rapidly expanding world population is a potential crisis that may cause environmental and human disaster by the middle of the twenty-first century.

Map 56   Infant Mortality Rate

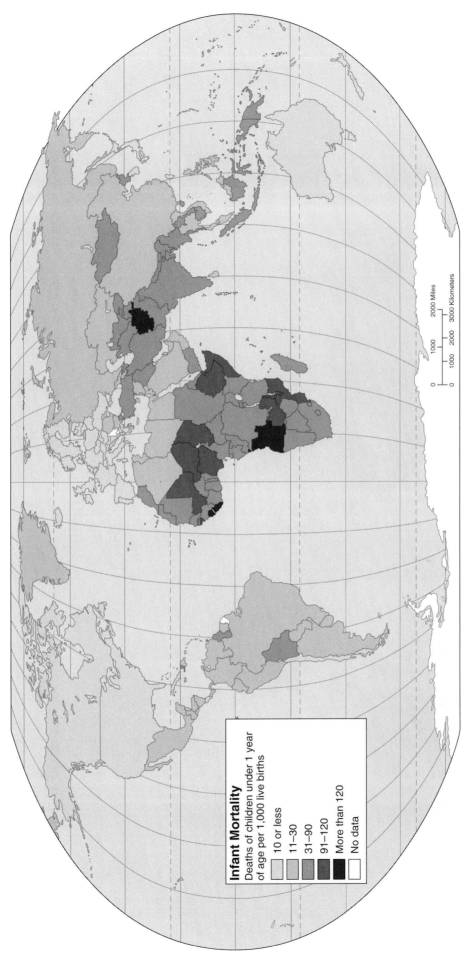

Infant Mortality

Deaths of children under 1 year
of age per 1,000 live births

- 10 or less
- 11–30
- 31–90
- 91–120
- More than 120
- No data

Infant mortality rates are calculated by dividing the number of children born in a given year who die before their first birthday by the total number of children born that year and then multiplying by 1,000; this shows how many infants have died for every 1,000 births. Infant mortality rates are prime indicators of economic development. In highly developed economies, with advanced medical technologies, sufficient diets, and adequate public sanitation, infant mortality rates tend to be quite low. By contrast, in less developed countries, with the disadvantages of poor diet, limited access to medical technology, and the other problems of poverty, infant mortality rates tend to be high. Although worldwide infant mortality has decreased significantly during the last two decades, many regions of the world still experience infant mortality above the 10 percent level (100 deaths per 1,000 live births). Such infant mortality rates not only represent human tragedy at its most basic level, but also are powerful inhibiting factors for the future of human development. Comparing infant mortality rates in the midlatitudes and the tropics shows that children in most African countries are more than 10 times as likely to die within a year of birth as children in European countries.

Map 57 Average Life Expectancy at Birth

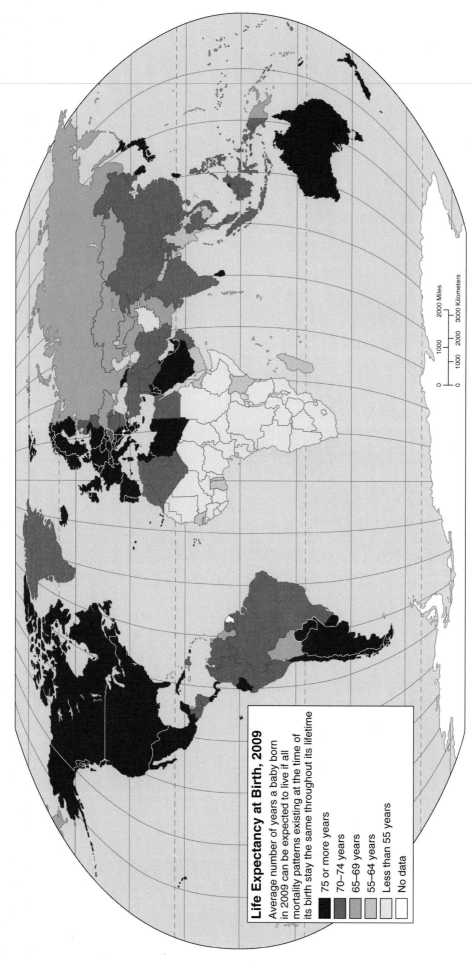

Life Expectancy at Birth, 2009

Average number of years a baby born in 2009 can be expected to live if all mortality patterns existing at the time of its birth stay the same throughout its lifetime

- 75 or more years
- 70–74 years
- 65–69 years
- 55–64 years
- Less than 55 years
- No data

Average life expectancy at birth is a measure of the average longevity of the population of a country. Like all average measures, it is distorted by extremes. For example, a country with a high mortality rate among children will have a low average life expectancy. Thus, an average life expectancy of 45 years does not mean that everyone can be expected to die at the age of 45. More normally, what the figure means is that a substantial number of children die between birth and 5 years of age, thus reducing the average life expectancy for the entire popu-

lation. In spite of the dangers inherent in misinterpreting the data, average life expectancy (along with infant mortality and several other measures) is a valid way of judging the relative health of a population. It reflects the nature of the health care system, public sanitation and disease control, nutrition, and a number of other key human need indicators. As such, it is a measure of well-being that is significant in indicating economic development and predicting political stability.

Map 58 Population by Age Group

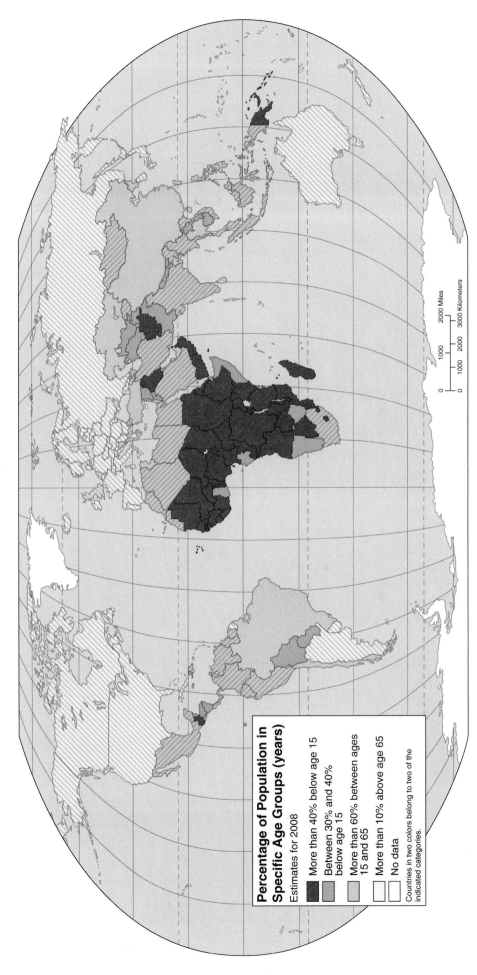

Percentage of Population in Specific Age Groups (years)

Estimates for 2008

- More than 40% below age 15
- Between 30% and 40% below age 15
- More than 60% between ages 15 and 65
- More than 10% above age 65
- No data

Countries in two colors belong to two of the indicated categories.

Of all the measurements that illustrate the dynamics of a population, age distribution may be the most significant, particularly when viewed in combination with average growth rates. The particular relevance of age distribution is that it tells us what to expect from a population in terms of growth over the next generation. If, for example, approximately 40–50 percent of a population is below the age of 15, that suggests that in the next generation about one-quarter of the total population will be women of childbearing age. When age distribution is combined with fertility rates (the average number of children born per woman in a population), an especially valid measurement of future growth potential may be derived. A simple example: Nigeria, with a 2002 population of 130 million, has 43.6 percent of its population below the age of 15 and a fertility rate of 5.5; the United States, with a 2002 population of 280 million, has 21 percent of its population below the age of 15 and a fertility rate of 2.07. During the period in which those women presently under the age of 15 are in their childbearing years, Nigeria can be expected to add a total of approximately 155 million persons to its total population. Over the same period, the United States can be expected to add only 61 million.

Map 59 International Migrant Populations

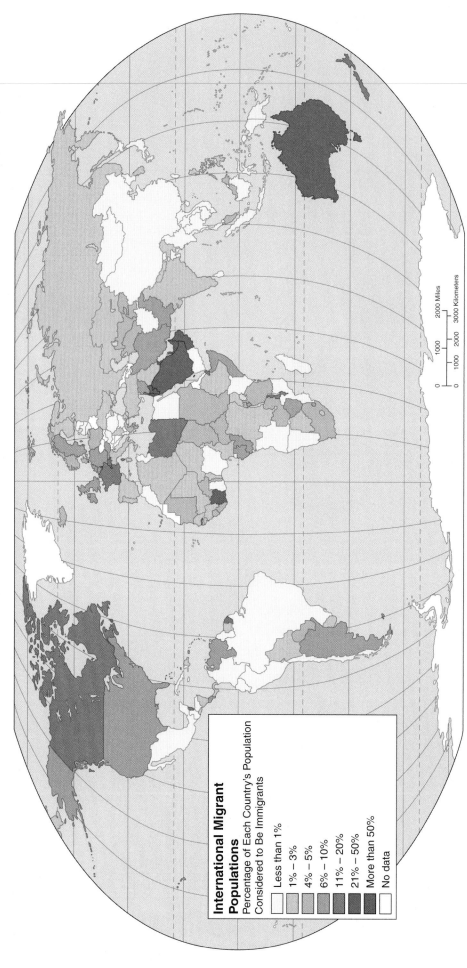

International Migrant Populations

Percentage of Each Country's Population
Considered to Be Immigrants

- Less than 1%
- 1% – 3%
- 4% – 5%
- 6% – 10%
- 11% – 20%
- 21% – 50%
- More than 50%
- No data

Migration—the movement from one place to another—takes a number of different forms. It may be a move within a country from an old job to a new one. It may also mean a migration, either forced or voluntary, from one country to another. The map here depicts international migration: migration between countries. Migration is distinguished from a refugee movement in that migrants are not defined as refugees granted a humanitarian and temporary protection status under international law. The nearly 2 million people who have fled Iraq for Iran are refugees who expect and hope to return to Iraq after the present civil war is ended. The Middle Americans who leave the Central American countries, Mexico, or the Caribbean for the United States plan to live in the United States permanently, although still retaining cultural and family ties to their native country. This map clearly shows that those countries viewed as having the most favorable opportunities for improvement in personal living conditions are those with the highest numbers of in-migrants; those countries that are overcrowded, with little economically upward mobility, or international conflict tend to be those with the greatest number of out-migrants.

Map 60 Urban Population

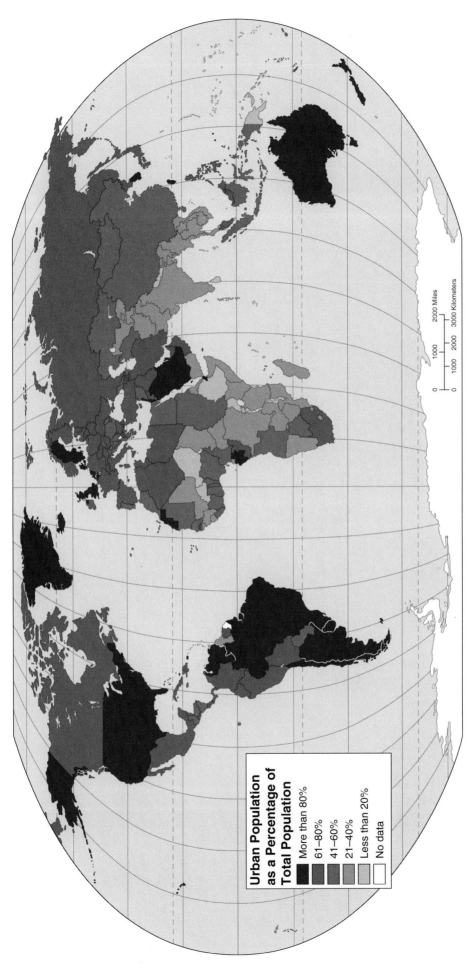

Urban Population as a Percentage of Total Population

- More than 80%
- 61–80%
- 41–60%
- 21–40%
- Less than 20%
- No data

The proportion of a country's population that resides in urban areas was formerly considered a measure of relative economic development, with countries possessing a large urban population ranking high on the development scale and countries with a more rural population ranking low. Given the rapid rate of urbanization in developing countries, however, this traditional measure is no longer so valuable. What relative urbanization rates now tell us is something about levels of economic development in a negative sense. Latin American, African, and Asian countries with more than 40 percent of their populations living in urban areas generally suffer from a variety of problems: rural overpopulation and flight from the land, urban poverty and despair, high unemployment, and poor public services. The rate of urbanization in less developed nations is such that many cities in these nations will outstrip those in North America and Europe by the end of this century. It has been estimated, for example, that Mexico City—now the world's second largest metropolis—has over 19 million inhabitants. Urbanization was once viewed as an indicator of economic health and political maturity. For many countries it is instead a harbinger of potential economic and environmental disaster.

Map **61**   Illiteracy Rates

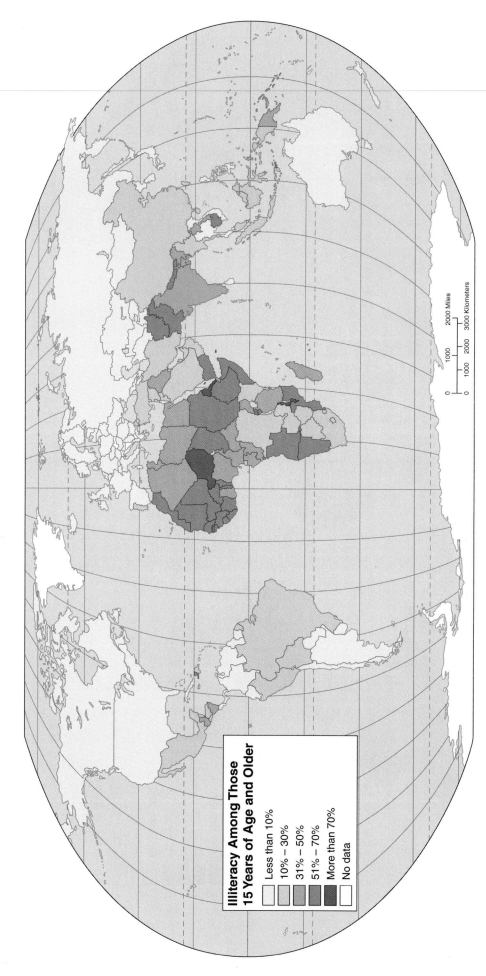

Illiteracy Among Those 15 Years of Age and Older

- Less than 10%
- 10% – 30%
- 31% – 50%
- 51% – 70%
- More than 70%
- No data

0   1000   2000 Miles
0   1000   2000   3000 Kilometers

Illiteracy rates are based on the percentages of people age 15 or above (classed as adults in most countries) who are not able to write and read, with understanding, a brief, simple statement about everyday life written in their home- or official language. As might be expected, illiteracy rates tend to be higher in the less-developed states, where educational systems are a low government priority. Rates of literacy or illiteracy also tend to be gender-differentiated, with women in many countries experiencing educational neglect or discrimination that makes it more likely they will be illiterate. In many developing countries, between five and ten times as many women will be illiterate as men, and the illiteracy rate for women may even exceed 90 percent. Both male and female illiteracy severely compromises economic development.

-88-

Map 62 Primary School Education

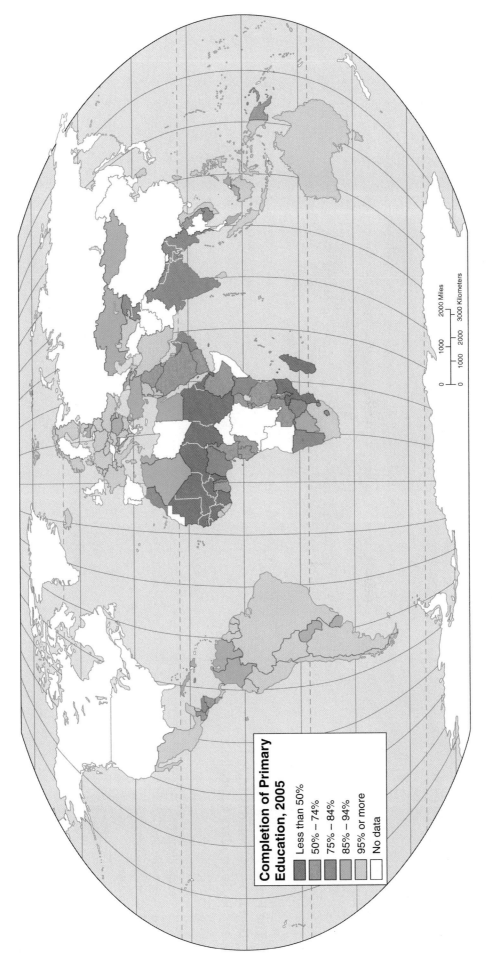

Completion of Primary Education, 2005

- Less than 50%
- 50% – 74%
- 75% – 84%
- 85% – 94%
- 95% or more
- No data

0   1000   2000 Miles
0   1000   2000   3000 Kilometers

Nearly one in five of the world's children of primary school age are not in school. Of this number, more than half are girls. The most critical area of the world in terms of primary school enrollment is sub-Saharan Africa, where 19 countries have primary school completion rates of 50 percent or less. In many of these countries, children are held out of school because of their importance in the agricultural workforce. But the global economy is changing to more knowledge-driven activities, and a lack of education will hurt those countries with low primary school enrollments the most. The need for flexible and skilled workforces, able to read and write, cannot be met unless that generation entering the workforce is educated— if only at minimal levels. Of all the measures necessary to establish sustainable economic development and to alleviate poverty, education is the most important.

Map 63 The Gender Gap: Inequalities in Education and Employment

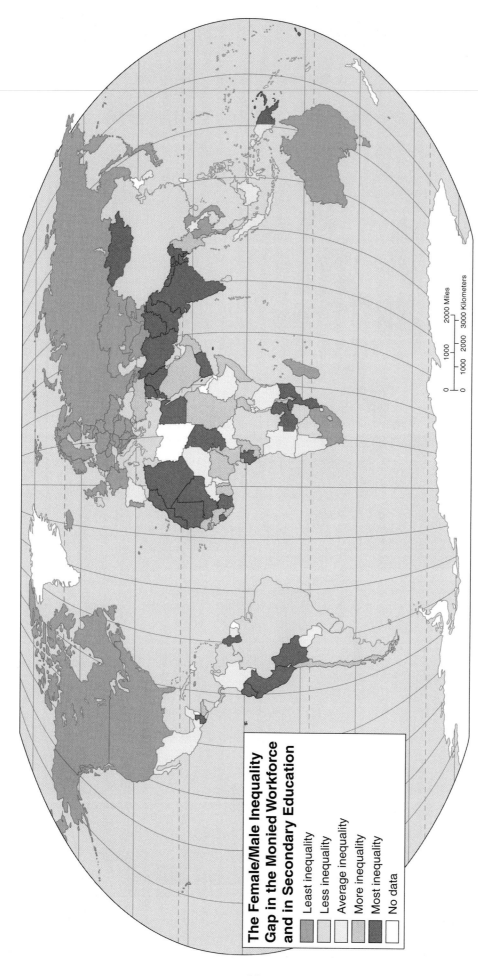

The Female/Male Inequality
Gap in the Monied Workforce
and in Secondary Education

- Least inequality
- Less inequality
- Average inequality
- More inequality
- Most inequality
- No data

0   1000   2000 Miles
0 1000 2000 3000 Kilometers

Although women in developed countries, particularly in North America and Europe, have made significant advances in socioeconomic status in recent years, in most of the world females suffer from significant inequality when compared with their male counterparts. Women have received the right to vote in most of the world's countries, but in over 90 percent of these countries that right has only been granted in the last 50 years. In most regions, literacy rates for women still fall far short of those for men; in Africa and Asia, for example, only about half as many women are literate as are men. Women marry con-siderably younger than men and attend school for shorter periods of time. Inequalities in education and employment are perhaps the most telling indicators of the unequal status of women in most of the world. Lack of secondary education in comparison with men prevents women from entering the workforce with equally high-paying jobs. Even where women are employed in positions similar to those held by men, they still tend to receive less compensation. The gap between rich and poor involves not only a clear geographic differentiation, but a clear gender differentiation as well.

Map 64   The Global Security Threat of Infectious Diseases

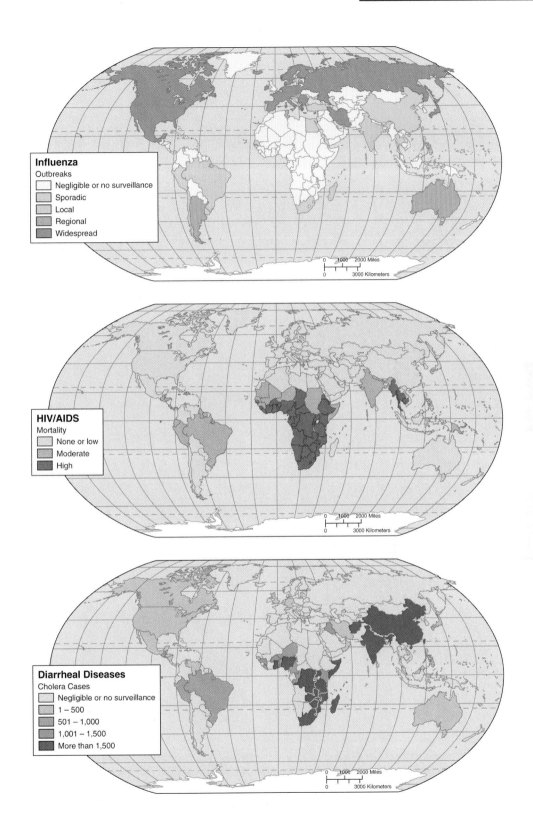

Influenza
Outbreaks
- Negligible or no surveillance
- Sporadic
- Local
- Regional
- Widespread

HIV/AIDS
Mortality
- None or low
- Moderate
- High

Diarrheal Diseases
Cholera Cases
- Negligible or no surveillance
- 1 – 500
- 501 – 1,000
- 1,001 – 1,500
- More than 1,500

The infectious diseases shown in these maps account for more than 9 out of every 10 deaths worldwide from infectious disease. They are spread through various mechanisms, some—such as HIV/AIDS—requiring direct contact, while others such as tuberculosis or influenza may be contracted through airborne transmissions from an infected host. Still others, such as malaria and diarrheal diseases like cholera, require transmission by a vector or carrier. In malaria, the vector is the mosquito (most commonly *Aenopheles*) while the diarrheal diseases are transmitted by microscopic vectors such as bacteria or viruses that commonly live in the water that people drink. Infectious diseases such as these six do tend to have specific geographic distributions, sometimes as the result of climatic factors

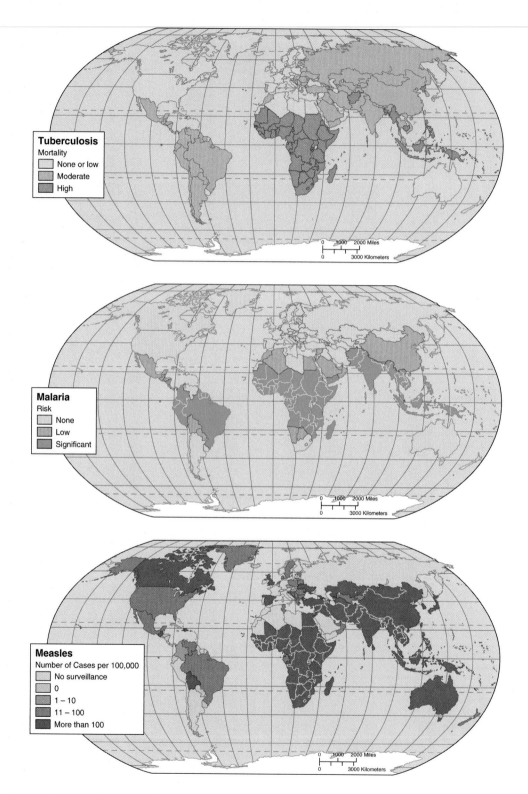

(malaria depends upon warm and moist conditions) and sometimes the result of cultural factors such as rapid and widespread travel. It is the latter that helps to explain why influenza tends to have a greater impact in the developed world, even though the influenza viruses themselves often have their origins in less developed regions of Asia. One good way to avoid influenza is to never travel on a common carrier such as an airplane, train, or bus! None of these diseases has yet been controlled (to the extent that, say, poliomyelitis or smallpox have been controlled). But neither have they wrought the havoc caused by the bubonic plague in late medieval Europe. The sites where future concerns about the transmission of infectious diseases ought to be focused are the increasingly large urban concentrations in South America, Africa, and Asia.

Map 65 Global Scourges: Major Infectious Diseases

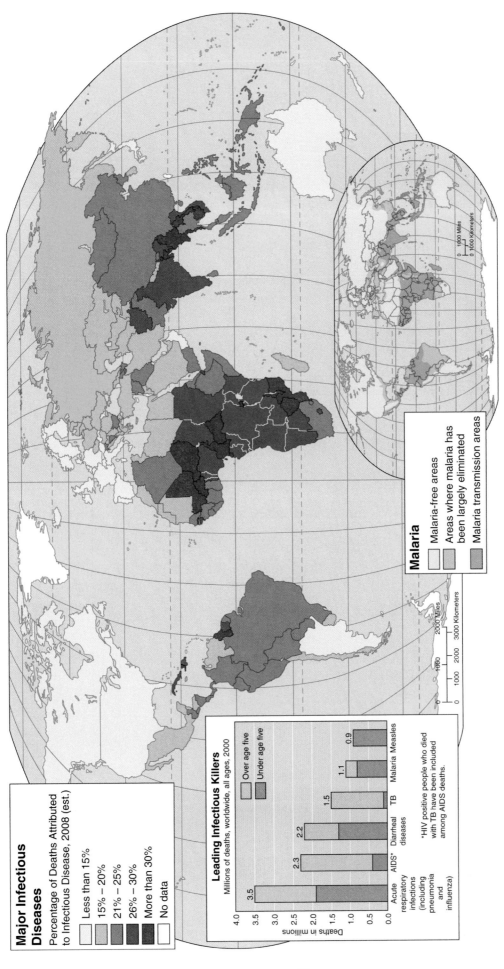

Major Infectious Diseases

Percentage of Deaths Attributed to Infectious Disease, 2008 (est.)

- Less than 15%
- 15% – 20%
- 21% – 25%
- 26% – 30%
- More than 30%
- No data

Malaria

- Malaria-free areas
- Areas where malaria has been largely eliminated
- Malaria transmission areas

Leading Infectious Killers
Millions of deaths, worldwide, all ages, 2000

- Over age five
- Under age five

*HIV positive people who died with TB have been included among AIDS deaths.

Disease	Deaths (millions)
Acute respiratory infections (including pneumonia and influenza)	3.5
AIDS*	2.3
Diarrheal diseases	2.2
TB	1.5
Malaria	1.1
Measles	0.9

Infectious diseases are the world's leading cause of premature death and at least half of the world's population is, at any time, at risk of contracting an infectious disease. Although we often think of infectious diseases as being restricted to the tropical world (malaria, dengue fever), many if not most of them have attained global proportions. A major case in point is HIV/AIDS, which quite probably originated in Africa but has, over the last two decades, spread throughout the entire world. Major diseases of the nineteenth century, such as cholera and tuberculosis, are making a major comeback in many parts of the world, in spite of being preventable or treatable. Part of the problem with infectious diseases is that they tend to be associated with poverty (poor nutrition, poor sanitation, substandard housing, and so on) and, therefore, are

seen as a problem of undeveloped countries, with the consequent lack of funding for prevention and treatment. Infectious diseases are also tending to increase because lifesaving drugs, such as antibiotics and others used in the fight against diseases, are losing their effectiveness as bacteria develop genetic resistance to them. The problem of global warming is also associated with a spread of infectious diseases as many disease vectors (certain species of mosquito, for example) are spreading into higher latitudes with increasingly warm temperatures and are spreading disease into areas where populations have no resistance to them. Infectious diseases have become something greater than simply a health issue of poor countries. They are now major social problems with potentially enormous consequences for the entire world.

Map **66**   Adult Incidence of HIV/AIDS, 2007

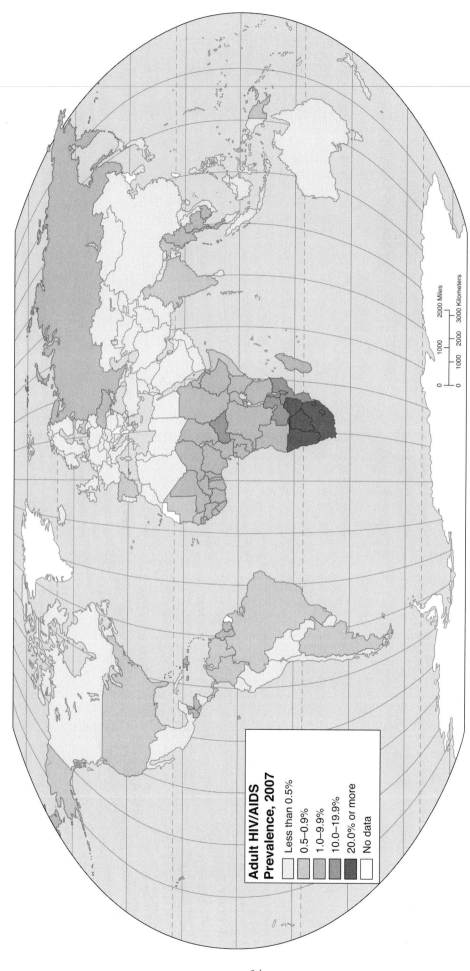

Adult HIV/AIDS Prevalence, 2007

- Less than 0.5%
- 0.5—0.9%
- 1.0—9.9%
- 10.0—19.9%
- 20.0% or more
- No data

Of all the infectious diseases, the one that poses the greatest risks to public health worldwide is human immune deficiency which, if untreated, progresses to the deadly autoimmune deficiency, or AIDS. The highest incidence of AIDS among adult populations occurs in sub-Saharan Africa, where public health systems are too poorly funded and developed to treat HIV cases, and the medications needed to preserve health and reasonable longevity are too expensive. Since the rate of adult cases is high, large numbers of children are also infected, having been born HIV-positive. Indeed, among all the world's children living with HIV, approximately 90 percent live in Sub-Saharan Africa. Other countries in the developing world also are high on the scale of HIV/AIDS incidence and the suspicion is that the official figures could go even higher if accurately reported. China, for example, may have rates that are 3 to 4 times greater than the official figures. Worldwide, HIV/AIDS has a devastating impact on family structures (many children are orphaned by both parents dying of AIDS) and on the economic growth of the developing countries.

Map **67**   Undernourished Populations

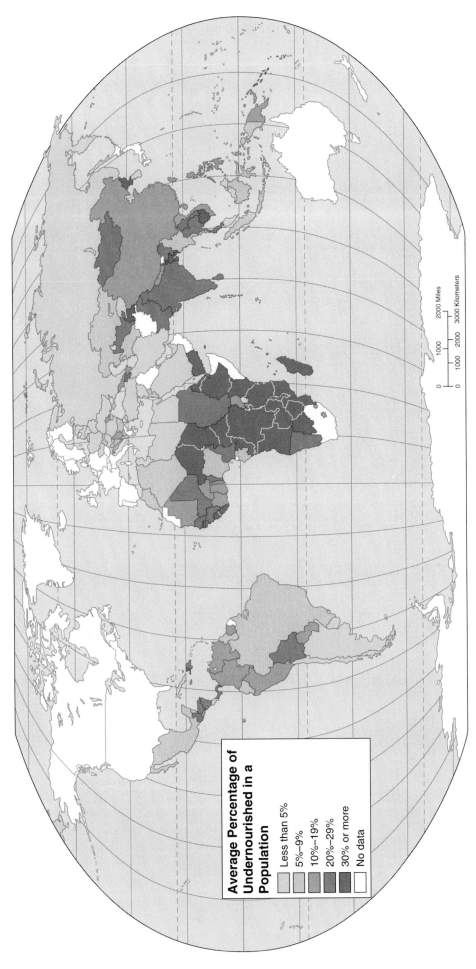

Average Percentage of Undernourished in a Population

- Less than 5%
- 5%–9%
- 10%–19%
- 20%–29%
- 30% or more
- No data

A number of international organizations, including the Food and Agriculture Organization (FAO) of the UN and the World Bank, have established a "Millenium Development Goal" of halving global hunger by 2015. Thus far, only the Latin America and Caribbean region (with several notable exceptions such as Haiti and the Dominican Republic) have succeeded in reducing hunger sufficiently to reach the goals set by the FAO. Most of the world's hungry are the rural poor—living in areas where agricultural overcrowding and the use of land for cash crops rather than food produces hunger where logic suggests there should be relative abundance. Moreover, the largest percentage of undernourished people live in areas where environmental degradation and climate change are taking the greatest toll on the ability of the land to support a human population. While people rarely starve to death, undernourishment opens up populations to a large number of wasting diseases that accompany inadequate diets. It is these wasting diseases that debilitate and, eventually, kill.

Map **68**   The Index of Human Development

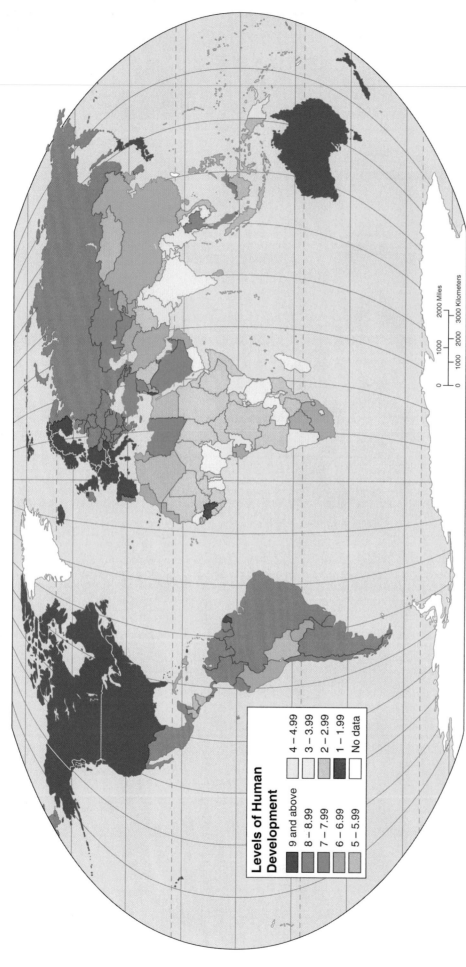

Levels of Human Development

	9 and above
	8 – 8.99
	7 – 7.99
	6 – 6.99
	5 – 5.99
	4 – 4.99
	3 – 3.99
	2 – 2.99
	1 – 1.99
	No data

The development index upon which this map is based takes into account a wide variety of demographic, health, and educational data, including population growth, per capita gross domestic income, longevity, literacy, and years of schooling. The map reveals significant improvement in the quality of life in Middle and South America, although it is questionable whether the gains made in those regions can be maintained in the face of the dramatic population increases expected over the next 30 years. More clearly than anything else, the map illustrates the near-desperate situation in Africa and South Asia. In those regions, the unparalleled growth in population threatens to overwhelm all efforts to improve the quality of life. In Africa, for example, the population is increasing by 20 million persons per year. With nearly 45 percent of the continent's population aged 15 years or younger, this growth rate will accelerate as the women reach childbearing age. Africa, along with South Asia, faces the very difficult challenge of providing basic access to health care, education, and jobs for a rapidly increasing population. The map also illustrates the striking difference in quality of life between those who inhabit the world's equatorial and tropical regions and those fortunate enough to live in the temperate zones, where the quality of life is significantly higher.

Map **69**   Demographic Stress: The Youth Bulge

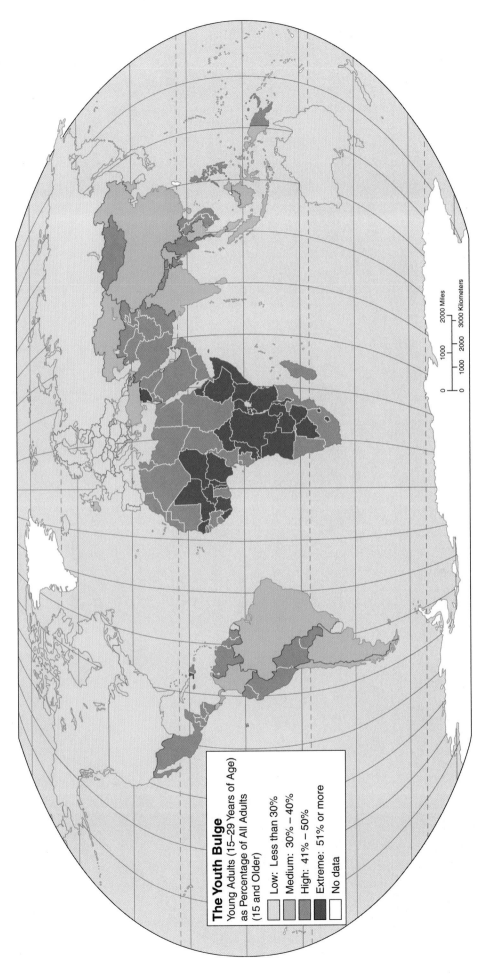

The Youth Bulge
Young Adults (15–29 Years of Age)
as Percentage of All Adults
(15 and Older)

- Low: Less than 30%
- Medium: 30% – 40%
- High: 41% – 50%
- Extreme: 51% or more
- No data

One of the greatest stresses of the demographic transition is when the death rate drops as the result of better public health and sanitation and the birth rate remains high for the same reasons it has always been high in traditional, agricultural societies: (1) the need for enough children to supply labor, which is one of the few ways to increase agricultural production in a non-mechanized agricultural system, and (2) the need for enough children to offset high infant and child mortality rates so that some children will survive to take care of parents in their old age. With declining death rates and steady birth rates, population growth skyrockets—particularly among the youngest cohorts of a popula-

tion (between the ages of birth and 15). While this is, on the one hand, a demographic benefit since it increases the size of the labor force in the next generation and thereby helps to accelerate economic growth, it also means more people of childbearing age in the next generation and, hence, greater numbers of births, which continue to swell the population in the youngest, most vulnerable, and most dependent portion of the population. The literature on population and conflict suggests that the larger the percentage of a population below the age of 25, the greater the chance for political violence and warfare.

Map 70 Demographic Stress: Rapid Urban Growth

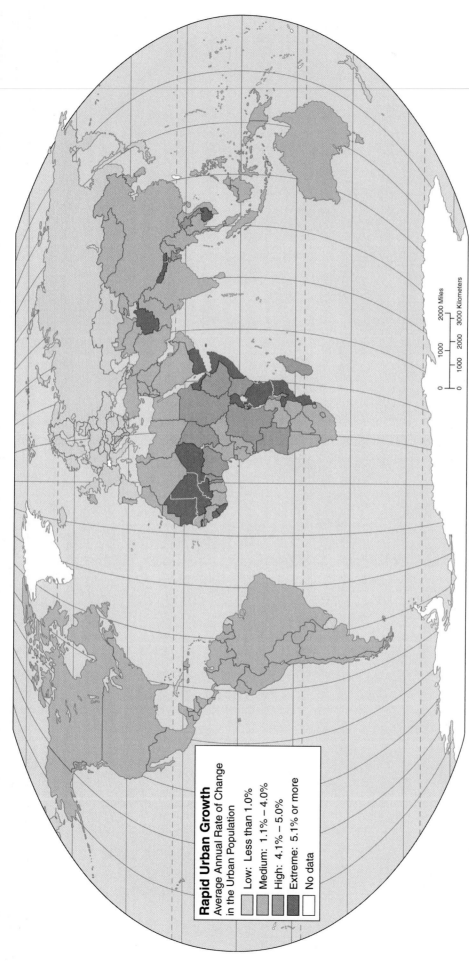

Rapid Urban Growth
Average Annual Rate of Change
in the Urban Population

Low: Less than 1.0%
Medium: 1.1% – 4.0%
High: 4.1% – 5.0%
Extreme: 5.1% or more
No data

0   1000   2000 Miles
0   1000   2000   3000 Kilometers

The trend toward urbanization—an increasing percentage of a country's population living in a city—is normally a healthy, modern trend. But in many of the world's developing countries, increasing urbanization is the consequence of high physiologic population densities (too many people for the available agricultural land) and the flight of poorly educated, untrained rural poor to the cities where they hope (often in vain) to find employment. High urbanization exists in many of the world's poorest countries, where the urban poor live in conditions that make the worst living conditions in the inner cities of devel-oped countries look positively luxurious. In the urban slums of South America, Africa, and South Asia, millions of people live in temporary housing of cardboard and flattened aluminum cans, with no public services such as water, sewage, or electricity. In Africa, where only 40% of the population is urbanized (in comparison with more than 90% in North America and Europe), the population of urban poor is greater than the total urban population of the United States and the European Union. This represents an increasingly destabilizing element of modern urban societies.

Map 71   Demographic Stress: Competition for Cropland

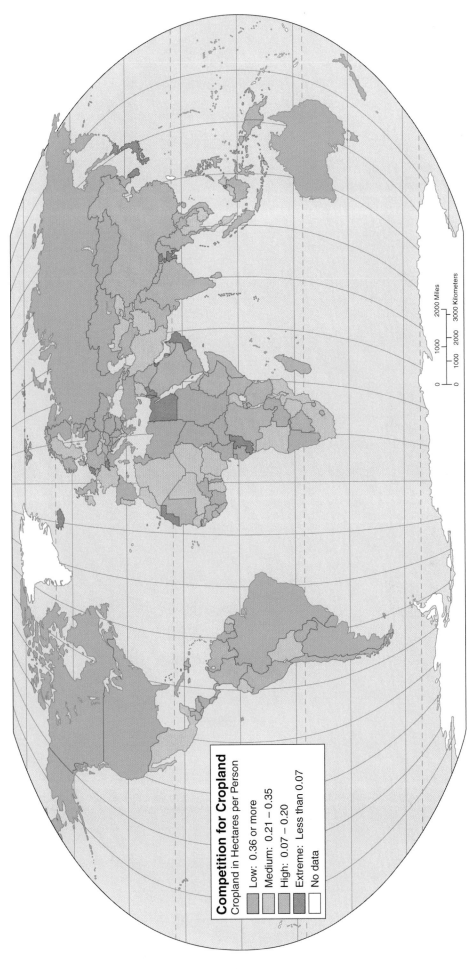

Competition for Cropland
Cropland in Hectares per Person

- Low: 0.36 or more
- Medium: 0.21 – 0.35
- High: 0.07 – 0.20
- Extreme: Less than 0.07
- No data

Many of the world's countries have reached the point where available acres or hectares in cropland are less than the numbers of people wishing to occupy them. For developed countries, who pay for agricultural imports with industrial exports, this is not an alarming trend and therefore countries like Germany or Italy (where the ratio between cropland and farmers is very low) have little to worry about. But in countries in South America, Africa, and South and East Asia, the trend toward more farmers and less available land *is* an alarming trend. In these developing regions, farmers depend on their crops for a relatively meager subsistence diet and—if they are lucky—a few bushels of rice or corn to take to the local market to sell or exchange for the small surpluses of other farmers. Despite the broad global trends toward urbanization and more productive agriculture (and this generally means mechanized agriculture), farm occupation and subsistence cropping remain mainstays of the economy in Africa south of the Sahara, in much of western South America, and in much of South and East Asia. Here, the increasingly small margin between the numbers of farmers and the amount of available farmland can lead to conflict among tribal communities or even among members of a single family.

-99-

Map 72 Demographic Stress: Competition for Fresh Water

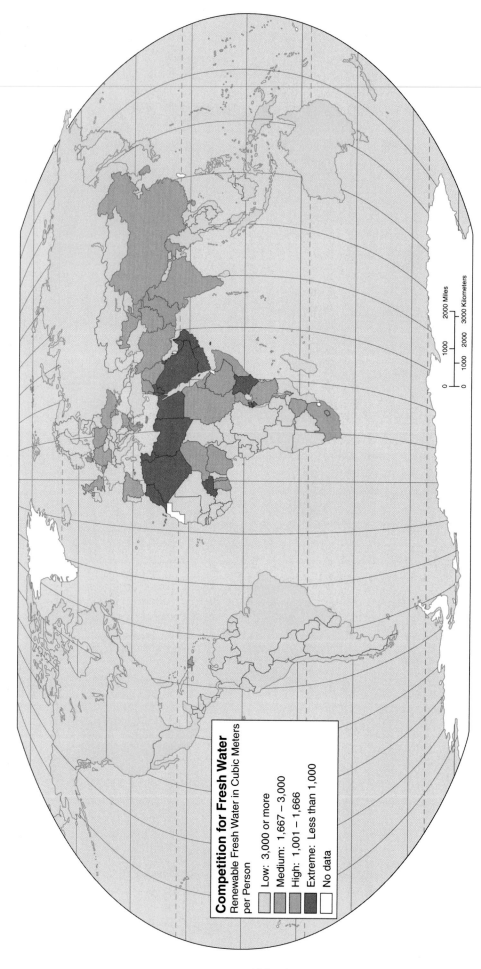

Competition for Fresh Water
Renewable Fresh Water in Cubic Meters per Person

Low: 3,000 or more
Medium: 1,667 – 3,000
High: 1,001 – 1,666
Extreme: Less than 1,000
No data

As rates of urbanization have increased, the competition between city dwellers and farmers for water has also increased. And as the population of farmers relative to the available surface or groundwater supply has accelerated, so rural competition for access to fresh water for irrigation has increased. Obviously, this trend is most obvious in the world's drier regions. On this map, the greatest stress factors relating to water availability are in North and East Africa, the Middle East, and Central and East Asia. The current conflict between Israelis and Palestinians in the West Bank goes far beyond religion or politics: Some is the result of the more affluent Israeli farmers being able to drill wells to tap groundwater, which lowers the water table and causes previously accessible surface wells in Palestinian villages to go dry. And part of the horrific Hutu-Tutsi civil war in Rwanda and the taking of European farmlands by the current government of Zimbabwe have more to do with the need for access to fresh water than to racial or ethnic differences. Given that fresh water is, for all practical purposes, a nonrenewable resource, more conflicts over access to water are going to erupt in the future.

Map 73 Demographic Stress: Death in the Prime of Life

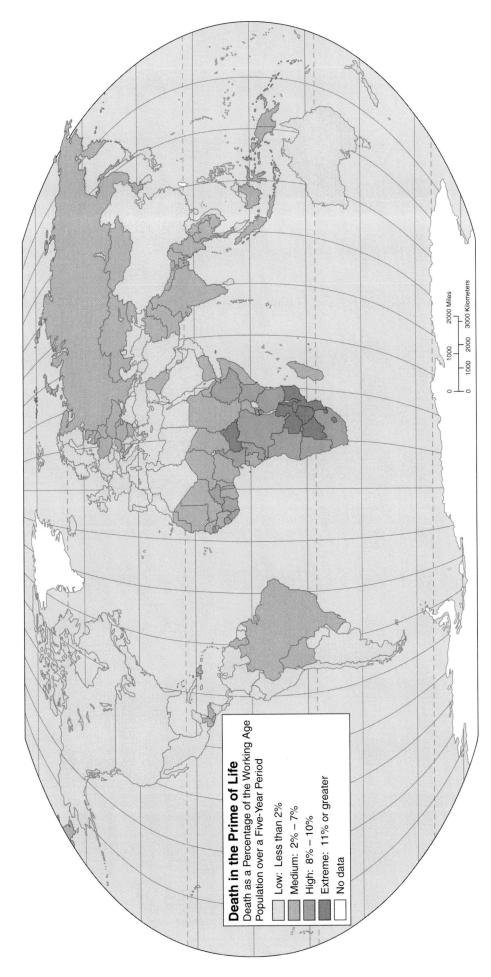

Death in the Prime of Life
Death as a Percentage of the Working Age
Population over a Five-Year Period

Low: Less than 2%
Medium: 2% – 7%
High: 8% – 10%
Extreme: 11% or greater
No data

Most infectious diseases lay waste to the oldest and the youngest sectors of a population, leaving the healthier working-age population able to reproduce itself and to continue to grow an economy. Modern infectious diseases—most particularly HIV/AIDS—impacts not the youngest or oldest but those in the prime of life, in their most productive and reproductive years. Indeed, medical data from the United Nations show that 90% of HIV/AIDS-related deaths occur in people of working age. Some of the most severely impacted countries in southern Africa lose between 10% and 20% of their working age population every 5 years. Rates in the developed world are from 0.10% to 0.02% of this level.

A prominent fact of life in much of the developing world—particularly in sub-Saharan Africa—is the long-distance labor migration. In this pattern, a man leaves his wife and family for extended periods of time (10 or more months of the year) to work in mines, on docks, as sailors. These men are highly vulnerable to the acquisition of HIV, which is then transmitted to wives when the husband returns home on his annual visit. Thus both the male and the female portion of the working-age population are impacted by early mortality from AIDS. None of this bodes well for economic development in those affected areas of the world.

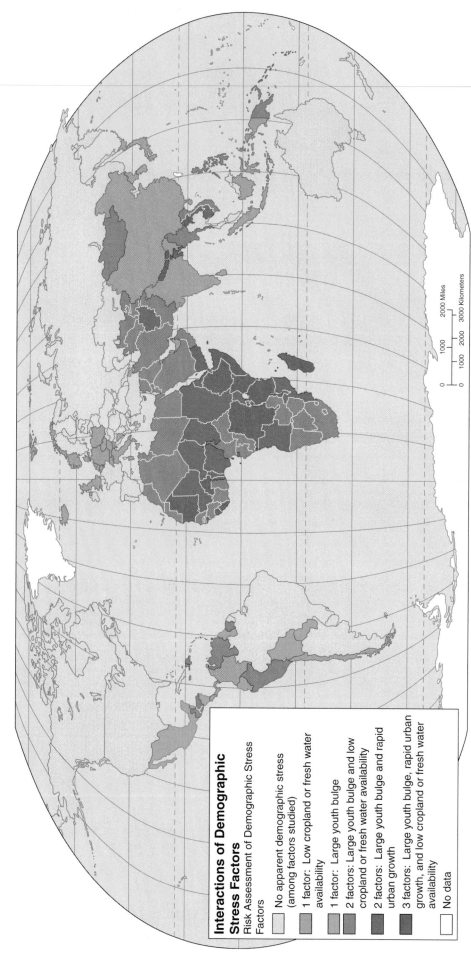

Interactions of Demographic Stress Factors

Risk Assessment of Demographic Stress Factors

No apparent demographic stress (among factors studied)

1 factor: Low cropland or fresh water availability

1 factor: Large youth bulge

2 factors: Large youth bulge and low cropland or fresh water availability

2 factors: Large youth bulge and rapid urban growth

3 factors: Large youth bulge, rapid urban growth, and low cropland or fresh water availability

No data

We have persisted in viewing internal and international conflicts as conflicts produced by religious differences, the acceptance or rejection of "freedom" or "democracy," or even, as argued by a prominent historian, a "Clash of Civilizations." While religious, political, or historical differences cannot be ignored in interpreting the causes of conflict, neither can simple demographic stresses produced by too many new urban dwellers without jobs or hopes of jobs, by too many farmers and too little farmland, by too many deaths among people who should be in the most productive portions of their lives. A massive study by Population Action International, from which these last half-dozen or so maps have been drawn, shows quite clearly that countries suffering from multiple demographic risk factors are, were, and will be much more prone to civil conflict than countries with only one or two demographic risk factors. A look at this map provides a predictor of future civil unrest, violence, and even civil war.

Unit IV

The Global Economy

Map 75   Membership in the World Trade Organization
Map 76   Regional Trade Organizations
Map 77   Relative Wealth of Nations: Purchasing Power Parity
Map 78   Inequality of Income and Consumption
Map 79   The World's Poorest
Map 80   Economic Output Per Sector
Map 81   Employment by Economic Activity
Map 82   Unemployment by Economic Activity
Map 83   Central Government Expenditures Per Capita
Map 84   The Indebtedness of States
Map 85   Global Flows of Investment Capital
Map 86   Inflation Rates
Map 87   Dependence on Trade
Map 88   Trade with Neighboring Countries
Map 89   Aiding Economic Development
Map 90   The Cost of Consumption, 2008
Map 91   A Wired World: Internet Users
Map 92   The Rise of the Personal Computer
Map 93   Traditional Links: The Telephone

Map 75 Membership in the World Trade Organization

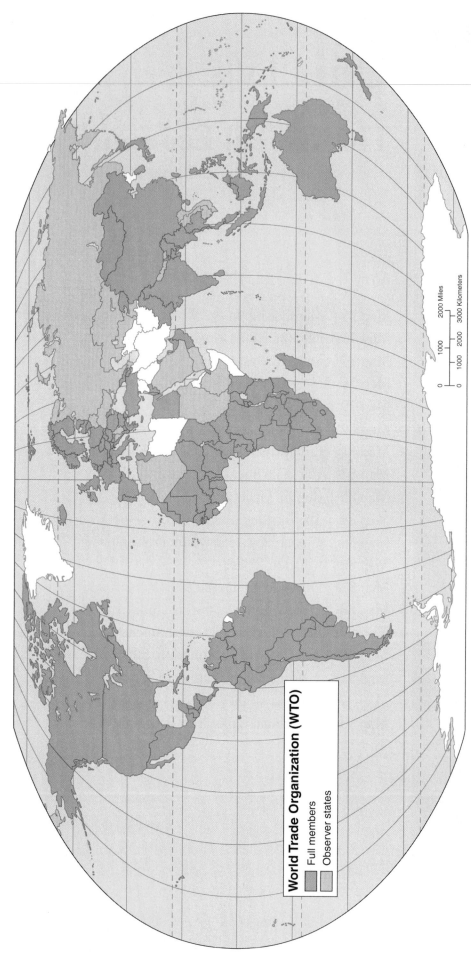

World Trade Organization (WTO)
- Full members
- Observer states

0   1000   2000 Miles
0   1000   2000   3000 Kilometers

After World War II, the General Agreement on Tariffs and Trade (GATT) sponsored several rounds of negotiations, especially related to lower tariffs but also considering issues such as dumping and other nontariff questions. The last round of negotiations under GATT took place in Uruguay in 1986–1994 and set the stage for the World Trade Organization (WTO), which was formally established in 1995. Today the WTO has 146 members with more than 30 "observer" governments. With the exception of the Holy See (Vatican), observer governments are expected to begin negotiations for full membership within five years of becoming observers. The objective of the WTO is to help international trade flow smoothly and fairly and to assure more stable and secure supplies of goods to consumers. To this end, it administers trade agreements, acts as a forum for trade negotiations, settles trade disputes, reviews national trade policies, assists developing countries through technical assistance and training programs, and cooperates with other international organizations. Increased globalization of the world's economy makes the administrative role of the WTO of increasing importance in the twenty-first century. The headquarters of the WTO is in Geneva, Switzerland.

Map 76 Regional Trade Organizations

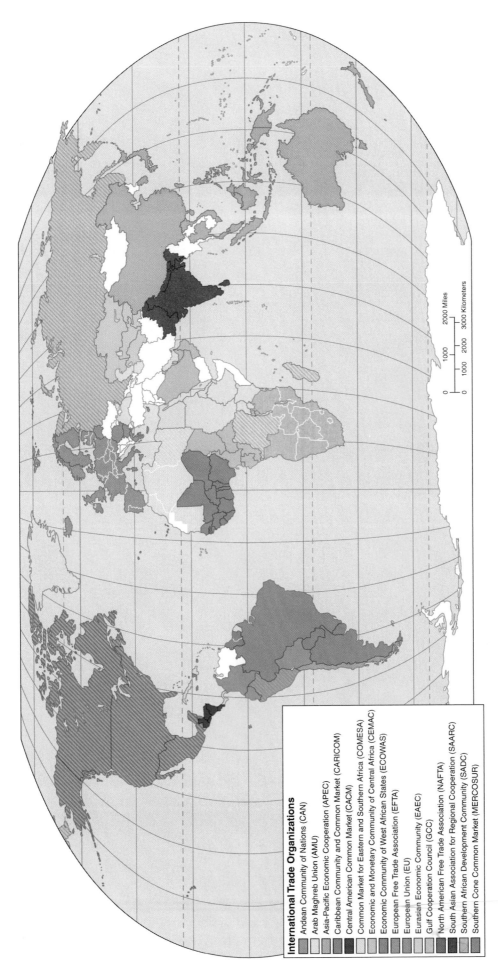

International Trade Organizations

Andean Community of Nations (CAN)
Arab Maghreb Union (AMU)
Asia-Pacific Economic Cooperation (APEC)
Caribbean Community and Common Market (CARICOM)
Central American Common Market (CACM)
Common Market for Eastern and Southern Africa (COMESA)
Economic and Monetary Community of Central Africa (CEMAC)
Economic Community of West African States (ECOWAS)
European Free Trade Association (EFTA)
European Union (EU)
Eurasian Economic Community (EAEC)
Gulf Cooperation Council (GCC)
North American Free Trade Association (NAFTA)
South Asian Association for Regional Cooperation (SAARC)
Southern African Development Community (SADC)
Southern Cone Common Market (MERCOSUR)

One of the most pervasive influences in the global economy over the last half century, particularly since the end of the Cold War, has been that international trade organizations. The role pioneered by the European Eco-nomic Community, founded in part to assist in rebuilding the European economy after World War II, these organizations have become major players in global movements of goods, services, and labor. Some have integrated to form financial and political unions, such as the European Community, which has grown into the European Union. Others, like the Asia-Pacific Economic Cooperation, and the Southern African Development Community, incorporate vastly different regions, states, and even economic systems, and are attempts to anticipate the direction of future economic growth. The role of international trade organizations is likely to grow greater in the next fifty years. In terms of purchasing power parity GDP, the North American Free Trade Agreement (NAFTA) is the largest trade bloc in the world and has restructured many segments of the Canadian, American, and Mexican economies (particularly in Mexico).

0   1000   2000 Miles
0   1000   2000   3000 Kilometers

Map 77   Relative Wealth of Nations: Purchasing Power Parity

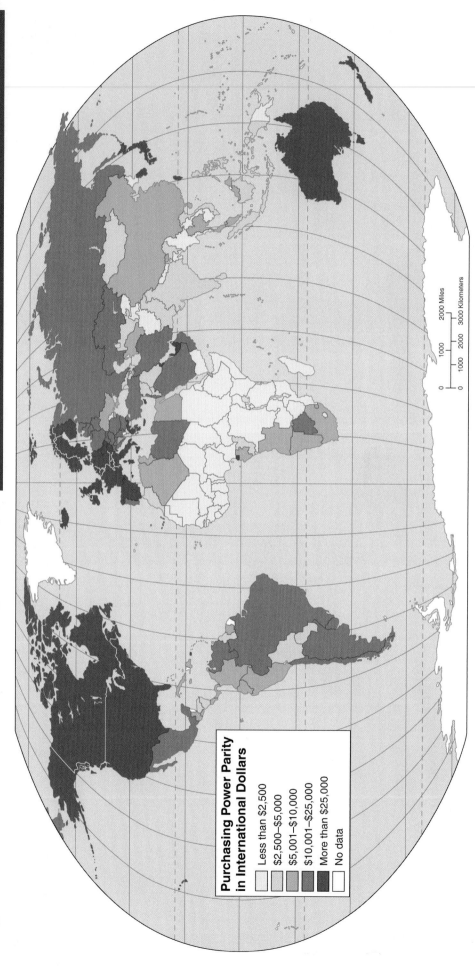

Purchasing Power Parity in International Dollars

- Less than $2,500
- $2,500–$5,000
- $5,001–$10,000
- $10,001–$25,000
- More than $25,000
- No data

0   1000   2000 Miles

0   1000   2000   3000 Kilometers

Of all the economic measures that separate the "haves" from the "have-nots," perhaps per capita purchasing power parity (PPP) is the most meaningful. While per capita figures can mask significant uneven distributions within a country, they are generally useful for demonstrating important differences between countries. Per capita GNP and GDP (gross domestic product) figures, and even per capita income, have the limitation of seldom reflecting the true purchasing power of a country's currency at home. In order to get around this limitation, international economists seeking to compare national currencies developed the PPP measure, which shows the level of goods and services that holders of a country's money can acquire locally. By converting all currencies to the "international dollar," the World Bank and other organizations using PPP can now show more truly comparative values, since the new currency value shows the number of units of a coun-

try's currency required to buy the same quantity of goods and services in the local market as one U.S. dollar would buy in an average country. The use of PPP currency values can alter the perceptions about a country's true comparative position in the world economy. More than per capita income figures, PPP provides a valid measurement of the ability of a country's population to provide for itself the things that people in the developed world take for granted: adequate food, shelter, clothing, education, and access to medical care. A glance at the map shows a clear-cut demarcation between temperate and tropical zones, with most of the countries with a PPP above $5,000 in the midlatitude zones and most of those with lower PPPs in the tropical and equatorial regions. Where exceptions to this pattern occur, they usually stem from a tremendous maldistribution of wealth among a country's population.

Map 78 Inequality of Income and Consumption

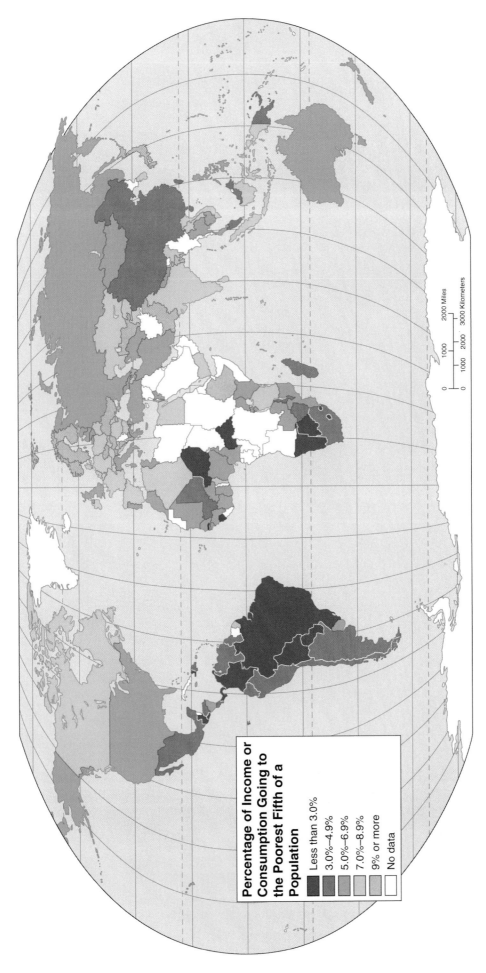

Percentage of Income or Consumption Going to the Poorest Fifth of a Population

- Less than 3.0%
- 3.0%–4.9%
- 5.0%–6.9%
- 7.0%–8.9%
- 9% or more
- No data

0   1000   2000 Miles
0   1000   2000   3000 Kilometers

While it is more than arguably true that the poor get poorer and the rich get richer (and that, by the way, is just as true in some highly developed areas such as the United States and the United Kingdom as it is in the lesser-developed regions), what is often ignored is the breadth of the inequality in distribution of incomes or in the levels of consumption of basic goods. In many of the world's developing countries—despite the rapid increases in economic growth of China and India over the last two decades—the poorest 20% of the population receives less than 7% of the income or consumption share. Although school participation rates have risen worldwide, in countries with the greatest inequalities of income, access to education remains low. If translated into ratios, the inequality ratio of many of the world's countries (including, as noted above, some in the highly developed world) is 8 or higher, meaning that the top 20% of the population spends and consumes at least 8 times as much per person as the bottom 20% of the population.

-107-

Map 79 The World's Poorest

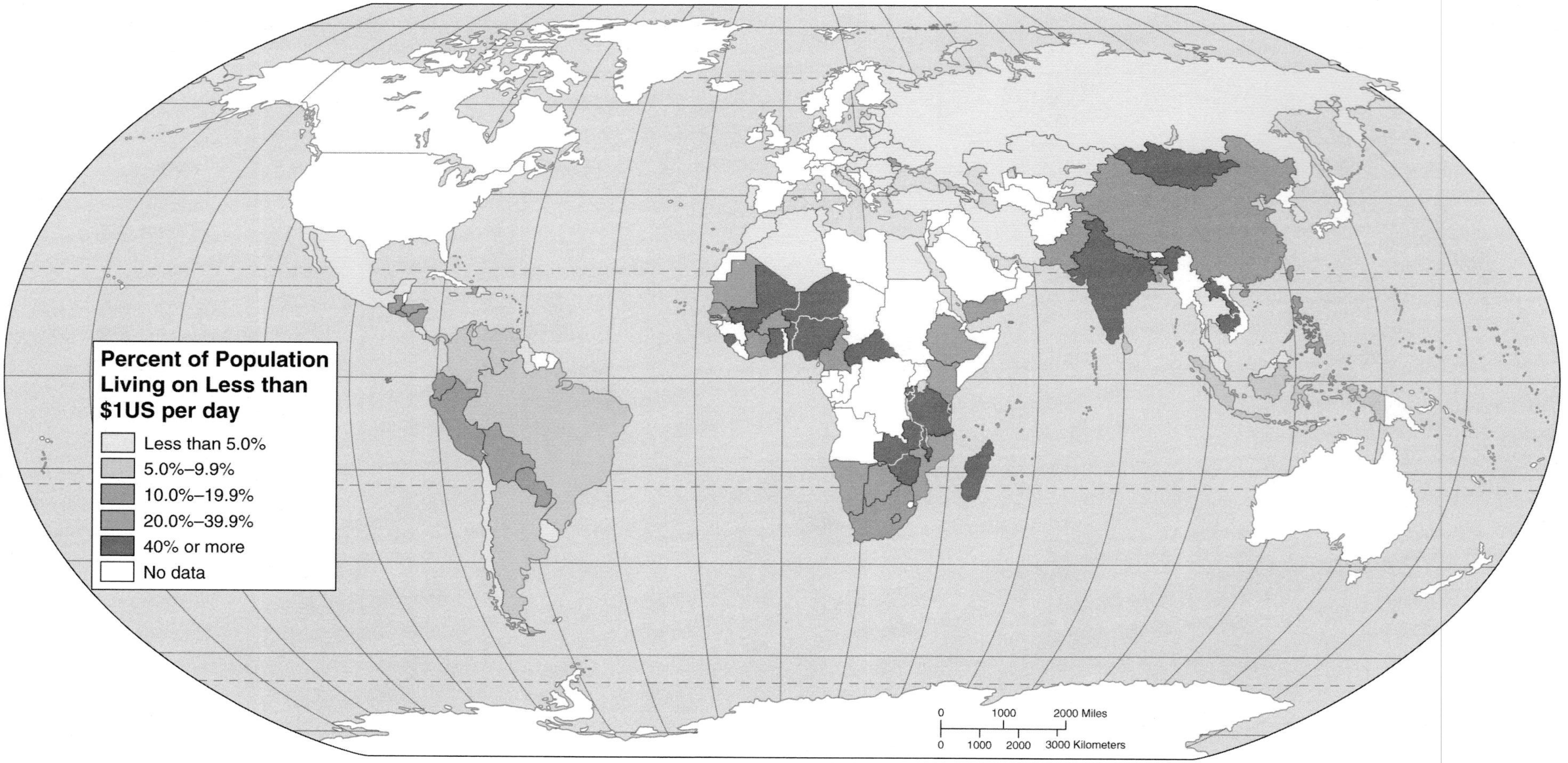

Percent of Population Living on Less than $1US per day

- Less than 5.0%
- 5.0%–9.9%
- 10.0%–19.9%
- 20.0%–39.9%
- 40% or more
- No data

```
0        1000        2000 Miles
0   1000   2000   3000 Kilometers
```

Extreme poverty, represented by annual per capita incomes of approximately $300US, is found in rural areas (particularly those of subsistence rather than commercial agriculture) and in the urban slums of the developing world where rural poor have fled the countryside for the city and the hope for jobs and a better life. The greatest number of countries with high percentages of extremely poor people is in sub-Saharan Africa; the greatest populations of the extremely poor are in South Asia where nearly half a bil-

lion people live under conditions of the most severe poverty. Few developing countries are on track to halve poverty by the UN and World Bank target date of 2015. Poverty begets poverty as the poor have the lowest levels of access to education, transportation, job training, health facilities, and other "amenities" of the better well-off. As a consequence, the children of the poorest are more than likely to end up in the same classification as their parents.

Map 80   Economic Output Per Sector

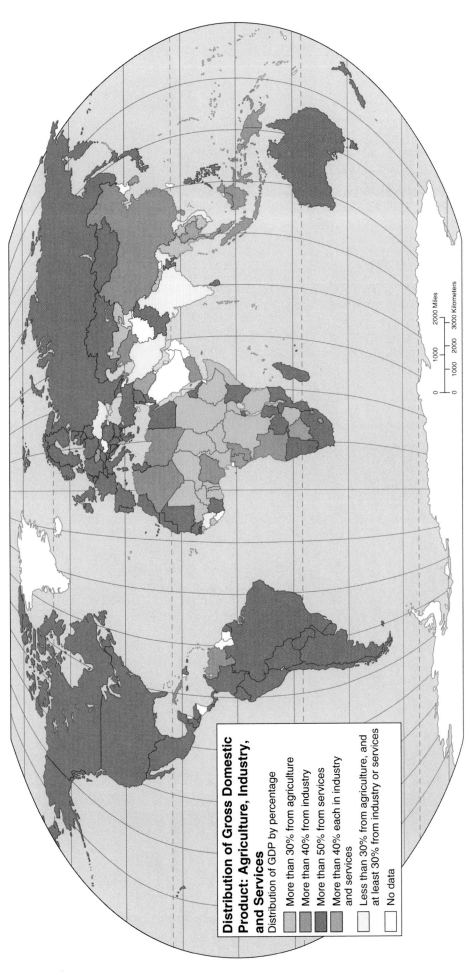

Distribution of Gross Domestic Product: Agriculture, Industry, and Services

Distribution of GDP by percentage

- More than 30% from agriculture
- More than 40% from industry
- More than 50% from services
- More than 40% each in industry and services
- Less than 30% from agriculture, and at least 30% from industry or services
- No data

The percentage of the gross domestic product (the final output of goods and services produced by the domestic economy, including net exports of goods and nonfactor—nonlabor, noncapital—services) that is devoted to agricultural, industrial, and service activities is considered a good measure of the level of economic development. In general, countries with more than 40 percent of their GDP derived from agriculture are still in a *colonial dependency economy*—that is, raising agricultural goods primarily for the export market and dependent upon that market (usually the richer countries). Similarly, countries with more than 40 percent of GDP devoted to both agriculture and services often emphasize resource extractive (primarily mining and forestry) activities. These also tend to be *colonial dependency* countries, providing raw materials for foreign markets. Countries with more than 40 percent of their GDP obtained from industry are normally well along the path to economic development. Countries with more than half of their GDP based on service activities fall into two ends of the development spectrum. On the one hand are countries heavily dependent upon both extractive activities and tourism and other low-level service functions. On the other hand are countries that can properly be termed *postindustrial*: they have already passed through the industrial stage of their economic development and now rely less on the manufacture of products than on finance, research, communications, education, and other service-oriented activities.

Map 81   Employment by Economic Activity

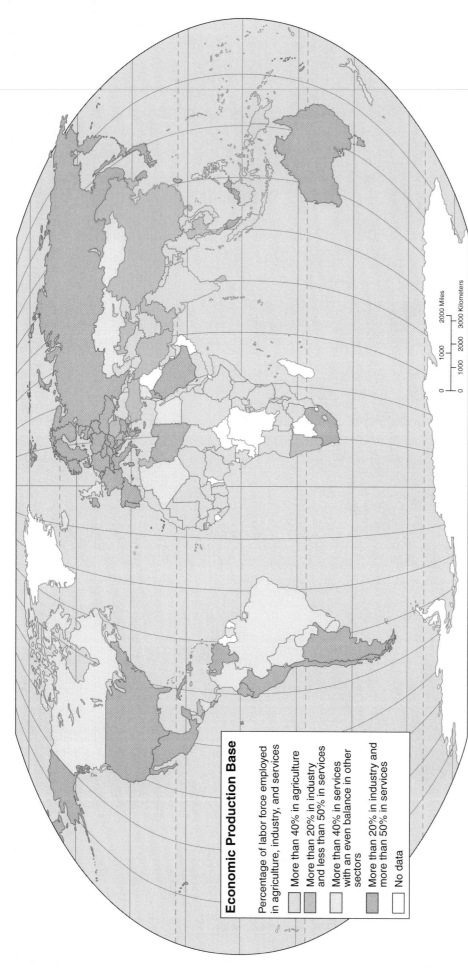

Economic Production Base

Percentage of labor force employed
in agriculture, industry, and services

- More than 40% in agriculture
- More than 20% in industry
  and less than 50% in services
- More than 40% in services
  with a fairly even balance in other
  sectors
- More than 20% in industry and
  more than 50% in services
- No data

The employment structure of a country's population is one of the best indicators of the country's position on the scale of economic development. At one end of the scale are those countries with more than 40 percent of their labor force employed in agriculture. These are almost invariably the least developed, with high population growth rates, poor human services, significant environmental problems, and so on. In the middle of the scale are two types of countries: those with more than 20 percent of their labor force employed in industry and those with a fairly even balance among agricultural, industrial, and service employment but with at least 40 percent of their labor force employed in service activities. Generally, these countries have undergone the industrial revolution fairly recently

and are still developing an industrial base while building up their service activities. This category also includes countries with a disproportionate share of their economies in service activities primarily related to resource extraction. On the other end of the scale from the agricultural economies are countries with more than 20 percent of their labor force employed in industry and more than 50 percent in service activities. These countries are, for the most part, those with a highly automated industrial base and a highly mechanized agricultural system (the "postindustrial," developed countries). They also include, particularly in Middle and South America and Africa, industrializing countries that are also heavily engaged in resource extraction as a service activity.

Map 82 Unemployment by Economic Activity

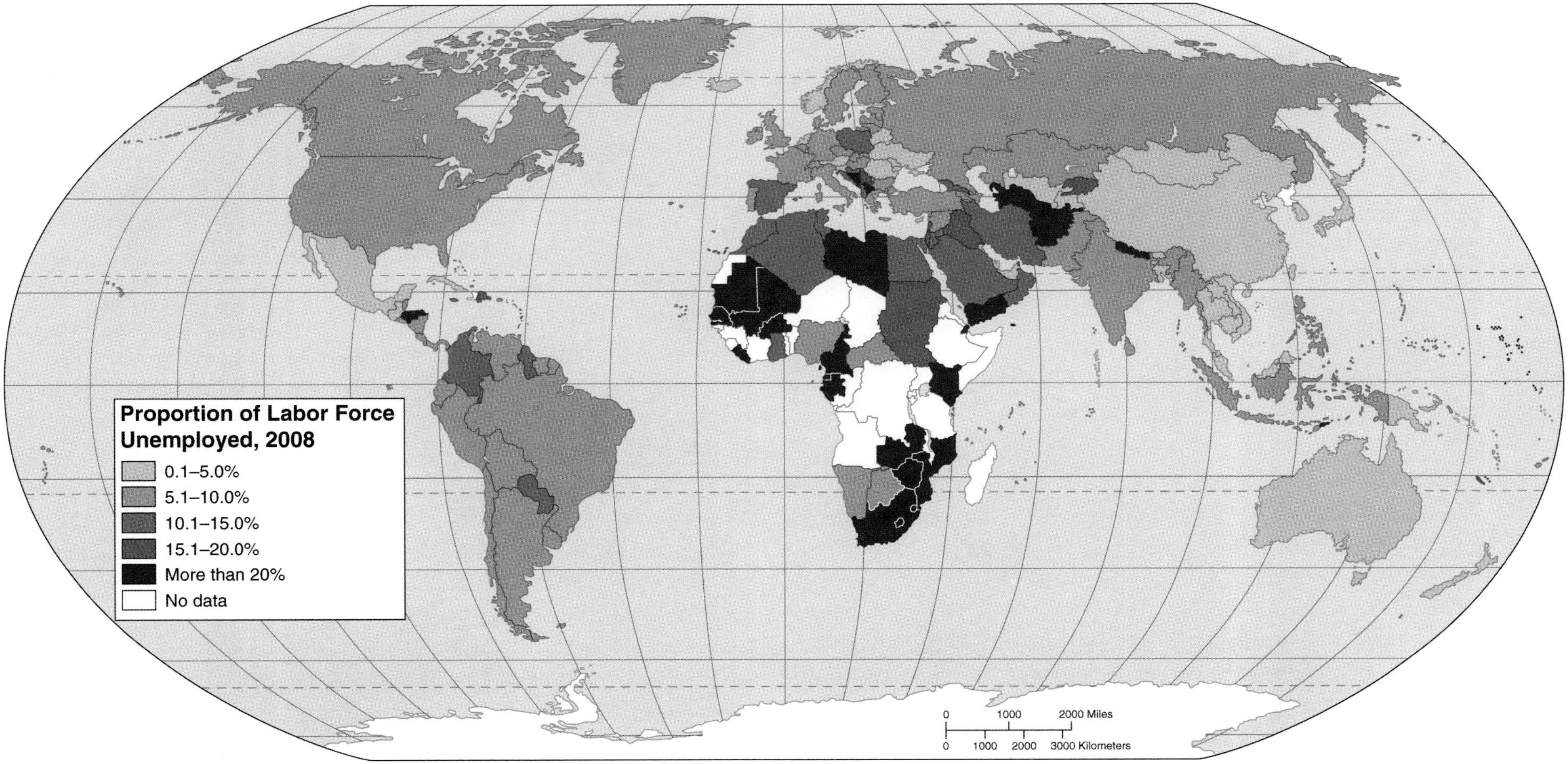

Proportion of Labor Force Unemployed, 2008

- 0.1–5.0%
- 5.1–10.0%
- 10.1–15.0%
- 15.1–20.0%
- More than 20%
- No data

0   1000   2000 Miles

0   1000   2000   3000 Kilometers

The percentage of a country's labor force that is classified as "unemployed" includes those without work but who are available for work and seeking employment. Countries may define the labor force in different ways, however. In many developing countries, for example, "employability" based on age may be more extensive than in more highly developed economies with stringent child labor laws. Generally, countries with higher percentages of their labor forces employed will be countries with higher levels of economic development. Where unemployment tends to be high, the out-migration of labor also tends to be high as workers unable to find employment at home cross international boundaries in search of work. Again, there tends to be a difference based on levels of economic development with the more developed countries experiencing inflows of labor while the reverse is true in the less developed world.

Map 83 Central Government Expenditures Per Capita

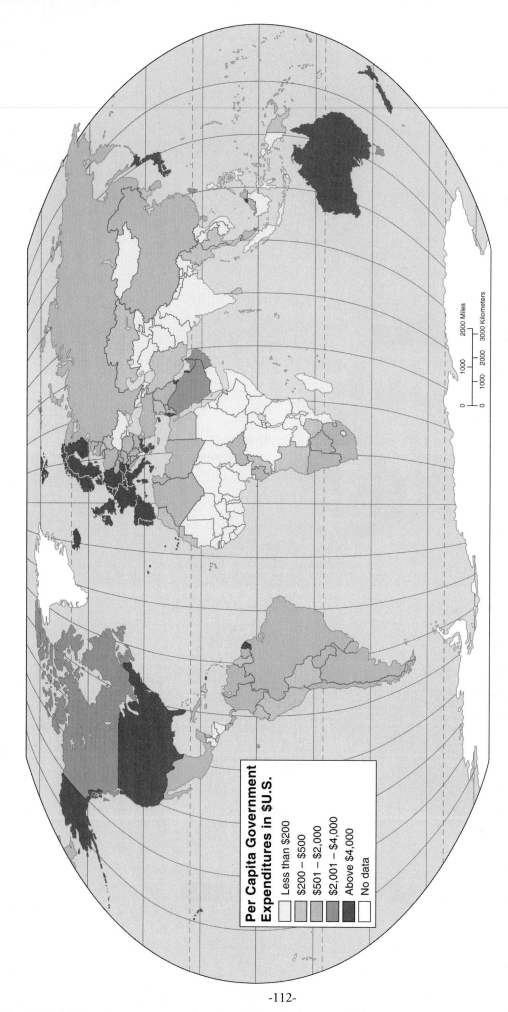

Per Capita Government Expenditures in $U.S.

Less than $200
$200 – $500
$501 – $2,000
$2,001 – $4,000
Above $4,000
No data

2000 Miles
1000 2000 3000 Kilometers
0 1000 2000

The amount of money that the central government of a country spends upon a variety of essential governmental functions is a measure of relative economic development, particularly when it is viewed on a per-person basis. These functions include such governmental responsibilities as agriculture, communications, culture, defense, education, fishing and hunting, health, housing, recreation, religion, social security, transportation, and welfare. Generally, the higher the level of economic development, the greater the per capita expenditures on these services. However, the data do mask some internal variations. For example, countries that spend 20 percent or more of their

central government expenditures on defense will often show up in the more developed category when, in fact, all that the figures really show is that a disproportionate amount of the money available to the government is devoted to purchasing armaments and maintaining a large standing military force. Thus, the fact that Libya spends more than the average for Africa does not suggest that the average Libyan is much better off than the average Tanzanian. Nevertheless, this map—particularly when compared with Map 101, Energy Consumption Per Capita—does provide a reasonable approximation of economic development levels.

Map 84 The Indebtedness of States

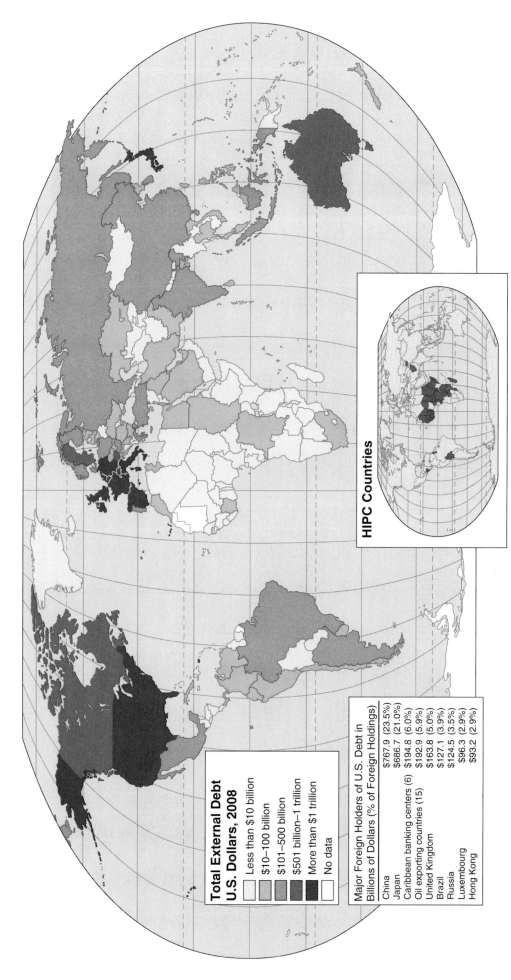

Total External Debt U.S. Dollars, 2008

- Less than $10 billion
- $10–100 billion
- $101–500 billion
- $501 billion–1 trillion
- More than $1 trillion
- No data

Major Foreign Holders of U.S. Debt in Billions of Dollars (% of Foreign Holdings)

China	$767.9 (23.5%)
Japan	$686.7 (21.0%)
Caribbean banking centers (6)	$194.8 (6.0%)
Oil exporting countries (15)	$192.9 (5.9%)
United Kingdom	$163.8 (5.0%)
Brazil	$127.1 (3.9%)
Russia	$124.5 (3.5%)
Luxembourg	$96.3 (2.9%)
Hong Kong	$93.2 (2.9%)

HIPC Countries

External debt is money or credit owed to foreign lenders. It generally is comprised of bonds and treasury bills (in the case of the United States) that are sold to foreign lenders and money owed to banks, governments, and international financial institutions. External debt is highly fluid and many countries of the world have "sustainable debt"—where a country can meet its debt service obligations. Other countries, particularly those in the developing world, have levels of debt, typically to international financial institutions such as the IMF and World Bank, that are beyond the governments' ability to repay. These countries typically are in a constant "catch-up" situation in which they fall increasingly further into debt and cannot meet their obligations without receiving partial or total forgiveness of debt. The IMF and World Bank have jointly put together debt reduction packages for 35 of the 41 countries identified as Heavily Indebted Poor Countries (HIPC). As of 2009 the level of structured debt relief was approximately $50 billion. As of 2009 approximately one-third of the U.S. national debt is that owed to foreign countries, with China and Japan accounting for over 44 percent of those holdings. Given the level of debt held by foreign countries, it is in the best interest of these countries to have the economy of the U.S. healthy.

Map 85 Global Flows of Investment Capital

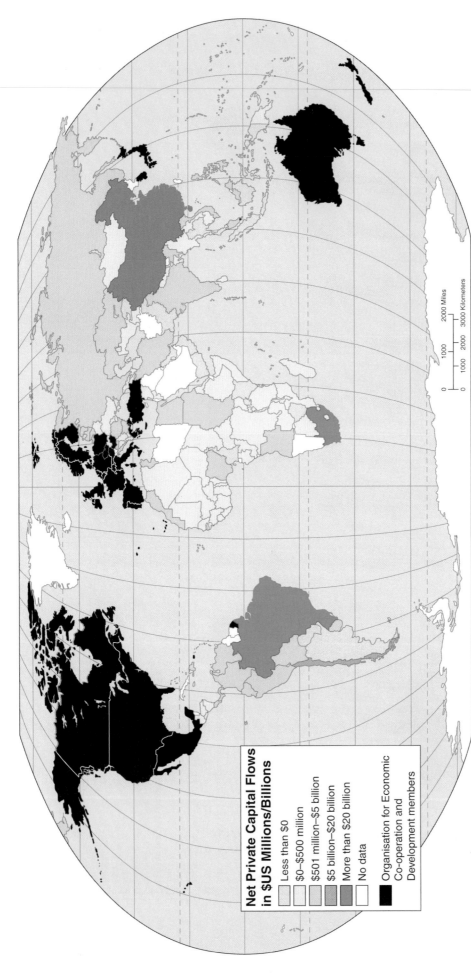

Net Private Capital Flows in $US Millions/Billions

- Less than $0
- $0–$500 million
- $501 million–$5 billion
- $5 billion–$20 billion
- More than $20 billion
- No data
- Organisation for Economic Co-operation and Development members

International capital flows include private debt and nondebt flows from one country to another, shown on the map as flows into a country. Nearly all of the capital comes from those countries that are members of the Organisation for Economic Co-operation and Development (OECD), shown in black on the map. Capital flows include commercial bank lending, bonds, other private credits, foreign direct investment, and portfolio investment. Most of these flows are indicators of the increasing influence developed countries exert over the developing economies. Foreign direct investment or FDI, for example, is a measure of the net inflow of investment monies used to acquire long-term management interest in businesses located

somewhere other than in the economy of the investor. Usually this means the acquisition of at least 10 percent of the stock of a company by a foreign investor and is, then, a measure of what might be termed "economic colonialism": control of a region's economy by foreign investors that could, in the world of the future, be as significant as colonial political control was in the past. International capital flows have increased greatly in the last decade as the result of the increasing liberalization of developing countries, the strong economic growth exhibited by many developing countries, and the falling costs and increased efficiency of communication and transportation services.

Map 86   Inflation Rates

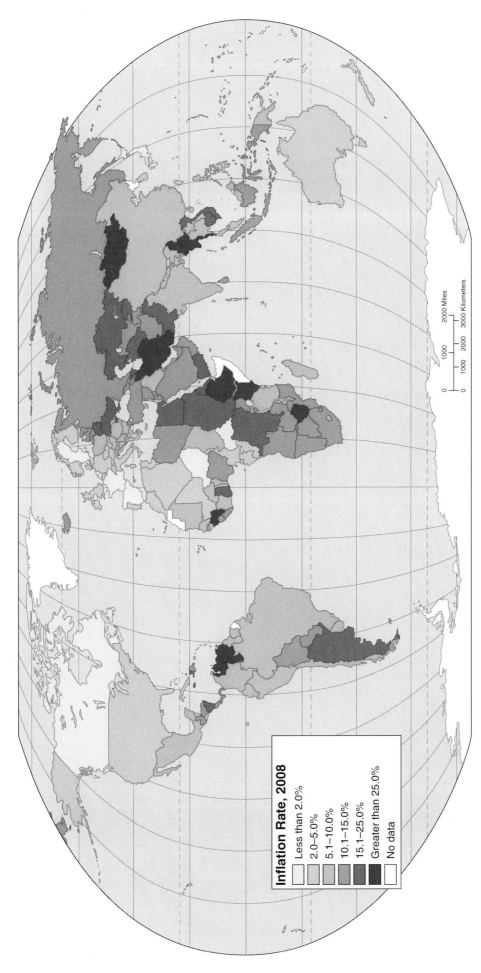

Inflation Rate, 2008

- Less than 2.0%
- 2.0–5.0%
- 5.1–10.0%
- 10.1–15.0%
- 15.1–25.0%
- Greater than 25.0%
- No data

The last half of the first decade of the twenty-first century saw economic decline on a global scale at levels not seen since the 1930s. In 2008, growth in GDP (Gross Domestic Product —the market value of a country's goods and services produced during a year) began slowing. In many countries, the slowing growth of GDP has been accompanied by rising inflation rates. The inflation rate is a measure of the rise in the prices of goods and services. Inflation can influence economies both positively and negatively, but hyperinflation—extremely high

or out-of-control inflation—can seriously hinder a country's ability to produce goods and services. The most noteworthy example of recent hyperinflation is Zimbabwe. During the late twentieth century Zimbabwe's inflation rate was relatively high—typically between 15 percent and 40 percent. During the early 2000s, hyperinflation set in, reaching as high as 11.2 million percent in 2008. In 2009 the country gained international notoriety when it issued a 100 trillion Zimbabwean Dollar note.

Map **87**   Dependence on Trade

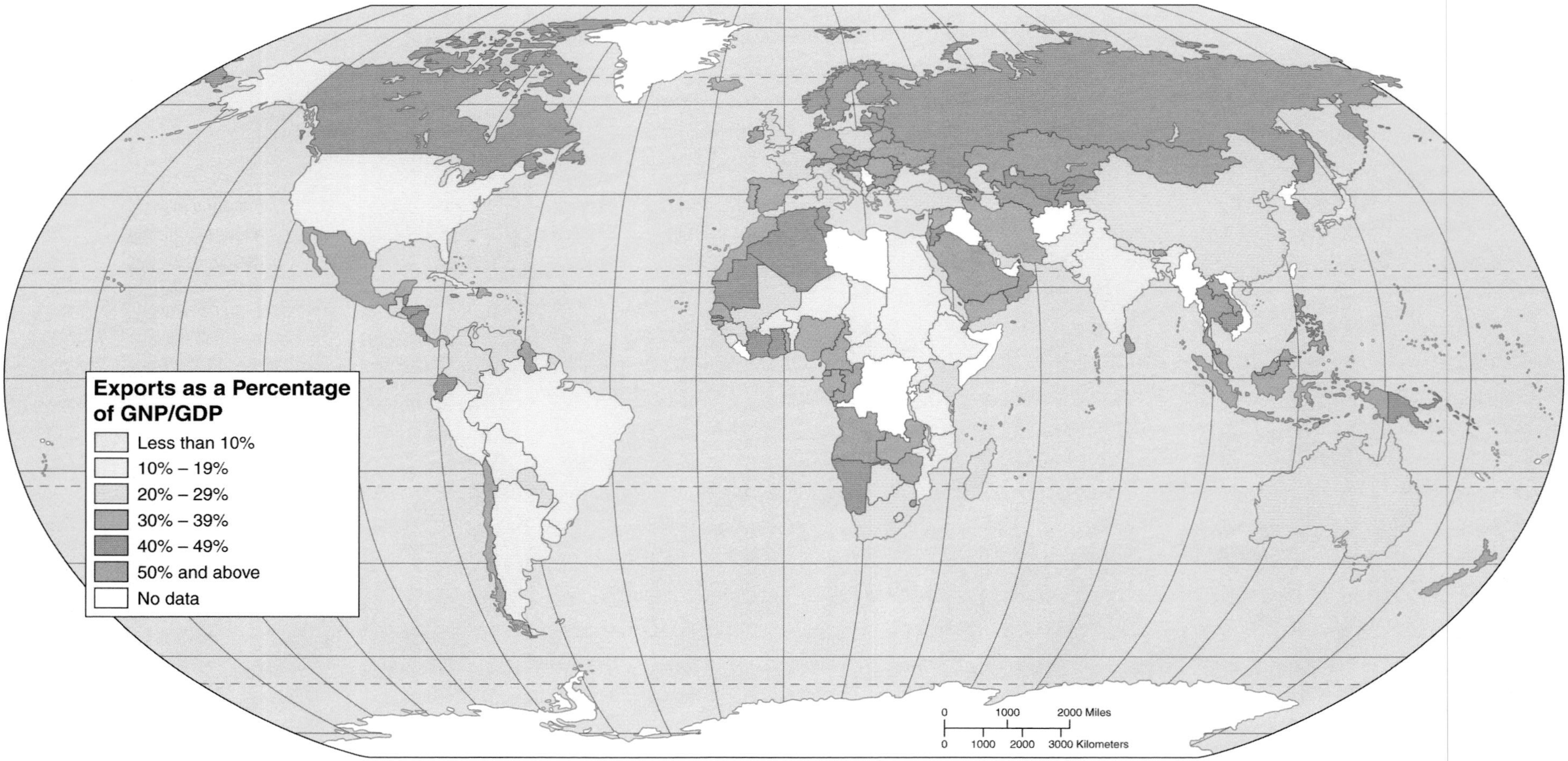

Exports as a Percentage of GNP/GDP

Less than 10%
10% – 19%
20% – 29%
30% – 39%
40% – 49%
50% and above
No data

0   1000   2000
0   1000   2000   3000 Kilometers
0   1000   2000 Miles

As the global economy becomes more and more a reality, the economic strength of virtually all countries is increasingly dependent upon trade. For many developing nations, with relatively abundant resources and limited industrial capacity, exports provide the primary base upon which their economies rest. Even countries like the United States, Japan, and Germany, with huge and diverse economies, depend on exports to generate a significant percentage of their employment and wealth. Without imports, many products that consumers want would be unavailable or more expensive; without exports, many jobs would be eliminated.

Map 88 Trade with Neighboring Countries

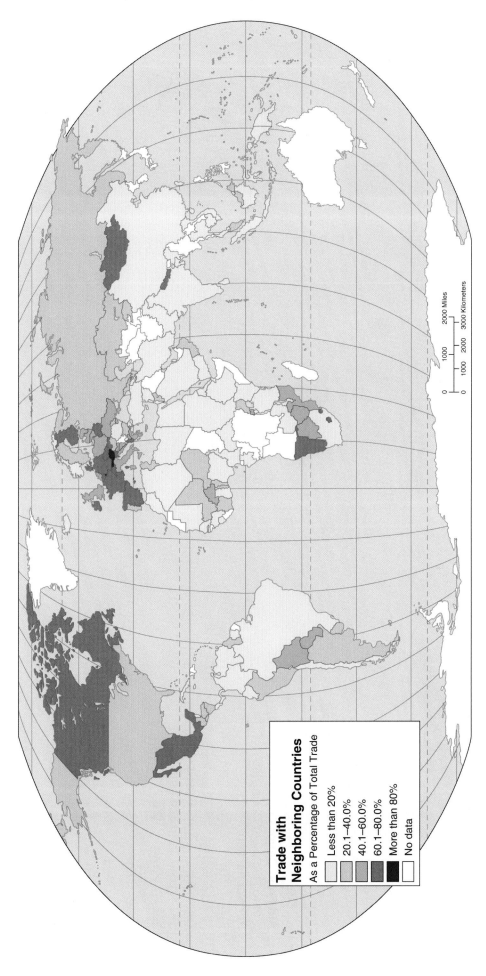

Trade with Neighboring Countries

As a Percentage of Total Trade

- Less than 20%
- 20.1–40.0%
- 40.1–60.0%
- 60.1–80.0%
- More than 80%
- No data

Two important factors influencing international trade are proximity and relative wealth of trading partners. Proximity is important because transportation costs can be a large part of an economic activity. Relative wealth is an important influence on the goods and services a country may produce for export. Of course, the percentage of trade with neighboring countries isn't necessarily a strong indicator of a country's wealth or future growth, but the patterns exhibited on this map are telling. The world's countries are increasingly interconnecting through regional trade agreements (see Map 76), and the influence of connectivity among EU and NAFTA states is evident here. Much of Africa, South Asia, and South America trades more with more distant countries such as the United States, Japan, and EU states. As regional trade blocs mature, look for the levels of cross-border trade to increase.

Map **89**   Aiding Economic Development

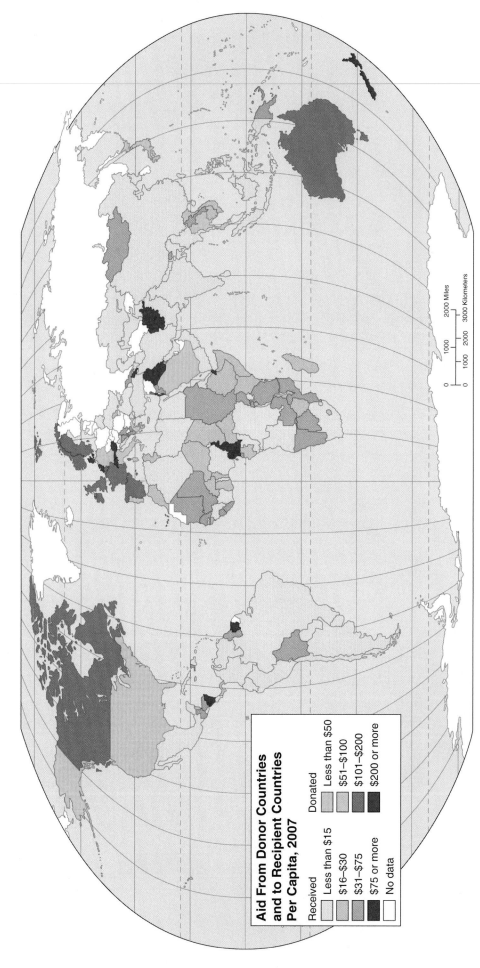

**Aid From Donor Countries
and to Recipient Countries
Per Capita, 2007**

Received

Less than $15
$16–$30
$31–$75
$75 or more
No data

Donated

Less than $50
$51–$100
$101–$200
$200 or more

0   1000   2000 Miles
0   1000   2000   3000 Kilometers

Over the last few years, official development assistance to developing countries from the member countries of the Organisation for Economic Co-operation and Development has risen dramatically, with the United States as the world's number one donor country, giving over 25 percent of the total of development assistance. Development assistance—or "foreign aid," as it is sometimes called—is widely recognized as benefiting both the donor and the recipient. Developing countries that increase their levels of per capita income through economic development have more money to spend on products from more highly developed countries. Increased development increases the capacity to foster not just economic but political change. In some parts of the world, such as Sub-Saharan Africa, foreign aid is the largest single source of external finance, far exceeding foreign investments.

Map 90 The Cost of Consumption, 2008

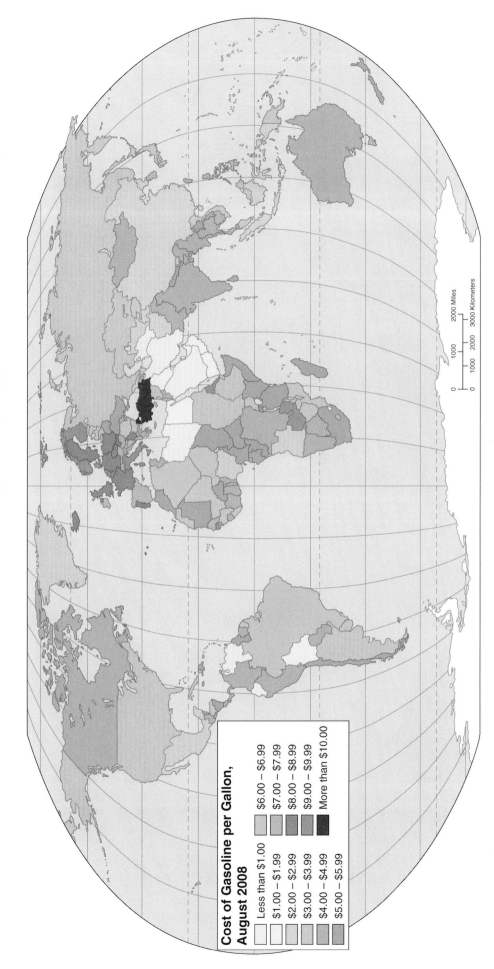

Cost of Gasoline per Gallon, August 2008

- Less than $1.00
- $1.00 – $1.99
- $2.00 – $2.99
- $3.00 – $3.99
- $4.00 – $4.99
- $5.00 – $5.99
- $6.00 – $6.99
- $7.00 – $7.99
- $8.00 – $8.99
- $9.00 – $9.99
- More than $10.00

The year 2008 brought massive increases in the price of gasoline at the pump, creating considerable consternation among the American driving population, in particular. It is one thing to point out that gasoline prices are and historically have been considerably higher in Europe than in North America. But it is another to note that European spatial patterns of places of work and places of residence are significantly different than in North America. The North American metropolitan area evolved its spatial patterns in conjunction with the rise of privately owned automobiles; European cities, on the other hand, had spatial patterns well established centuries or even millennia before the automobile emerged as a common mode of transportation. As a consequence, such things as the journey to work are very different for many Europeans, who can walk from where they live to where they work, than it is for Ameri-

cans and Canadians who often live considerable distances from their places of employment. A daily commute of 75 miles one way would not be considered unusual in America. In Europe it is virtually unheard of. There is also the component of the scale of organization of human activities: because of the very large country in which Americans live, their spatial movements are customarily more extensive than those of Europeans, who live in countries the size of American states. So, yes, gasoline is much more expensive in Europe than in North America. But in North America, the increase in the cost of gasoline to and above $4.00 per gallon produces significantly more economic impact than proportionally similar increases in Europe. Similarly, the reduction in gasoline prices in late 2008 and throughout 2009 had a greater impact in North America—although its impact was overshadowed by larger forces.

Map 91 A Wired World: Internet Users

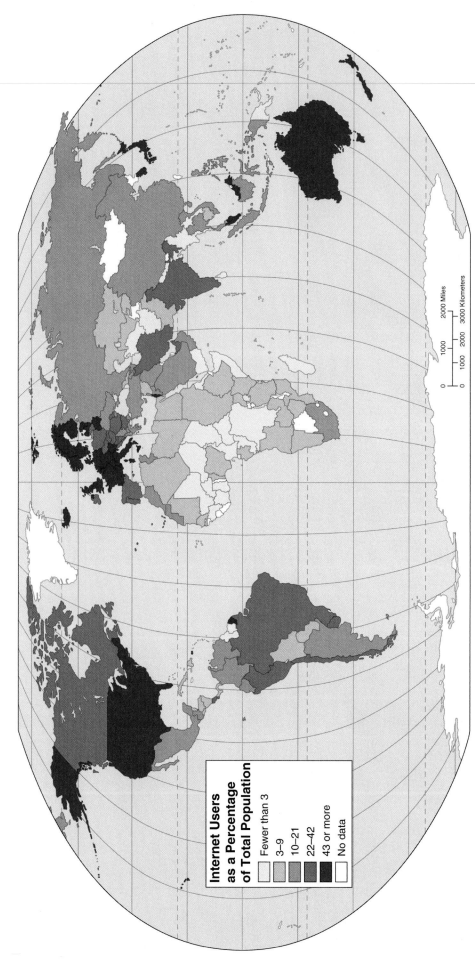

Internet Users as a Percentage of Total Population

- Fewer than 3
- 3–9
- 10–21
- 22–42
- 43 or more
- No data

It is interesting to contemplate that a short quarter of a century ago, such a map could not have been created. The emergence of immediate, long-distance connectivity via the Internet has been one of the most important components of globalization. We now live, as author Thomas Friedman has noted, in a "flat world" where lines of connection are more important than distance and where virtually instantaneous connections have altered—perhaps forever—the way that we do business, exchange information, and transform our cultures. Some of the recent transformations we have seen in the emergence of countries like China and India as major players in the international economy are, in part, the consequence of access to the Internet. Originally conceived as a quick way for academics to exchange information, the Internet has become a cultural and social phenomenon that far exceeds its original purpose. Whether or not this will result in an eventual benefit to human well-being remains to be seen. Does the benefit of quick communication result in a cost to the complexity and richness of human cultures worldwide?

Map 92　The Rise of the Personal Computer

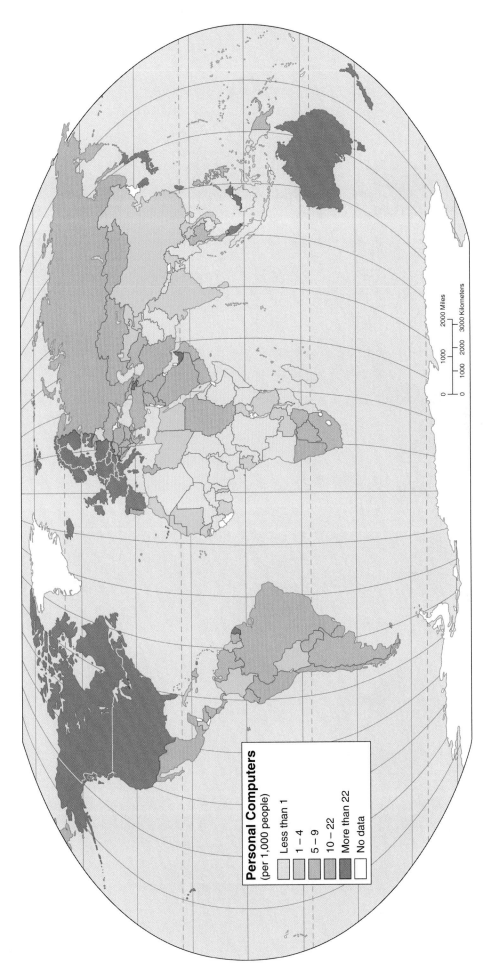

Personal Computers
(per 1,000 people)

- Less than 1
- 1 – 4
- 5 – 9
- 10 – 22
- More than 22
- No data

The Internet connections shown in the previous map would not be possible without personal computers—or at least not possible at their present scale. But personal computers do a great deal more than simply act as high-speed transmitters of information. They are incredibly powerful devices for the storage and analysis of data and are becoming, seemingly exponentially, even more powerful. When the use of mainframe computers became common on university campuses in the 1960s, they were used primarily for faculty and graduate student research. Now, an undergraduate can run on his or her laptop computer—in a matter of seconds—a program that would have required hours to run on an institutional computer that occupied spaces similar to those required for medium-sized classrooms. Certainly computers have changed the way that businesses are run. But they have, perhaps, changed the daily lives of personal computer users even more.

Map 93 Traditional Links: The Telephone

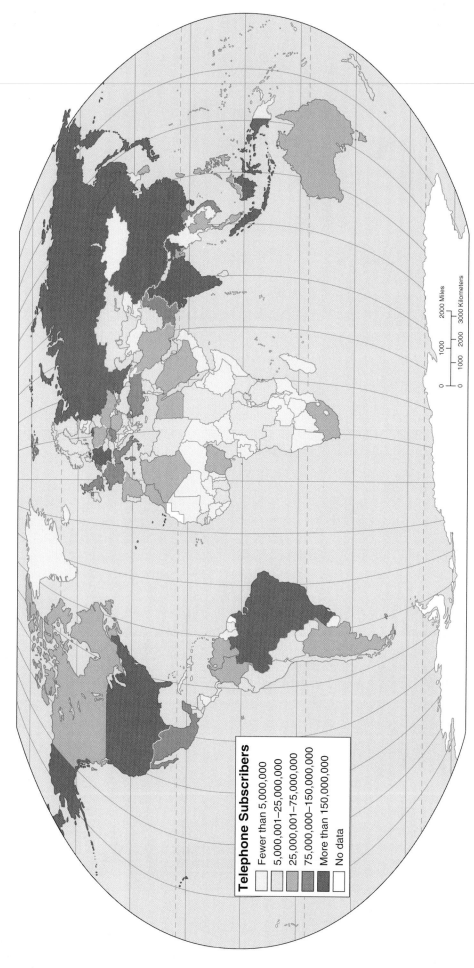

Telephone Subscribers

- Fewer than 5,000,000
- 5,000,001–25,000,000
- 25,000,001–75,000,000
- 75,000,000–150,000,000
- More than 150,000,000
- No data

2000 Miles

3000 Kilometers

1000

1000   2000

0   1000   2000

0

Not all of the world's communications take place via computers and the Internet. A lot of person-to-person connection is still carried out via the telephone, and access to telephone connections is perhaps as good an indication of economic development or, more important, the potential for economic development, as anything else. The map clearly shows the prevalence of telephone connectivity in the developed world. But it also shows an increasingly high degree of access to telephones in major countries in the developing world, such as India and China. If these countries are to continue to develop their econo-

mies at the pace of the last decade, then their degree of communication—including access to telephones—will also have to increase. The data shown on this map include users of both land lines and cellular phones. By the end of 2008, for the first time, the number of cellular phone users worldwide exceeded the number of those using the traditional land lines. As cellular phone complexity increases to include e-mail and other computer functions, the gap between cellular users and traditional phone users can be expected to widen.

Unit V

Food and Energy

Map 94   The Value of Agriculture

Map 95   Average Daily Per Capita Supply of Calories (Kilocalories)

Map 96   Food Supply from Marine and Freshwater Systems

Map 97   Cropland Per Capita: Changes, 1996–2007

Map 98   World Pastureland, 2005

Map 99   Fertilizer Use, 2007

Map 100   Energy Production Per Capita

Map 101   Energy Consumption Per Capita

Map 102   Energy Dependency

Map 103   Flows of Oil

Map 94 The Value of Agriculture

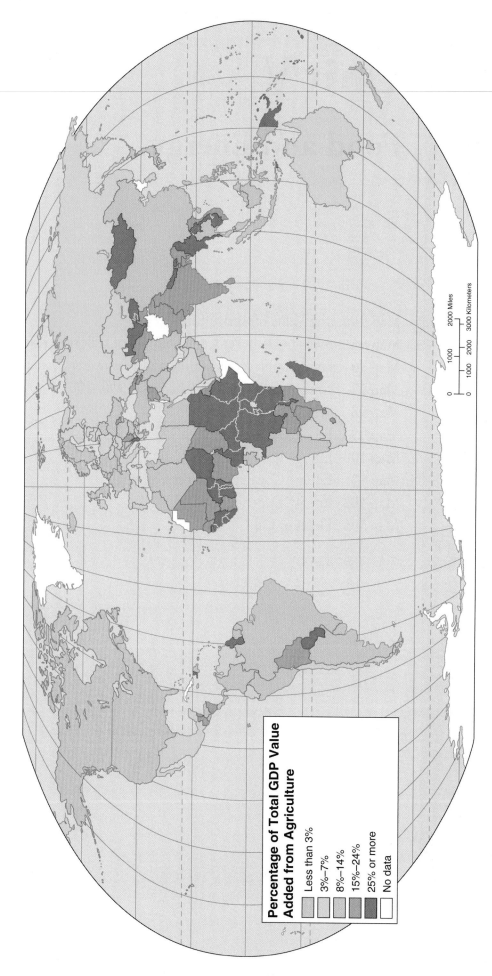

Percentage of Total GDP Value Added from Agriculture

- Less than 3%
- 3%–7%
- 8%–14%
- 15%–24%
- 25% or more
- No data

When compared with the service and industrial sectors of the global economy, agriculture grew more slowly between 1990 and 2005. The highest rates of growth were recorded in the Sub-Saharan African region, where agriculture grew more than either service or industrial economies. It is clear from the Sub-Saharan African figures, as well as those from Middle and South America and Asia, that agriculture is still of vital economic importance to the developing regions of the world. Not only does agriculture

contribute significantly to the gross domestic product of these countries but it represents the primary source of employment in nearly two-thirds of the world's countries. Even in the rapidly expanding service and industrial economies of India and China, agriculture still counts for nearly half of all employment. This contrasts with 4 percent of total employment in the United States and Germany, and only 1 percent in the United Kingdom.

Map 95   Average Daily Per Capita Supply of Calories (Kilocalories)

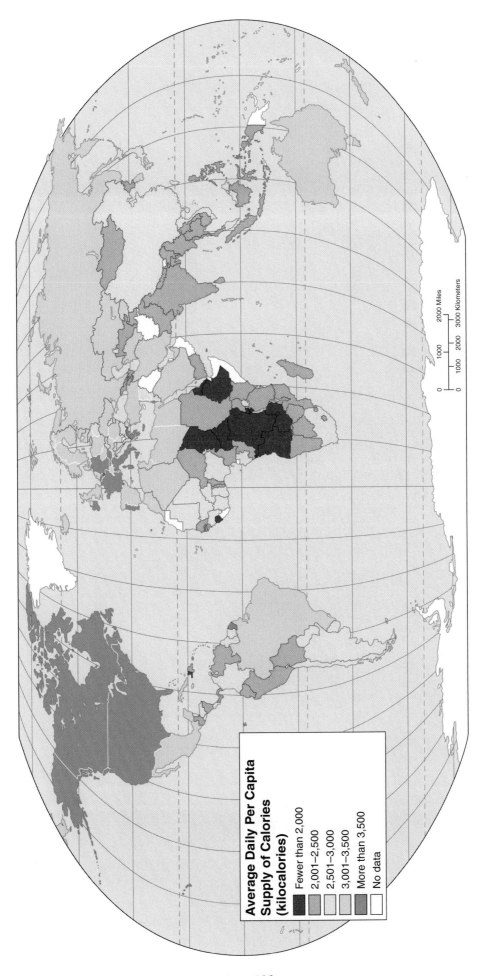

**Average Daily Per Capita
Supply of Calories
(kilocalories)**

Fewer than 2,000
2,001–2,500
2,501–3,000
3,001–3,500
More than 3,500
No data

The data shown on this map, which indicate the presence or absence of critical food shortages, do not necessarily indicate the presence of starvation or famine. But they certainly do indicate potential problem areas for the next decade. The measurements are in calories from *all* food sources: domestic production, international trade, drawdown on stocks or food reserves, and direct foreign contributions or aid. The quantity of calories available is that amount, estimated by the UN's Food and Agriculture Organization (FAO), that reaches consumers. The calories actually consumed may be lower than the figures shown, depending on how much is lost in a variety of ways: in home storage (to pests such as rats and mice), in preparation and cooking, through consumption by pets and domestic animals, and as discarded foods, for example. The estimate of need is not a global uniform value but is calculated for each country on the basis of the age and sex distribution of the population and the estimated level of activity of the population.

-125-

Map 96 Food Supply from Marine and Freshwater Systems

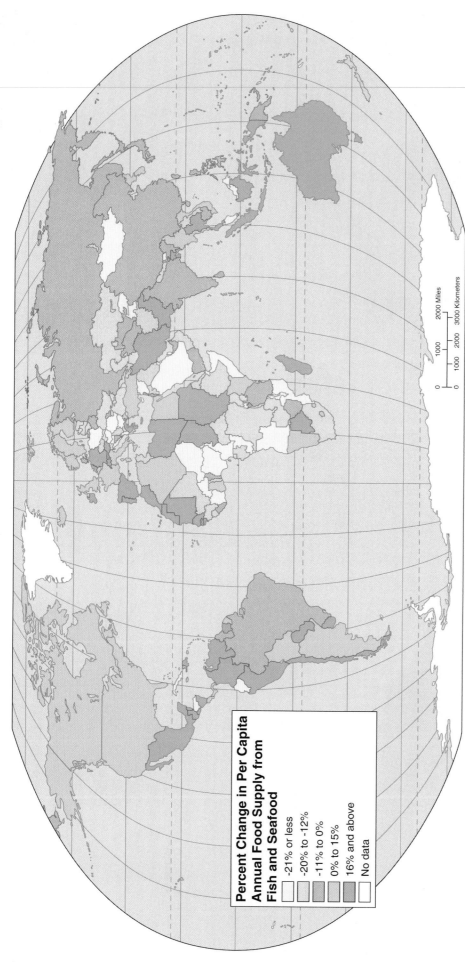

Percent Change in Per Capita Annual Food Supply from Fish and Seafood

- -21% or less
- -20% to -12%
- -11% to 0%
- 0% to 15%
- 16% and above
- No data

0   1000   2000 Miles
0   1000   2000   3000 Kilometers

Not that many years ago, food supply experts were confidently predicting that the "starving millions" of the world of the future could be fed from the unending bounty of the world's oceans. While the annual catch from the sea helped to keep hunger at bay for a time, by the late 1980s it had become apparent that without serious human intervention in the form of aquaculture, the supply of fish would not be sufficient to offset the population/food imbalance that was beginning to affect so many of the world's regions. The development of factory-fishing with advanced equipment to locate fish and process them before they went to market increased the supply of food from the ocean, but in that increase was sown the seeds of future problems. The factory-fishing system, efficient in

terms of economics, was costly in terms of fish populations. In some well-fished areas, the stock of fish that was viewed as near infinite just a few decades ago has dwindled nearly to the point of disappearance. This map shows both increases and decreases in the amount of individual countries' food supplies from the ocean. The increases are often the result of more technologically advanced fishing operations. The decreases are usually the result of the same thing: increased technology has brought increased harvests, which has reduced the supply of fish and shellfish and that, in turn, has increased prices. Most of the countries that have experienced sharp decreases in their supply of food from the world's oceans are simply no longer able to pay for an increasingly scarce commodity.

Map 97 Cropland Per Capita: Changes, 1996–2007

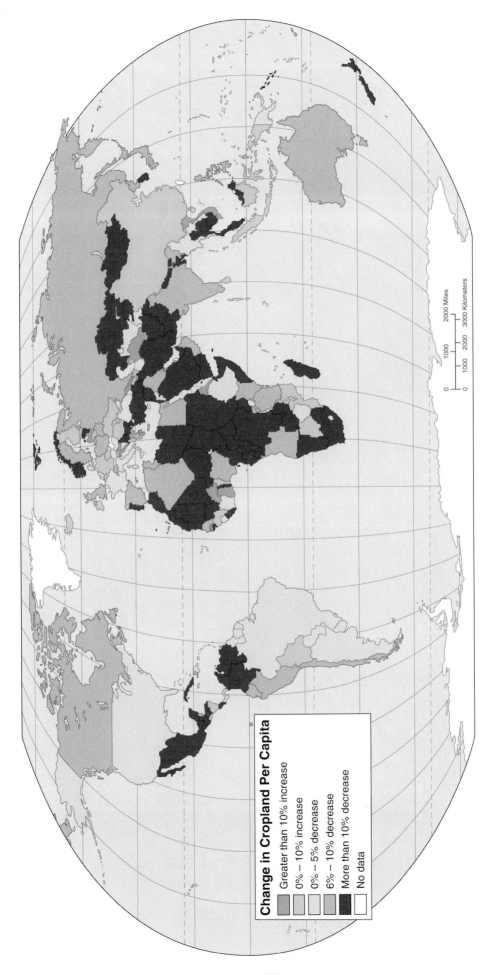

Change in Cropland Per Capita

- Greater than 10% increase
- 0% – 10% increase
- 0% – 5% decrease
- 6% – 10% decrease
- More than 10% decrease
- No data

0   1000   2000 Miles

0   1000   2000   3000 Kilometers

As population has increased rapidly throughout the world, the area of cultivated land has increased at the same time; in fact, the amount of farmland per person has gone up slightly. Unfortunately, the figures that show this also tell us that since most of the best (or even good) agricultural land in 1985 was already under cultivation, most of the agricultural area added since the mid-1990s involves land that would have been viewed as marginal by the fathers and grandfathers of present farmers—marginal in that it was too dry, too wet, too steep to cultivate, too far from a market, and so on. The continued expansion of agricultural area is one reason that serious famine and starvation have struck only a few regions of the globe. But land, more than any other resource we deal with, is finite, and the expansion cannot continue indefinitely. Future gains in agricultural production are most probably going to come through more intensive use of existing cropland, heavier applications of fertilizers and other agricultural chemicals, and genetically engineered crops requiring heavier applications of energy and water, than from an increase in the amount of the world's cropland.

Map 98 World Pastureland, 2005

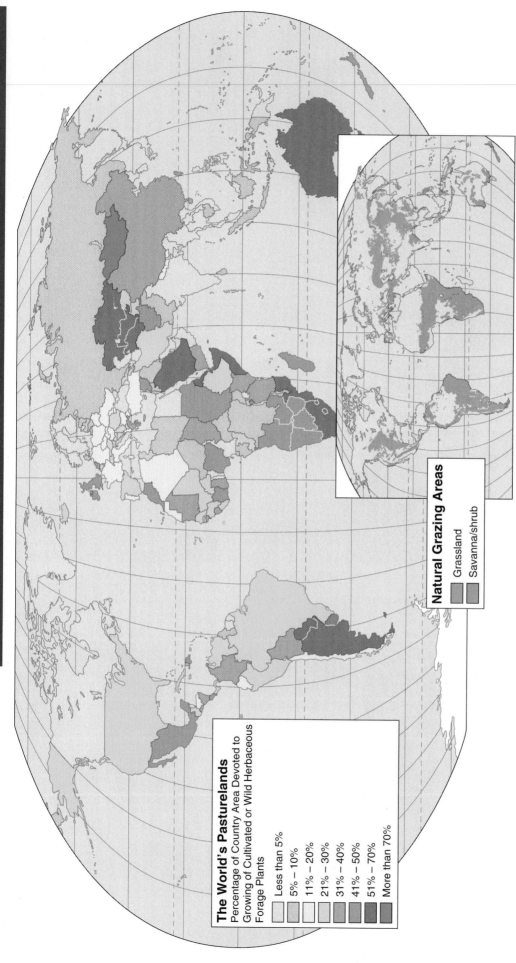

The World's Pasturelands

Percentage of Country Area Devoted to Growing of Cultivated or Wild Herbaceous Forage Plants

- Less than 5%
- 5% – 10%
- 11% – 20%
- 21% – 30%
- 31% – 40%
- 41% – 50%
- 51% – 70%
- More than 70%

Natural Grazing Areas

- Grassland
- Savanna/shrub

More than 25 percent of the world's surface is considered pastureland—either native wild grasses or human-made pastures created by clearing forests and planting grass and other herbaceous forage plants for livestock feed. Two types of pasture predominate: the prairie and steppe grasses of the mid-latitudes and the savanna grasses of the sub-tropics and tropics. These two primary grassland biomes are shown in the inset map. The larger map depicts pastureland as a proportion of land area of individual countries. You will note that many of the countries with high levels of pastureland (Argentina and Australia, for example) are among the world's leading exporters of livestock products. Other countries with high levels of pastureland (Saudi Arabia and the Central Asian states) consume the bulk of their products domestically. The significance of the distribution and use of pastureland is that—whether it is in the African Sahel, China, Brazil, or the United States—the world's pasturelands are deteriorating rapidly under increasing demands to produce more animal products than even a wealthier world can afford to pay for. Grassland degradation, particularly in areas where pastoral nomads use their animals as their chief source of food and income, creates woody scrublands where the carrying capacity for grazing animals is sharply diminished. In short, most of the world's pasturelands are overgrazed, and the world's supply of animal products is in jeopardy.

Map 99 Fertilizer Use, 2007

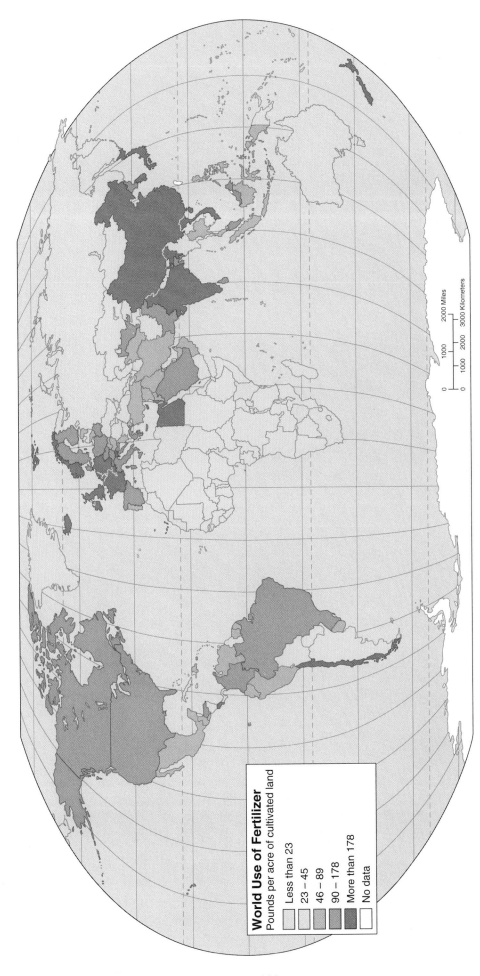

World Use of Fertilizer
Pounds per acre of cultivated land

- Less than 23
- 23 – 45
- 46 – 89
- 90 – 178
- More than 178
- No data

The use of fertilizer to maintain the productivity of agricultural lands is a wonderful agricultural invention—as long as the fertilizers used are natural rather than artificial. In most of the world's developed countries, such as those in Europe and North America, the use of animal manure to fertilize fields has decreased dramatically over the past century, in favor of artificial fertilizers that are cheaper and easier to use and—what is most important—increase crop yields more dramatically. The danger here is that artificial fertilizers normally have high concentrations of nitrates that tend to convert to nitrites in the soil, reducing the ability of soil bacteria to extract "free" nitrogen from the atmosphere. As

more artificial fertilizer is used, natural soil fertility is decreased, creating the demand for more artificial fertilizers. In some areas, overuse of artificial fertilizers has actually created soils that are too "hot" chemically to produce crops. Countries with high fertilizer use in the developing world—northern South America, and Southwest, South, and East Asia— still tend to use more natural fertilizers. But as farmers in those areas gain more ability to buy and use artificial fertilizers, their soils will also begin to suffer from overfertilization. Global agriculture needs to come to grips with the need to maintain productivity but to do so in a manner that is sustainable.

Map 100   Energy Production Per Capita

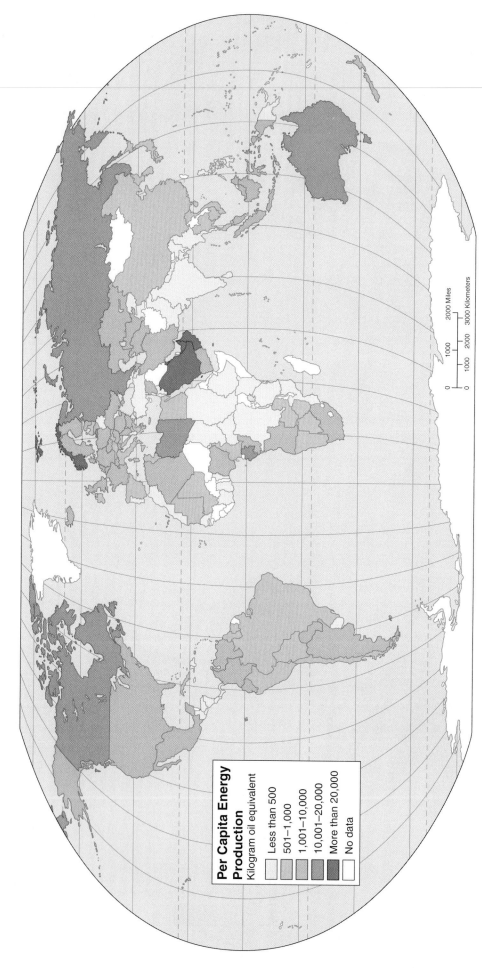

Per Capita Energy Production
Kilogram oil equivalent

- Less than 500
- 501–1,000
- 1,001–10,000
- 10,001–20,000
- More than 20,000
- No data

Energy production per capita is a measure of the availability of mechanical energy to assist people in their work. This map shows the amount of all kinds of energy—solid fuel (primarily coal), liquid fuel (primarily petroleum), natural gas, geothermal, wind, solar, hydroelectric, nuclear, waste recycling, and indigenous heat pumps—produced per person in each country. With some exceptions, wealthier countries produce more energy per capita than poor ones. Countries such as Japan and many European states rank among the world's wealthiest, but are energy-poor and produce relatively little of their own energy.

They have the ability, however, to pay for imports. On the other hand, countries such as those of the Persian Gulf or the oil-producing states of Central and South America may rank relatively low on the scale of economic development but rank high as producers of energy. In many poor countries, especially in Central and South America, Africa, South Asia, and East Asia, large proportions of energy come from traditional fuels such as fire-wood and animal dung. Indeed, for many in the developing world, the real energy crisis is a shortage of wood for cooking and heating.

Map 101 Energy Consumption Per Capita

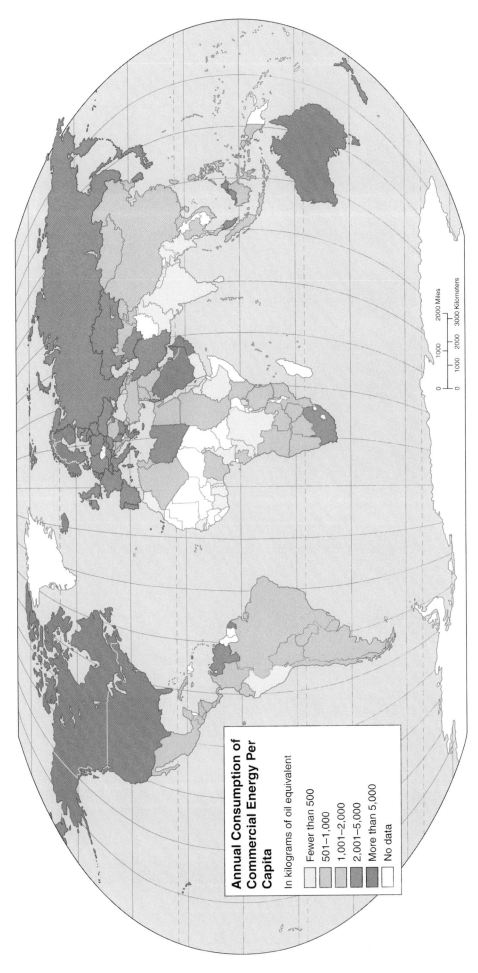

Annual Consumption of Commercial Energy Per Capita

In kilograms of oil equivalent

- Fewer than 500
- 501–1,000
- 1,001–2,000
- 2,001–5,000
- More than 5,000
- No data

Of all the quantitative measures of economic well-being, energy consumption per capita may be the most expressive. All of the countries defined by the World Bank as having high incomes consume at least 100 gigajoules of commercial energy (the equivalent of about 3.5 metric tons of coal) per person per year, with some, such as the United States and Canada, having consumption rates in the 300-gigajoule range (the equivalent of more than 10 metric tons of coal per person per year). With the exception of the oil-rich Persian Gulf states, where consumption figures include the costly "burning off" of excess energy in the form of natural gas flares at wellheads, most of the highest-consuming countries are in the Northern Hemisphere, concentrated in North America and Western Europe. At the other end of the scale are low-income countries, whose consumption rates are often less than 1 percent of those of the United States and other high consumers. These figures do not, of course, include the consumption of noncommercial energy—the traditional fuels of firewood, animal dung, and other organic matter—widely used in the less developed parts of the world.

-131-

Map 102 Energy Dependency

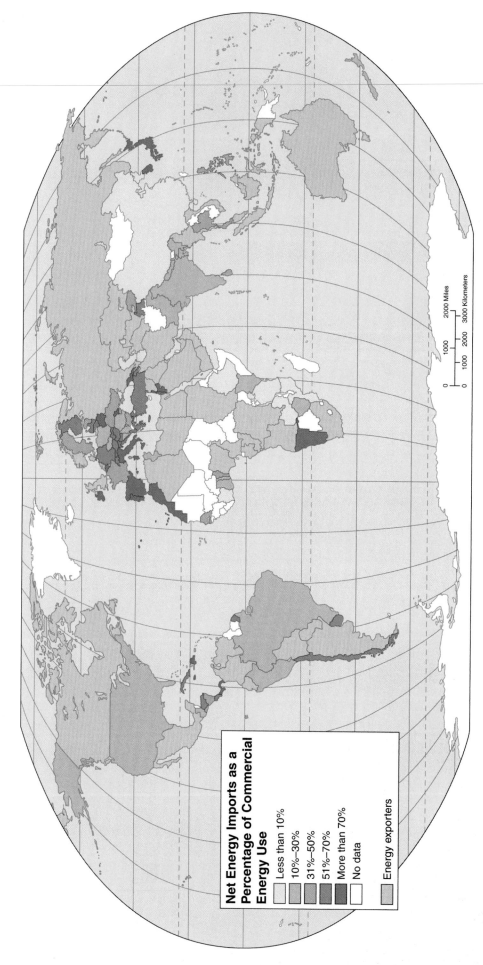

Net Energy Imports as a Percentage of Commercial Energy Use

- Less than 10%
- 10%–30%
- 31%–50%
- 51%–70%
- More than 70%
- No data

- Energy exporters

0   1000   2000 Miles
0   1000   2000   3000 Kilometers

The patterns on the map show dependence on commercial energy to other end-use fuels such as electricity or refined petroleum products; energy from traditional sources such as fuelwood or dried animal dung is not included. Energy dependency is the difference between domestic consumption and domestic production of commercial energy and is most often expressed as a net energy import or export. A few of the world's countries are net exporters of energy: most are importers. The growth in global commercial energy use over the last decade indicates growth in the modern sectors of the economy—industry, transportation, and urbanization—particularly in the lesser developed countries. Still, the primary consumers of energy—and those having the greatest dependence on foreign sources of energy—are the more highly developed countries of Europe, North America, and Japan.

Map 103   Flows of Oil

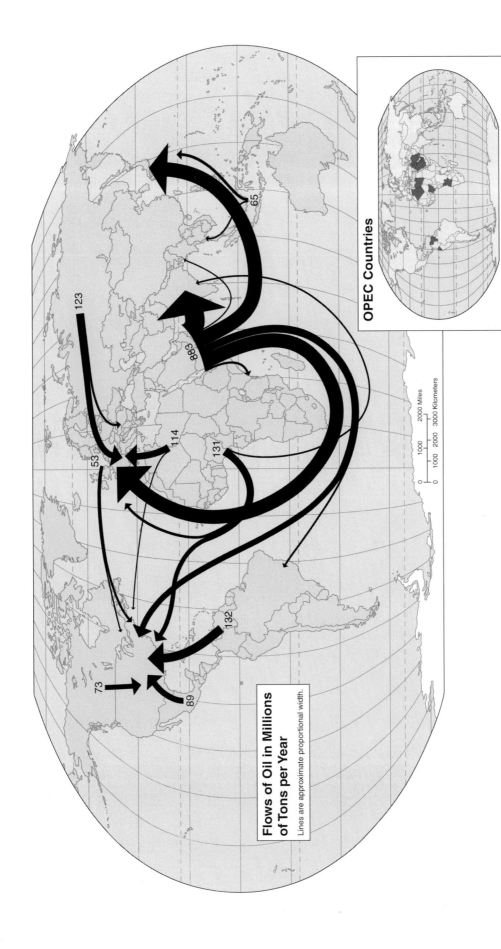

Flows of Oil in Millions of Tons per Year

Lines are approximate proportional width.

OPEC Countries

0   1000   2000 Miles
0 1000 2000 3000 Kilometers

The pattern of oil movements from producing region to consuming region is one of the dominant facts of contemporary international maritime trade. Supertankers carry a million tons of crude oil and charge rates in excess of $0.10 per ton per mile, making the transportation of oil not only a necessity for the world's energy-hungry countries, but also an enormously profitable proposition. One of the major negatives of these massive oil flows is the damage done to the oceanic ecosystems—not just from the well-publicized and dramatic events like the wrecking of the *Exxon Valdez* but from the incalculable amounts of oil from leakage, scrubbings, purgings, and so on, which are a part of the oil transport technology. As seen above, much of the supply of the world's oil comes from countries belonging to the Organization of the Petroleum Exporting Countries (OPEC). In 1999, OPEC members controlled nearly two-thirds of the world's known oil reserves and over one-third of the world's production. It is clear from the map that the primary recipients of these oil flows are the world's most highly developed economies.

-133-

Unit VI

Environmental Conditions

Map 104 Deforestation and Desertification

Map 105 Forest Loss and Gain, 1990–2005

Map 106 Soil Degradation

Map 107 Global Air Pollution: Sources and Wind Currents

Map 108 The Acid Deposition Problem: Air, Water, Soil

Map 109 Pollution of the Oceans

Map 110 Water Resources: Availability of Renewable Water Per Capita

Map 111 Water Resources: Annual Withdrawal Per Capita

Map 112 Water Stress: Shortage, Abundance, and Population Density

Map 113 Carbon Dioxide Emissions

Map 114 Potential Global Temperature Change

Map 115 The Loss of Biodiversity: Globally Threatened Animal Species

Map 116 The Loss of Biodiversity: Globally Threatened Plant Species

Map 117 Global Hotspots of Biodiversity

Map 118 Degree of Human Disturbance

Map 119 The Green and Not-So-Green World

Map 104 Deforestation and Desertification

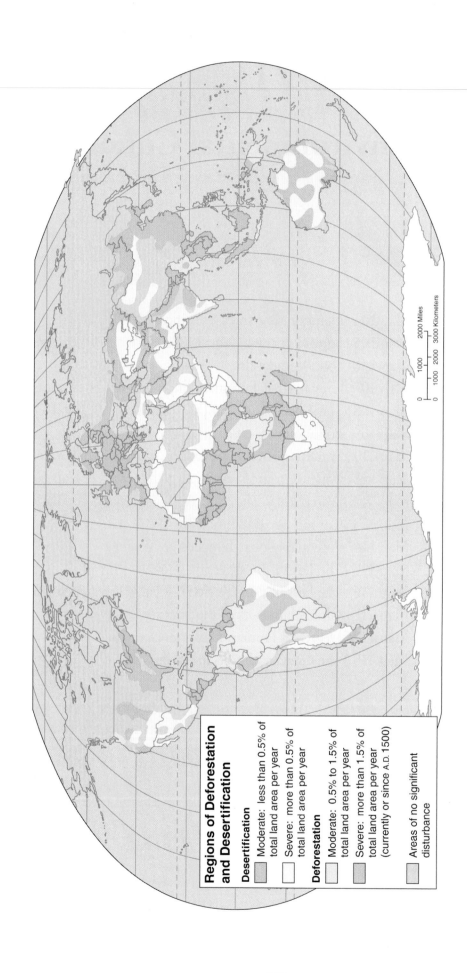

Regions of Deforestation and Desertification

Desertification

- Moderate: less than 0.5% of total land area per year
- Severe: more than 0.5% of total land area per year

Deforestation

- Moderate: 0.5% to 1.5% of total land area per year
- Severe: more than 1.5% of total land area per year (currently or since A.D. 1500)

- Areas of no significant disturbance

0   1000   2000 Miles
0 1000 2000 3000 Kilometers

While those of us in the developed countries of the world tend to think of environmental deterioration as the consequence of our heavily industrialized economies, in fact the worst examples of current environmental degradation are found within the world's less developed regions. There, high population growth rates and economies limited primarily to farming have forced the increasing use of more marginal (less suited to cultivation) land. In the world's grassland and arid environments, which occupy approximately 40 percent of the world's total land area, increasing cultivation pressures are turning vulnerable areas into deserts incapable of sustaining agricultural productivity. In the world's forested regions, particularly in the tropical forests of Middle and South America, Africa, and Asia, a similar process is occurring: increasing pressure for more farmland is creating a process of deforestation or forest clearing that destroys the soil, reduces the biological diversity of the forest regions, and ultimately may have the capacity to alter the global climate by contributing to an increase in carbon dioxide in the atmosphere. This increases the heat trapped in the atmosphere and enhances the greenhouse effect.

Map 105 Forest Loss and Gain, 1990–2005

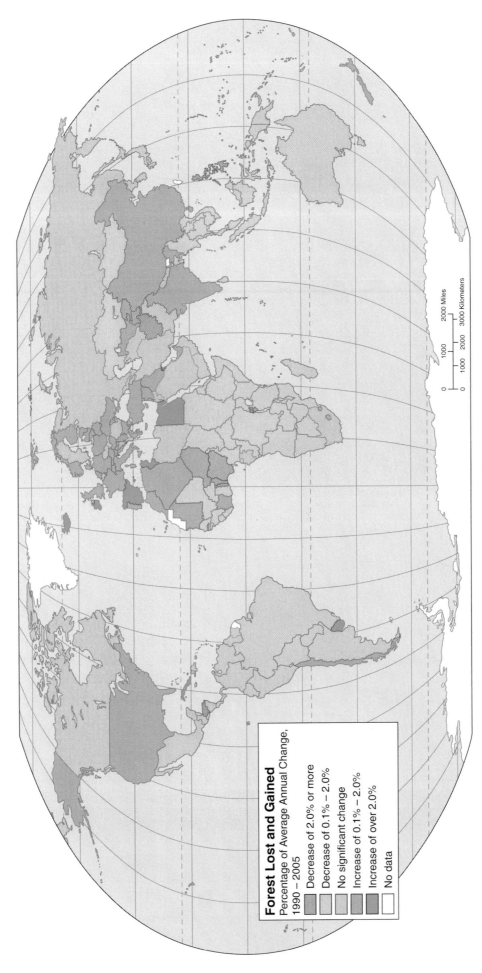

Forest Lost and Gained
Percentage of Average Annual Change, 1990 – 2005

- Decrease of 2.0% or more
- Decrease of 0.1% – 2.0%
- No significant change
- Increase of 0.1% – 2.0%
- Increase of over 2.0%
- No data

During the 15 years included in this analysis, the world lost approximately 20 million acres of forest land each year or a total of 256 million acres. About 50 percent of the world's total loss came in Africa—most of this loss represented land clearance for agricultural purposes. Nearly 40 percent of the world's total loss was in Brazil and, again, the majority of this loss resulted from land clearance for agriculture. At the global level, forest clearance seems to be slowing somewhat—but it still is an area of concern for a variety of reasons. Healthy forests act as a "carbon sink" and withdraw carbon dioxide from the at-

mosphere, aiding in the reduction of this important greenhouse gas and helping to reduce the impact of carbon dioxide on global warming. Equally important is the fact that forest clearance disturbs all other components of an ecosystem, from soil chemistry to water quality and quantity. There is a temptation to blame countries in Africa, Middle America or South America for failing to protect these forests. But the agricultural products grown on cleared land, or the livestock pastured on forests cleared and replaced by grasslands, are generally consumed by the market of the more highly developed world.

-137-

Map 106   Soil Degradation

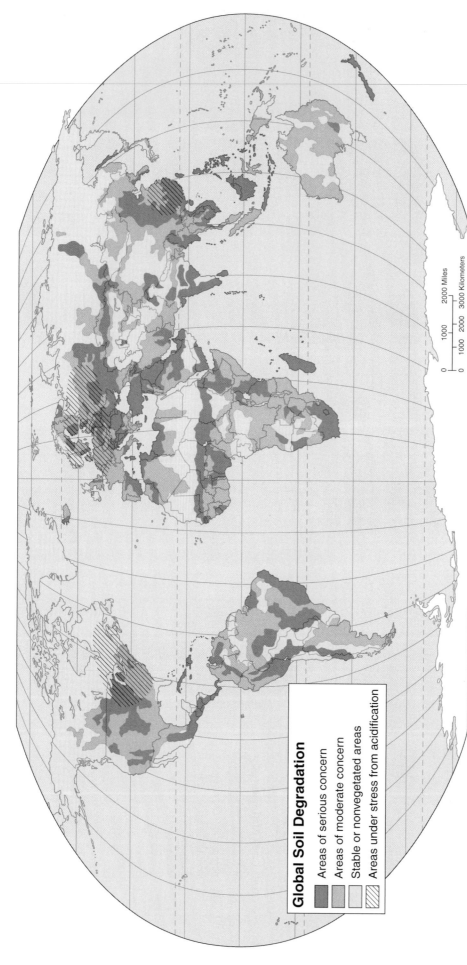

Global Soil Degradation

- Areas of serious concern
- Areas of moderate concern
- Stable or nonvegetated areas
- Areas under stress from acidification

0   1000   2000 Miles
0   1000   2000   3000 Kilometers

Recent research has shown that more than 3 billion acres of the world's surface suffer from serious soil degradation, with more than 22 million acres so severely eroded or poisoned with chemicals that they can no longer support productive crop agriculture. Most of this soil damage has been caused by poor farming practices, overgrazing of domestic livestock, and deforestation. These activities strip away the protective cover of natural vegetation—forests and grasslands—allowing wind and water erosion to remove the topsoil that contains the necessary nutrients and soil microbes for plant growth. But millions of acres of topsoil have been degraded by chemicals as well. In some instances

these chemicals are the result of overapplication of fertilizers, herbicides, pesticides, and other agricultural chemicals. In other instances, chemical deposition from industrial and urban wastes and from acid precipitation has poisoned millions of acres of soil. As the map shows, soil erosion and pollution are problems not just in developing countries with high population densities and increasing use of marginal lands but in the more highly developed regions of mechanized, industrial agriculture as well. While many methods for preventing or reducing soil degradation exist, they are seldom used because of ignorance, cost, or perceived economic inefficiency.

Map 107 Global Air Pollution: Sources and Wind Currents

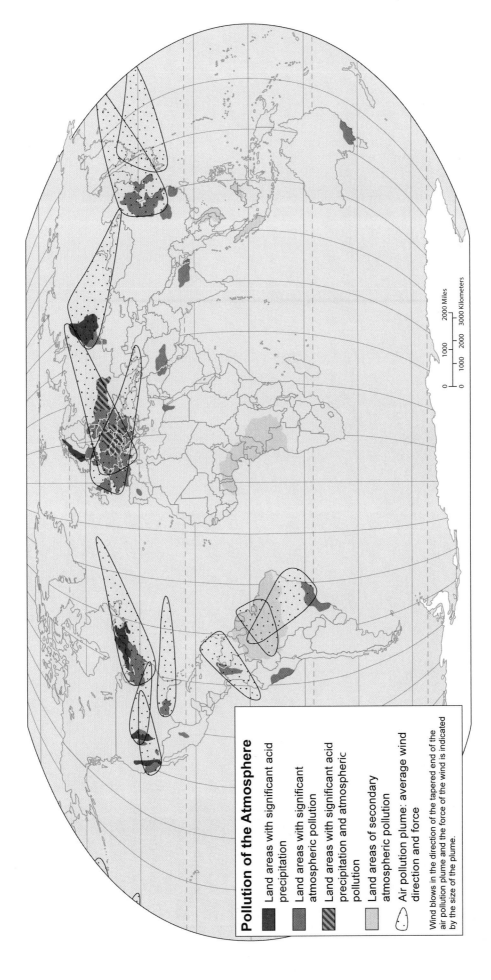

Pollution of the Atmosphere

- Land areas with significant acid precipitation
- Land areas with significant atmospheric pollution
- Land areas with significant acid precipitation and atmospheric pollution
- Land areas of secondary atmospheric pollution
- Air pollution plume: average wind direction and force

Wind blows in the direction of the tapered end of the air pollution plume and the force of the wind is indicated by the size of the plume.

| 0 | 1000 | 2000 Miles |
| 0 | 1000 2000 | 3000 Kilometers |

Almost all processes of physical geography begin and end with the flows of energy and matter among land, sea, and air. Because of the primacy of the atmosphere in this exchange system, air pollution is potentially one of the most dangerous human modifications in environmental systems. Pollutants such as various oxides of nitrogen or sulfur cause the development of acid precipitation, which damages soil, vegetation, and wildlife and fish.

Air pollution in the form of smog is often dangerous for human health. And most atmospheric scientists believe that the efficiency of the atmosphere in retaining heat—the so-called greenhouse effect—is being enhanced by increased carbon dioxide, methane, and other gases produced by agricultural and industrial activities. The result, they fear, will be a period of global warming that will dramatically alter climates in all parts of the world.

Map 108 The Acid Deposition Problem: Air, Water, Soil

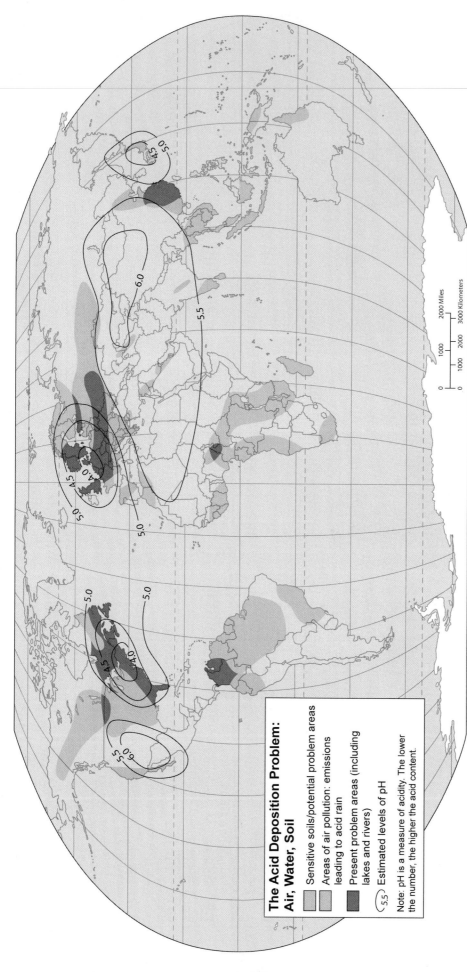

The Acid Deposition Problem: Air, Water, Soil

- Sensitive soils/potential problem areas
- Areas of air pollution: emissions leading to acid rain
- Present problem areas (including lakes and rivers)
- ⟨5.5⟩ Estimated levels of pH

Note: pH is a measure of acidity. The lower the number, the higher the acid content.

The term "acid precipitation" refers to increasing levels of acidity in snowfall and rainfall caused by atmospheric pollution. Oxides of nitrogen and sulfur resulting from incomplete combustion of fossil fuels (coal, oil, and natural gas) combine with water vapor in the atmosphere to produce weak acids that then "precipitate" or fall along with water or ice crystals. Some atmospheric acids formed by this process are known as "dry-acid" precipitates and they too will fall to earth, although not necessarily along with rain or snow. In some areas of the world, the increased acidity of streams and lakes stemming from high levels of acid precipitation or dry acid fallout has damaged or destroyed aquatic life. Acid precipitation and dry acid fallout also harm soil systems and vegetation, producing a characteristic burned appearance in forests that lends the same quality to landscapes that forest fires would. The region most dramatically impacted by acid precipitation is Central Europe, where decades of destructive environmental practices, including the burning of high sulfur coal for commercial, industrial, and residential purposes, has produced the destruction of hundreds of thousands of acres of woodlands—a phenomenon described by the German foresters who began their study of the area following the lifting of the Iron Curtain as "Waldsterben": Forest Death.

-140-

Map 109   Pollution of the Oceans

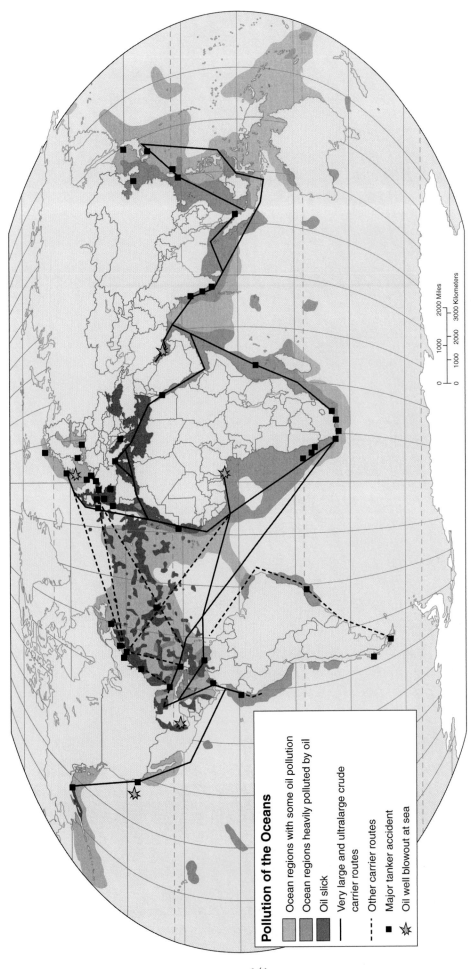

Pollution of the Oceans

- Ocean regions with some oil pollution
- Ocean regions heavily polluted by oil
- Oil slick
- —— Very large and ultralarge crude carrier routes
- - - Other carrier routes
- ■ Major tanker accident
- ☆ Oil well blowout at sea

0   1000   2000 Miles
0   1000   2000   3000 Kilometers

The pollution of the world's oceans has long been a matter of concern to physical geographers, oceanographers, and other environmental scientists. The great circulation systems of the ocean are one of the controlling factors of the earth's natural environment, and modifications to those systems have unknown consequences. This map is based on what we can measure: (1) areas of oceans where oil pollution has been proven to have inflicted significant damage to ocean ecosystems and life forms (including phytoplankton, the oceans' primary food producers, equivalent to land-based vegetation) and (2) areas of oceans where unusually high concentrations of hydrocarbons from oil spills may have inflicted some damage to the oceans' biota. A glance at the map shows that there are few areas of the world's oceans where some form of pollution is not a part of the environmental system. What the map does not show in detail, because of the scale, are the dramatic consequences of large individual pollution events: the wreck of the *Exxon Valdez* and the polluting of Prince William Sound, or the environmental devastation produced by the 1991 Gulf War in the Persian Gulf.

Map 110 Water Resources: Availability of Renewable Water Per Capita

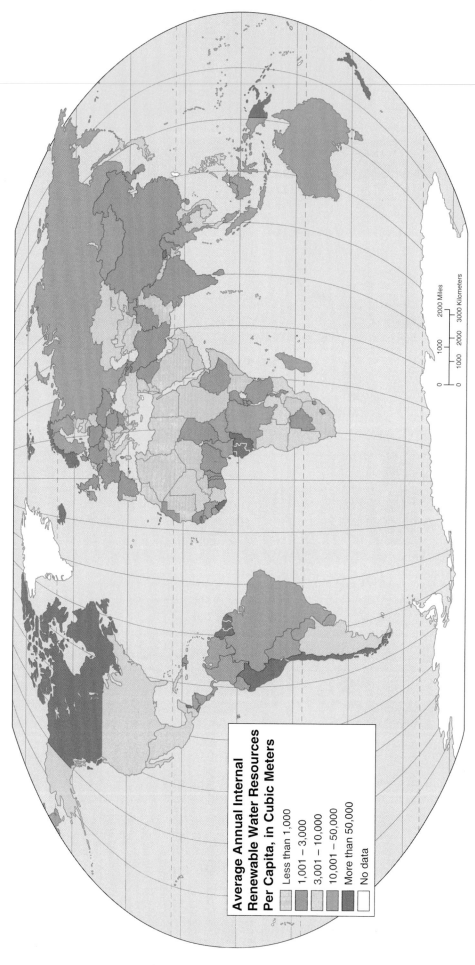

Average Annual Internal Renewable Water Resources Per Capita, in Cubic Meters

- Less than 1,000
- 1,001 – 3,000
- 3,001 – 10,000
- 10,001 – 50,000
- More than 50,000
- No data

0 1000 2000 Miles
0 1000 2000 3000 Kilometers

Renewable water resources are usually defined as the total water available from streams and rivers (including flows from other countries), ponds and lakes, and groundwater storage or aquifers. Not included in the total of renewable water would be water that comes from such nonrenewable sources as desalinization plants or melted icebergs. While the concept of renewable or flow resources is a traditional one in resource management, in fact, few resources, including water, are truly renewable when their use is excessive. The water resources shown here are indications of that principle. A country like the United States possesses truly enormous quantities of water. But the United States also uses enormous quantities of water. The result is that, largely because of excessive use, the availability of renewable water is much less than in many other parts of the world where the total supply of water is significantly less.

Map 111 Water Resources: Annual Withdrawal Per Capita

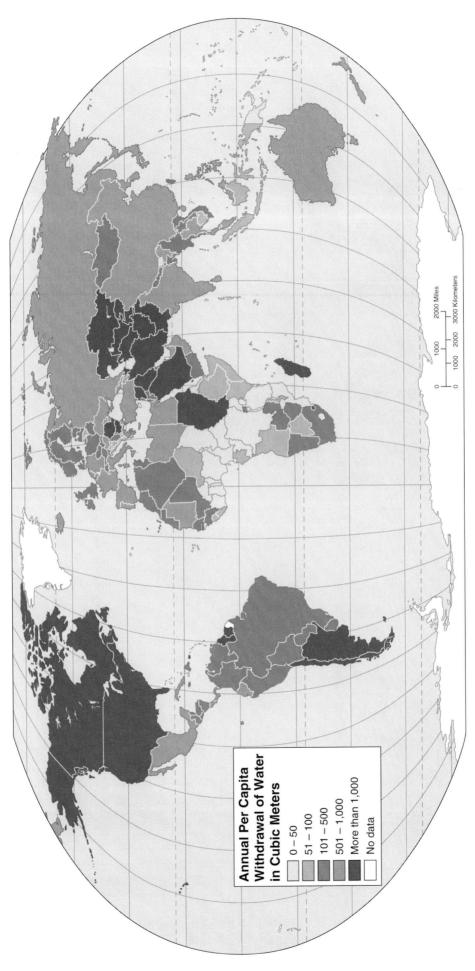

Annual Per Capita Withdrawal of Water in Cubic Meters

- 0 – 50
- 51 – 100
- 101 – 500
- 501 – 1,000
- More than 1,000
- No data

Water resources must be viewed like a bank account in which deposits and withdrawals are made. As long as the deposits are greater than the withdrawals, a positive balance remains. But when the withdrawals begin to exceed the deposits, sooner or later (depending on the relative sizes of the deposits and withdrawals) the account becomes overdrawn. For many of the world's countries, annual availability of water is insufficient to cover the demand. In these countries, reserves stored in groundwater are being tapped, resulting in depletion of the water supply (think of this as shifting money from a savings account to a checking account). The water supply can maintain its status as a renewable resource only if deposits continue to be greater than withdrawals, and that seldom happens. In general, countries with high levels of economic development and countries that rely on irrigation agriculture are the most spendthrift when it comes to their water supplies.

Map 112 Water Stress: Shortage, Abundance, and Population Density

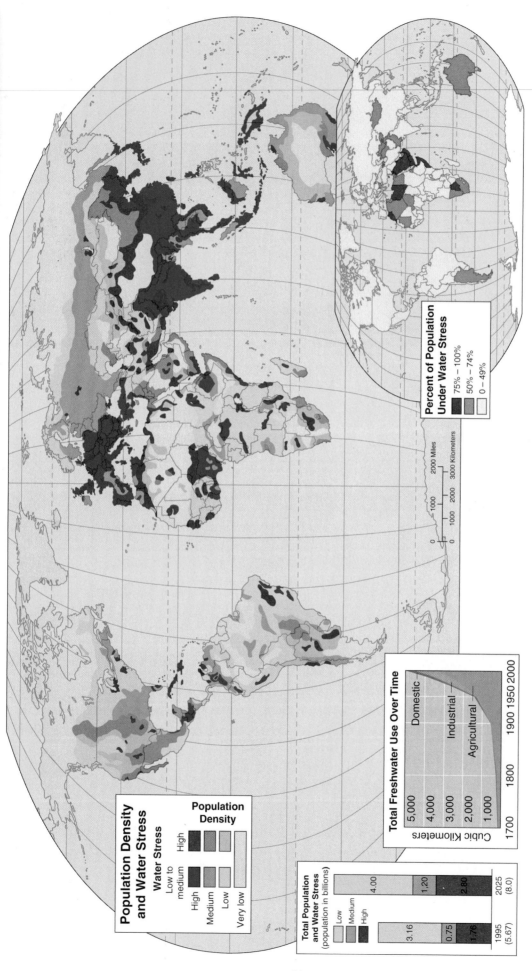

Population Density and Water Stress

Water Stress
Low to medium | High

Population Density

	Water Stress Low to medium	High
High		
Medium		
Low		
Very low		

Total Population and Water Stress
(population in billions)

Low | Medium | High

	1995 (5.67)	2025 (8.0)
Low	3.16	4.00
Medium	0.75	1.20
High	1.76	2.80

Total Freshwater Use Over Time

Cubic Kilometers

5,000
4,000
3,000
2,000
1,000

1700 1800 1900 1950 2000

Domestic
Industrial
Agricultural

0   1000   2000 Miles
0 1000 2000 3000 Kilometers

Percent of Population Under Water Stress

75% – 100%
50% – 74%
0 – 49%

Maps such as the previous two, based on national-level data for water consumption and availability, should be used only to obtain national-level understanding. Information on water withdrawal and availability are regionally and locally based geographic phenomena and are linked not just with water supplies but with the density of human populations. Even areas (such as New England in the United States) in which water availability is high and withdrawal rates are relatively low show areas of stress in regions of high population density (cities such as Boston). This map, originally produced by scientists at the University of New Hampshire, attempts to show those areas of the world where populations will tend to be at high, medium, and low risk of stress because of water availability. It is important to note that many of the world's prime agricultural regions, such as the Great Plains of the United States or the Argentine Pampas, show the potential for high risk of water stress in the immediate future. Why is this important? Because the greatest single use of water on the planet is for irrigation (nearly 70 percent of the world's water use), and it is the continued expansion of irrigation systems that allows the increase in agricultural production that feeds the Earth's more than 6 billion persons.

-144-

Map **113** Carbon Dioxide Emissions

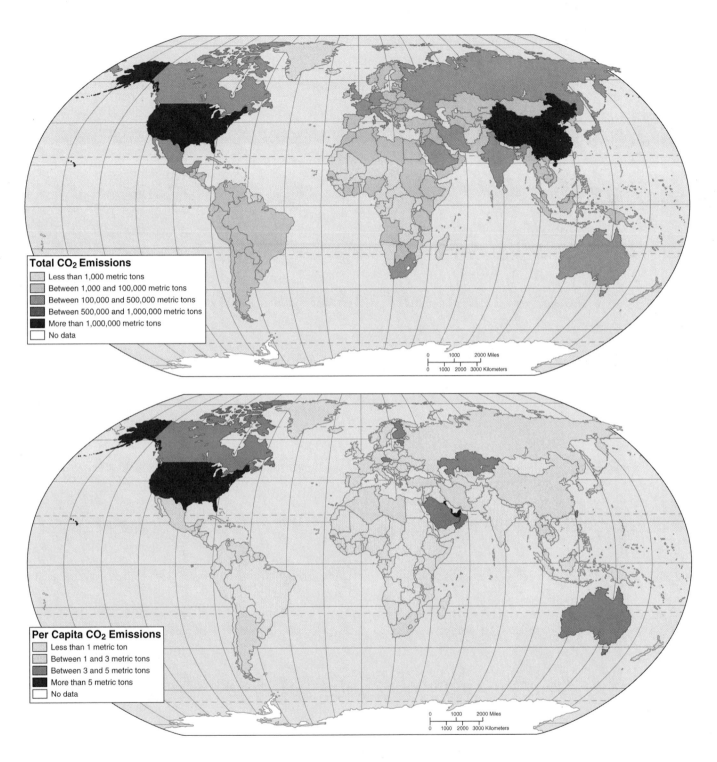

Total CO$_2$ Emissions
- Less than 1,000 metric tons
- Between 1,000 and 100,000 metric tons
- Between 100,000 and 500,000 metric tons
- Between 500,000 and 1,000,000 metric tons
- More than 1,000,000 metric tons
- No data

Per Capita CO$_2$ Emissions
- Less than 1 metric ton
- Between 1 and 3 metric tons
- Between 3 and 5 metric tons
- More than 5 metric tons
- No data

Carbon dioxide emissions are a major indicator of economic development, since they are generated largely by burning of fossil fuels for electrical power generation, for industrial processes, for domestic and commercial heating, and for the internal combustion engines of automobiles, trucks, buses, planes, and trains. Scientists have long known that carbon dioxide in the atmosphere increases the ability of the atmosphere to retain heat, a phenomenon known as the greenhouse effect. While the greenhouse effect is a natural process (and life on earth as we know it would not be possible without it), many scientists are concerned that an increase in carbon dioxide in the atmosphere is augmenting this process, creating a global warming trend and a potential worldwide change of climate patterns. These climatological changes threaten disaster for many regions and their peoples in both the developed and less developed areas of the world. You will note from the maps that China and the United States are the leading producers of carbon dioxide emissions—both emit carbon dioxide at levels nearly four times that of the Russia, the third-leading emitter. When examined on a per capita basis, note that the countries of the mid-latitudes generate extremely high levels of carbon dioxide.

Map 114 Potential Global Temperature Change

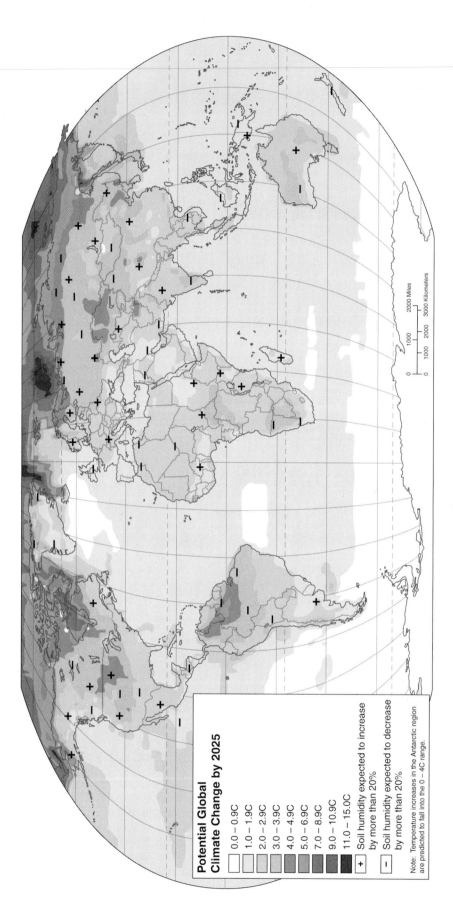

Potential Global Climate Change by 2025

- 0.0 – 0.9C
- 1.0 – 1.9C
- 2.0 – 2.9C
- 3.0 – 3.9C
- 4.0 – 4.9C
- 5.0 – 6.9C
- 7.0 – 8.9C
- 9.0 – 10.9C
- 11.0 – 15.0C

+ Soil humidity expected to increase by more than 20%

- Soil humidity expected to decrease by more than 20%

Note: Temperature increases in the Antarctic region are predicted to fall into the 0 – 4C range.

According to atmospheric scientists, one of the major problems of the twenty-first century will be "global warming," produced as the atmosphere's natural ability to trap and retain heat is enhanced by increased percentages of carbon dioxide, methane, chlorinated fluorocarbons or "CFCs," and other "greenhouse gases" in the earth's atmosphere. Computer models based on atmospheric percentages of carbon dioxide resulting from present use of fossil fuels show that warming is not just a possibility but a probability. Increased temperatures would cause precipitation patterns to alter significantly as well and would produce a number of other harmful effects, including a rise in the level of the world's oceans that could flood most coastal cities. International conferences on the topic of the enhanced greenhouse effect have resulted in several international agreements to reduce the emission of carbon dioxide or to maintain it at present levels. Unfortunately, the solution is not that simple since reduction of carbon dioxide emissions is, in the short run,

expensive—particularly as long as the world's energy systems continue to be based on fossil fuels. Chief among the countries that could be hit by serious international mandates to reduce emissions are those highest on the development scale who use the highest levels of fossil fuels and, therefore, produce the highest emissions, and those on the lowest end of the development scale whose efforts to industrialize could be severely impeded by the more expensive energy systems that would replace fossil fuels. In April 2007, the Intergovernmental Panel on Climate Change—an international body of diplomats and scientists—issued the direst warning yet about the virtual certainty of human-induced global warming and the impacts it would have on water supplies, species extinction, and sea levels. The report represented the best scientific conclusions possible but was criticized by many scientists as not going far enough. As severe as the language of the IPCC report was, it was toned down by the threat of refusal to sign by China and the United States.

Map 115   The Loss of Biodiversity: Globally Threatened Animal Species

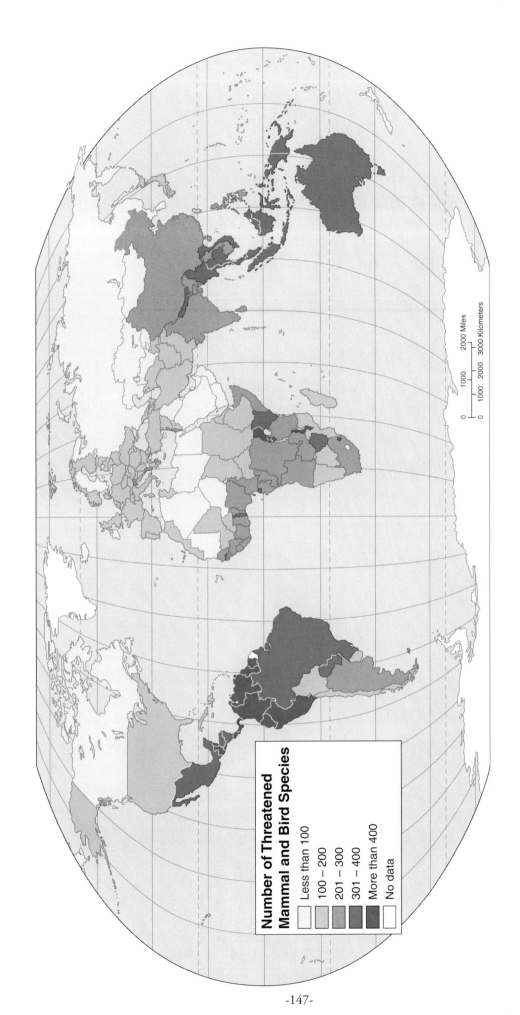

Number of Threatened Mammal and Bird Species

- Less than 100
- 100 – 200
- 201 – 300
- 301 – 400
- More than 400
- No data

0   1000   2000 Miles

0   1000   2000   3000 Kilometers

Threatened species are those in grave danger of going extinct. Their populations are becoming restricted in range, and the size of the populations required for sustained breeding is nearing a critical minimum. *Endangered species* are in immediate danger of becoming extinct. Their range is already so reduced that the animals may no longer be able to move freely within an ecozone, and their populations are at the level where the species may no longer be able to sustain breeding. Most species become threatened first and then endangered as their range and numbers continue to decrease. When people think of animal extinction, they think of large herbivorous species like the rhinoceros or fierce carnivores like lions, tigers, or grizzly bears. Certainly these animals make almost any list of endangered or threatened species. But there are literally hundreds of less conspicuous animals that are equally threatened. Extinction is normally nature's way of informing a species that it is inefficient. But conditions in the early twenty-first century are controlled more by human activities than by natural evolutionary processes. Species that are endangered or threatened fall into that category because, somehow, they are competing with us or with our domesticated livestock for space and food. And in that competition the animals are always going to lose.

Map 116   The Loss of Biodiversity: Globally Threatened Plant Species

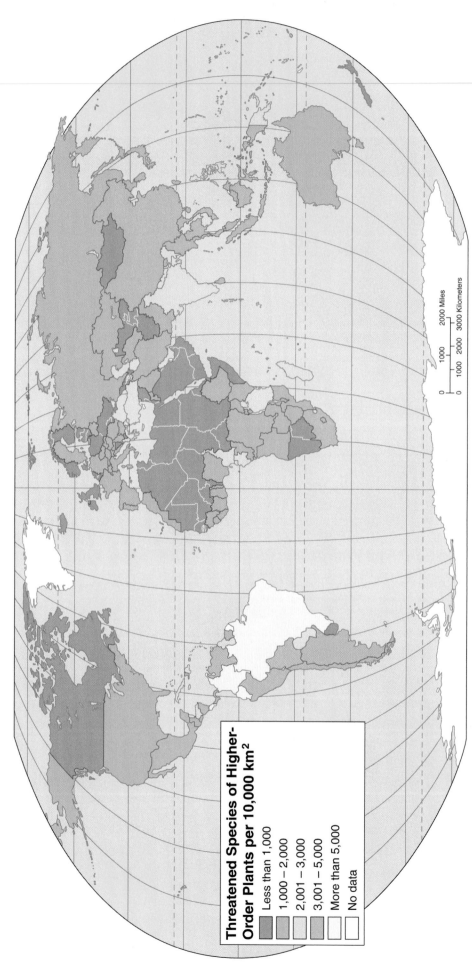

Threatened Species of Higher-Order Plants per 10,000 km²

- Less than 1,000
- 1,000 – 2,000
- 2,001 – 3,000
- 3,001 – 5,000
- More than 5,000
- No data

0   1000   2000 Miles
0   1000   2000   3000 Kilometers

While most people tend to be more concerned about the animals on threatened and endangered species lists, the fact is that many more plants are in jeopardy, and the loss of plant life is, in all ecological regions, a more critical occurrence than the loss of animal populations. Plants are the primary producers in the ecosystem; that is, plants produce the food upon which all other species in the food web, including human beings, depend for sustenance. It is plants from which many of our critical medicines come, and it is plants that maintain the delicate balance between soil and water in most of the world's regions. When environmental scientists speak of a loss of biodiversity, what they are most often describing is a loss of the richness and complexity of plant life that lends stability to ecosystems. Systems with more plant life tend to be more stable than those with less. For these and other reasons, the scientific concern over extinction is greater when applied to plants than to animals. It is difficult for people to become as emotional over a teak tree as they would over an elephant. But as great a tragedy as the loss of the elephant would be, the loss of the teak would be greater.

Map 117   Global Hotspots of Biodiversity

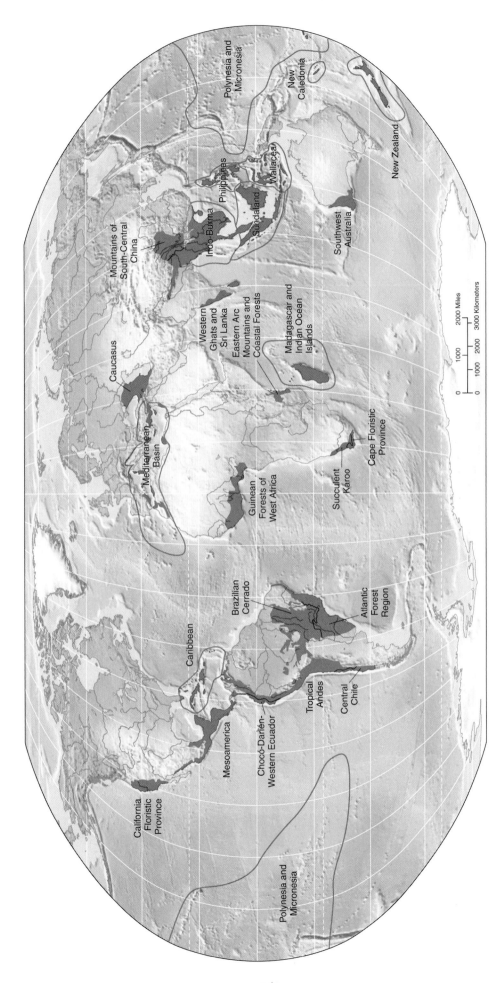

Where we have normally thought of tropical forest basins such as Amazonia as the world's most biologically diverse ecosystems, recent research has discovered the surprising fact that a number of hotspots of biological diversity exist outside the major tropical forest regions. These hotspot regions contain slightly less than 2 percent of the world's total land area but may contain up to 60 percent of the total world's terrestrial species of plants and animals. Geographically, the hotspot areas are characterized by vertical zonation (that is, they tend to be hilly to mountainous regions), long known to be a factor in biological complexity. They are also in coastal locations or near large bodies of water, locations that stimulate climatic variability and, hence, biological complexity. Although some of the hotspots are sparsely populated, others, such as "Sundaland," are among the world's most densely populated areas. Protection of the rich biodiversity of these hotspots is, most biologists feel, of crucial importance to the preservation of the world's biological heritage.

Map 118   Degree of Human Disturbance

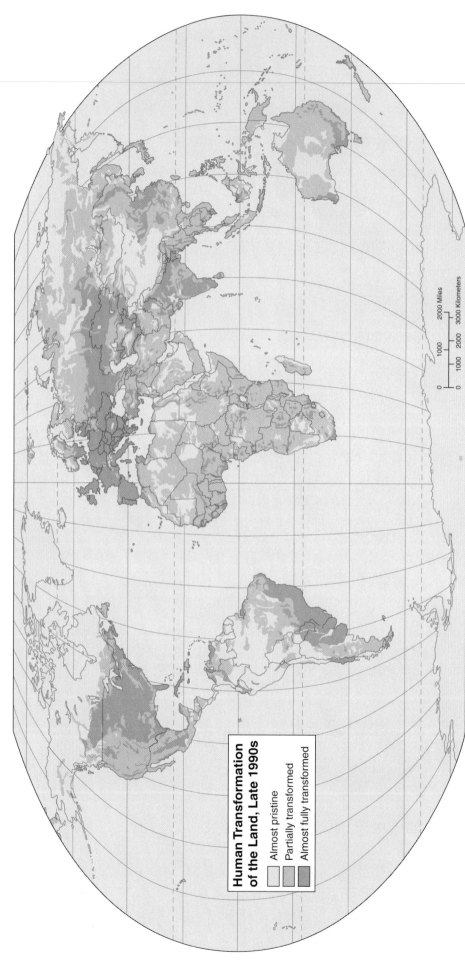

Human Transformation of the Land, Late 1990s

- Almost pristine
- Partially transformed
- Almost fully transformed

2000 Miles

1000   2000   3000 Kilometers

0   1000   2000

The data on human disturbance have been gathered from a wide variety of sources, some of them conflicting and not all of them reliable. Nevertheless, at a global scale this map fairly depicts the state of the world in terms of the degree to which humans have modified its surface. The almost pristine areas, covered with natural vegetation, generally have population densities under 10 persons per square mile. These areas are, for the most part, in the most inhospitable parts of the world: too high, too dry, too cold for permanent human habitation in large numbers. The partially transformed areas are normally agricultural areas, either subsistence (such as shifting cultivation) or extensive (such as livestock grazing). They often contain areas of second-

ary vegetation, regrown after removal of original vegetation by humans. They are also often marked by a density of livestock in excess of carrying capacity, leading to overgrazing, which further alters the condition of the vegetation. The almost fully transformed areas are those of permanent and intensive agriculture and urban settlement. The primary vegetation of these regions has been removed, with no evidence of regrowth or with current vegetation that is quite different from natural (potential) vegetation. Soils are in a state of depletion and degradation, and, in drier lands, desertification is a factor of human occupation. The disturbed areas match closely those areas of the world with the densest human populations.

Map 119 The Green and Not-So-Green World

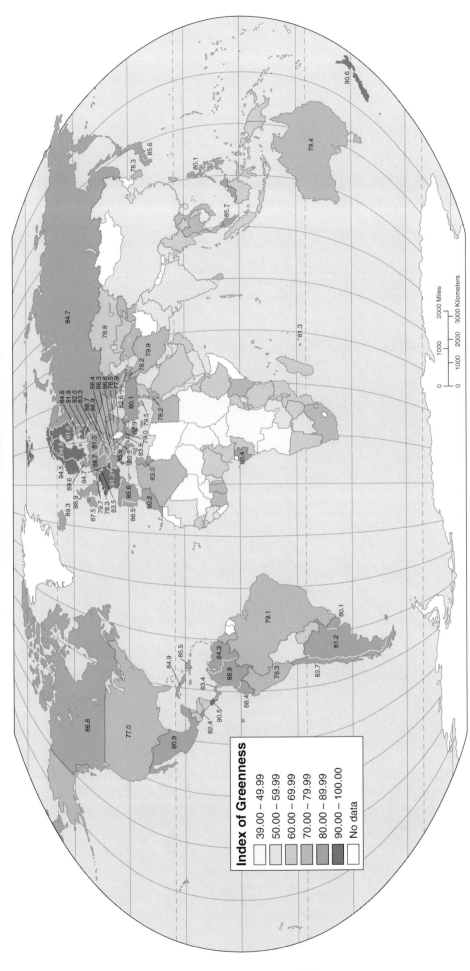

Index of Greenness

- 39.00 – 49.99
- 50.00 – 59.99
- 60.00 – 69.99
- 70.00 – 79.99
- 80.00 – 89.99
- 90.00 – 100.00
- No data

The index of "greenness" ranks countries according to their greenhouse gas emissions, the quality of their water resources, their protection of plant and animal habitats, and other factors. As might be expected, the "greenest" countries also tend to be relatively affluent and in cooler climates. There are obvious exceptions to this generalization (Mexico, for example) but, in general, we find countries like Sweden (no. 1), Switzerland, Norway, Finland, France, New Zealand, and Denmark ranking high on the index while poorer countries in warmer climates (much of South and East Asia, much of Sub-Saharan Africa) generally tend to rank lower on the index. There is a pretty clear correlation between affluence and "greenness"—that is, wealthy countries not only recognize the importance of "being green" but have the ability to pay for it. Still, some of the world's more affluent countries, like the United States and Australia, rank rather lower on the scale. The relatively low ranking (not quite in the top third of the countries in the index) attained

by the United States—despite its excellent record on controlling water and air pollution—results from its persistent reliance on fossil fuels and a correspondingly high release of greenhouse gas emissions. Sweden, whose per capita income is similar to that of the United States, uses renewable resources (particularly hydroelectric power) to keep its emissions low and its ranking on the scale of "greenness" high. Similarly, France (no. 7) maintains a high rank because of a reliance on nuclear power, which curbs greenhouse gas emissions. In Sub-Saharan Africa, the level of carbon dioxide emissions is low but water quality and sanitation are poor. Rapid industrialization in countries like Brazil, India, and China have impacted emissions levels, as well as water and sanitation levels. These countries appear rather lower on the index (China, for example, ranks 134 among 186 countries). The rankings shown on the map are based on 2008 data; it will be interesting to see how the patterns have changed in 20 years.

-151-

Unit VII

Regions of the World

Map 120 North America: Physical Features
Map 121 North America: Political Divisions
Map 122 North American Land Use
Map 123 South America: Physical Features
Map 124 South America: Political Divisions
Map 125 South American Land Use
Map 126 Europe: Physical Features
Map 127 Europe: Political Divisions
Map 128 European Land Use
Map 129 Asia: Physical Features
Map 130 Asia: Political Divisions
Map 131 Asian Land Use
Map 132 Africa: Physical Features
Map 133 Africa: Political Divisions
Map 134 African Land Use
Map 135 Australia and Oceania: Physical Features
Map 136 Australia and Oceania: Political Divisions
Map 137 Australia and Oceania: Land Use
Map 138 The World Ocean
Map 139 The Arctic
Map 140 Antarctica

Map 120 North America: Physical Features

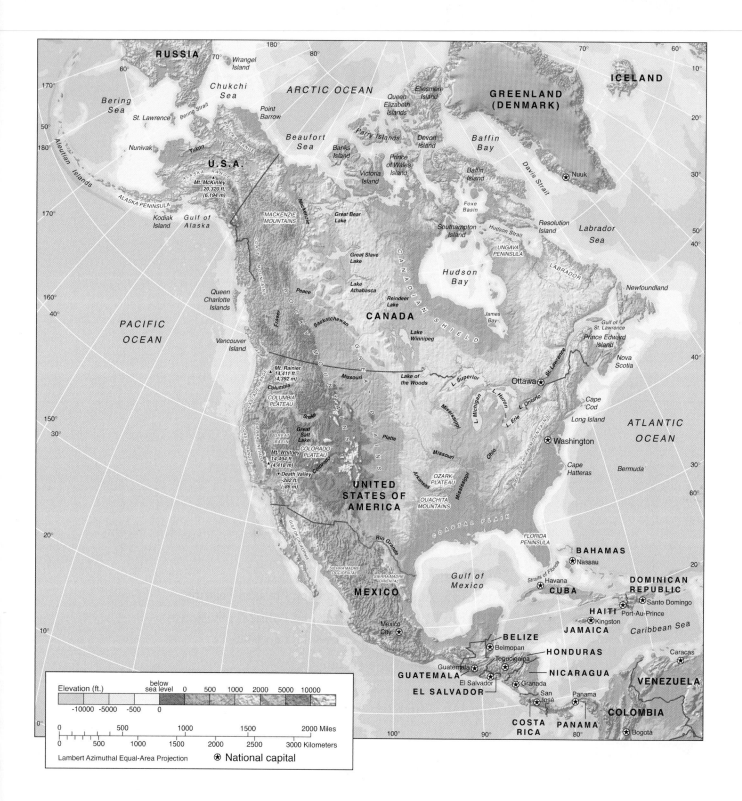

Elevation (ft.)

below sea level	0	500	1000	2000	5000	10000

-10000   -5000   -500   0

0	500	1000	1500	2000 Miles

0	500	1000	1500	2000	2500	3000 Kilometers

Lambert Azimuthal Equal-Area Projection   ⊛ National capital

Map 121 North America: Political Divisions

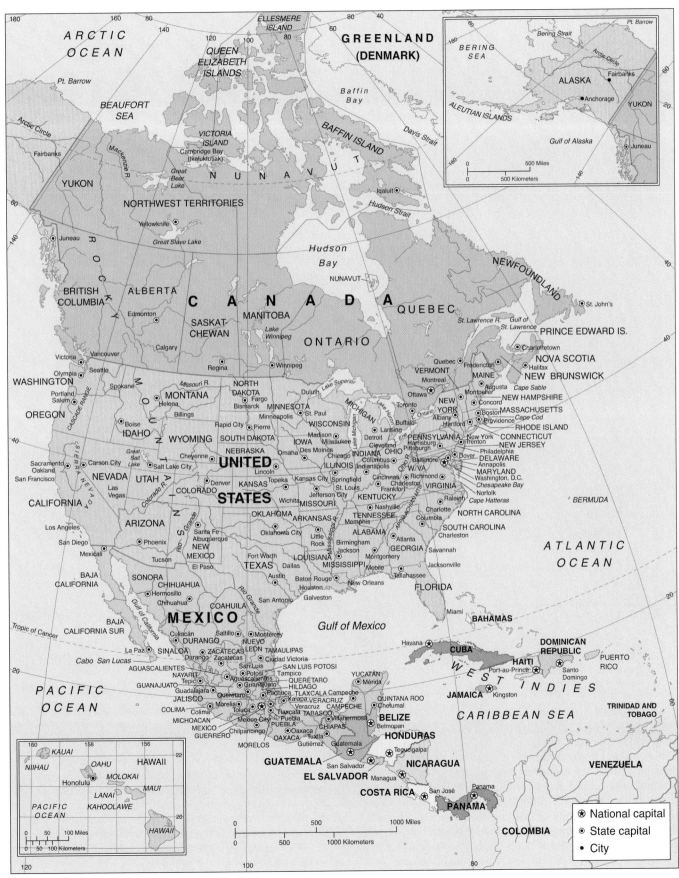

Map 122 North American Land Use

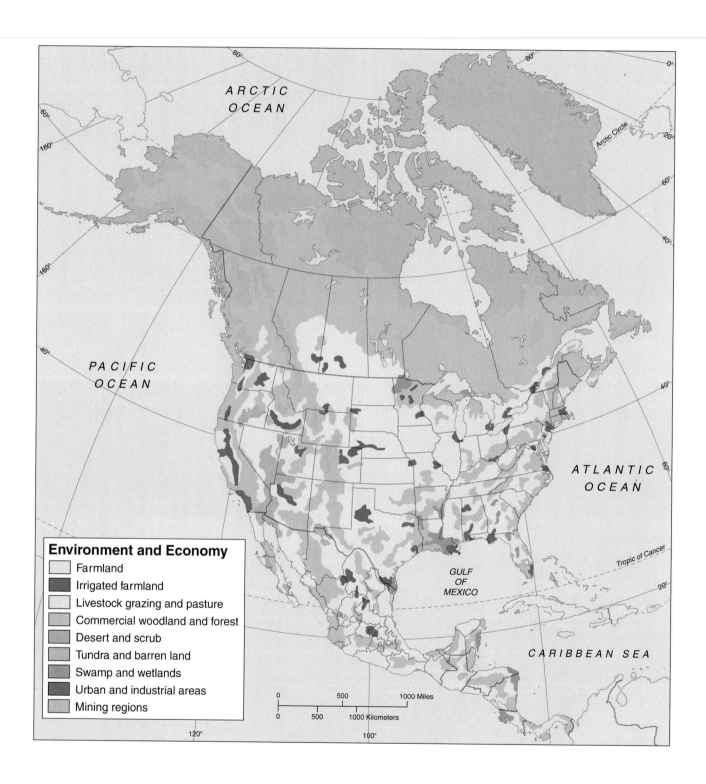

Environment and Economy
- Farmland
- Irrigated farmland
- Livestock grazing and pasture
- Commercial woodland and forest
- Desert and scrub
- Tundra and barren land
- Swamp and wetlands
- Urban and industrial areas
- Mining regions

The use of land in North America represents a balance between agriculture, resource extraction, and manufacturing that is unmatched. The United States, as the world's leading industrial power, is also the world's leader in commercial agricultural production. Canada, despite its small population, is a ranking producer of both agricultural and industrial products, and Mexico has begun to emerge from its developing nation status to become an important industrial and agricultural nation as well.

The countries of Middle America and the Caribbean are just beginning the transition from agriculture to modern industrial economies. Part of the basis for the high levels of economic productivity in North America is environmental: a superb blend of soil, climate, and raw materials. But just as important is the cultural and social mix of the plural societies of North America, a mix that historically aided the growth of the economic diversity necessary for developed economies.

Map 123

South America: Physical Features

NICARAGUA

Caribbean Sea

Lake Maracaibo

Port-of-Spain

TRINIDAD AND TOBAGO

ATLANTIC OCEAN

COSTA RICA

PANAMA

Caracas

Orinoco

VENEZUELA

Georgetown

Paramaribo

GUYANA

SURINAME

FRENCH GUIANA (FR.)

Gulf of Panama

Bogotá

Angel Falls

GUIANA HIGHLANDS

COLOMBIA

Marajó Island

Equator

Quito

ECUADOR

Putumayo

Japurá

Negro

Amazon

Amazon

Equator

Gulf of Guayaquil

PERU

Marañón

AMAZON BASIN

Amazon

Punta Negra

Ucayali

Purus

Madeira

Tapajós

Xingu

BRAZIL

PACIFIC OCEAN

Nevado Huascarán 22,205 ft. (6,768 m)

Araguaia

Tocantins

São Francisco

Lima

ANDES MOUNTAINS

Beni

MATO GROSSO PLATEAU

Lake Titicaca

BOLIVIA

La Paz

Sucre

PANTANAL

Brasília

BRAZILIAN HIGHLANDS

ATACAMA DESERT

GRAN CHACO

Paranaíba

PARAGUAY

Tropic of Capricorn

Mt. Ojos del Salado 22,572 ft. (6,880 m)

Asunción

Iguazú Falls

Cape Frio

Tropic of Capricorn

Paraná

Juan Fernández Islands

Patos Lagoon

ARGENTINA

Mt. Aconcagua 22,834 ft. (6,960 m)

Uruguay

Santiago

PAMPAS

URUGUAY

Montevideo

Buenos Aires

Rio de la Plata

CHILE

ATLANTIC OCEAN

Chiloé Island

San Matías Gulf

Chonos Archipelago

PATAGONIA

Gulf of San Jorge

Strait of Magellan

Falkland Islands

Tierra del Fuego

Cape Horn

Elevation (ft.)

below sea level   0   500   1000   2000   5000   10000

-10000 -5000 -500   0

0   500   1000   1500   2000 Miles

0   500   1000   1500   2000   2500   3000 Kilometers

Lambert Azimuthal Equal-Area Projection   ⊗ National capital

Map 124   South America: Political Divisions

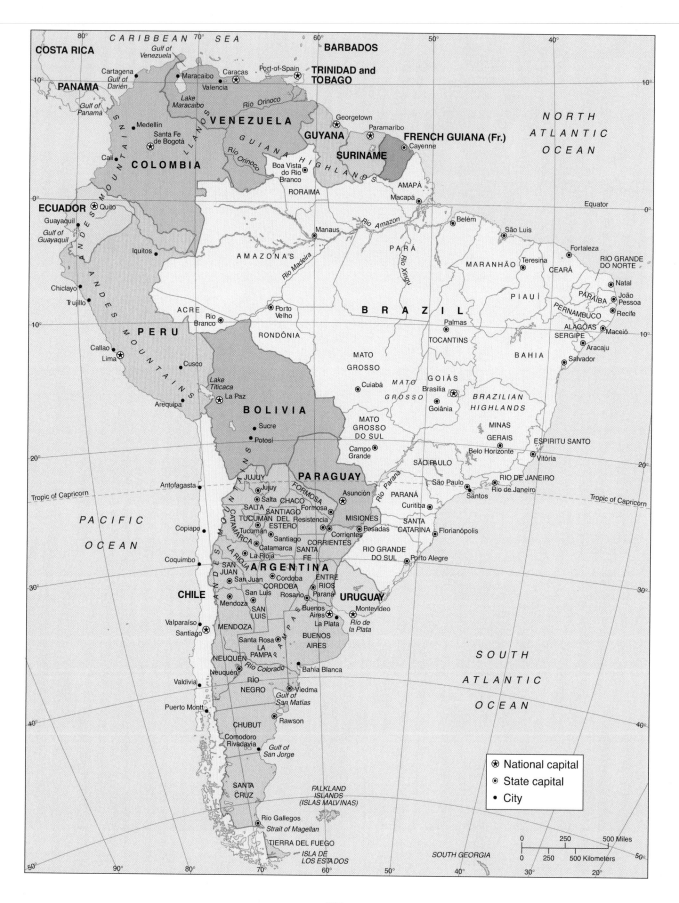

Map 125   South American Land Use

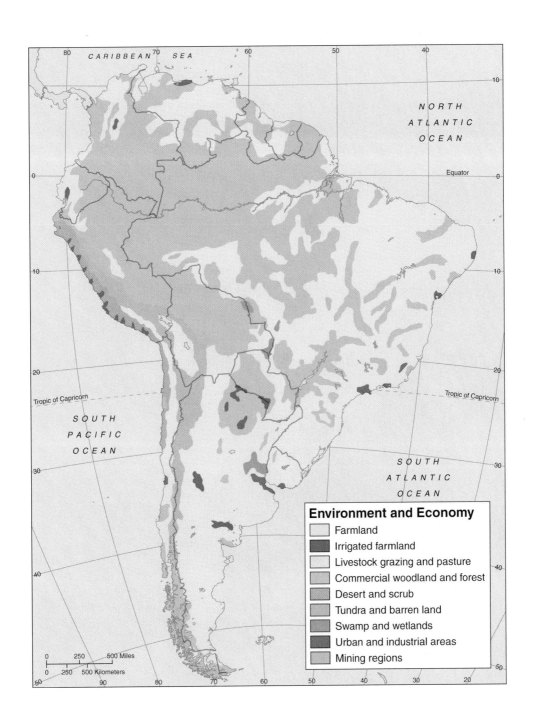

Environment and Economy
- Farmland
- Irrigated farmland
- Livestock grazing and pasture
- Commercial woodland and forest
- Desert and scrub
- Tundra and barren land
- Swamp and wetlands
- Urban and industrial areas
- Mining regions

South America is a region just beginning to emerge from a colonial-dependency economy in which raw materials flowed from the continent to more highly developed economic regions. With the exception of Brazil, Argentina, Chile, and Uruguay, most of the continent's countries still operate under the traditional mode of exporting raw materials in exchange for capital that tends to accumulate in the pockets of a small percentage of the population. The land use patterns of the continent are, therefore, still dominated by resource extrac-tion and agriculture. A problem posed by these patterns is that little of the continent's land area is actually suitable for either commercial forestry or commercial crop agriculture without extremely high environmental costs. Much of the agriculture, then, is based on high value tropical crops that can be grown in small areas profitably, or on extensive livestock grazing. Even within the forested areas of the Amazon Basin where forest clearance is taking place at unprecedented rates, much of the land use that replaces forest is grazing.

Map 126   Europe: Physical Features

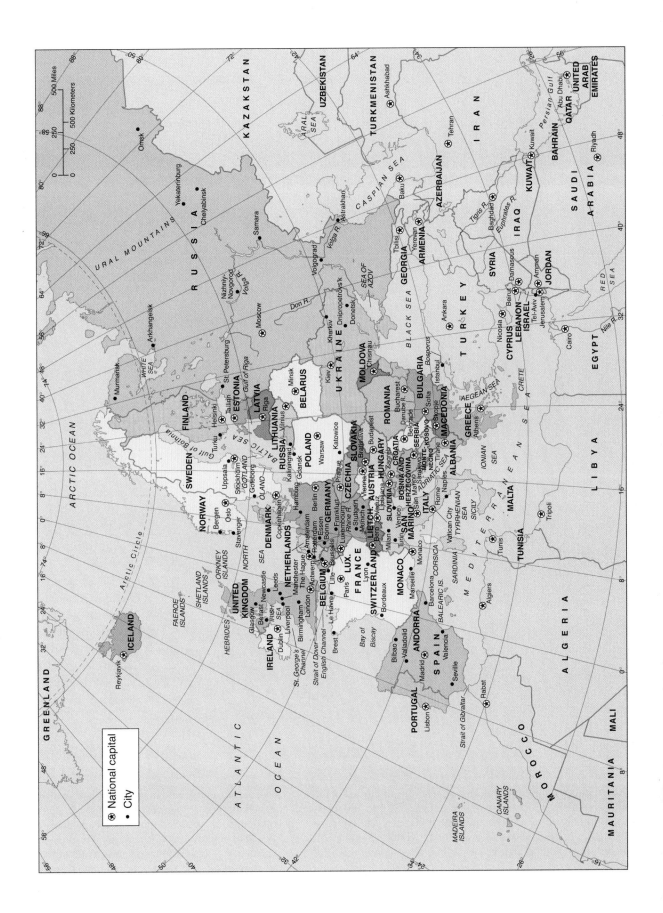

Map 127 Europe: Political Divisions

Map **128**   European Land Use

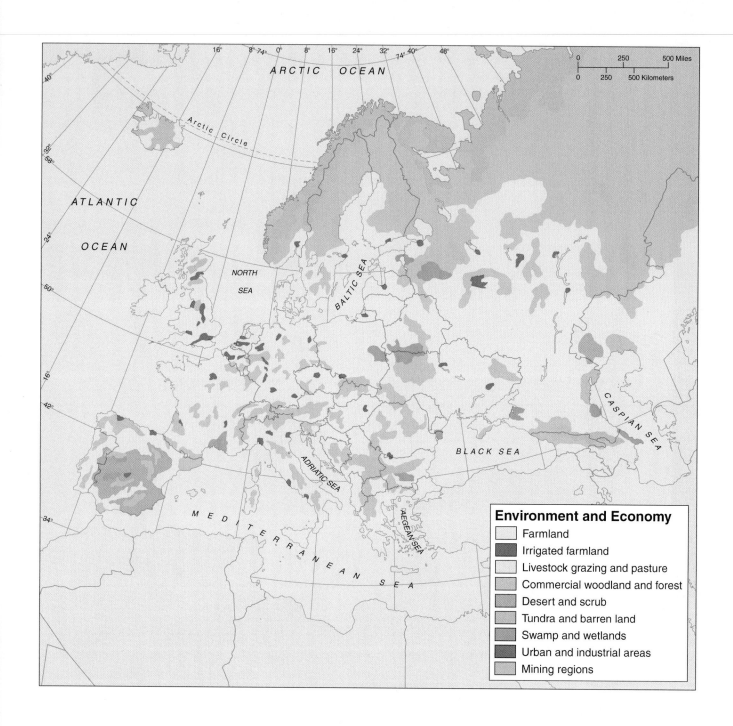

Environment and Economy

- Farmland
- Irrigated farmland
- Livestock grazing and pasture
- Commercial woodland and forest
- Desert and scrub
- Tundra and barren land
- Swamp and wetlands
- Urban and industrial areas
- Mining regions

More than any other continent, Europe bears the imprint of human activity—mining, forestry, agriculture, industry, and urbanization. Virtually all of western and central Europe's natural forest vegetation is gone, lost to clearing for agriculture beginning in prehistory, to lumbering that began in earnest during the Middle Ages, or, more recently, to disease and destruction brought about by acid precipitation. Only in the far north and the east do some natural stands remain. The region is the world's most heavily industrialized, and the industrial areas on the map represent only the largest and most significant. Not shown are the industries that are found in virtually every small town and village and smaller city throughout the industrial countries for Europe. Europe also possesses abundant raw materials and a very productive agricultural base. The mineral resources have long been in a state of active exploitation and the mining regions shown on the map are, for the most part, old regions in upland areas that are somewhat less significant now than they may have been in the past. Agriculturally, the northern European plain is one of the world's great agricultural regions but most of Europe contains decent land for agriculture.

Map 129   Asia: Physical Features

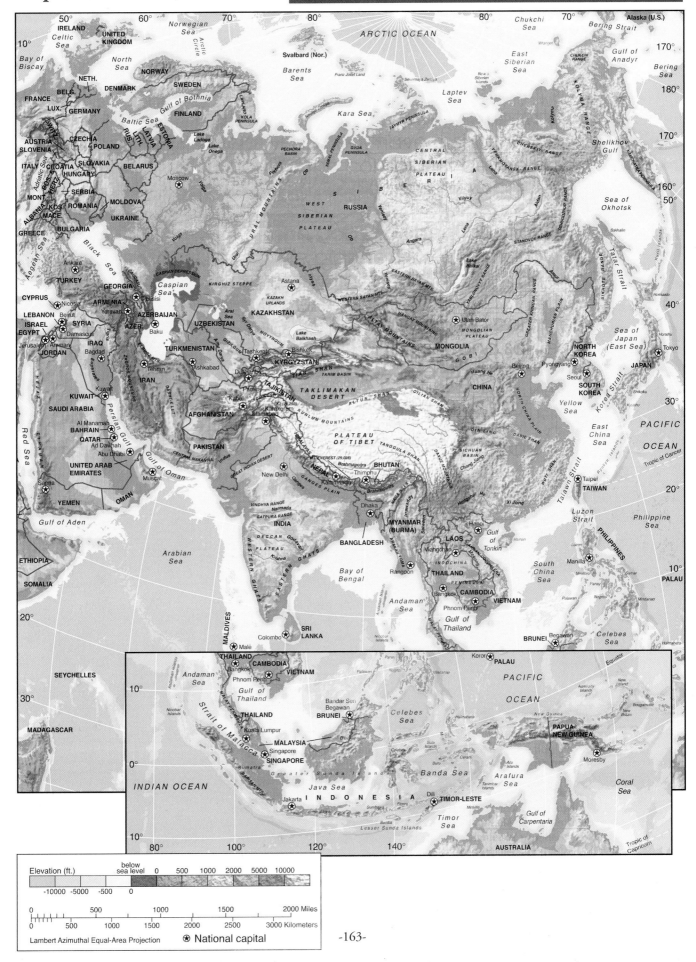

Elevation (ft.)

below sea level   0   500   1000   2000   5000   10000

-10000   -5000   -500   0

0   500   1000   1500   2000 Miles

0   500   1000   1500   2000   2500   3000 Kilometers

Lambert Azimuthal Equal-Area Projection   ⊛ National capital

Map 130   Asia: Political Divisions

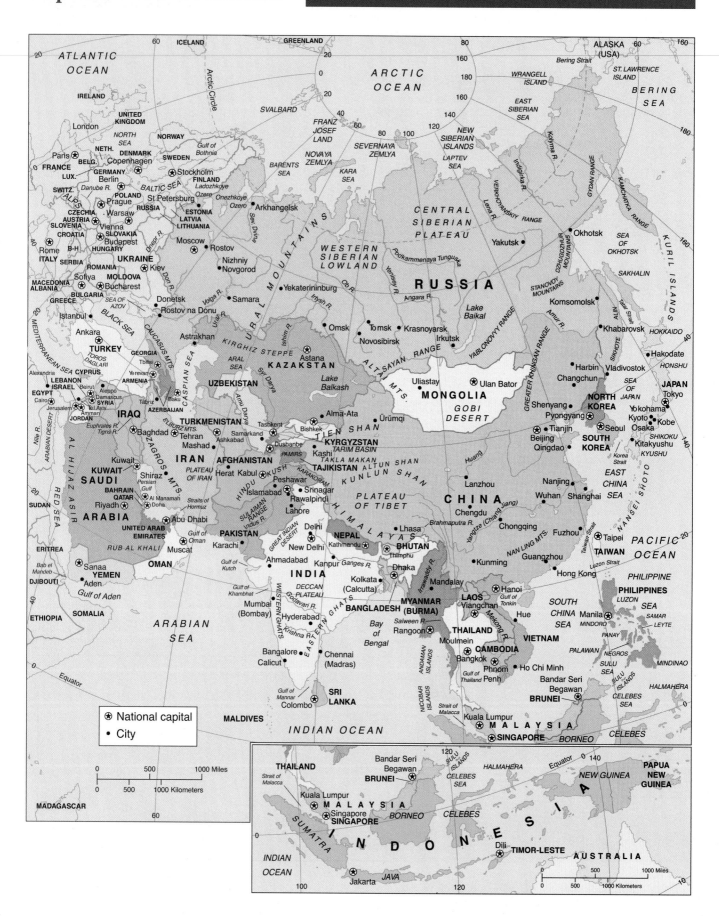

Map **131**   Asian Land Use

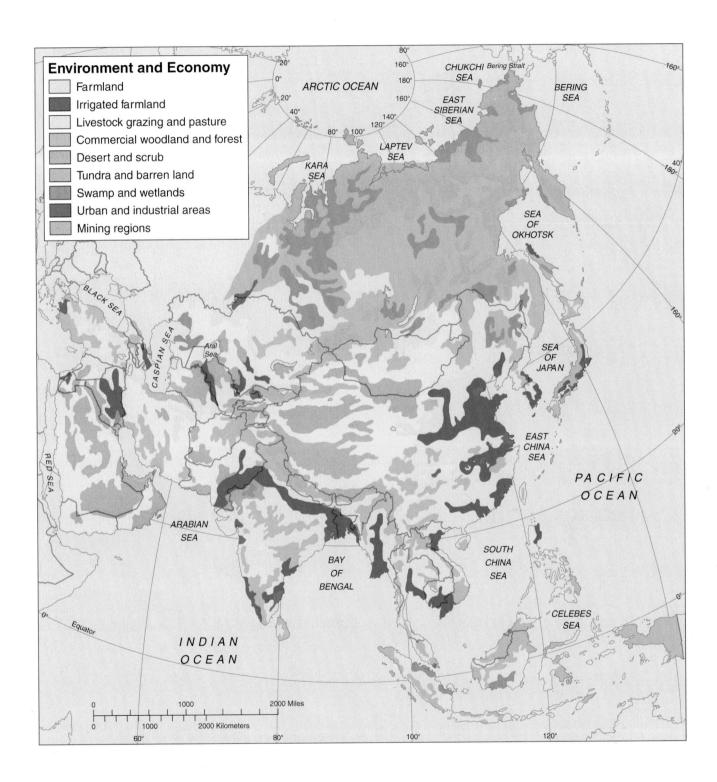

Environment and Economy
- Farmland
- Irrigated farmland
- Livestock grazing and pasture
- Commercial woodland and forest
- Desert and scrub
- Tundra and barren land
- Swamp and wetlands
- Urban and industrial areas
- Mining regions

Asia is a land of extremes of land use with some of the world's most heavily industrialized regions, barren and empty areas, and productive and densely populated farm regions. Asia is a region of rapid industrial growth. Yet Asia remains an agricultural region with three out of every four workers engaged in agriculture. Asian commercial agriculture and intensive subsistence agriculture is characterized by irrigation. Some of Asia's irrigated lands are desert requiring additional water. But most of the Asian irrigated regions have sufficient precipitation for crop agriculture, and irrigation is a way of coping with seasonal drought—the wet-and-dry cycle of the monsoon—often gaining more than one crop per year on irrigated farms. Agricultural yields per unit area in many areas of Asia are among the world's highest. Because the Asian population is so large and the demands for agricultural land so great, Asia is undergoing rapid deforestation, and some areas of the continent have only small remnants of a once-abundant forest reserve.

Map 132   Africa: Physical Features

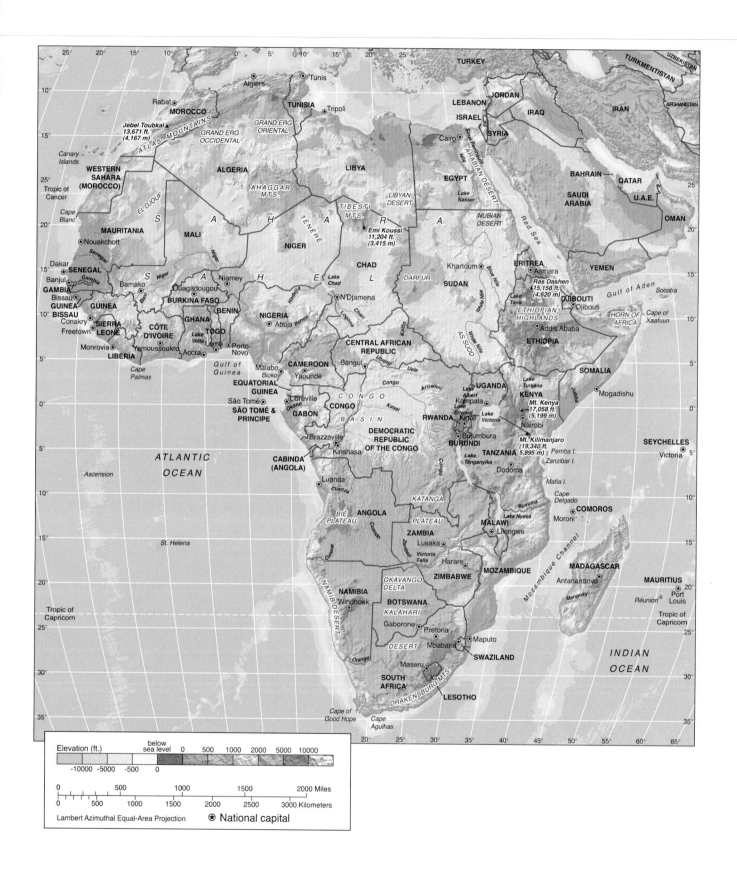

Map 133 Africa: Political Divisions

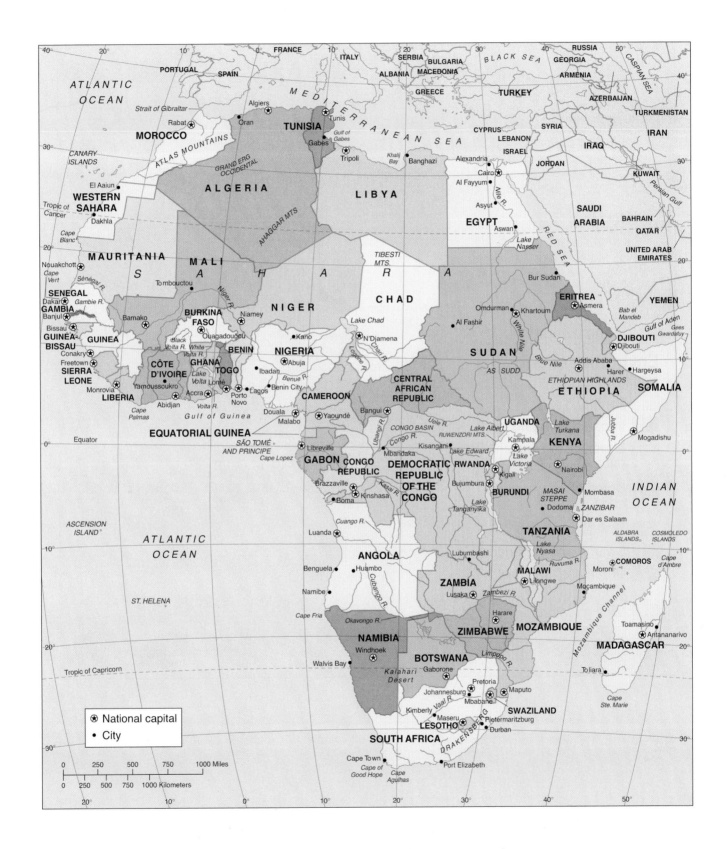

Map 134   African Land Use

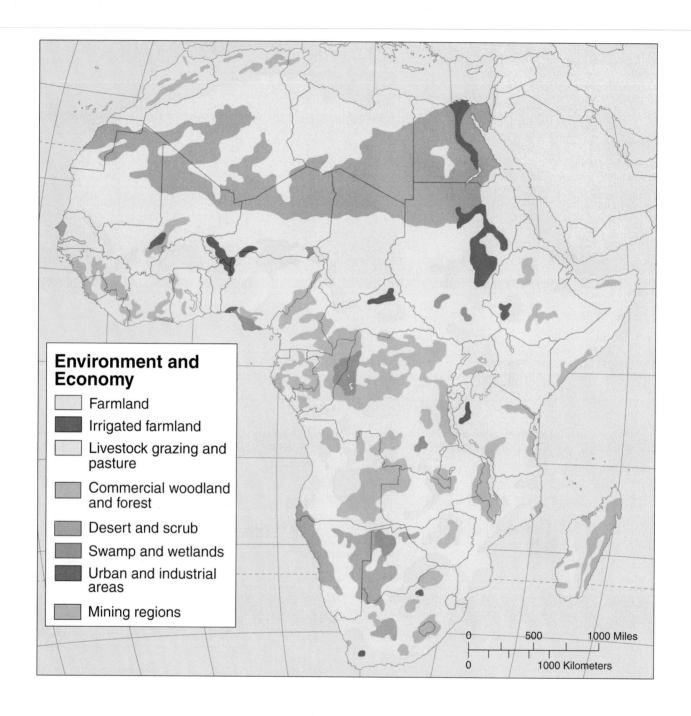

Environment and Economy

- ☐ Farmland
- ■ Irrigated farmland
- ☐ Livestock grazing and pasture
- ▨ Commercial woodland and forest
- ▨ Desert and scrub
- ▨ Swamp and wetlands
- ■ Urban and industrial areas
- ▨ Mining regions

0   500   1000 Miles

0   1000 Kilometers

Africa's economic landscape is dominated by subsistence, or marginally commercial agricultural activities and raw material extraction, engaging three-fourths of Africa's workers. Much of this grazing land is very poor desert scrub and bunch grass that is easily impacted by cattle, sheep, and goats. Growing human and livestock populations place enormous stress on this fragile support capacity and the result is desertification: the conversion of even the most minimal of grazing environments or land suitable for crop farming to virtual desert conditions. Although the continent has approximately 20 percent of the world's total land area, the proportion of Africa's arable land is small. The agricultural environment is also uncertain; unpredictable precipitation and poor soils hamper crop agriculture.

Map 135 Australia and Oceania: Physical Features

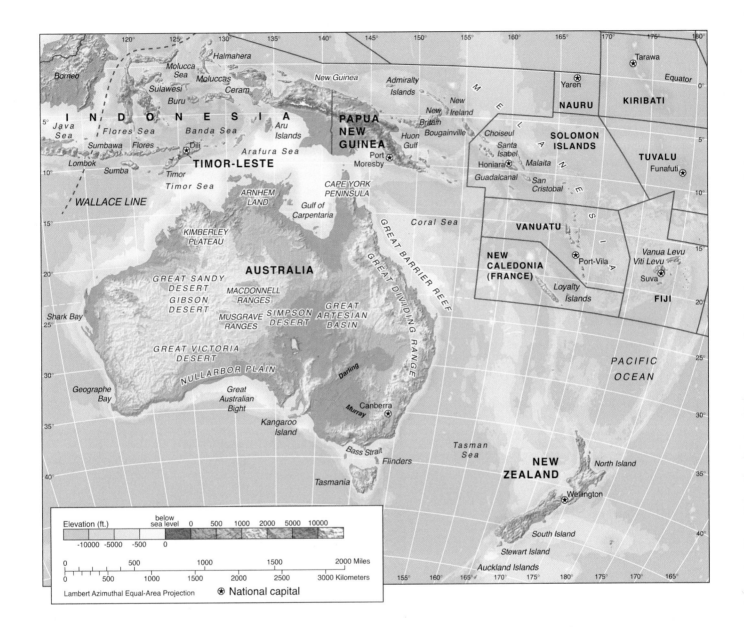

Map 135 Australia and Oceania: Physical Features

Elevation (ft.)

below sea level | 0 | 500 | 1000 | 2000 | 5000 | 10000

-10000 -5000 -500 0

0 ... 500 ... 1000 ... 1500 ... 2000 Miles

0 ... 500 ... 1000 ... 1500 ... 2000 ... 2500 ... 3000 Kilometers

Lambert Azimuthal Equal-Area Projection

⊛ National capital

Map 136 Australia and Oceania: Political Divisions

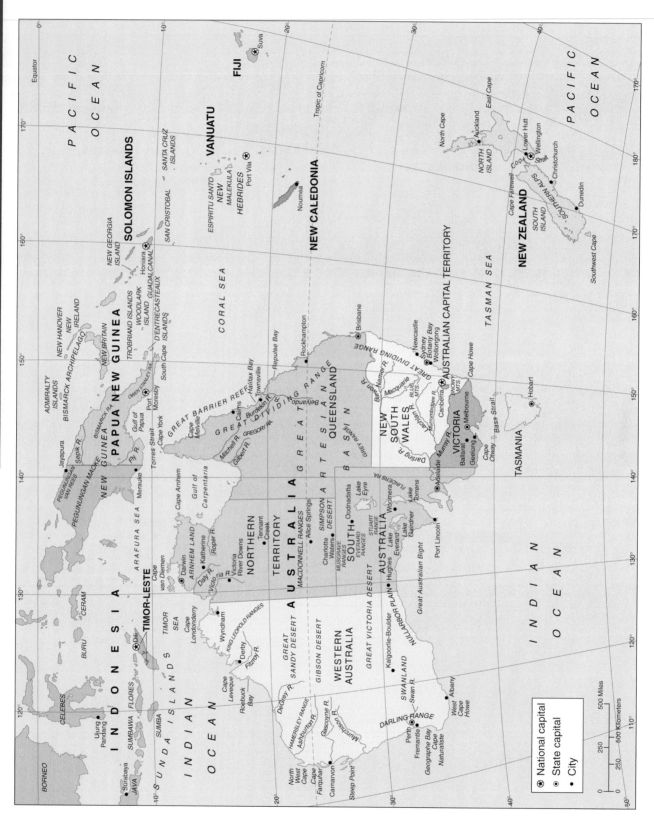

Map 137 Australia and Oceania: Land Use

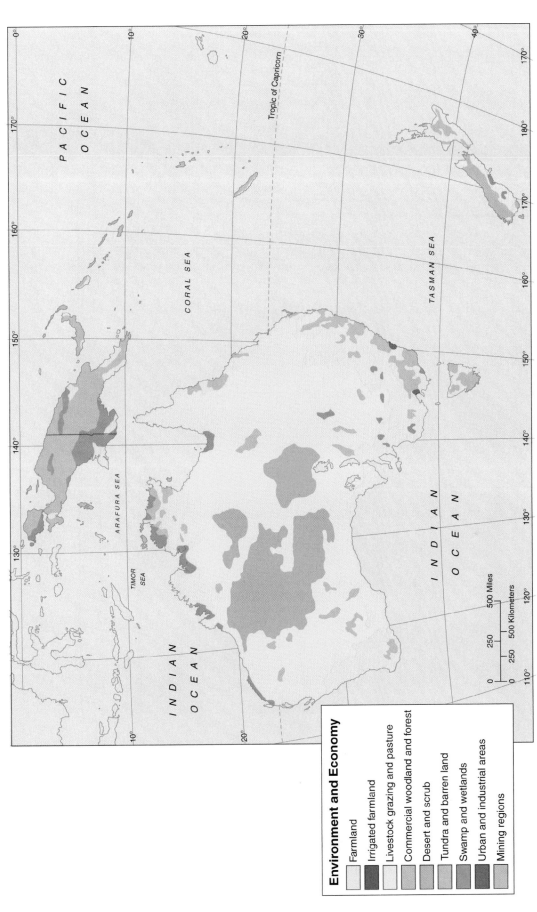

Environment and Economy

- Farmland
- Irrigated farmland
- Livestock grazing and pasture
- Commercial woodland and forest
- Desert and scrub
- Tundra and barren land
- Swamp and wetlands
- Urban and industrial areas
- Mining regions

Australasia is dominated by the world's smallest and most uniform continent. Flat, dry, and mostly hot, Australia has the simplest of land use patterns: where rainfall exists so does agricultural activity. Two agricultural patterns dominate the map: livestock grazing, primarily sheep, and wheat farming, although some sugar cane production exists in the north and some cotton is grown elsewhere. Only about 6 percent of the continent consists of arable land, so the areas of wheat farming, dominant as they may be in the context of Australian agriculture, are small.

Australia also supports a healthy mineral resource economy, with iron and copper and precious metals making up the bulk of the extraction. Elsewhere in the region, tropical forests dominate Papua New Guinea, with some subsistence agriculture and livestock. New Zealand's temperate climate with abundant precipitation supports a productive livestock industry and little else besides tourism—which is an important economic element throughout the remainder of the region as well.

-171-

Map 138 The World Ocean

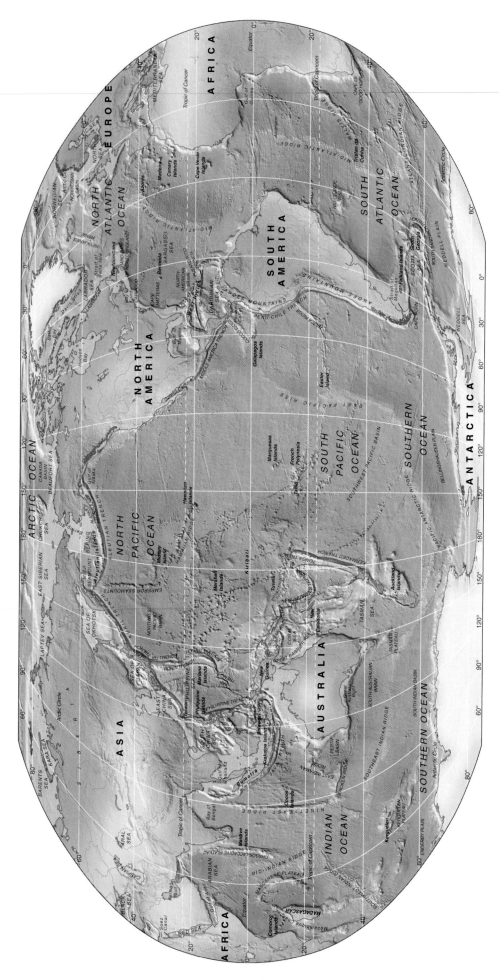

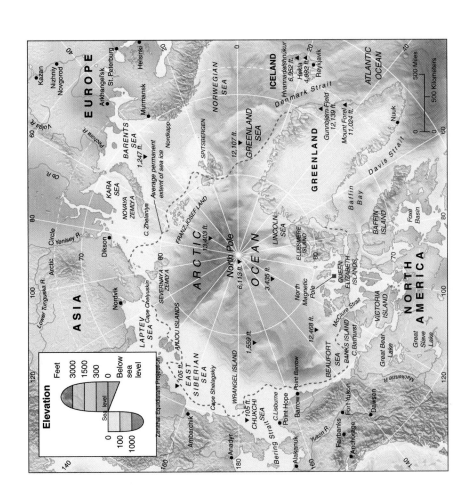

Map 140 Antarctica

Elevation

Feet
3000
1500
300
0
Below sea level

Sea level
0
100
1000

Zenithal Equidistant Projection

ATLANTIC OCEAN

NORWEGIAN CLAIM

INDIAN OCEAN

SOUTH GEORGIA
▼ 8,426 ft.

S. ORKNEY IS.
FALKLAND IS.
S. SHETLAND IS.
SCOTIA SEA
TIERRA DEL FUEGO
SOUTH AMERICA
Drake Passage

C. Norvegia
▼ 840 ft.
Average permanent extent of sea ice

▼ 6,972 ft.

Dronning Maud Land

B R I T I S H   C L A I M

CHILEAN CLAIM

Graham Land
Larsen Ice Shelf
▼ 4,380 ft.
WEDDELL SEA
ARGENTINE CLAIM
BERKNER I.
877 ft.

Coats Land
Robertson Land
Mac Robertson Land
Enderby Land
C. Darnley
Amery Ice Shelf

ALEXANDER I.
Antarctic Peninsula
Ronne Ice Shelf
PENSACOLA MTNS.
South Pole
PR. CHARLES MTNS.
AMERICAN HIGHLAND
AUSTRALIAN CLAIM
Queen Mary Land
70
Shackleton Ice Shelf
▼ 6,089 ft.

5,010 ft. ▼
PALMER ARCHIPELAGO
CHARCOT I.
BELLINGHAUSEN SEA
Ellsworth Land
GREATER ANTARCTICA
80
Knox Coast

5,240 ft. ▼
PACIFIC OCEAN
THURSTON I.
AMUNDSEN SEA
Walgreen Coast
SIPLE I.
Mt. Vinson Massif 16,864 ft.
Mt. Sidley 13,717 ft.
Marie Byrd Land
Mt. Seelig 9,915 ft.
LESSER ANTARCTICA
SENTINEL MTNS.
TRANSANTARCTIC MTNS.
Wilkes Land
C. Poinsett
Antarctic Circle
INDIAN OCEAN
100

C. Colbeck
ROOSEVELT I.
Ross Ice Shelf
ROSS SEA
Mt. Kirkpatrick 14,856 ft.
Mt. Markham 14,275 ft.
QUEEN MAUD MTNS.
Victoria Land
George V
Oates Land
Terre Adélie
120

STURGE I.
BALLENY IS.
C. Adare
677 ft. ▼
South Magnetic Pole
AUSTRALIAN CLAIM
FRENCH CLAIM

NEW ZEALAND CLAIM

180

160

140

Unit VIII

Country and Dependency Profiles

Country and Dependency Profiles

Afghanistan

Afghanestan

Official Name: Islamic Republic of Afghanistan
Capital: Kabul
Area: 250,001 sq mi (647,500 sq km)
Population: 33,609,937
Major Language(s): Dari, Pashto
Major Religion(s): Sunni Islam
Currency: afghani

Albania

Shqiperia

Official Name: Republic of Albania
Capital: Tirana
Area: 11,100 sq mi (28,748 sq km)
Population: 3,639,453
Major Language(s): Albanian
Major Religion(s): Sunni Islam
Currency: lek

Algeria

Al Jaza'ir

Official Name: People's Democratic Republic of Algeria
Capital: Algiers
Area: 919,595 sq mi (2,381,740 sq km)
Population: 34,178,188
Major Language(s): Arabic, French, Berber dialects
Major Religion(s): Sunni Islam
Currency: Algerian dinar

American Samoa

(territory of the United States)

Official Name: Territory of American Samoa
Capital: Pago Pago
Area: 77 sq mi (199 sq km)
Population: 65,628
Major Language(s): Samoan
Major Religion(s): Protestant Christianity
Currency: US dollar

Andorra

Official Name: Principality of Andorra
Capital: Andorra la Vella
Area: 181 sq mi (468 sq km)
Population: 83,888
Major Language(s): Catalan, Spanish, French
Major Religion(s): Roman Catholic Christianity
Currency: Euro

Angola

Official Name: Republic of Angola
Capital: Luanda
Area: 481,354 sq mi (1,246,700 sq km)
Population: 12,799,293
Major Language(s): Portuguese, Bantu languages
Major Religion(s): Indigenous beliefs, Christianity
Currency: kwanza

Anguilla

(overseas territory of the United Kingdom)

Official Name: Anguilla
Capital: Valley, The
Area: 39 sq mi (102 sq km)
Population: 14,436
Major Language(s): English
Major Religion(s): Protestant Christianity
Currency: East Caribbean dollar

Antigua and Barbuda

Official Name: Antigua and Barbuda
Capital: Saint John's
Area: 171 sq mi (443 sq km)
Population: 85,632
Major Language(s): English
Major Religion(s): Protestant Christianity
Currency: East Caribbean dollar

Argentina

Official Name: Argentine Republic
Capital: Buenos Aires
Area: 1,068,302 sq mi (2,766,890 sq km)
Population: 40,913,584
Major Language(s): Spanish
Major Religion(s): Roman Catholic Christianity
Currency: Argentine peso

Armenia

Hayastan

Official Name: Republic of Armenia
Capital: Yerevan
Area: 11,484 sq mi (29,743 sq km)
Population: 2,967,004
Major Language(s): Armenian
Major Religion(s): Armenian Apostolic Christianity
Currency: dram

Aruba

(part of the Kingdom of the Netherlands)

Official Name: Aruba
Capital: Oranjestad
Area: 75 sq mi (193 sq km)
Population: 103,065
Major Language(s): Papiamento, Dutch
Major Religion(s): Roman Catholic Christianity
Currency: Arubian guilder/florin

Australia

Official Name: Commonwealth of Australia
Capital: Canberra
Area: 2,967,909 sq mi (7,686,850 sq km)
Population: 21,262,641
Major Language(s): English, Aboriginal languages
Major Religion(s): Christianity
Currency: Australian dollar

Austria

Oesterreich

Official Name: Republic of Austria
Capital: Vienna
Area: 32,382 sq mi (83,870 sq km)
Population: 8,210,281
Major Language(s): German
Major Religion(s): Roman Catholic Christianity
Currency: Euro

Azerbaijan

Azarbaycan

Official Name: Republic of Azerbaijan
Capital: Baku
Area: 33,436 sq mi (86,600 sq km)
Population: 8,238,672
Major Language(s): Azerbaijani
Major Religion(s): Shia Islam
Currency: manats

Bahamas, The

Official Name: Commonwealth of the Bahamas
Capital: Nassau
Area: 5,382 sq mi (13,940 sq km)
Population: 309156
Major Language(s): English
Major Religion(s): Protestant
Currency: Bahamian dollar

Bahrain

Al Bahrayn

Official Name: Kingdom of Bahrain
Capital: Manama
Area: 257 sq mi (665 sq km)
Population: 727,785
Major Language(s): Arabic, English
Major Religion(s): Sunni Islam
Currency: Bahraini dollar

Country and Dependency Profiles

Bangladesh

Banladesh

Official Name: People's Republic of Bangladesh
Capital: Dhaka
Area: 55,599 sq mi (144,000 sq km)
Population: 156,050,883
Major Language(s): Bangla, English
Major Religion(s): Sunni Islam
Currency: taka

Belize

Official Name: Belize
Capital: Belmopan
Area: 8,867 sq mi (22,966 sq km)
Population: 307,899
Major Language(s): Spanish, Creole, English
Major Religion(s): Roman Catholic Christianity
Currency: Belizian dollar

Barbados

Official Name: Barbados
Capital: Bridgetown
Area: 166 sq mi (431 sq km)
Population: 284,589
Major Language(s): English
Major Religion(s): Protestant Christianity
Currency: Barbadian dollar

Benin

Official Name: Republic of Benin
Capital: Porto-Novo
Area: 43,483 sq mi (112,620 sq km)
Population: 8,791,832
Major Language(s): French, Fon, Yoruba, other African languages
Major Religion(s): Indigenous beliefs, Christianity
Currency: CFA franc

Belarus

Byelarus'

Official Name: Republic of Belarus
Capital: Minsk
Area: 80,155 sq mi (207,600 sq km)
Population: 9,648,533
Major Language(s): Belarusian, Russian
Major Religion(s): Eastern Orthodox Christianity
Currency: Belarusian ruble

Bermuda

(overseas territory of the United Kingdom)

Official Name: Bermuda
Capital: Hamilton
Area: 20 sq mi (53 sq km)
Population: 67,837
Major Language(s): English
Major Religion(s): Protestant Christianity
Currency: Bermudian dollar

Belgium

Belgique/Belgie

Official Name: Kingdom of Belgium
Capital: Brussels
Area: 11,787 sq mi (30,528 sq km)
Population: 10,414,336
Major Language(s): Dutch, French, German
Major Religion(s): Roman Catholic Christianity
Currency: Euro

Bhutan

Druk Yul

Official Name: Kingdom of Bhutan
Capital: Thimphu
Area: 18,147 sq mi (47,000 sq km)
Population: 691,141
Major Language(s): Dzongkha, Tibetan dialects, Nepalese dialects
Major Religion(s): Buddhism
Currency: ngultrum

Bolivia

Official Name: Plurinational State of Bolivia
Capital: La Paz (administrative), Sucre (constitutional)
Area: 424,164 sq mi (1,098,580 sq km)
Population: 9,775,246
Major Language(s): Spanish, Quechua, Aymara
Major Religion(s): Roman Catholic Christianity
Currency: boliviano

Brunei

Official Name: Brunei Darussalam
Capital: Bandar Seri Begawan
Area: 2,228 sq mi (5,770 sq km)
Population: 388,190
Major Language(s): Malay, English
Major Religion(s): Sunni Islam
Currency: Bruneian dollar

Bosnia and Herzegovina

Bosna i Hercegovina

Official Name: Bosnia and Herzegovina
Capital: Sarajevo
Area: 19,772 sq mi (51,209 sq km)
Population: 4,613,414
Major Language(s): Bosnian, Croatian, Serbian
Major Religion(s): Christianity, Islam
Currency: konvertibilna mark

Bulgaria

Balgariya

Official Name: Republic of Bulgaria
Capital: Sofia
Area: 42,823 sq mi (110,910 sq km)
Population: 7,204,687
Major Language(s): Bulgarian
Major Religion(s): Eastern Orthodox Christianity
Currency: leva

Botswana

Official Name: Republic of Botswana
Capital: Gaborone
Area: 231,804 sq mi (600,370 sq km)
Population: 1,990,876
Major Language(s): Setswana, Kalanga, English
Major Religion(s): Christianity
Currency: pula

Burkina Faso

Official Name: Burkina Faso
Capital: Ouagadougou
Area: 105,869 sq mi (274,200 sq km)
Population: 15,746,232
Major Language(s): French, many African languages
Major Religion(s): Sunni Islam
Currency: CFA franc

Brazil

Brasil

Official Name: Federative Republic of Brazil
Capital: Brasilia
Area: 3,286,488 sq mi (8,511,965 sq km)
Population: 198,739,269
Major Language(s): Portuguese, many Amerindian languages
Major Religion(s): Roman Catholic Christianity
Currency: real

Burma (Myanmar)

Myanma Naingngandaw

Official Name: Union of Burma
Capital: Rangoon
Area: 261,970 sq mi (678,500 sq km)
Population: 48,137,741
Major Language(s): Burmese
Major Religion(s): Buddhism
Currency: kyat

Country and Dependency Profiles

Burundi

Official Name: Republic of Burundi
Capital: Bujumbura
Area: 10,745 sq mi (27,830 sq km)
Population: 8,988,091
Major Language(s): Kirundi, French, Swahili
Major Religion(s): Roman Catholic Christianity
Currency: Burundi franc

Cambodia

Kampuchea

Official Name: Kingdom of Cambodia
Capital: Phnom Penh
Area: 69,900 sq mi (181,040 sq km)
Population: 14,494,293
Major Language(s): Khmer
Major Religion(s): Buddhism
Currency: riel

Cameroon

Cameroun

Official Name: Republic of Cameroon
Capital: Yaounde
Area: 183,568 sq mi (475,440 sq km)
Population: 18,879,301
Major Language(s): English, French, many African languages
Major Religion(s): Indigenous beliefs, Christianity
Currency: CFA franc

Canada

Official Name: Canada
Capital: Ottawa
Area: 3,855,103 sq mi (9,984,670 sq km)
Population: 33,487,208
Major Language(s): English, French, Amerindian languages
Major Religion(s): Roman Catholic Christianity
Currency: Canadian dollar

Cape Verde

Cabo Verde

Official Name: Republic of Cape Verde
Capital: Praia
Area: 1,557 sq mi (4,033 sq km)
Population: 429,474
Major Language(s): Portuguese
Major Religion(s): Roman Catholic Christianity
Currency: escudo

Cayman Islands

(overseas territory of the United Kingdom)

Official Name: Cayman Islands
Capital: George Town
Area: 101 sq mi (262 sq km)
Population: 49,035
Major Language(s): English
Major Religion(s): Christianity
Currency: Caymanian dollar

Central African Republic

Official Name: Central African Republic
Capital: Bangui
Area: 240,535 sq mi (622,984 sq km)
Population: 4,511,488
Major Language(s): French, Sangho
Major Religion(s): Indigenous beliefs, Christianity
Currency: CFA franc

Chad

Tchad/Tshad

Official Name: Republic of Chad
Capital: N'Djamena
Area: 495,755 sq mi (1,284,000 sq km)
Population: 10,329,208
Major Language(s): French, Arabic, many African languages
Major Religion(s): Sunni Islam
Currency: CFA franc

Chile

Official Name: Republic of Chile
Capital: Santiago
Area: 292,260 sq mi (756,950 sq km)
Population: 16,601,707
Major Language(s): Spanish
Major Religion(s): Roman Catholic Christianity
Currency: Chilean peso

China

Zhongguo

Official Name: People's Republic of China
Capital: Beijing
Area: 3,705,407 sq mi (9,596,960 sq km)
Population: 1,338,612,968
Major Language(s): Chinese (Mandarin), Yue (Cantonese), many other dialects
Major Religion(s): Officially atheist
Currency: Renminbi yuan

Colombia

Official Name: Republic of Colombia
Capital: Bogotá
Area: 439,736 sq mi (1,138,910 sq km)
Population: 45,644,023
Major Language(s): Spanish
Major Religion(s): Roman Catholic Christianity
Currency: Colombian peso

Comoros

Komori/Comores/Juzur al Qamar

Official Name: Union of the Comoros
Capital: Moroni
Area: 838 sq mi (2,170 sq km)
Population: 752,438
Major Language(s): Arabic, French
Major Religion(s): Sunni Islam
Currency: Comoran franc

Costa Rica

Official Name: Republic of Costa Rica
Capital: San Jose
Area: 19,730 sq mi (51,100 sq km)
Population: 4,253,877
Major Language(s): Spanish
Major Religion(s): Roman Catholic Christianity
Currency: colón

Cote d'Ivoire

Official Name: Republic of Cote d'Ivoire
Capital: Yamoussoukro
Area: 124,503 sq mi (322,460 sq km)
Population: 20,617,068
Major Language(s): French, many African languages
Major Religion(s): Sunni Islam, Christianity
Currency: CFA franc

Croatia

Hrvatska

Official Name: Republic of Croatia
Capital: Zagreb
Area: 21,831 sq mi (56,542 sq km)
Population: 4,489,409
Major Language(s): Croatian
Major Religion(s): Roman Catholic Christianity
Currency: kuna

Cuba

Official Name: Republic of Cuba
Capital: Havana
Area: 42,803 sq mi (110,860 sq km)
Population: 11,451,652
Major Language(s): Spanish
Major Religion(s): Roman Catholic Christianity
Currency: Cuban peso

Country and Dependency Profiles

Cyprus

Kypros/Kibris

Official Name: Republic of Cyprus
Capital: Nicosia
Area: 3,571 sq mi (9,250 sq km)
Population: 796,740
Major Language(s): Greek, Turkish
Major Religion(s): Eastern Orthodox Christianity
Currency: Euro

Czechia

Cesko

Official Name: Czech Republic
Capital: Prague
Area: 30,450 sq mi (78,866 sq km)
Population: 10,211,904
Major Language(s): Czech
Major Religion(s): Roman Catholic Christianity
Currency: koruny

Denmark
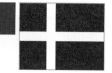

Danmark

Official Name: Kingdom of Denmark
Capital: Copenhagen
Area: 16,639 sq mi (43,094 sq km)
Population: 5,500,510
Major Language(s): Danish
Major Religion(s): Protestant Christianity
Currency: Danish kroner

Djibouti

Jibuti

Official Name: Republic of Djibouti
Capital: Djibouti
Area: 8,880 sq mi (23,000 sq km)
Population: 516,055
Major Language(s): French, Arabic
Major Religion(s): Sunni Islam
Currency: Djiboutian franc

Dominica

Official Name: Commonwealth of Dominica
Capital: Roseau
Area: 291 sq mi (754 sq km)
Population: 72,660
Major Language(s): English
Major Religion(s): Roman Catholic Christianity
Currency: East Caribbean dollar

Dominican Republic

La Dominicana

Official Name: Dominican Republic
Capital: Santo Domingo
Area: 18,815 sq mi (48,730 sq km)
Population: 9,650,054
Major Language(s): Spanish
Major Religion(s): Roman Catholic Christianity
Currency: Dominican peso

Ecuador

Official Name: Republic of Ecuador
Capital: Quito
Area: 109,483 sq mi (283,560 sq km)
Population: 14,573,101
Major Language(s): Spanish, many Amerindian languages
Major Religion(s): Roman Catholic Christianity
Currency: US dollar

Egypt

Misr

Official Name: Arab Republic of Egypt
Capital: Cairo
Area: 386,662 sq mi (1,001,450 sq km)
Population: 83,082,869
Major Language(s): Arabic
Major Religion(s): Sunni Islam
Currency: Egyptian pound

El Salvador

Official Name: Republic of El Salvador
Capital: San Salvador
Area: 8,124 sq mi (21,040 sq km)
Population: 7,185,218
Major Language(s): Spanish
Major Religion(s): Roman Catholic Christianity
Currency: US dollar

Ethiopia

Ityop'iya

Official Name: Federal Democratic Republic of Ethiopia
Capital: Addis Ababa
Area: 435,186 sq mi (1,127,127 sq km)
Population: 85,237,338
Major Language(s): Amarigna, Oromigna, English
Major Religion(s): Ethiopian Orthodox Christianity, Islam
Currency: birr

Equatorial Guinea

Guinea Ecuatorial/Guinee equatoriale

Official Name: Republic of Equatorial Guinea
Capital: Malabo
Area: 10,831 sq mi (28,051 sq km)
Population: 633,441
Major Language(s): Spanish, French, Fang, Bubi
Major Religion(s): Roman Catholic Christianity
Currency: CFA franc

Falkland Islands (Islas Malvinas)

(overseas territory of the United Kingdom, claimed by Argentina)

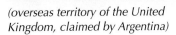

Official Name: Falkland Islands (Islas Malvinas)
Capital: Stanley
Area: 4,700 sq mi (12,173 sq km)
Population: 3,140
Major Language(s): English
Major Religion(s): Christianity
Currency: British pound

Eritrea

Ertra

Official Name: State of Eritrea
Capital: Asmara
Area: 46,842 sq mi (121,320 sq km)
Population: 5,647,168
Major Language(s): Tigrinya, Arabic
Major Religion(s): Sunni Islam, Christianity
Currency: nakfa

Faroe Islands

Foroyar
(part of the Kingdom of Denmark)

Official Name: Faroe Islands
Capital: Torshavn
Area: 540 sq mi (1,399 sq km)
Population: 48,856
Major Language(s): Faroese
Major Religion(s): Protestant Christianity
Currency: Danish kroner

Estonia

Eesti

Official Name: Republic of Estonia
Capital: Tallinn
Area: 17,462 sq mi (45,226 sq km)
Population: 1,299,371
Major Language(s): Estonian, Russian
Major Religion(s): Protestant Christianity
Currency: krooni

Fiji

Fiji/Viti

Official Name: Republic of the Fiji Islands
Capital: Suva
Area: 7,054 sq mi (18,270 sq km)
Population: 944,720
Major Language(s): English, Fijian
Major Religion(s): Christianity
Currency: Fijian dollar

Country and Dependency Profiles

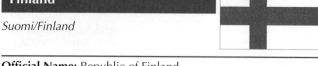

Finland
Suomi/Finland

Official Name: Republic of Finland
Capital: Helsinki
Area: 130,559 sq mi (338,145 sq km)
Population: 5,250,275
Major Language(s): Finnish
Major Religion(s): Protestant Christianity
Currency: Euro

Georgia
Sak'art'velo

Official Name: Georgia
Capital: T'bilisi
Area: 26,911 sq mi (69,700 sq km)
Population: 4,615,807
Major Language(s): Georgian, Russian
Major Religion(s): Eastern Orthodox Christianity
Currency: laris

France

Official Name: French Republic
Capital: Paris
Area: 248,429 sq mi (643,427 sq km)
Population: 64,057,792
Major Language(s): French
Major Religion(s): Roman Catholic Christianity
Currency: Euro

Germany
Deutschland

Official Name: Federal Republic of Germany
Capital: Berlin
Area: 137,847 sq mi (357,021 sq km)
Population: 82,329,758
Major Language(s): German
Major Religion(s): Christianity
Currency: Euro

Gabon

Official Name: Gabonese Republic
Capital: Libreville
Area: 103,347 sq mi (267,667 sq km)
Population: 1,514,993
Major Language(s): French, Fang
Major Religion(s): Christianity
Currency: CFA franc

Ghana

Official Name: Republic of Ghana
Capital: Accra
Area: 92,456 sq mi (239,460 sq km)
Population: 23,832,495
Major Language(s): English, many African languages
Major Religion(s): Christianity
Currency: cedi

Gambia, The

Official Name: Republic of The Gambia
Capital: Banjul
Area: 4,363 sq mi (11,300 sq km)
Population: 1,782,893
Major Language(s): English, Mandinka, Wolof, Fula
Major Religion(s): Sunni Islam
Currency: dalasis

Greece
Ellas or Ellada

Official Name: Hellenic Republic
Capital: Athens
Area: 50,942 sq mi (131,940 sq km)
Population: 10,737,428
Major Language(s): Greek
Major Religion(s): Eastern Orthodox Christianity
Currency: Euro

Greenland

Kalaallit Nunaat
(part of the Kingdom of Denmark)

Official Name: Greenland
Capital: Nuuk
Area: 836,330 sq mi (2,166,086 sq km)
Population: 57,600
Major Language(s): Greenlandic, Danish, English
Major Religion(s): Protestant Christianity
Currency: Danish kroner

Guinea

Guinee

Official Name: Republic of Guinea
Capital: Conakry
Area: 94,926 sq mi (245,857 sq km)
Population: 10,057,975
Major Language(s): French, many African languages
Major Religion(s): Sunni Islam
Currency: Guinean franc

Grenada

Official Name: Grenada
Capital: Saint George's
Area: 133 sq mi (344 sq km)
Population: 90,739
Major Language(s): English, French patois
Major Religion(s): Roman Catholic Christianity
Currency: East Caribbean dollar

Guinea-Bissau

Guine-Bissau

Official Name: Republic of Guinea-Bissau
Capital: Bissau
Area: 13,946 sq mi (36,120 sq km)
Population: 1,533,964
Major Language(s): Portuguese, Crioulo
Major Religion(s): Sunni Islam, Indigenous beliefs
Currency: CFA franc

Guatemala

Official Name: Republic of Guatemala
Capital: Guatemala
Area: 42,043 sq mi (108,890 sq km)
Population: 13,276,517
Major Language(s): Spanish, many Amerindian languages
Major Religion(s): Roman Catholic Christianity
Currency: quetzal

Guyana

Official Name: Cooperative Republic of Guyana
Capital: Georgetown
Area: 83,000 sq mi (214,970 sq km)
Population: 772,298
Major Language(s): English, Amerindian dialects
Major Religion(s): Hinduism, Christianity
Currency: Guyanese dollar

Guernsey

(British crown dependency)

Official Name: Bailiwick of Guernsey
Capital: Saint Peter Port
Area: 30 sq mi (78 sq km)
Population: 65,870
Major Language(s): English
Major Religion(s): Protestant Christianity
Currency: British pound

Haiti

Haiti/Ayiti

Official Name: Republic of Haiti
Capital: Port-au-Prince
Area: 10,714 sq mi (27,750 sq km)
Population: 9,035,536
Major Language(s): French, Creole
Major Religion(s): Roman Catholic Christianity
Currency: gourde

Country and Dependency Profiles

Holy See (Vatican City)

Santa Sede (Citta del Vaticano)

Official Name: The Holy See (State of the Vatican City)
Capital: Vatican City
Area: 0.4 sq mi (1.1 sq km)
Population: 826
Major Language(s): Italian, Latin
Major Religion(s): Roman Catholic Christianity
Currency: Euro

India

India/Bharat

Official Name: Republic of India
Capital: New Delhi
Area: 1,269,346 sq mi (3,287,590 sq km)
Population: 1,166,079,217
Major Language(s): Hindi, English, 17 other languages
Major Religion(s): Hinduism, Sunni Islam
Currency: Indian rupee

Honduras

Official Name: Republic of Honduras
Capital: Tegucigalpa
Area: 43,278 sq mi (112,090 sq km)
Population: 7,792,854
Major Language(s): Spanish, Amerindian dialects
Major Religion(s): Roman Catholic Christianity
Currency: lempira

Indonesia

Official Name: Republic of Indonesia
Capital: Jakarta
Area: 741,100 sq mi (1,919,440 sq km)
Population: 240,271,522
Major Language(s): Bahasa Indonesia, many local dialects
Major Religion(s): Sunni Islam
Currency: rupiah

Hungary

Magyarorszag

Official Name: Republic of Hungary
Capital: Budapest
Area: 35,919 sq mi (93,030 sq km)
Population: 9,905,596
Major Language(s): Hungarian
Major Religion(s): Roman Catholic Christianity
Currency: forint

Iran

Official Name: Islamic Republic of Iran
Capital: Tehran
Area: 636,296 sq mi (1,648,000 sq km)
Population: 66,429,284
Major Language(s): Persian, Turkic dialects, Kurdish
Major Religion(s): Shia Islam
Currency: Iranian rial

Iceland

Island

Official Name: Republic of Iceland
Capital: Reykjavik
Area: 39,769 sq mi (103,000 sq km)
Population: 306,694
Major Language(s): Icelandic
Major Religion(s): Protestant Christianity
Currency: kronur

Iraq

Al Iraq

Official Name: Republic of Iraq
Capital: Baghdad
Area: 168,754 sq mi (437,072 sq km)
Population: 28,945,657
Major Language(s): Arabic, Kurdish
Major Religion(s): Shia and Sunni Islam
Currency: New Iraqi dinar

Ireland

Eire

Official Name: Ireland
Capital: Dublin
Area: 27,135 sq mi (70,280 sq km)
Population: 4,203,200
Major Language(s): English, Irish
Major Religion(s): Roman Catholic Christianity
Currency: Euro

Japan

Nihon/Nippon

Official Name: Japan
Capital: Tokyo
Area: 145,883 sq mi (377,835 sq km)
Population: 127,078,679
Major Language(s): Japanese
Major Religion(s): Shintoism
Currency: yen

Israel

Yisra'el

Official Name: State of Israel
Capital: Jerusalem (proclaimed), Tel Aviv (de facto)
Area: 8,019 sq mi (20,770 sq km)
Population: 7,233,701
Major Language(s): Hebrew, Arabic
Major Religion(s): Judaism
Currency: Israeli new shekel

Jersey

(British crown dependency)

Official Name: Bailiwick of Jersey
Capital: Saint Helier
Area: 45 sq mi (116 sq km)
Population: 91,626
Major Language(s): English
Major Religion(s): Protestant Christianity
Currency: British pound

Italy

Italia

Official Name: Italian Republic
Capital: Rome
Area: 116,306 sq mi (301,230 sq km)
Population: 58,126,212
Major Language(s): Italian, German, French
Major Religion(s): Roman Catholic Christianity
Currency: Euro

Jordan

Al Urdun

Official Name: Hashemite Kingdom of Jordan
Capital: Amman
Area: 35,637 sq mi (92,300 sq km)
Population: 6,342,948
Major Language(s): Arabic
Major Religion(s): Sunni Islam
Currency: Jordanian dinar

Jamaica

Official Name: Jamaica
Capital: Kingston
Area: 4,244 sq mi (10,991 sq km)
Population: 2,825,928
Major Language(s): English, English patois
Major Religion(s): Protestant Christianity
Currency: Jamaica dollar

Kazakhstan

Astana

Official Name: Republic of Kazakhstan
Capital: Almaty
Area: 1,049,155 sq mi (2,717,300 sq km)
Population: 15,399,437
Major Language(s): Kazakh, Russian
Major Religion(s): Sunni Islam, Eastern Orthodox Christianity
Currency: tenge

Country and Dependency Profiles

Kenya

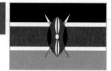

Official Name: Republic of Kenya
Capital: Nairobi
Area: 224,962 sq mi (582,650 sq km)
Population: 39,002,772
Major Language(s): English, Kiswahili
Major Religion(s): Christianity
Currency: Kenyan shilling

Kosovo

Kosova

Official Name: Republic of Kosovo
Capital: Pristina
Area: 4,203 sq mi (10,887 sq km)
Population: 1,804,838
Major Language(s): Albanian, Serbian
Major Religion(s): Sunni Islam
Currency: Euro

Kiribati

Official Name: Republic of Kiribati
Capital: Taraw
Area: 313 sq mi (811 sq km)
Population: 112,850
Major Language(s): I-Kiribati, English
Major Religion(s): Roman Catholic Christianity
Currency: Australian Dollar

Kuwait

Al Kuwayt

Official Name: State of Kuwait
Capital: Kuwait
Area: 6,880 sq mi (17,820 sq km)
Population: 2,691,158
Major Language(s): Arabic
Major Religion(s): Sunni Islam
Currency: Kuwaiti dinar

Korea, North

Choson

Official Name: Democratic People's Republic of Korea
Capital: P'yongyang
Area: 46,541 sq mi (120,540 sq km)
Population: 22,665,345
Major Language(s): Korean
Major Religion(s): Buddhism
Currency: North Korean won

Kyrgyzstan

Official Name: Kyrgyz Republic
Capital: Bishkek
Area: 76,641 sq mi (198,500 sq km)
Population: 5,431,747
Major Language(s): Kyrgyz, Uzbek, Russian
Major Religion(s): Sunni Islam, Eastern Orthodox Christianity
Currency: som

Korea, South

Han'guk

Official Name: Republic of Korea
Capital: Seoul
Area: 38,023 sq mi (98,480 sq km)
Population: 48,508,972
Major Language(s): Korean
Major Religion(s): Buddhism
Currency: South Korean won

Laos

Pathet Lao

Official Name: Lao People's Democratic Republic
Capital: Vientiane
Area: 91,429 sq mi (236,800 sq km)
Population: 6,834,942
Major Language(s): Lao, French, English
Major Religion(s): Buddhism
Currency: kip

Latvia

Latvija

Official Name: Republic of Latvia
Capital: Riga
Area: 24,938 sq mi (64,589 sq km)
Population: 2,231,503
Major Language(s): Latvian, Russian
Major Religion(s): Protestant Christianity
Currency: lati

Libya

Ar-Libya

Official Name: Great Socialist People's Libyan Arab Jamahiriya
Capital: Tripoli
Area: 679,362 sq mi (1,759,540 sq km)
Population: 6,310,434
Major Language(s): Arabic
Major Religion(s): Sunni Islam
Currency: Libyan dinar

Lebanon

Lubnan

Official Name: Lebanese Republic
Capital: Beirut
Area: 4,015 sq mi (10,400 sq km)
Population: 4,017,095
Major Language(s): Arabic, French, English, Armenian
Major Religion(s): Islam, Christianity
Currency: Lebanese pound

Liechtenstein

Official Name: Principality of Liechtenstein
Capital: Vaduz
Area: 62 sq mi (160 sq km)
Population: 34,761
Major Language(s): German
Major Religion(s): Roman Catholic Christianity
Currency: Swiss franc

Lesotho

Official Name: Kingdom of Lesotho
Capital: Maseru
Area: 11,720 sq mi (30,355 sq km)
Population: 2,130,819
Major Language(s): Sesotho, English, Zulu, Xhosa
Major Religion(s): Christianity, Indigenous beliefs
Currency: maloti

Lithuania

Lietuva

Official Name: Republic of Lithuania
Capital: Vilnius
Area: 25,212 sq mi (65,300 sq km)
Population: 3,555,179
Major Language(s): Lithuanian, Russian
Major Religion(s): Roman Catholic Christianity
Currency: litai

Liberia

Official Name: Republic of Liberia
Capital: Monrovia
Area: 43,000 sq mi (111,370 sq km)
Population: 3,441,790
Major Language(s): English, many African languages
Major Religion(s): Christianity, Indigenous beliefs
Currency: Liberian dollar

Luxembourg

Official Name: Grand Duchy of Luxembourg
Capital: Luxembourg
Area: 998 sq mi (2,586 sq km)
Population: 491,775
Major Language(s): Luxembourgish, German, French
Major Religion(s): Roman Catholic Christianity
Currency: Euro

Country and Dependency Profiles

Macedonia

Makedonija

Official Name: Republic of Macedonia
Capital: Skopje
Area: 9,781 sq mi (25,333 sq km)
Population: 2,066,718
Major Language(s): Macedonian, Albanian
Major Religion(s): Eastern Orthodox Christianity, Sunni Islam
Currency: Macedonian denar

Madagascar

Madagascar/Madagasikara

Official Name: Republic of Madagascar
Capital: Antananarivo
Area: 226,657 sq mi (587,040 sq km)
Population: 20,653,556
Major Language(s): English, French, Malagasy
Major Religion(s): Indigenous beliefs, Christianity
Currency: ariary

Malawi

Official Name: Republic of Malawi
Capital: Lilongwe
Area: 45,745 sq mi (118,480 sq km)
Population: 14,268,711
Major Language(s): Chichewa, Chinyanja, other African languages
Major Religion(s): Christianity, Islam
Currency: Malawian kwacha

Malaysia

Official Name: Malaysia
Capital: Kuala Lumpur
Area: 127,317 sq mi (329,750 sq km)
Population: 25,715,819
Major Language(s): Bahasa Malaysia, Chinese, Tamil
Major Religion(s): Islam, Buddhism
Currency: ringgit

Maldives

Dhivehi Raajje

Official Name: Republic of Maldives
Capital: Male
Area: 116 sq mi (300 sq km)
Population: 396,334
Major Language(s): Maldivian Dhivehi
Major Religion(s): Sunni Islam
Currency: rufiyaa

Mali

Official Name: Republic of Mali
Capital: Bamako
Area: 478,767 sq mi (1,240,000 sq km)
Population: 12,666,987
Major Language(s): Bambara, French, many African languages
Major Religion(s): Sunni Islam
Currency: CFA franc

Malta

Official Name: Republic of Malta
Capital: Valletta
Area: 122 sq mi (316 sq km)
Population: 405,165
Major Language(s): Maltese
Major Religion(s): Roman Catholic Christianity
Currency: Euro

Marshall Islands

Official Name: Republic of the Marshall Islands
Capital: Majuro
Area: 70 sq mi (181 sq km)
Population: 64,522
Major Language(s): Marshallese
Major Religion(s): Protestant Christianity
Currency: US dollar

Mauritania

Muritaniyah

Official Name: Islamic Republic of Mauritania
Capital: Nouakchott
Area: 397,955 sq mi (1,030,700 sq km)
Population: 3,129,486
Major Language(s): Arabic, Pulaar, Soninke, Wolof, French
Major Religion(s): Sunni Islam
Currency: ouguiya

Mauritius

Official Name: Republic of Mauritius
Capital: Port Louis
Area: 788 sq mi (2,040 sq km)
Population: 1,284,264
Major Language(s): Creole, Bhojpuri, French
Major Religion(s): Hinduism
Currency: Mauritian rupee

Mayotte

(territorial overseas collectivity of France)

Official Name: Territorial Collectivity of Mayotte
Capital: Mamoutzou
Area: 144 sq mi (374 sq km)
Population: 223,765
Major Language(s): Mahorian, French
Major Religion(s): Sunni Islam
Currency: Euro

Mexico

Official Name: United Mexican States
Capital: Mexico City
Area: 761,606 sq mi (1,972,550 sq km)
Population: 111,211,789
Major Language(s): Spanish, Amerindian dialects
Major Religion(s): Roman Catholic Christianity
Currency: Mexican peso

Micronesia

Official Name: Federated States of Micronesia
Capital: Palikir
Area: 271 sq mi (702 sq km)
Population: 107,434
Major Language(s): English
Major Religion(s): Roman Catholic Christianity
Currency: US dollar

Moldova

Official Name: Republic of Moldova
Capital: Chisinau
Area: 13,067 sq mi (33,843 sq km)
Population: 4,320,748
Major Language(s): Moldovan, Russian
Major Religion(s): Eastern Orthodox Christianity
Currency: lei

Monaco

Official Name: Principality of Monaco
Capital: Monaco
Area: 1 sq mi (2 sq km)
Population: 32,965
Major Language(s): French, English, Italian, Monegasque
Major Religion(s): Roman Catholic Christianity
Currency: Euro

Mongolia

Mongol Uls

Official Name: Mongolia
Capital: Ulaanbaatar
Area: 603,909 sq mi (1,564,116 sq km)
Population: 3,041,142
Major Language(s): Khalkha Mongol
Major Religion(s): Buddhism
Currency: tögrög

Country and Dependency Profiles

Montenegro

Crna Gora

Official Name: Montenegro
Capital: Cetinje
Area: 5,415 sq mi (14,026 sq km)
Population: 672,180
Major Language(s): Montenegrin, Serbian
Major Religion(s): Eastern Orthodox Christianity, Sunni Islam
Currency: Euro

Montserrat

(overseas territory of the United Kingdom)

Official Name: Montserrat
Capital: Plymouth
Area: 39 sq mi (102 sq km)
Population: 5,097
Major Language(s): English
Major Religion(s): Protestant Christianity
Currency: East Caribbean dollar

Morocco

Al Maghrib

Official Name: Kingdom of Morocco
Capital: Rabat
Area: 172,414 sq mi (446,550 sq km)
Population: 34,859,364
Major Language(s): Arabic, French, Berber dialects
Major Religion(s): Sunni Islam
Currency: Moroccan dirham

Mozambique

Moçambique

Official Name: Republic of Mozambique
Capital: Maputo
Area: 309,496 sq mi (801,590 sq km)
Population: 21,669,278
Major Language(s): Emakhuwa, Xichangana, Portuguese
Major Religion(s): Christianity, Sunni Islam
Currency: metical

Namibia

Official Name: Republic of Namibia
Capital: Windhoek
Area: 318,696 sq mi (825,418 sq km)
Population: 2,108,665
Major Language(s): Afrikaans, English, German
Major Religion(s): Christianity, Indigenous beliefs
Currency: Namibian dollar

Nepal

Official Name: Federal Democratic Republic of Nepal
Capital: Kathmandu
Area: 56,827 sq mi (147,181 sq km)
Population: 28,563,377
Major Language(s): Nepali, Maithali, Bhojpuri
Major Religion(s): Hinduism, Buddhism
Currency: Nepalese rupee

Netherlands

Nederland

Official Name: Kingdom of the Netherlands
Capital: Amsterdam
Area: 16,033 sq mi (41,526 sq km)
Population: 16,715,999
Major Language(s): Dutch, Frisian
Major Religion(s): Christianity
Currency: Euro

Netherlands Antilles

Nederlandse Antillen
(part of the Kingdom of the Netherlands)

Official Name: Netherlands Antilles
Capital: Willemstad
Area: 371 sq mi (960 sq km)
Population: 227,049
Major Language(s): Papiamento, English, Dutch
Major Religion(s): Roman Catholic Christianity
Currency: Netherlands Antilles guilder

New Caledonia

Nouvelle-Caledonie
(self-governing territory of France)

Official Name: Territory of New Caledonia and Dependencies
Capital: Noumea
Area: 7,359 sq mi (19,060 sq km)
Population: 227,436
Major Language(s): French, many Melanesian-Polynesian dialects
Major Religion(s): Roman Catholic Christianity
Currency: CFP franc

New Zealand

Official Name: New Zealand
Capital: Wellington
Area: 103,738 sq mi (268,680 sq km)
Population: 4,213,418
Major Language(s): English, Maori
Major Religion(s): Christianity
Currency: New Zealand dollar

Nicaragua

Official Name: Republic of Nicaragua
Capital: Managua
Area: 49,998 sq mi (129,494 sq km)
Population: 5,891,199
Major Language(s): Spanish
Major Religion(s): Roman Catholic Christianity
Currency: cordoba

Niger

Official Name: Republic of Niger
Capital: Niamey
Area: 489,191 sq mi (1,267,000 sq km)
Population: 15,306,252
Major Language(s): French, Hausa, Djerma
Major Religion(s): Sunni Islam
Currency: CFA franc

Nigeria

Official Name: Federal Republic of Nigeria
Capital: Abuja
Area: 356,669 sq mi (923,768 sq km)
Population: 149,229,090
Major Language(s): English, Hausa, Yoruba, Igbo, Fulani
Major Religion(s): Sunni Islam, Christianity
Currency: naira

Niue

*(self-governing territory in
free association with New Zealand)*

Official Name: Niue
Capital: Alofi
Area: 100 sq mi (260 sq km)
Population: 1,398
Major Language(s): Niuean, English
Major Religion(s): Protestant Christianity
Currency: New Zealand dollar

Norfolk Island

(self-governing territory of Australia)

Official Name: Territory of Norfolk Island
Capital: Kingston
Area: 14 sq mi (35 sq km)
Population: 2,141
Major Language(s): English
Major Religion(s): Protestant Christianity
Currency: Australian dollar

Norway

Norge

Official Name: Kingdom of Norway
Capital: Oslo
Area: 125,021 sq mi (323,802 sq km)
Population: 4,660,539
Major Language(s): Norwegian
Major Religion(s): Protestant Christianity
Currency: Norwegian kroner

Country and Dependency Profiles

Oman
Uman

Official Name: Sultanate of Oman
Capital: Muscat
Area: 82,031 sq mi (212,460 sq km)
Population: 3,418,085
Major Language(s): Arabic
Major Religion(s): Sunni Islam
Currency: Omani rial

Papua New Guinea
Papuaniugini

Official Name: Independent State of Papua New Guinea
Capital: Port Moresby
Area: 178,704 sq mi (462,840 sq km)
Population: 6,057,263
Major Language(s): Tok Pisin, English, Hiri Motu
Major Religion(s): Protestant Christianity
Currency: kina

Pakistan

Official Name: Islamic Republic of Pakistan
Capital: Islamabad
Area: 310,403 sq mi (803,940 sq km)
Population: 176,242,949
Major Language(s): Punjabi, Sindhi, Siraiki, Pashtu, Urdu
Major Religion(s): Sunni Islam
Currency: Pakistani rupee

Paraguay

Official Name: Republic of Paraguay
Capital: Asuncion
Area: 157,047 sq mi (406,750 sq km)
Population: 6,995,655
Major Language(s): Spanish, Guarani
Major Religion(s): Roman Catholic Christianity
Currency: guaraní

Palau
Belau

Official Name: Republic of Palau
Capital: Koror
Area: 177 sq mi (458 sq km)
Population: 20,796
Major Language(s): Palauan, Tobi, English
Major Religion(s): Christianity
Currency: US dollar

Peru

Official Name: Republic of Peru
Capital: Lima
Area: 496,226 sq mi (1,285,220 sq km)
Population: 29,546,963
Major Language(s): Spanish, Quechua, Aymara
Major Religion(s): Roman Catholic Christianity
Currency: nuevo sol

Panama

Official Name: Republic of Panama
Capital: Panama
Area: 30,193 sq mi (78,200 sq km)
Population: 3,360,474
Major Language(s): Spanish, English
Major Religion(s): Roman Catholic Christianity
Currency: balboa

Philippines
Pilipinas

Official Name: Republic of the Philippines
Capital: Manila
Area: 115,831 sq mi (300,000 sq km)
Population: 97,976,603
Major Language(s): Filipino, Tagalog, English
Major Religion(s): Roman Catholic Christianity
Currency: Philippine peso

Pitcairn Islands

*(overseas territory of the
United Kingdom)*

Official Name: Pitcairn, Henderson, Ducie, and Oeno Islands
Capital: Adamstown
Area: 18 sq mi (47 sq km)
Population: 48
Major Language(s): English
Major Religion(s): Protestant Christianity
Currency: New Zealand dollar

Poland

Polska

Official Name: Republic of Poland
Capital: Warsaw
Area: 120,726 sq mi (312,679 sq km)
Population: 38,482,919
Major Language(s): Polish
Major Religion(s): Roman Catholic Christianity
Currency: zloty

Portugal

Official Name: Portuguese Republic
Capital: Lisbon
Area: 35,672 sq mi (92,391 sq km)
Population: 10,707,924
Major Language(s): Portuguese
Major Religion(s): Roman Catholic Christianity
Currency: Euro

Puerto Rico

*(territory of the United States
with commonwealth status)*

Official Name: Commonwealth of Puerto Rico
Capital: San Juan
Area: 5,324 sq mi (13,790 sq km)
Population: 3,971,020
Major Language(s): Spanish, English
Major Religion(s): Roman Catholic Christianity
Currency: US dollar

Qatar

Official Name: State of Qatar
Capital: Doha
Area: 4,416 sq mi (11,437 sq km)
Population: 833,285
Major Language(s): Arabic
Major Religion(s): Sunni Islam
Currency: Qatari rial

Romania

Official Name: Romania
Capital: Bucharest
Area: 91,699 sq mi (237,500 sq km)
Population: 22,215,421
Major Language(s): Romanian, Hungarian
Major Religion(s): Eastern Orthodox Christianity
Currency: lei

Russia

Rossiya

Official Name: Russian Federation
Capital: Moscow
Area: 6,592,772 sq mi (17,075,200 sq km)
Population: 140,041,247
Major Language(s): Russian, many minority languages
Major Religion(s): Russian Orthodox, Muslim
Currency: Russian ruble

Rwanda

Official Name: Republic of Rwanda
Capital: Kigali
Area: 10,169 sq mi (26,338 sq km)
Population: 10,473,282
Major Language(s): Kinyarwanda, French, English
Major Religion(s): Roman Catholic Christianity
Currency: Rwandan franc

Country and Dependency Profiles

Saint Helena

(overseas territory of the United Kingdom)

Official Name: Saint Helena
Capital: Jamestown
Area: 159 sq mi (413 sq km)
Population: 7,637
Major Language(s): English
Major Religion(s): Protestant Christianity
Currency: Saint Helenanian pound

Saint Kitts and Nevis

Official Name: Federation of Saint Kitts and Nevis
Capital: Basseterre
Area: 101 sq mi (261 sq km)
Population: 40,131
Major Language(s): English
Major Religion(s): Protestant Christianity
Currency: East Caribbean dollar

Saint Lucia

Official Name: Saint Lucia
Capital: Castries
Area: 238 sq mi (616 sq km)
Population: 160,267
Major Language(s): English, French patois
Major Religion(s): Roman Catholic Christianity
Currency: East Caribbean dollar

Saint Pierre and Miquelon

Saint-Pierre et Miquelon
(territorial overseas collectivity of France)

Official Name: Territorial Collectivity of Saint Pierre and Miquelon
Capital: Saint-Pierre
Area: 93 sq mi (242 sq km)
Population: 7,051
Major Language(s): French
Major Religion(s): Roman Catholic Christianity
Currency: Euro

Saint Vincent and the Grenadines

Official Name: Saint Vincent and the Grenadines
Capital: Kingstown
Area: 150 sq mi (389 sq km)
Population: 104,574
Major Language(s): English, French patois
Major Religion(s): Protestant Christianity
Currency: East Caribbean dollar

Samoa

Official Name: Independent State of Samoa
Capital: Apia
Area: 1,137 sq mi (2,944 sq km)
Population: 219,998
Major Language(s): Samoan, English
Major Religion(s): Protestant Christianity
Currency: tala

San Marino

Official Name: Republic of San Marino
Capital: San Marino
Area: 24 sq mi (61 sq km)
Population: 30,324
Major Language(s): Italian
Major Religion(s): Roman Catholic Christianity
Currency: Euro

São Tomé and Príncipe

São Tomé e Príncipe

Official Name: Democratic Republic of São Tomé and Príncipe
Capital: São Tomé
Area: 386 sq mi (1,001 sq km)
Population: 212,679
Major Language(s): Portuguese
Major Religion(s): Roman Catholic Christianity
Currency: dobra

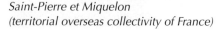

Saudi Arabia

Al Arabiyah as Suudiyah

Official Name: Kingdom of Saudi Arabia
Capital: Riyadh
Area: 830,000 sq mi (2,149,690 sq km)
Population: 28,686,633
Major Language(s): Arabic
Major Religion(s): Sunni Islam
Currency: Saudi riyal

Sierra Leone

Official Name: Republic of Sierra Leone
Capital: Freetown
Area: 27,699 sq mi (71,740 sq km)
Population: 6,440,053
Major Language(s): Mende, Temne, English, Krio
Major Religion(s): Sunni Islam
Currency: leone

Senegal

Official Name: Republic of Senegal
Capital: Dakar
Area: 75,749 sq mi (196,190 sq km)
Population: 13,711,597
Major Language(s): French, Wolof, Pulaar, Jola, Mandinka
Major Religion(s): Sunni Islam
Currency: CFA franc

Singapore

Official Name: Republic of Singapore
Capital: Singapore
Area: 268 sq mi (693 sq km)
Population: 4,657,542
Major Language(s): Mandarin Chinese, English, Malay, Hokkien
Major Religion(s): Buddhism, Sunni Islam
Currency: Singapore dollar

Serbia

Srbija

Official Name: Republic of Serbia
Capital: Belgrade
Area: 29,913 sq mi (77,474 sq km)
Population: 7,379,339
Major Language(s): Serbian
Major Religion(s): Eastern Orthodox Christianity
Currency: Serbian dinal

Slovakia

Slovensko

Official Name: Slovak Republic
Capital: Bratislava
Area: 18,859 sq mi (48,845 sq km)
Population: 5,463,046
Major Language(s): Slovak, Hungarian
Major Religion(s): Roman Catholic Christianity
Currency: Euro

Seychelles

Official Name: Republic of Seychelles
Capital: Victoria
Area: 176 sq mi (455 sq km)
Population: 87,476
Major Language(s): Creole
Major Religion(s): Roman Catholic Christianity
Currency: Seychelles rupee

Slovenia

Slovenija

Official Name: Republic of Slovenia
Capital: Ljubljana
Area: 7,827 sq mi (20,273 sq km)
Population: 2,005,692
Major Language(s): Slovenian
Major Religion(s): Roman Catholic Christianity
Currency: Euro

Country and Dependency Profiles

Solomon Islands

Official Name: Solomon Islands
Capital: Honiara
Area: 10,985 sq mi (28,450 sq km)
Population: 595,613
Major Language(s): English, many indigenous languages
Major Religion(s): Protestant Christianity
Currency: Solomon Islands dollar

Somalia

Soomaaliya

Official Name: Somalia
Capital: Mogadishu
Area: 246,201 sq mi (637,657 sq km)
Population: 9,832,017
Major Language(s): Somali, Arabic, Italian
Major Religion(s): Sunni Islam
Currency: Somali shilling

South Africa

Official Name: Republic of South Africa
Capital: Bloemfontein (judicial), Cape Town (legislative),
Area: 471,011 sq mi (1,219,912 sq km)
Population: 49,052,489
Major Language(s): Zulu, Xhosa, Afrikaans, Sepedi, English, Setswana, Sesotho
Major Religion(s): Protestant Christianity
Currency: rand

Spain

España

Official Name: Kingdom of Spain
Capital: Madrid
Area: 194,897 sq mi (504,782 sq km)
Population: 40,525,002
Major Language(s): Spanish, Catalan, Galician, Basque
Major Religion(s): Roman Catholic Christianity
Currency: Euro

Sri Lanka

Shri Lamka/Ilankai

Official Name: Democratic Socialist Republic of Sri Lanka
Capital: Colombo
Area: 25,332 sq mi (65,610 sq km)
Population: 21,324,791
Major Language(s): Sinhala, Tamil
Major Religion(s): Buddhism
Currency: Sri Lankan rupee

Sudan

As-Sudan

Official Name: Republic of the Sudan
Capital: Khartoum
Area: 967,499 sq mi (2,505,810 sq km)
Population: 41,087,825
Major Language(s): Arabic, English
Major Religion(s): Sunni Islam
Currency: Sudanese pound

Suriname

Official Name: Republic of Suriname
Capital: Paramaribo
Area: 63,039 sq mi (163,270 sq km)
Population: 481,267
Major Language(s): Dutch, English
Major Religion(s): Hinduism, Christianity
Currency: Surinamese dollar

Swaziland

eSwatini

Official Name: Kingdom of Swaziland
Capital: Mbabane
Area: 6,704 sq mi (17,363 sq km)
Population: 1,123,913
Major Language(s): English, siSwati
Major Religion(s): Christianity, Indigenous beliefs
Currency: emalangeni

Sweden

Sverige

Official Name: Kingdom of Sweden
Capital: Stockholm
Area: 173,732 sq mi (449,964 sq km)
Population: 9,059,651
Major Language(s): Swedish
Major Religion(s): Protestant Christianity
Currency: Swedish kronor

Switzerland

Schweiz/Suisse/Svizzera/Svizra

Official Name: Swiss Confederation
Capital: Bern
Area: 15,942 sq mi (41,290 sq km)
Population: 7,604,467
Major Language(s): German, French, Italian, Romansch
Major Religion(s): Christianity
Currency: Swiss franc

Syria

Suriyah

Official Name: Syrian Arab Republic
Capital: Damascus
Area: 71,498 sq mi (185,180 sq km)
Population: 20,178,485
Major Language(s): Arabic
Major Religion(s): Sunni Islam
Currency: Syrian pound

Taiwan

*T'ai-wan
(unresolved status; has limited
international recognition as the
legitimate representative of China)*

Official Name: Taiwan
Capital: Taipei
Area: 13,892 sq mi (35,980 sq km)
Population: 22,974,347
Major Language(s): Mandarin Chinese, Taiwanese
Major Religion(s): Buddhism
Currency: New Taiwan dollar

Tajikistan

Tojikiston

Official Name: Republic of Tajikistan
Capital: Dushanbe
Area: 55,251 sq mi (143,100 sq km)
Population: 7,349,145
Major Language(s): Tajik, Russian
Major Religion(s): Sunni Islam
Currency: somoni

Tanzania

Official Name: United Republic of Tanzania
Capital: Dar es Salaam
Area: 364,900 sq mi (945,087 sq km)
Population: 41,048,532
Major Language(s): Swahili, English
Major Religion(s): Sunni Islam, Christianity
Currency: Tanzanian shilling

Thailand

Prathet Thai

Official Name: Kingdom of Thailand
Capital: Bangkok
Area: 198,457 sq mi (514,000 sq km)
Population: 65,905,410
Major Language(s): Thai
Major Religion(s): Buddhism
Currency: baht

Timor-Leste

Timor Lorosa'e/Timor-Leste

Official Name: Democratic Republic of Timor-Leste
Capital: Dili
Area: 5,794 sq mi (15,007 sq km)
Population: 1,131,612
Major Language(s): Tetum, Portuguese, Indonesian
Major Religion(s): Roman Catholic Christianity
Currency: US dollar

Country and Dependency Profiles

Togo

Official Name: Togolese Republic
Capital: Lome
Area: 21,925 sq mi (56,785 sq km)
Population: 6,019,877
Major Language(s): French, many African languages
Major Religion(s): Indigenous beliefs, Christianity
Currency: CFA franc

Turkey
Turkiye

Official Name: Republic of Turkey
Capital: Ankara
Area: 301,384 sq mi (780,580 sq km)
Population: 76,805,524
Major Language(s): Turkish, Kurdish
Major Religion(s): Sunni Islam
Currency: lira

Tonga

Official Name: Kingdom of Tonga
Capital: Nuku'alofa
Area: 289 sq mi (748 sq km)
Population: 120,898
Major Language(s): Tongan, English
Major Religion(s): Protestant Christianity
Currency: pa'anga

Turkmenistan

Official Name: Turkmenistan
Capital: Ashgabat
Area: 188,456 sq mi (488,100 sq km)
Population: 4,884,887
Major Language(s): Turkmen, Russian, Uzbek
Major Religion(s): Sunni Islam
Currency: manats

Trinidad and Tobago

Official Name: Republic of Trinidad and Tobago
Capital: Port-of-Spain
Area: 1,980 sq mi (5,128 sq km)
Population: 1,229,953
Major Language(s): English, French, Spanish
Major Religion(s): Roman Catholic Christianity, Hinduism
Currency: Trinidad and Tobago dollar

Turks and Caicos Islands
(overseas territory of the United Kingdom)

Official Name: Turks and Caicos Islands
Capital: Grand Turk
Area: 166 sq mi (430 sq km)
Population: 22,942
Major Language(s): English
Major Religion(s): Protestant Christianity
Currency: US dollar

Tunisia
Tunis

Official Name: Tunisian Republic
Capital: Tunis
Area: 63,170 sq mi (163,610 sq km)
Population: 10,486,339
Major Language(s): Arabic, French
Major Religion(s): Sunni Islam
Currency: Tunisian dinar

Tuvalu

Official Name: Tuvalu
Capital: Funafuti
Area: 10 sq mi (26 sq km)
Population: 12,373
Major Language(s): Tuvaluan, English, Samoan
Major Religion(s): Protestant Christianity
Currency: Tuvaluan dollar

Uganda

Official Name: Republic of Uganda
Capital: Kampala
Area: 91,136 sq mi (236,040 sq km)
Population: 32,369,558
Major Language(s): English, Ganda, Swahili, other African languages
Major Religion(s): Christianity
Currency: Ugandan shilling

United States

Official Name: United States of America
Capital: Washington
Area: 3,794,083 sq mi (9,826,630 sq km)
Population: 307,212,123
Major Language(s): English, Spanish
Major Religion(s): Christianity
Currency: US dollar

Ukraine

Ukrayina

Official Name: Ukraine
Capital: Kyiv
Area: 233,090 sq mi (603,700 sq km)
Population: 45,700,395
Major Language(s): Ukrainian, Russian
Major Religion(s): Eastern Orthodox Christianity
Currency: hryvnia

Uruguay

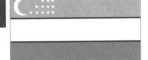

Official Name: Oriental Republic of Uruguay
Capital: Montevideo
Area: 68,039 sq mi (176,220 sq km)
Population: 3,494,382
Major Language(s): Spanish
Major Religion(s): Christianity
Currency: Uruguayan peso

United Arab Emirates

Al Imarat al Arabiyah al Muttahidah

Official Name: United Arab Emirates
Capital: Abu Dhabi
Area: 32,278 sq mi (83,600 sq km)
Population: 4,798,491
Major Language(s): Arabic
Major Religion(s): Sunni Islam
Currency: Emirati dirham

Uzbekistan

Ozbekiston

Official Name: Republic of Uzbekistan
Capital: Tashkent
Area: 172,742 sq mi (447,400 sq km)
Population: 27,606,007
Major Language(s): Uzbek, Russian
Major Religion(s): Sunni Islam
Currency: soum

United Kingdom

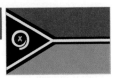

Official Name: United Kingdom of Great Britain and Northern Ireland
Capital: London
Area: 94,526 sq mi (244,820 sq km)
Population: 61,113,205
Major Language(s): English, Welsh, Scottish Gaelic
Major Religion(s): Christianity
Currency: British pound

Vanuatu

Official Name: Republic of Vanuatu
Capital: Port-Vila
Area: 4,710 sq mi (12,200 sq km)
Population: 218,519
Major Language(s): Many local languages
Major Religion(s): Protestant Christianity
Currency: vatu

Country and Dependency Profiles

Venezuela

Official Name: Bolivarian Republic of Venezuela
Capital: Caracas
Area: 352,144 sq mi (912,050 sq km)
Population: 26,814,843
Major Language(s): Spanish, many Amerindian languages
Major Religion(s): Roman Catholic Christianity
Currency: bolivar

Yemen

Al Yaman

Official Name: Republic of Yemen
Capital: Sanaa
Area: 203,850 sq mi (527,970 sq km)
Population: 23,822,783
Major Language(s): Arabic
Major Religion(s): Sunni Islam
Currency: Yemeni rial

Vietnam

Viet Nam

Official Name: Socialist Republic of Vietnam
Capital: Hanoi
Area: 127,244 sq mi (329,560 sq km)
Population: 86,967,524
Major Language(s): Vietnamese, French, Chinese
Major Religion(s): Non-religious beliefs dominate
Currency: dong

Zambia

Official Name: Republic of Zambia
Capital: Lusaka
Area: 290,586 sq mi (752,614 sq km)
Population: 11,862,740
Major Language(s): English, many African (Bantu) languages
Major Religion(s): Christianity, Islam
Currency: Zambian kwacha

Virgin Islands

(territory of the United States)

Official Name: United States Virgin Islands
Capital: Charlotte Amalie
Area: 737 sq mi (1,910 sq km)
Population: 109,825
Major Language(s): English, Spanish
Major Religion(s): Christianity
Currency: US dollar

Zimbabwe

Official Name: Republic of Zimbabwe
Capital: Harare
Area: 150,804 sq mi (390,580 sq km)
Population: 11,392,629
Major Language(s): English, many African (Bantu) languages
Major Religion(s): Christianity, Indigenous beliefs
Currency: Zimbabwean dollar

Wallis and Futuna

Wallis et Futuna
(overseas collectivity of France)

Official Name: Territory of the Wallis and Futuna Islands
Capital: Mata-Utu
Area: 106 sq mi (274 sq km)
Population: 15,289
Major Language(s): Wallisian, Futunian, French
Major Religion(s): Roman Catholic Christianity
Currency: CFP franc

Unit IX

Geographic Index

GEOGRAPHIC INDEX

NAME/DESCRIPTION	LATITUDE & LONGITUDE	PAGE	NAME/DESCRIPTION	LATITUDE & LONGITUDE	PAGE
Abidjan, Côte d'Ivoire (city, nat. cap.)	5N 4W	167	Aleppo, Syria (city)	36N 37E	164
Abu Dhabi, U.A.E. (city, nat. cap.)	24N 54E	164	Aleutian Islands	55N 175W	154
Abuja, Nigeria (city, nat. cap.)	9N 7E	167	Alexander Island	71S 70W	173
Accra, Ghana (city, nat. cap.)	64N 0	167	Alexandria, Egypt (city)	31N 30E	167
Aconcagua, Mt. 22,834	38S 78W	157	Algeria (country)	28N 15E	167
Acre (st., Brazil)	9S 70W	158	Algiers, Algeria (city, nat. cap.)	37N 3E	167
Adan (riv., Asia)	60N 135E	163	Alice Springs, Aust. (city)	24S 134E	170
Addis Ababa, Ethiopia (city, nat. cap.)	9N 39E	167	Allier (riv., Europe)	46N 3E	160
Adelaide, S. Australia (city, st. cap., Aust.)	35S 139E	170	Almaty, Kazakhstan (city, nat. cap.)	43N 77E	164
Aden, Gulf of	12N 46E	163	Alps Mountains	46N 6E	160
Aden, Yemen (city)	13N 45E	164	Altay Mountains	49N 87E	163
Adige (riv., Europe)	46N 11E	160	Altun Shan	45N 90E	163
Admiralty Islands	1S 146E	169	Amapá (st., Brazil)	2N 52W	158
Adriatic Sea	44N 14E	160	Amazon (riv., S.Am.)	2S 53W	157
Aegean Sea	39N 25E	160	Amazon Basin	3S 61W	157
Afghanistan (country)	35N 65E	164	Amazonas (st., Brazil)	2S 64W	158
Aguascalientes (st., Mex.)	22N 110W	155	American Highland	74S 90E	173
Aguascalientes, Aguas. (city, st. cap., Mex.)	22N 102W	155	Amery Ice Shelf	69S 71E	173
Agulhas, Cape	35S 20E	166	Amman, Jordan (city, nat. cap.)	32N 36E	164
Ahaggar Mountains	23N 6E	166	Amsterdam, Netherlands (city)	52N 5E	161
Ahmadabad, India (city)	23N 73E	164	Amu Darya (riv., Asia)	40N 62E	163
Al Fashir, Sudan (city)	14N 25E	167	Amur (riv., Asia)	52N 156E	163
Al Fayyum, Egypt (city)	29N 31E	167	Anadyr, Gulf of	35N 175W	163
Al Manamah, Bahrain (city, nat. cap.)	26N 50E	164	Anchorage, AK (city)	61N 150W	155 inset
Alabama (st., US)	33N 87W	155	Andaman Islands	12N 92E	163
Alagoas (st., Brazil)	9S 37W	158	Andaman Islands	12N 92E	163 inset
Alaska (st., US)	63N 153W	155 inset	Andaman Sea	12N 95E	163
Alaska Peninsula	57N 155W	154	Andes Mountains	25S 70W	157
Alaska Range	60N 150W	154	Angara (riv., Asia)	60N 100E	163
Alaska, Gulf of	58N 150W	155 inset	Angel Falls	6N 62W	157
Albania (country)	41N 20E	161	Angola (country)	11S 18E	167
Albany, Australia (city)	35S 118E	170	Ankara, Turkey (city, nat. cap.)	40N 33E	164
Albany, New York (city, st. cap., US)	43N 74W	155	Annam Cordillera	17N 107E	163
Albert Edward, Mt. 13,090	8S 147E	169	Annapolis, Maryland (city, st. cap., US)	39N 76W	155
Albert, Lake	2N 30E	166	Antananarivo, Madagascar (city, nat. cap.)	19S 48E	167
Alberta (prov., Can.)	55N 117W	155	Antarctic Peninsula	69S 65W	173
Albuquerque, NM	35N 107W	155	Antofogasta, Chile (city)	24S 70W	158
Aldabra Islands	9S 44E	167	Antwerp, Belgium (city)	51N 4E	161

The geographic index contains approximately 1,500 names of cities, states, countries, rivers, lakes, mountain ranges, oceans, capes, bays, and other geographic features. The name of each geographical feature in the index is accompanied by a geographical coordinate (latitude and longitude) in degrees and by the page number of the primary map on which the geographical feature appears. Where the geographical coordinates are for specific places or points, such as a city or a mountain peak, the latitude and longitude figures give the location of the map symbol denoting that point. Thus, Los Angeles, California, is at 34N and 118W and the location of Mt. Everest is 28N and 87E.

The coordinates for political features (countries or states) or physical features (oceans, deserts) that are areas rather than points are given according to the location of the name of the feature on the map, except in those cases where the name of the feature is separated from the feature (such as a country's name appearing over an adjacent ocean area because of space requirements). In such cases, the feature's coordinates will indicate the location of the center of the feature. The coordinates for the Sahara Desert will lead the reader to the place name "Sahara Desert" on the map; the coordinates for North Carolina will show the center location of the state since the name appears over the adjacent Atlantic Ocean. Finally, the coordinates for geographical features that are lines rather than points or areas will also appear near the center of the text identifying the geographical feature.

Alphabetizing follows general conventions; the names of physical features such as lakes, rivers, mountains are given as: proper name, followed by the generic name. Thus "Mount Everest" is listed as "Everest, Mt." Where an article such as "the," "le," or "al" appears in a geographic name, the name is alphabetized according to the article. Hence, "La Paz" is found under "L" and not under "P."

GEOGRAPHIC INDEX

NAME/DESCRIPTION	LATITUDE & LONGITUDE	PAGE	NAME/DESCRIPTION	LATITUDE & LONGITUDE	PAGE
Appalachian Mountains	37N 80W	154	Baffin Island	70N 72W	154
Appenines Mountains	32N 14E	160	Baghdad, Iraq (city, nat. cap.)	33N 44E	164
Arabian Desert	25N 33E	166	Bahamas (island)	25N 75W	154
Arabian Sea	18N 61E	163	Bahia (st., Brazil)	13S 42W	158
Aracaju, Sergipe (city, st. cap., Braz.)	11S 37W	158	Bahia Blanca, Argentina (city)	39S 62W	158
Arafura Sea	9S 133E	169	Bahrain	26N 50E	164
Araguaia, Rio (riv., Brazil)	10S 50W	157	Baikal, Lake	52N 105E	163
Arakan Yoma	19N 94E	163	Baja California (st., Mex.)	30N 110W	155
Aral Sea	45N 60E	163	Baja California Sur (st., Mex.)	25N 110W	155
Arctic Ocean	75N 160W	173	Baku, Azerbaijan (city, nat. cap.)	40N 50E	161
Arequipa, Peru (city)	16S 71W	158	Balearic Islands	29N 3E	160
Argentina (country)	39S 67W	158	Balkan Peninsula	40N 21E	160
Arizona (st., US)	34N 112W	155	Balkash, Lake	47N 75E	163
Arkansas (st., US)	37N 94W	155	Ballarat, Aust. (city)	38S 144E	170
Arkhangelsk, Russia (city)	75N 160W	161	Balleny Islands	67S 163E	173
Armenia (country)	40N 45E	161	Baltic Sea	56N 18E	160
Arnhem Land	12S 133E	169	Baltimore, MD (city)	39N 77W	155
Arnhem, Cape	11S 139E	170	Bamako, Mali (city, nat. cap.)	13N 8W	167
Arno (riv., Europe)	44N 11E	160	Banda Sea	5N 127E	163 inset
Aru Islands	6S 134E	163 inset	Bandar Seri Begawan, Brunei (city, nat. cap.)	4N 114E	164 inset
Aruwimi (riv., Africa)	2N 27E	166	Bangalore, India (city)	13N 75E	164
As Sudd	9N 26E	166	Banghazi, Libya (city)	32N 20E	167
Ascension (island)	9S 13W	166	Bangkok, Thailand (city, nat. cap.)	14N 100E	164
Ashburton (riv., Australasia)	23S 115W	170	Bangladesh (country)	23N 92E	164
Ashkhabad, Turkmenistan (city, nat. cap.)	38N 58E	164	Bangui, Cent. African Rep. (city, nat. cap.)	4N 19E	167
Asmera, Eritrea (city, nat. cap.)	15N 39E	167	Bani (riv., Africa)	14n 4W	166
Astana, Kazakhstan (city)	51N 72E	164	Banjul, Gambia (city, nat. cap.)	13N 17W	167
Astrakhan, Russia (city)	46N 48E	161	Banks Island	73N 125W	154
Asuncion, Paraguay (city, nat. cap.)	25S 57W	158	Barbados (country)	13N 60W	158
Aswan, Egypt (city)	24N 33E	167	Barcelona, Spain (city)	41N 2E	161
Asyut, Egypt (city)	27N 31E	167	Barents Sea	69N 40E	163
Atacama Desert	23S 70W	157	Barwon (riv., Australasia)	29S 148E	170
Athabasca, Lake (lake, N.Am.)	60N 109W	154	Bass Strait	40S 146E	169
Athabaska (riv., N.Am.)	58N 114W	154	Baton Rouge, Louisiana (city, st. cap., US)	30N 91W	155
Athens, Greece (city, nat. cap.)	38N 24E	161	Beaufort Sea	72N 135W	154
Atlanta, Georgia (city, st. cap., US)	34N 84W	155	Beijing, China (city, nat. cap.)	40N 116E	164
Atlantic Ocean	30N 40W	154	Beirut, Lebanon (city, nat. cap.)	34N 35E	164
Atlas Mountains	31N 6W	166	Belarus (country)	52N 27E	161
Auckland Islands	50S 166E	169	Belém, Para (city, st. cap., Braz.)	1S 48W	158
Auckland, New Zealand (city)	37S 175E	170	Belfast, Northern Ireland, UK (city)	55N 6W	161
Augusta, Maine (city, st. cap., US)	44N 70W	155	Belgium (country)	51N 4E	161
Austin, Texas (city, st. cap., US)	30N 98W	155	Belgrade, Serbia (city, nat. cap.)	45N 21E	161
Australia (country)	20S 135W	170	Belhuka, Mt. 14,483	50N 86E	163
Austria (country)	47N 14E	161	Belize (country)	18S 102W	155
Azerbaijan (country)	38N 48E	161	Bellinghausen Sea	72S 85W	173
Azov, Sea of	48N 36E	161	Belmopan, Belize (city, nat. cap.)	18S 89W	155
Bab el Mandeb (strait)	13N 42E	167	Belo Horizonte, M.G. (city, st. cap., Braz.)	20S 43W	158
Baffin Bay	74N 65W	154	Belyando (riv., Australasia)	22S 147W	170

GEOGRAPHIC INDEX

NAME/DESCRIPTION	LATITUDE & LONGITUDE	PAGE
Bengal, Bay of	15N 90E	163
Benguela, Angola (city)	13S 13E	167
Beni, Rio (riv., S.Am.)	14S 67W	157
Benin (country)	10N 4E	167
Benin City, Nigeria (city)	6N 6E	167
Benue (riv., Africa)	8N 9E	166
Bergen, Norway (city)	60N 5E	161
Bering Sea	57N 175W	154
Bering Strait	65N 168W	163
Berkner Island	79S 47W	173
Berlin, Germany (city)	52N 13E	161
Bermuda (island)	30S 66W	154
Bern, Switzerland (city, nat. cap.)	46N 7E	161
Bhutan (country)	28N 110E	164
Bie Plateau	13S 16E	166
Bilbao, Spain (city)	43N 2W	161
Billings, MT (city)	46N 108W	155
Birmingham, AL (city)	34N 87W	155
Birmingham, England, UK (city)	52N 2W	161
Biscay, Bay of	45N 5W	160
Bishkek, Kyrgyzstan (city, nat. cap.)	43N 75E	164
Bismarck Archipelago	4S 147E	170
Bismarck Range	6S 145E	170
Bismarck, North Dakota (city, st. cap., US)	47N 101W	155
Bissau, Guinea-Bissau (city, nat. cap.)	12N 16W	167
Black Sea	46N 34E	160
Blanc, Cape	21N 18W	166
Blue Mountains	33S 150E	170
Blue Nile (riv., Africa)	10N 36E	166
Boa Vista do Rio Branco, Roraima (city, st. cap., Braz.)	3N 61W	158
Boise, Idaho (city, st. cap., US)	44N 116W	155
Bolivia (country)	17S 65W	158
Boma, Congo Republic (city)	5S 13E	167
Bombay, (Mumbai) India (city)	19N 73E	164
Bonn, Germany (city)	51N 7E	161
Bordeaux, France (city)	45N 0	161
Borneo (island)	0 11E	163
Bosnia and Herzegovina (country)	45N 18E	161
Bosporus, Strait of	41N 29E	160
Boston, Massachusetts (city, st. cap., US)	42N 71W	155
Botany Bay	35S 153E	170
Bothnia, Gulf of	62N 20E	160
Botswana (country)	23S 25E	167
Bougainville (island)	6S 155E	169
Brahmaputra (riv., Asia)	30N 100E	163
Brasilia, Brazil (city, nat. cap.)	16S 48W	158
Bratislava, Slovakia (city, nat. cap.)	48N 17E	161
Brazil (country)	10S 52W	158

NAME/DESCRIPTION	LATITUDE & LONGITUDE	PAGE
Brazilian Highlands	18S 45W	157
Brazzaville, Congo (city, nat. cap.)	4S 15E	167
Brest, France (city)	48N 4W	161
Brisbane, Queensland (city, st. cap., Aust.)	27S 153E	170
British Columbia (prov., Can.)	54N 130W	155
Brooks Range	67N 155W	154
Brunei (country)	4N 114E	164 inset
Brussels, Belgium (city, nat. cap.)	51N 4E	161
Bucharest, Romania (city, nat. cap.)	44N 26E	161
Budapest, Hungary (city, nat. cap.)	47N 19E	161
Buenos Aires (st., Argentina)	36S 60W	158
Buenos Aires, Argentina (city, nat. cap.)	34S 58W	158
Buffalo, NY (city)	43N 79W	155
Bug (riv., Europe)	54N 24E	160
Bujumbura, Burundi (city, nat. cap.)	3S 29E	167
Bulgaria (country)	44N 26E	161
Bur Sudan, Sudan (city)	19N 37E	167
Burdekin (riv., Australasia)	19S 146W	170
Burkina Faso (country)	11N 2W	167
Buru (island)	4S 127E	169
Burundi (country)	4S 30E	167
Cairns, Aust. (city)	17S 145E	170
Cairo, Egypt (city, nat. cap.)	30N 31E	167
Calgary, Canada (city)	51N 114W	155
Cali, Colombia (city)	3N 76W	158
Calicut, India (city)	11N 76E	164
California (st., US)	35N 120W	155
California, Gulf of	29N 110W	154
Callao, Peru (city)	13S 77W	158
Camarvon, Australia (city)	25S 113E	170
Cambodia (country)	10N 106E	164
Cameroon (country)	5N 13E	167
Campeche (st., Mex.)	19N 90W	155
Campeche, Campeche (city, st. cap., Mex.)	19N 90W	155
Campo Grande, M.G.S. (city, st. cap., Braz.)	20S 55W	158
Canada (country)	52N 100W	155
Canadian Shield	55N 95W	154
Canary Islands	29N 18W	166
Canberra, Australia (city, nat. cap.)	35S 149E	170
Cape Adams	75S 62W	173
Cape Colbeck	78S 158W	173
Cape Norvegia	71S 12E	173
Cape Poinsett	65S 113E	173
Cape Town, South Africa (city)	34S 18E	167
Cape York Peninsula	13S 142E	169
Caracas, Venezuela (city, nat. cap.)	10N 67W	158
Caribbean Sea	18N 75W	157
Carpathian Mountains	48N 24E	160

GEOGRAPHIC INDEX

NAME/DESCRIPTION	LATITUDE & LONGITUDE	PAGE
Carpentaria, Gulf of	14S 140E	169
Carson City, Nevada (city, st. cap., US)	39N 120W	155
Cartagena, Colombia (city)	10N 76W	158
Cascade Range	45N 120W	154
Caspian Depression	49N 48E	163
Caspian Sea	42N 48E	163
Catamarca (st., Argentina)	25S 70W	158
Catamarca, Catamarca (city, st. cap., Argen.)	28S 66W	158
Caucasus Mountains	42N 40E	163
Cayenne, French Guiana (city, nat. cap.)	5N 52W	158
Ceará (st., Brazil)	4S 40W	158
Celebes (island)	0 120E	163 inset
Celebes Sea	2N 120E	163
Celebes Sea	3N 122E	163
Celtic Sea	51N 7W	160
Central African Republic (country)	5N 20E	167
Central Massif	45N 3E	160
Central Siberian Plateau	66N 100E	163
Ceram (island)	3S 129E	163
Chaco (st., Argentina)	25S 60W	158
Chad (country)	15N 20E	167
Chad, Lake	12N 12E	166
Changchun, China (city)	44N 125E	164
Channel Islands	49N 2W	160
Charcot Island	69S 75W	173
Chari (riv., Africa)	11N 16E	166
Charleston, SC (city)	33N 80W	155
Charleston, West Virginia (city, st. cap., US)	38N 82W	155
Charlotte Waters, Aust. (city)	26S 135E	170
Charlotte, NC (city)	35N 81W	155
Charlottetown, P.E.I. (city, prov. cap., Can.)	46N 63W	155
Chelyabinsk, Russia (city)	55N 61E	161
Chengdu, China (city)	30N 104E	164
Chetumal, Quintana Roo (city, st. cap., Mex.)	19N 88W	155
Cheyenne, Wyoming (city, st. cap., US)	41N 105W	155
Chiapas (st., Mex.)	17N 92W	155
Chicago, IL (city)	42N 87W	155
Chiclayo, Peru (city)	7S 80W	158
Chihuahua (st., Mex.)	30N 110W	155
Chihuahua, Chihuahua (city, st. cap., Mex.)	29N 106W	155
Chile (country)	32S 75W	158
Chiloe (island)	43S 74W	157
Chilpancingo, Guerrero (city, st. cap., Mex.)	17N 99W	155
China (country)	38N 105E	164
Chisinau, Moldova (city, nat. cap.)	47N 29E	161
Choiseul (island)	7S 157E	169
Chongqing, China (city)	30N 107E	164
Chonos Archipelago	45S 74W	157

NAME/DESCRIPTION	LATITUDE & LONGITUDE	PAGE
Christchurch, New Zealand (city)	43S 173E	170
Chubut (st., Argentina)	44S 70W	158
Cincinnati, OH (city)	39N 84W	155
Cleveland (city)	41N 82W	155
Coahuila (st., Mex.)	30N 105W	155
Coast Mountains	55N 130W	154
Coast Ranges	40N 120W	154
Coastal Plain	31N 90W	154
Coats Land	77S 15E	173
Cocos Islands	12S 97E	172
Cod, Cape	42N 70W	154
Colima (st., Mex.)	18N 104W	155
Colima, Colima (city, st. cap., Mex.)	19N 104W	155
Colombia (country)	4N 73W	158
Colombo, Sri Lanka (city, nat. cap.)	7N 80E	164
Colorado (riv., N.Am.)	36N 110W	154
Colorado (st., US)	38N 104W	155
Colorado Plateau	39N 113W	154
Columbia (riv., N.Am.)	45N 120W	154
Columbia Plateau	43N 118W	154
Columbia, South Carolina (city, st. cap., US)	34N 81W	155
Columbus, Ohio (city, st. cap., US)	40N 83W	155
Comodoro Rivadavia, Argentina (city)	68S 70W	158
Comoros (country)	12S 44E	167
Conakry, Guinea (city, nat. cap.)	9N 14W	167
Concord, New Hampshire (city, st. cap., US)	43N 71W	155
Congo (riv., Africa)	3N 22E	166
Congo Basin	4N 22E	166
Congo Republic (country)	3S 15E	167
Congo, Democratic Republic of (country)	5S 15E	167
Connecticut (st., US)	43N 76W	155
Cook Strait	42S 175E	170
Copenhagen, Denmark (city, nat. cap.)	56N 12E	161
Copiapo, Chile (city)	27S 70W	158
Coquimbo, Chile (city)	30S 70W	158
Coral Sea	15S 155E	169
Cordoba (st., Argentina)	32S 67W	158
Cordoba, Cordoba (city, st. cap., Argen.)	32S 64W	158
Corrientes (st., Argentina)	27S 60W	158
Corrientes, Corrientes (city, st. cap., Argen.)	27S 59W	158
Corsica (island)	42N 9E	160
Cosmoledo Islands	9S 48E	167
Costa Rica (country)	15N 84W	155
Côte d'Ivoire (country)	7N 86W	167
Crete (island)	36N 25W	160
Croatia (country)	46N 20W	161
Cuando (riv., Africa)	10S 16E	166
Cuanza (riv., Africa)	9S 13E	166

GEOGRAPHIC INDEX

NAME/DESCRIPTION	LATITUDE & LONGITUDE	PAGE	NAME/DESCRIPTION	LATITUDE & LONGITUDE	PAGE
Cuba (country)	22N 78W	155	Donetsk, Ukraine (city)	48N 38E	161
Cuiabá , Mato Grosso (city, st. cap., Braz.)	16S 56W	158	Douro (riv., Europe)	41N 8W	160
Cuidad Victoria, Tamaulipas (city, st. cap., Mex.)	24N 99W	155	Dover, Delaware (city, st. cap., US)	39N 75W	155
Culiacan, Sinaloa (city, st. cap., Mex.)	25N 107W	155	Drake Passage	58S 63W	173
Cunene (riv., Africa)	17S 11E	166	Drakensberg Mountains	30S 30E	166
Curitiba, Paraná (city, st. cap., Braz.)	26S 49W	158	Drava (riv., Europe)	47N 17E	160
Cusco, Peru (city)	14S 72W	158	Dronning Maud Land	72S 10E	173
Cyprus (country)	36N 34E	161	Dublin, Ireland (city, nat. cap.)	53N 6W	161
Czechia (country)	50N 16E	161	Duluth, MN (city)	47N 92W	155
D'Entrecasteaux Islands	10S 153E	170	Dunedin, New Zealand (city)	46S 171E	170
Dabie Shan	31N 115E	163	Durango (st., Mex.)	25N 108W	155
Dakar, Senegal (city, nat. cap.)	15N 17W	167	Durango, Durango (city, st. cap., Mex.)	24N 105W	155
Dakhla, Western Sahara (city)	24N 16W	167	Durban, South Africa (city)	30S 31E	167
Dallas, TX (city)	33N 97W	155	Dushanbe, Tajikistan (city, nat. cap.)	39N 69E	164
Daly (riv., Australasia)	14S 132E	170	Dzhugdzhur Range	58N 138E	163
Damascus, Syria (city, nat. cap.)	34N 36E	164	East Cape (NZ)	37S 180E	170
Danube (riv., Europe)	44N 24E	160	East China Sea	30N 128E	163
Danube (riv., Europe)	45N 25E	160	East Siberian Sea	75N 170E	163
Dar es Salaam, Tanzania (city, nat. cap.)	7S 39E	167	Easter Island	28S 109W	172
Dardanelles, Strait	40N 26E	160	Eastern Ghats	15N 80E	163
Darfur	10N 23E	166	Ebro (riv., Europe)	42N 1W	160
Darling (riv., Australasia)	35S 144E	169	Ecuador (country)	3S 78W	158
Darling Range	33S 116W	170	Edmonton, Alberta (city, prov. Cap., Can.)	54N 114W	155
Darwin, Northern Terr. (city, st. cap., Aust.)	12S 131E	170	Edward, Lake	0 30E	166
Dasht-e Lut	30N 58E	163	Egypt (country)	23N 30E	167
Davis Strait	57N 59W	154	El Aaiun, Western Sahara (city)	27N 13W	167
Deccan Plateau	20N 80E	163	El Djouf	25N 15W	166
DeGrey (riv., Australasia)	22S 120E	170	El Paso, TX (city)	32N 106W	155
Delaware (st., US)	38N 75W	155	El Salvador (country)	15N 90W	155
Delgado, Cape	11S 41E	166	Elbe (riv., Europe)	54N 10E	160
Delhi, India (city)	30N 78E	164	Elburz Mountains	28N 60E	163
Denmark (country)	55N 10E	161	Ellesmere Island	80N 79W	154
Denver, Colorado (city, st. cap., US)	40N 105W	155	Emi Koussi 11,204	19N 18E	166
Derby, Australia (city)	17S 124E	170	Enderby Land	51S 59E	173
Des Moines, Iowa (city, st. cap., US)	42N 92W	155	English Channel	50N 0	160
Desna (riv., Europe)	52N 33E	160	Entre Rios (st., Argentina)	32S 60W	158
Detroit, MI (city)	42N 83W	155	Equatorial Guinea (country)	3N 10E	167
Devon Island	75N 87W	154	Erie, Lake (lake, N.Am.)	42N 85W	154
Dhaka, Bangladesh (city, nat. cap.)	24N 90E	164	Eritrea (country)	16N 38E	167
Dili, Timor-Leste (city, nat. cap.)	8S 125E	164 inset	Espiritu Santo (island)	15S 168E	170
Djibouti (country)	12N 43E	167	Espiritu Santo (st., Brazil)	20S 42W	158
Djibouti, Djibouti (city, nat. cap.)	12N 43E	167	Essen, Germany (city)	52N 8E	161
Dnieper (riv., Europe)	50N 34E	160	Estonia (country)	60N 26E	161
Dnipropetrovsk, Ukraine (city)	48N 35E	161	Ethiopia (country)	8N 40E	167
Dodoma, Tanzania (city)	6S 36E	167	Ethiopian Highlands	8N 40E	166
Doha (city, nat. cap.)	25N 51E	164	Euphrates (riv., Asia)	28N 50E	163
Dominican Republic (country)	20N 70W	155	Everard Ranges	28S 135E	170
Don (riv., Europe)	53N 39E	161	Everard, Lake	32S 135E	170

GEOGRAPHIC INDEX

NAME/DESCRIPTION	LATITUDE & LONGITUDE	PAGE
Everest, Mt. 29,028	28N 84E	163
Eyre, Lake	29S 136E	170
Faeroe Islands	62N 11W	160
Fairbanks, AK (city)	63N 146W	155
Falkland Islands (Islas Malvinas)	52S 60W	157
Farewell, Cape (NZ)	40S 170E	170
Fargo, ND (city)	47N 97W	155
Farquhar, Cape	24S 114E	170
Fiji (country)	17S 178E	170
Finland (country)	62N 28E	161
Finland, Gulf of	60N 20E	160
Fitzroy (riv., Australasia)	17S 125E	170
Flinders (island)	40S 148E	169
Flinders Ranges	31S 139E	170
Flores (island)	8S 121E	163
Florianópolis, Sta. Catarina (city, st. cap., Braz.)	27S 48W	158
Florida (st., US)	28N 83W	155
Florida Peninsula	26N 82W	154
Florida, Straits of	28N 80W	154
Fly (riv., Australasia)	8S 143E	170
Forel, Mount 11,024	67N 35W	173
Formosa (st., Argentina)	23S 60W	158
Formosa, Formosa (city, st. cap., Argen.)	27S 58W	158
Fort Worth, TX (city)	33N 97W	155
Fortaleza, Ceara (city, st. cap., Braz.)	4S 39W	158
Foxe Basin	66N 77W	154
France (country)	46N 4E	161
Frankfort, Kentucky (city, st. cap., US)	38N 85W	155
Frankfurt, Germany (city)	50N 9E	161
Franz Josef Land (island)	80N 40E	163
Fraser (riv., N.Am.)	52N 122W	154
Fredericton, N.B. (city, prov. Cap., Can.)	46N 67W	155
Freetown, Sierra Leone (city, nat. cap.)	8N 13W	167
Fremantle, Australia (city)	33S 116E	170
French Guiana (dept., France)	4N 52W	158
Fria, Cape	18S 12E	167
Fuzhou, China (city)	26N 119E	164
Gabes, Gulf of	33N 12E	167
Gabes, Tunisia (city)	34N 10E	167
Gabon (country)	2S 12E	167
Gaborone, Botswana (city, nat. cap.)	25S 25E	167
Gairdiner, Lake	32S 136E	170
Galveston, TX (city)	29N 95W	155
Gambia (country)	13N 15W	167
Gambia (riv., Africa)	13N 15W	166
Ganges (riv., Asia)	27N 85E	163
Ganges Plain	27N 82E	163
Garonne (riv., Europe)	45N 1E	160

NAME/DESCRIPTION	LATITUDE & LONGITUDE	PAGE
Gascoyne (riv., Australasia)	25S 115E	170
Gdansk, Poland (city)	54N 19E	161
Geelong, Aust. (city)	38S 144E	170
Gees Gwardafuy (island)	15N 50E	167
Geographe Bay	35S 115E	169
George V Land	68S 148E	173
Georgetown, Guyana (city, nat. cap.)	8N 58W	158
Georgia (country)	42N 44E	161
Georgia (st., US)	30N 82W	155
Germany (country)	50N 12E	161
Ghana (country)	8N 3W	167
Gibraltar, Strait of	37N 6W	160
Gibson Desert	24S 124E	169
Gilbert (riv., Australasia)	8S 142E	170
Glama (riv., Europe)	61N 11E	160
Glasgow, Scotland, UK (city)	56N 6W	161
Gobi Desert	48N 105E	163
Godavari (riv., Asia)	18N 82E	163
Goiania, Goias (city, st. cap., Braz.)	17S 49W	158
Goiás (st., Brazil)	15S 50W	158
Good Hope, Cape of	33S 18E	166
Goteborg, Sweden (city)	58N 12E	161
Gotland (island)	57N 20E	160
Gran Chaco	23S 70W	157
Grand Erg Occidental	29N 0	166
Grand Erg Oriental	30N 7E	166
Great Artesian Basin	25S 145E	169
Great Australian Bight	33S 130E	169
Great Barrier Reef	15S 145E	169
Great Basin	39N 117W	154
Great Basin	40N 116W	154
Great Bear Lake (lake, N.Am.)	67N 120W	154
Great Dividing Range	20S 145E	169
Great Indian Desert	25N 72E	163
Great Plains	40N 105W	154
Great Salt Lake (lake, N.Am.)	40N 113W	154
Great Sandy Desert	23S 125E	169
Great Slave Lake (lake, N.Am.)	62N 110W	154
Great Victoria Desert	30S 125E	169
Greater Khingan Range	50N 120E	163
Greece (country)	39N 21E	161
Greenland (island)	78N 40W	154
Gregory Range	18S 145E	170
Grey Range	26S 145E	170
Guadalajara, Jalisco (city, st. cap., Mex.)	21N 103W	155
Guadalcanal (island)	9S 160E	169
Guadalquivir (riv., Europe)	37N 5W	160
Guadiana (riv., Europe)	39N 6W	160

GEOGRAPHIC INDEX

NAME/DESCRIPTION	LATITUDE & LONGITUDE	PAGE	NAME/DESCRIPTION	LATITUDE & LONGITUDE	PAGE
Guanajuato (st., Mex.)	22N 100W	155	Honduras (country)	16N 87W	155
Guanajuato, Guanajuato (city, st. cap., Mex.)	21N 101W	155	Honiara, Solomon Islands (city, nat. cap.)	9S 160E	170
Guangzhou, China (city)	23N 113E	164	Honolulu, Hawaii (city, st. cap., US)	21N 158W	155 inset
Guatemala (country)	14N 90W	155	Honshu (island)	38N 140E	163
Guatemala, Guatemala (city, nat. cap.)	15N 91W	155	Horn of Africa	10N 50E	166
Guayaquil, Ecuador (city)	2S 80W	158	Horn, Cape	55S 70W	157
Guayaquil, Gulf of	3S 83W	157	Houston, TX (city)	30N 95W	155
Guerrero (st., Mex.)	18N 102W	155	Howe, Cape	37S 150E	170
Guiana Highlands	5N 60W	157	Huambo, Angola (city)	13S 16E	167
Guinea (country)	10N 10W	167	Huang He (riv., Asia)	30N 105E	163
Guinea, Gulf of	3N 0	166	Hudson Bay	60N 90W	154
Guinea-Bissau (country)	12N 15W	167	Hudson Strait	63N 70W	154
Gunnbjørn Fjeld 12,139	69N 30W	173	Hue, Vietnam (city)	15N 110E	164
Guyana (country)	6N 57W	158	Hughes, Aust. (city)	30S 130E	170
Gydan Range	62N 155E	163	Hungary (country)	48N 20E	161
Hadejia (riv., Africa)	12N 10E	166	Huon Gulf	7S 147E	169
Hainan (island)	19N 110E	163	Huron, Lake (lake, N.Am.)	45N 85W	154
Haiti (country)	18N 72W	155	Hyderabad, India (city)	17N 79E	164
Hakodate, Japan (city)	42N 140E	164	Ibadan, Nigeria (city)	7N 4E	167
Halifax Bay	18S 146E	170	Iberian Peninsula	42N 4W	160
Halifax, Nova Scotia (city, prov. Cap., Can.)	45N 64W	155	Iceland (country)	64N 20W	161
Halmahera (island)	1N 128E	163 inset	Idaho (st., US)	43N 113W	155
Hamburg, Germany (city)	54N 10E	161	Iguazu Falls	25S 55W	157
Hammersley Range	23S 116W	170	Illinois (st., US)	44N 90W	155
Hangay Mountains	16N 98E	163	India (country)	23N 80E	164
Hanoi, Vietnam (city, nat. cap.)	21N 106E	164	Indiana (st., US)	46N 88W	155
Harare, Zimbabwe (city, nat. cap.)	18S 31E	167	Indianapolis, Indiana (city, st. cap., US)	40N 86W	155
Harbin, China (city)	46N 126E	164	Indonesia (country)	2S 120E	164
Harer, Ethiopia (city)	10N 42E	167	Indus (riv., Asia)	25N 70E	163
Hargeysa, Somalia (city)	9N 44E	167	Ionian Sea	38N 19E	160
Harrisburg, Pennsylvania (city, st. cap., US)	40N 77W	155	Iowa (st., US)	43N 95W	155
Hartford, Connecticut (city, st. cap., US)	42N 73W	155	Iqaluit, Nunavut (city, terr. cap., Can.)	63N 68W	155
Hatteras, Cape	32N 73W	154	Iquitos, Peru (city)	4S 74W	158
Havana, Cuba (city, nat. cap.)	23N 82W	155	Iran (country)	30N 55E	164
Hawaii (st., US)	21N 156W	155 inset	Iraq (country)	30N 50E	164
Hawaiian Islands	23N 152W	172	Ireland (country)	54N 8W	161
Hebrides Islands	58N 8W	160	Irkutsk, Russia (city)	52N 104E	164
Hejaz	30N 40E	163	Irrawaddy (riv., Asia)	25N 95E	163
Helena, Montana (city, st. cap., US)	47N 112W	155	Irtysh (riv., Asia)	50N 70E	163
Helsinki, Finland (city, nat. cap.)	60N 25E	161	Islamabad, Pakistan (city, nat. cap.)	34N 73E	164
Herat Afghanistan (city)	34N 62E	164	Israel (country)	31N 36E	161
Hermosillo, Sonora (city, st. cap., Mex.)	29N 111W	155	Istanbul, Turkey (city)	41N 29E	161
Hidalgo (st., Mex.)	20N 98W	155	Italy (country)	42N 12E	161
Himalayas	26N 80E	163	Jackson, Mississippi (city, st. cap., US)	32N 84W	155
Hindu Kush	30N 70E	163	Jacksonville, FL (city)	30N 82W	155
Ho Chi Minh City, Vietnam (city)	11N 107E	164	Jakarta, Indonesia (city, nat. cap.)	6S 107E	164 inset
Hobart, Tasmania (city, st. cap., Aust.)	43S 147E	170	Jalisco (st., Mex.)	20N 105W	155
Hokkaido (island)	43N 142E	163	Jamaica (country)	18N 78W	155

GEOGRAPHIC INDEX

NAME/DESCRIPTION	LATITUDE & LONGITUDE	PAGE
James Bay	54N 81W	154
Japan (country)	35N 138E	164
Japan, Sea of	40N 135E	163
Japura, Rio (riv., S.Am.)	3S 65W	157
Java (island)	6N 110E	163 inset
Jayapura, Indonesia (city)	3S 141E	170
Jebel Toubkal 13,671	31N 8W	166
Jefferson City, Missouri (city, st. cap., US)	39N 92W	155
Jerusalem, Israel (city, nat. cap.)	32N 35E	161
João Pessoa, Paraiba (city, st. cap., Braz.)	7S 35W	158
Johannesburg, South Africa (city)	26S 27E	167
Jordan (country)	32N 36E	161
Juan Fernandez Islands	33S 80W	157
Jubba (riv., Africa)	3N 43E	166
Jujuy (st., Argentina)	23S 67W	158
Jujuy, Jujuy (city, st. cap., Argen.)	23S 66W	158
Juneau, Alaska (city, st. cap., US)	58N 134W	155
Jutland Peninsula	56N 9E	160
K2, Mt. 28,250	30N 70E	163
Kabul, Afghanistan (city, nat. cap.)	35N 69E	164
Kalahari Desert	25S 20E	166
Kalgourie-Boulder, Australia (city)	31S 121E	170
Kaliningrad, Russia (city)	55N 21E	161
Kamchatka Peninsula	55N 159E	163
Kampala, Uganda (city, nat. cap.)	0 33E	167
Kano, Nigeria (city)	12N 9E	167
Kanpur, India (city)	27N 80E	164
Kansas (st., US)	40N 98W	155
Kansas City, MO (city)	39N 95W	155
Kara Sea	69N 65E	163
Karachi, Pakistan (city)	25N 66E	164
Karakorum Range	32N 78E	164
Kasai (riv., Africa)	5S 18E	166
Kashi, China (city)	39N 76E	164
Katanga Plateau	11S 26E	166
Katherine, Aust. (city)	14S 132E	170
Kathmandu, Nepal (city, nat. cap.)	28N 85E	164
Katowice, Poland (city)	50N 19E	161
Kattegat, Strait of	57N 11E	160
Kazakh Uplands	49N 72E	163
Kazakhstan (country)	50N 70E	164
Kentucky (st., US)	37N 88W	155
Kenya (country)	0 35E	167
Kenya, Mt. 17,058	0 37E	166
Kerguélen (island)	49S 69E	172
Khabarovsk, Russia (city)	48N 135E	164
Khambhat, Gulf of	20N 73E	164
Kharkiv, Ukraine (city)	50N 36E	161

NAME/DESCRIPTION	LATITUDE & LONGITUDE	PAGE
Khartoum, Sudan (city, nat. cap.)	16N 33E	167
Kiev, Ukraine (city, nat. cap.)	50N 31E	161
Kigali, Rwanda (city, nat. cap.)	2S 30E	167
Kilimanjaro, Mt. 19,340	4N 35E	166
Kimberly Plateau	17S 127E	169
Kimberly, South Africa (city)	29S 25E	167
King Leopold Ranges	16S 125E	170
Kingston, Jamaica (city, nat. cap.)	18N 77W	155
Kinshasa, Dem. Rep. Congo (city, nat. cap.)	4S 15E	167
Kirghiz Steppe	40N 65E	163
Kirkpatrick, Mount 14,856	84S 166E	173
Kisangani, Dem. Rep. Congo (city)	1N 25E	167
Kitakyushu, Japan (city)	34N 130E	164
Kjollen Range	65N 12E	160
Knox Coast	66S 105E	173
Kobe, Japan (city)	34N 135E	164
Kodiak Island	58N 152W	154
Kola Peninsula	67N 36E	163
Kolkata (Calcutta) India (city)	23N 88E	164
Kolyma (riv., Asia)	70N 160E	163
Kolyma Range	65N 165E	163
Komsomolsk, Russia (city)	51N 137E	164
Korea Strait	32N 130W	163
Korea, North (country)	40N 128E	164
Korea, South (country)	3S 130W	164
Kosovo (country)	42N 21E	161
Kotto (riv., Africa)	7N 23E	166
Krasnoyarsk, Russia (city)	56N 93E	164
Krishna (riv., Asia)	15N 76E	163
Kuala Lumpur, Malaysia (city, nat. cap.)	3N 107E	164 inset
Kunlun Mountains	36N 90E	163
Kunming, China (city)	25N 106E	164
Kuril Islands	46N 147E	163
Kutch, Gulf of	23N 70E	164
Kuwait (country)	29N 48E	164
Kuwait, Kuwait (city, nat. cap.)	29N 48E	164
Kyoto, Japan (city)	35N 136E	164
Kyrgyzstan (country)	40N 75E	164
Kyushu (island)	30N 130W	163
La Pampa (st., Argentina)	36S 70W	158
La Paz, Baja California Sur (city, st. cap., Mex.)	24N 110W	155
La Paz, Bolivia (city, nat. cap.)	17S 68W	158
La Plata, Argentina (city)	35S 58W	158
La Rioja (st., Argentina)	30S 70W	158
La Rioja, La Rioja (city, st. cap., Argen.)	29S 67W	158
Labrador Peninsula	52N 60W	154
Labrador Sea	60N 55W	154
Lachlan (riv., Australasia)	34S 145E	170

GEOGRAPHIC INDEX

NAME/DESCRIPTION	LATITUDE & LONGITUDE	PAGE	NAME/DESCRIPTION	LATITUDE & LONGITUDE	PAGE
Ladoga, Lake	61N 31E	160	Lusaka, Zambia (city, nat. cap.)	15S 28E	167
Lagos, Nigeria (city)	7N 3E	167	Luxembourg (country)	50N 6E	161
Lahore, Pakistan (city)	34N 74E	164	Luxembourg, Luxembourg (city, nat. cap.)	50N 6E	161
Lake of the Woods	50N 92W	154	Luzon (island)	17N 121E	163
Lansing, Michigan (city, st. cap., US)	43N 85W	155	Luzon Strait	20N 121E	163
Lanzhou, China (city)	36N 104E	164	Lyon, France (city)	46N 5E	161
Laos (country)	20N 105E	164	Mac Robertson Land	70S 65E	173
Laptev Sea	73N 120E	163	Macapá, Amapa (city, st. cap., Braz.)	0 51W	158
Las Vegas, NV (city)	36N 115W	155	MacDonnell Ranges	23S 135E	169
Latvia (country)	56N 24E	161	Macedonia (country)	41N 21E	161
Le Havre, France (city)	50N 0	161	Maceió, Alagoas (city, st. cap., Braz.)	10S 36W	158
Lebanon (country)	34N 35E	161	Mackenzie (riv., N.Am.)	68N 130W	154
Leeds, England, UK (city)	54N 2W	161	Mackenzie Mountains	63N 130W	154
Lena (riv., Asia)	70N 125E	163	Macquarie (riv., Australasia)	33S 146E	170
Lesotho (country)	30S 27E	167	Madagascar (country)	20S 46E	167
Leveque, Cape	16S 123E	170	Madeira, Rio (riv., S.Am.)	5S 60W	157
Leyte (island)	12N 130E	164	Madison, Wisconsin (city, st. cap., US)	43N 89W	155
Lhasa, Tibet (China) (city)	30N 91E	164	Madras, (Chennai) India (city)	13N 80E	164
Liberia (country)	6N 10W	167	Madrid, Spain (city, nat. cap.)	40N 4W	161
Libreville, Gabon (city, nat. cap.)	0 9E	167	Mafia (island)	7S 39E	166
Libya (country)	27N 17E	167	Magdalena, Rio (riv., S.Am.)	8N 74W	157
Libyan Desert	27N 25E	166	Magellan, Strait of	54S 68W	157
Liechtenstein (country)	47N 9E	161	Main (riv., Europe)	50N 9E	160
Ligurian Sea	43N 9E	160	Maine (st., US)	46N 70W	155
Lille, France (city)	51N 3E	161	Malabo, Equatorial Guinea (city, nat. cap.)	4N 9E	167
Lilongwe, Malawi (city, nat. cap.)	14S 33E	167	Malacca, Strait of	3N 100E	163 inset
Lima, Peru (city, nat. cap.)	12S 77W	158	Malaita (island)	9S 161E	169
Limpopo (riv., Africa)	22S 30E	167	Malawi (country)	13S 35E	167
Lincoln, Nebraska (city, st. cap., US)	41N 97W	155	Malaysia (country)	3N 110E	164 inset
Lisbon, Portugal (city, nat. cap.)	39N 9W	161	Malekula (island)	16S 166E	170
Lithuania (country)	56N 24E	161	Mali (country)	17N 5W	167
Little Rock, Arkansas (city, st. cap., US)	35N 92W	155	Malta (country)	36N 16E	161
Liverpool, England, UK (city)	53N 3W	161	Managua, Nicaragua (city, nat. cap.)	12N 86W	155
Ljubljana, Slovenia (city, nat. cap.)	46N 14E	161	Manaus, Amazonas (city, st. cap., Braz.)	3S 60W	158
Llanos	33N 103W	157	Manchester, England, UK (city)	53N 2W	161
Logone (riv., Africa)	10N 14E	166	Manchurian Plain	45N 125E	163
Loire (riv., Europe)	47N 1E	160	Mandalay, Myanmar (city)	22N 96E	164
Lome, Togo (city, nat. cap.)	6N 1E	167	Mangoky (riv., Africa)	22S 46E	166
London, United Kingdom (city, nat. cap.)	51N 0	161	Manila, Philippines (city, nat. cap.)	115N 121E	164
Londonderry, Cape	14S 125E	170	Manitoba (prov., Can.)	52N 93W	155
Long Island	40N 73W	154	Maputo, Mozambique (city, nat. cap.)	26S 33E	167
Lopez, Cape	1S 8E	167	Maracaibo, Lake	10N 72W	157
Los Angeles, CA (city)	34N 118W	155	Maracaibo, Venezuela (city)	11N 72W	158
Louisiana (st., US)	30N 90W	155	Marajó Island	1S 49W	157
Lower Hutt, New Zealand (city)	45S 175E	170	Maranhao (st., Brazil)	4S 45W	158
Loyalty Islands	21S 167E	169	Maranon, Rio (riv., S.Am.)	5S 75W	157
Luanda, Angola (city, nat. cap.)	9S 13E	167	Marie Byrd Land	78S 125W	173
Lubumbashi, Dem. Rep. Congo (city)	12S 28E	167	Maritsa (riv., Europe)	42N 26E	160

GEOGRAPHIC INDEX

NAME/DESCRIPTION	LATITUDE & LONGITUDE	PAGE
Markham, Mount 14,275	83S 161E	173
Marne (riv., Europe)	49N 4E	160
Marquesas Islands	9S 139W	172
Marseille, France (city)	43N 5E	161
Marshall Islands	8N 171E	172
Maryland (st., US)	37N 76W	155
Masai Steppe	5S 35E	167
Maseru, Lesotho (city, nat. cap.)	29S 27E	167
Mashad, Iran (city)	36N 59E	164
Massachusetts (st., US)	42N 70W	155
Mato Grosso (st., Brazil)	15S 55W	158
Mato Grosso do Sul (st., Brazil)	20S 55W	158
Mato Grosso Plateau	16S 52W	157
Mauritania (country)	20N 10W	167
Mbandaka, Dem. Rep. Congo (city)	0 18E	167
McKinley, Mt. 20,320	62N 150W	154
Medellin, Colombia (city)	6N 76W	158
Mediterranean Sea	36N 16E	160
Mekong (riv., Asia)	15N 108E	163
Melanesia Islands	10S 165E	169
Melbourne, Victoria (city, st. cap., Aust.)	38S 145E	170
Melville, Cape	15S 145E	170
Memphis, TN (city)	35N 90W	155
Mendoza (st., Argentina)	35S 70W	158
Mendoza, Mendoza (city, st. cap., Argen.)	33S 69W	158
Merauke, Indonesia (city)	9S 140E	170
Merida, Yucatan (city, st. cap. Mex.)	21N 90W	155
Meuse (riv., Europe)	51N 4E	160
Mexicali, Baja California (city, st. cap., Mex.)	32N 115W	155
Mexico (country)	30N 110W	155
Mexico (st., Mex.)	18N 100W	155
Mexico City, Mexico (city, nat. cap.)	19N 99W	155
Mexico, Gulf of	26N 90W	154
Miami, FL (city)	26N 80W	155
Michigan (st., US)	45N 82W	155
Michigan, Lake (lake, N.Am.)	45N 90W	154
Michoacan (st., Mex.)	17N 107W	155
Midway Island	28N 177W	172
Milan, Italy (city)	45N 9E	161
Milwaukee, WI (city)	43N 88W	155
Minas Gerais (st., Brazil)	17S 45W	158
Mindanao (island)	8N 125E	163
Mindoro (island)	13N 120E	163
Minneapolis, MN (city)	45N 93W	155
Minnesota (st., US)	45N 90W	155
Minsk, Belarus (city, nat. cap.)	54N 28E	161
Misiones (st., Argentina)	25S 55W	158
Mississippi (riv., N.Am.)	28N 90W	154
Mississippi (st., US)	30N 90W	155
Missouri (riv., N.Am.)	41N 96W	154
Missouri (st., US)	35N 92W	155
Mitchell (riv., Australasia)	16S 143E	170
Mobile, AL (city)	31N 88W	155
Moçambique, Mozambique (city)	15S 40E	167
Mogadishu, Somalia (city, nat. cap.)	2N 45E	167
Moldova (country)	49N 28E	161
Mombasa, Kenya (city)	4S 40E	167
Monaco (country)	44N 8E	161
Monaco, Monaco (city)	44N 8E	161
Mongolia (country)	45N 100E	164
Mongolian Plateau	47N 110E	163
Monrovia, Liberia (city, nat. cap.)	6N 11W	167
Montana (st., US)	50N 110W	155
Montenegro (country)	42N 19E	161
Monterrey, Nuevo Leon (city, st. cap., Mex.)	26N 100W	155
Montevideo, Uruguay (city, nat. cap.)	35S 56W	158
Montgomery, Alabama (city, st. cap., US)	32N 86W	155
Montpelier, Vermont (city, st. cap., US)	44N 73W	155
Montreal, Canada (city)	45N 74W	155
Morava (riv., Europe)	44N 21E	160
Morelia, Michoacan (city, st. cap., Mex.)	20N 100W	155
Morelos (st., Mex.)	18N 99W	155
Morocco (country)	34N 10W	167
Moroni, Comoros (city, nat. cap.)	12S 42E	167
Moscow, Russia (city, nat. cap.)	56N 38E	161
Mozambique (country)	19N 35E	167
Mozambique Channel	19N 42E	166
Munich, Germany (city)	48N 12E	161
Murchison (riv., Australasia)	26S 115E	170
Murmansk, Russia (city)	69N 33E	161
Murray (riv., Australasia)	36S 143E	169
Murrumbidgee (riv., Australasia)	35S 146E	170
Muscat, Oman (city, nat. cap.)	23N 58E	164
Musgrave Ranges	28S 135E	170
Myanmar (Burma) (country)	20N 95E	164
N'Djamena, Chad (city, nat. cap.)	12N 15E	167
Nairobi, Kenya (city, nat. cap.)	1S 37E	167
Namib Desert	23S 10E	166
Namibe, Angola (city)	16S 13E	167
Namibia (country)	20S 16E	167
Namoi (riv., Australasia)	31S 150E	170
Nanjing, China (city)	32N 119E	164
Naples, Italy (city)	41N 14E	161
Nashville, Tennessee (city, st. cap., US)	36N 87W	155
Nasser, Lake	22N 32E	166
Natal, Rio Grande do Norte (city, st. cap., Braz.)	6S 5W	158

GEOGRAPHIC INDEX

NAME/DESCRIPTION	LATITUDE & LONGITUDE	PAGE	NAME/DESCRIPTION	LATITUDE & LONGITUDE	PAGE
Naturaliste, Cape	35S 115E	170	North Pole	90N 0	173
Nayarit (st., Mex.)	22N 106W	155	North Sea	56N 3E	160
Nebraska (st., US)	42N 100W	155	North West Cape	22S 115W	170
Negro, Rio (riv., S.Am.)	0 65W	157	Northern Territory (st., Aust.)	20S 134W	170
Negros (island)	10N 125E	163	Northwest Territories (terr. , Can.)	65N 125W	155
Nepal (country)	29N 85E	164	Norway (country)	62N 8E	161
Netherlands (country)	54N 6E	161	Norwegian Sea	65N 5E	160
Neuquen (st., Argentina)	38S 68W	158	Noth Magnetic Pole	84N 114W	173
Neuquen, Neuquen (city, st. cap., Argen.)	39S 68W	158	Nouakchott, Mauritania (city, nat. cap.)	18N 16W	167
Nevada (st., US)	37N 117W	155	Noumea, New Caledonia (city)	22S 167E	170
Nevado Huascarán 22,133	8N 79W	157	Nova Scotia (prov., Can.)	46N 67W	155
New Britain (island)	5S 152E	169	Novaya Zemlya (island)	72N 55E	163
New Brunswick (prov., Can.)	47N 67W	155	Novosibirsk, Russia (city)	55N 83E	164
New Caledonia (island)	21S 165E	169	Nubian Desert	20N 30E	166
New Delhi, India (city, nat. cap.)	29N 77E	164	Nuevo Leon (st., Mex.)	25N 100W	155
New Georgia (island)	8S 157E	170	Nullarbor Plain	34S 125W	169
New Guinea (island)	5S 142E	169	Nunavut (terr., Can)	70N 95w	155
New Hampshire (st., US)	45N 70W	155	Nyasa, Lake	10S 35E	166
New Hanover (island)	3S 153E	170	Oakland, CA (city)	38N 122W	155
New Hebrides (island)	15S 165E	170	Oates Land	69S 159E	173
New Ireland (island)	4S 154E	169	Oaxaca (st., Mex.)	17N 97W	155
New Jersey (st., US)	40N 75W	155	Oaxaca, Oaxaca (city, st. cap., Mex.)	17N 97W	155
New Mexico (st., US)	30N 108W	155	Ob (riv., Asia)	60N 78E	163
New Orleans, LA (city)	30N 90W	155	Oder (riv., Europe)	51N 16E	160
New Siberian Islands	74N 140E	163	Ohio (riv., N.Am.)	38N 85W	154
New South Wales (st., Aust.)	35S 145E	170	Ohio (st., US)	42N 85W	155
New York (city)	41N 74W	155	Okavango Delta	21S 23E	166
New York (st., US)	45N 75W	155	Okhotsk, Russia (city)	59N 140E	164
New Zealand (country)	40S 170E	170	Okhotsk, Sea of	57N 150E	163
Newcastle, Aust. (city)	33S 152E	170	Oklahoma (st., US)	36N 95W	155
Newcastle, England, UK (city)	55N 2W	161	Oklahoma City, Oklahoma (city, st. cap., US)	35N 98W	155
Newfoundland (island)	49N 56W	154	Olympia, Washington (city, st. cap., US)	47N 123W	155
Newfoundland (prov., Can.)	53N 60W	155	Omaha, NE (city)	41N 96W	155
Niamey, Niger (city, nat. cap.)	14N 2E	167	Oman (country)	20N 55E	164
Nicaragua (country)	10N 90W	155	Oman, Gulf of	23N 55E	163
Nicobar Islands	5N 93E	163	Omdurman, Sudan (city)	16N 32E	167
Niger (country)	10N 8E	167	Omsk, Russia (city)	55N 73E	164
Niger (riv., Africa)	12N 0	166	Onega, Lake	62N 35E	160
Nigeria (country)	8N 5E	167	Ontario (prov., Can.)	50N 90W	154
Nile (riv., Africa)	25N 31E	166	Ontario, Lake (lake, N.Am.)	45N 77W	154
Nizhny-Novgorod, Russia (city)	56N 44E	161	Oodnadatta, Aust. (city)	28S 135E	170
Norfolk, VA (city)	37N 76W	155	Oran, Algeria (city)	36N 1W	167
North Cape	36N 174W	170	Orange (riv., Africa)	27S 18E	166
North Carolina (st., US)	30N 78W	155	Oregon (st., US)	46N 120W	155
North China Plain	35N 117E	163	Orinoco, Rio (riv., S.Am.)	8N 65W	157
North Dakota (st., US)	49N 100W	155	Orkney Islands	60N 0	160
North European Plain	54N 15E	160	Osaka, Japan (city)	35N 135E	164
North Island	37S 175W	169	Oslo, Norway (city, nat. cap.)	60N 11W	161

GEOGRAPHIC INDEX

NAME/DESCRIPTION	LATITUDE & LONGITUDE	PAGE
Ottawa, Canada (city, nat. cap.)	45N 76W	155
Otway, Cape	40S 142W	170
Ouachita Mountains	34N 95W	154
Ougadougou, Burkina Faso (city, nat. cap.)	12N 2W	167
Owen Stanley Range	9S 148E	170
Ozark Plateau	37N 93W	154
Pachuca, Hidalgo (city, st. cap., Mex.)	20N 99W	155
Pacific Ocean	20N 115W	154
Pakistan (country)	25N 72E	164
Palawan (island)	10N 119E	163
Palmas, Cape	8N 8W	166
Palmas, Tocantins (city, st. cap., Braz.)	10S 49W	158
Palmer Archipelago	64S 63W	173
Palmer Land	71S 65W	173
Pamirs	32N 70E	163
Pampas	36S 73W	157
Panama (country)	10N 80W	155
Panama, Gulf of	10N 80W	157
Panama, Panama (city, nat. cap.)	9N 80W	155
Panay (island)	11N 122E	163
Pantanal	20S 58W	157
Papua New Guinea (country)	6S 144E	170
Papua, Gulf of	8S 144E	170
Pará (st., Brazil)	4S 54W	158
Paraguay (country)	23S 60W	158
Paraíba (st., Brazil)	6S 35W	158
Paramaribo, Suriname (city, nat. cap.)	5N 55W	158
Paraná (st., Brazil)	25S 55W	158
Paraná, Entre Rios (city, st. cap., Argen.)	32S 60W	158
Parana, Rio (riv., S.Am.)	20S 50W	157
Paranaiba, Rio (riv., S.Am.)	20S 55W	157
Paris, France (city, nat. cap.)	49N 2E	161
Pasadas, Misiones (city, st. cap., Argen.)	27S 56W	158
Patagonia	43S 70W	157
Peace (riv., N.Am.)	55N 120W	154
Pechora Basin	65N 58E	163
Pechora River	64N 58E	163
Peipas, Lake	59N 27E	160
Peloponnesus (peninsula)	37N 22E	160
Pempa (island)	5S 39E	166
Pennsylvania (st., US)	43N 80W	155
Pernambuco (st., Brazil)	7S 36W	158
Persian Gulf	28N 50E	163
Perth, W. Australia (city, st. cap., Aust.)	32S 116E	170
Peru (country)	10S 75W	158
Peshawar, Pakistan (city)	34N 72E	164
Philadelphia, PA (city)	40N 75W	155
Philippine Sea	15N 125E	163

NAME/DESCRIPTION	LATITUDE & LONGITUDE	PAGE
Philippines (country)	15N 120E	164
Phnom Penh, Cambodia (city, nat. cap.)	12N 105E	164
Phoenix, Arizona (city, st. cap., US)	33N 112W	155
Piauí (st., Brazil)	7S 44W	158
Pierre, South Dakota (city, st. cap., US)	44N 100W	155
Pietermaritzburg, South Africa (city)	30S 30E	167
Pittsburgh, PA (city)	40N 80W	155
Plateau of Iran	26N 60E	164
Plateau of Tibet	26N 85E	163
Platte (riv., N.Am.)	41N 105W	154
Po (riv., Europe)	45N 12E	160
Point Barrow	70N 156W	154
Poland (country)	54N 20E	161
Port Elizabeth, South Africa (city)	34S 26E	167
Port Lincoln, Aust. (city)	35S 135E	170
Port Moresby, Papua N. G. (city, nat. cap.)	10S 147E	170
Port Vila, Vanuatu (city, nat. cap.)	17S 169E	170
Port-au-Prince, Haiti (city, nat. cap.)	19N 72W	155
Portland, OR (city)	46N 123W	155
Porto Alegre, R. Gr. do Sul (city, st. cap., Braz.)	30S 51W	158
Porto Novo, Benin (city, nat. cap.)	7N 3E	167
Porto Velho, Rondonia (city, st. cap., Braz.)	9S 64W	158
Portugal (country)	38N 8W	161
Potosí, Bolivia (city)	20S 66W	158
Prague, Czechia (city, nat. cap.)	50N 14E	161
Pretoria, South Africa (city, nat. cap.)	26S 28E	167
Prince Charles Mountains	72S 67E	173
Prince Edward Island (island)	50N 67W	154
Prince Edward Island (prov., Can.)	50N 67W	155
Prince of Wales Island	73N 97W	154
Pripyat (riv., Europe)	52N 29E	160
Providence, Rhode Island (city, st. cap., US)	42N 71W	155
Puebla (st., Mex.)	18N 96W	155
Puebla, Puebla (city, st. cap., Mex.)	19N 98W	155
Puerto Monte, Chile (city)	42S 74W	158
Punta Negra	6S 81W	157
Purus, Rio (riv., S.Am.)	5S 68W	157
Putumayo, Rio (riv., S.Am.)	3S 74W	157
Pyongyang, Korea, North (city, nat. cap.)	39N 126E	164
Pyrenees Mountains	43N 2E	160
Qatar	25N 51E	164
Qilian Shan	39N 98E	163
Qingdao, China (city)	36N 120E	164
Qinling Mountains	33N 107E	163
Qizilqum	42N 65E	163
Quebec (prov., Can.)	52N 70W	155
Quebec, Quebec (city, prov. cap., Can.)	47N 71W	155
Queen Charlotte Islands	50N 130W	154

GEOGRAPHIC INDEX

NAME/DESCRIPTION	LATITUDE & LONGITUDE	PAGE
Queen Elizabeth Islands	75N 110W	154
Queensland (st., Aust.)	24S 145E	170
Querataro (st., Mex.)	22N 96W	155
Querataro, Querataro (city, st. cap., Mex.)	21N 100W	155
Quintana Roo (st., Mex.)	18N 88W	155
Quito, Ecuador (city, nat. cap.)	0 79W	158
Rabat, Morocco (city, nat. cap.)	34N 7W	167
Rainier, Mt. 14,410	48N 120W	154
Raleigh, North Carolina (city, st. cap., US)	36N 79W	155
Rangoon, Myanmar (Burma) (city, nat. cap.)	17N 96E	164
Rapid City, SD (city)	44N 103W	155
Rawalpindi, Pakistan (city)	34N 73E	164
Rawson, Chubuy (city, st. cap., Argen.)	43S 65W	158
Recife, Pernambuco (city, st. cap., Braz.)	8S 35W	158
Red (of the North) (riv., N.Am.)	50N 98W	158
Red Sea	20N 35E	166
Regina, Canada (city, prov. cap., Can.)	51N 104W	155
Reindeer Lake (lake, N.Am.)	57N 100W	154
Repulse Bay	22S 147E	170
Resistencia, Chaco (city, st. cap., Argen.)	27S 59W	158
Resolution Island	61N 65W	154
Réunion (island)	21S 55E	166
Reykjavik, Iceland (city, nat. cap.)	64N 22W	161
Rhine (riv., Europe)	50N 10E	160
Rhode Island (st., US)	42N 70W	155
Rhone (riv., Europe)	42N 8E	160
Richmond, Virginia (city, st. cap., US)	38N 77W	155
Riga, Gulf of	58N 24E	160
Riga, Latvia (city, nat. cap.)	57N 24E	161
Rio Branco, Acre (city, st. cap., Braz.)	10S 68W	158
Rio de Janeiro (st., Brazil)	22S 45W	158
Rio de Janeiro, R. de Jan. (city, st. cap., Braz.)	23S 43W	158
Rio de la Plata	35S 55W	157
Rio Gallegos, Santa Cruz (city, st. cap., Argen.)	52S 68W	158
Rio Grande (riv., N.Am.)	30N 100W	154
Rio Grande do Norte (st., Brazil)	5S 35W	158
Rio Grande do Sul (st., Brazil)	30S 55W	158
Río Negro (st., Argentina)	40S 70W	158
Riyadh, Saudi Arabia (city, nat. cap.)	25N 47E	164
Rockhampton, Aust. (city)	23S 150E	170
Rocky Mountains	50N 108W	154
Roebuck Bay	18S 125E	170
Romania (country)	46N 24E	161
Rome, Italy (city, nat. cap.)	42N 13E	161
Rondônia (st., Brazil)	12S 65W	158
Roper (riv., Australasia)	15S 135W	170
Roraima (st., Brazil)	2N 62W	158
Ros Dashen 15,158	12N 40E	166

NAME/DESCRIPTION	LATITUDE & LONGITUDE	PAGE
Rosario, Santa Fe (city, st. cap., Argen.)	33S 61W	158
Ross Ice Shelf	81S 174W	173
Ross Sea	77S 176W	173
Rostov na Donu, Russia (city)	47N 40E	164
Rotterdam, Netherlands (city)	52N 4E	161
Rub al Khali	20N 50E	164
Russia (country)	58N 56E	161
Ruvuma (riv., Africa)	12S 38E	166
Ruwenzori Mountains	0 30E	167
Rwanda (country)	3S 30E	167
Ryukyu Islands	27N 127E	163
Sacramento, California (city, st. cap., US)	39 121W	155
Sahara	18N 10E	166
Sahel	14N 10E	166
Sakhalin Island	50N 143E	163
Salem, Oregon (city, st. cap., US)	45N 123W	155
Salt Lake City, Utah (city, st. cap., US)	41N 112W	155
Salta (st., Argentina)	25S 70W	158
Salta, Salta (city, st. cap., Argen.)	25S 65W	158
Saltillo, Coahuila (city, st. cap., Mex.)	26N 101W	155
Salvador, Bahia (city, st. cap., Braz.)	13S 38W	158
Salween (riv., Asia)	18N 98E	163
Samar (island)	12N 124E	163
Samara, Russia (city)	53N 50E	161
Samarkand, Uzbekistan (city)	40N 67E	164
Samiland	68N 26E	160
San Antonio, TX (city)	29N 98W	155
San Cristobal (island)	12S 162E	169
San Diego, CA (city)	33N 117W	155
San Francisco, CA (city)	38N 122W	155
San Jorge, Gulf of	45S 68W	157
San Jose, Costa Rica (city, nat. cap.)	10N 84W	155
San Juan (st., Argentina)	30S 70W	158
San Juan, San Juan (city, st. cap., Arg.)	31S 68W	158
San Juan, San Juan (city, st. cap., Argen.)	18N 66W	158
San Luis (st., Argentina)	33S 66W	158
San Luis Potosi (st., Mex.)	22N 101W	155
San Luis Potosi, S. Luis P. (city, st. cap., Mex.)	22N 101W	155
San Luis, San Luis (st., Argentina)	33S 66W	158
San Marino (country)	43N 12E	161
San Marino, San Marino (city, nat. cap.)	43N 12E	161
San Matias Gulf	43S 65W	157
San Salvador, El Salvador (city, nat. cap.)	14N 89W	155
Sanaa, Yemen (city, nat. cap.)	16N 44E	164
Santa Catarina (st., Brazil)	28S 50W	158
Santa Cruz (st., Argentina)	50S 70W	158
Santa Cruz Islands	8S 168E	170
Santa Fe (st., Argentina)	30S 62W	158

GEOGRAPHIC INDEX

NAME/DESCRIPTION	LATITUDE & LONGITUDE	PAGE
Santa Fe de Bogotá Colombia (city, nat. cap.)	5N 74W	158
Santa Fe, New Mexico (city, st. cap., US)	35N 106W	155
Santa Isabel (island)	8S 159E	169
Santa Rosa, La Pampa (city, st. cap., Argen.)	37S 64W	158
Santiago del Estero (st., Argentina)	25S 65W	158
Santiago, Chile (city, nat. cap.)	33S 71W	158
Santiago, Sant. del Estero (city, st. cap., Argen.)	28S 64W	158
Santo Domingo, Dominican Rep. (city, nat. cap.)	18N 70W	155
Santos, Brazil (city)	24S 46W	158
Saõ Francisco, Rio (riv., S.Am.)	10S 40W	157
São Luis, Maranhao (city, st. cap., Braz.)	3S 43W	158
São Paulo (st., Brazil)	22S 50W	158
São Paulo, São Paulo (city, st. cap., Braz.)	24S 47W	158
Sarajevo, Bosnia-Herz. (city, nat. cap.)	43N 18E	161
Sardinia (island)	40N 10E	160
Sarmiento, Mt. 8,100	55S 72W	157
Saskatchewan (riv., N.Am.)	52N 108W	154
Saudi Arabia (country)	25N 50E	164
Savannah, GA (city)	32N 81W	155
Sayan Range	45N 90E	164
Scandanavia (peninsula)	63N 15E	160
Scotia Sea	57S 40W	173
Sea of Marmara	41N 28E	160
Seattle, WA (city)	48N 122W	155
Seelig, Mount 9,915	82S 104W	173
Seine (riv., Europe)	49N 3E	160
Senegal (country)	15N 15W	167
Senegal (riv., Africa)	15N 15W	166
Seoul, Korea, South (city, nat. cap.)	38N 127E	164
Sepik (riv., Australasia)	4S 142E	170
Serbia and Montenegro	44N 20E	161
Sergipe (st., Brazil)	12S 36W	158
Sev Dvina (riv., Asia)	60N 50E	164
Severnaya Zemlya (island)	80N 88E	163
Seville, Spain (city)	37N 6W	161
Shackleton Ice Shelf	66S 100E	173
Shanghai, China (city)	31N 121E	164
Shelikov Gulf	60N 158E	163
Shenyang, China (city)	42N 123E	164
Shetland Islands	60N 5W	160
Shikoku (island)	34N 130E	163
Shiraz, Iran (city)	30N 52E	164
Sicily (island)	38N 14E	160
Sidley, Mount 13,717	77S 126W	173
Sierra Leone (country)	6N 14W	167
Sierra Madre Occidental	27N 108W	154
Sierra Madre Oriental	27N 100W	154
Sierra Nevada	38N 120W	154

NAME/DESCRIPTION	LATITUDE & LONGITUDE	PAGE
Sikhote Range	45N 135E	163
Simpson Desert	25S 136E	169
Sinai Peninsula	28N 33E	166
Sinaloa (st., Mex.)	25N 110W	155
Singapore (city, nat. cap.)	1N 104E	164
Singapore (island)	1N 104E	163 inset
Skagerrak, Strait of	58N 8E	160
Skopje, Macedonia (city, nat. cap.)	42N 21E	161
Slovakia (country)	50N 20E	161
Slovenia (country)	47N 14E	161
Socotra (island)	12N 54E	166
Sofia, Bulgaria (city, nat. cap.)	43N 23E	161
Solomon Islands (country)	7S 160E	170
Somalia (country)	5N 45E	167
Sonora (st., Mex.)	30N 110W	155
South Africa (country)	30S 25E	167
South Australia (st., Aust.)	30S 125E	170
South Cape	8S 150E	170
South Carolina (st., US)	33N 79W	155
South China Sea	15N 115E	163
South China Sea	15N 115E	163
South Dakota (st., US)	45N 100W	155
South Georgia (island)	55S 40W	173
South Island	45S 170E	169
South Magnetic Pole	64S 138E	173
South Pole	90S 0	173
Southampton Island	68N 86W	154
Southern Alps	45S 170E	170
Southwest Cape	47S 167E	170
Spain (country)	38N 4W	161
Spokane, WA (city)	48N 117W	155
Springfield, Illinois (city, st. cap., US)	40N 90W	155
Sri Lanka (country)	8N 80E	164
Srinagar, India (city)	34N 75E	164
St. Helena (island)	16S 5W	166
St. John's, Nwfndlnd (city, prov. cap., Can.)	48N 53W	155
St. Lawrence (riv., N.Am.)	50N 65W	154
St. Lawrence, Gulf of	50N 65W	154
St. Louis, MO (city)	39N 90W	155
St. Marie, Cape	25S 45E	167
St. Paul, Minnesota (city, st. cap., US)	45N 93W	155
St. Petersburg, Russia (city)	60N 30E	161
Stanovoy Range	55N 125E	163
Stavanger, Norway (city)	59N 6E	161
Steep Point	25S 115E	170
Stewart Island	47S 167E	169
Stockholm, Sweden (city, nat. cap.)	59N 18E	161
Stuart Range	32S 135E	170

GEOGRAPHIC INDEX

NAME/DESCRIPTION	LATITUDE & LONGITUDE	PAGE	NAME/DESCRIPTION	LATITUDE & LONGITUDE	PAGE
Sturge Island	67S 164E	173	Tennant Creek, Aust. (city)	19S 134E	170
Stuttgart, Germany (city)	49N 9E	161	Tennessee (st., US)	37N 88W	155
Sucre, Bolivia (city)	19S 65W	158	Tepic, Nayarit (city, st. cap., Mex.)	22N 105W	155
Sudan (country)	10N 30E	167	Teresina, Piaui (city, st. cap., Braz.)	5S 43W	158
Sulaiman Range	28N 70E	164	Terre Adélie	66S 136E	173
Sulu Islands	8N 120E	164	Texas (st., US)	30N 95W	155
Sulu Sea	10N 120E	164	Thailand (country)	15N 105E	164
Sumatra (island)	0 100E	163 inset	Thailand, Gulf of	10N 105E	163
Sumba (island)	10S 120E	163	Thames (riv., Europe)	52N 4W	160
Sumbawa (island)	8S 116E	163	The Hague, Netherlands (city, nat. cap.)	52N 4E	161
Superior, Lake (lake, N.Am.)	50N 90W	154	Thimphu, Bhutan (city, nat. cap.)	28N 90E	164
Surabaya, Java (Indonesia) (city)	7S 113E	170	Thurston Island	72S 99W	173
Suriname (country)	5N 55W	158	Tianjin, China (city)	39N 117E	164
Svalbard Islands	75N 20E	163	Tiber (riv., Europe)	42N 13E	160
Swan (riv., Australasia)	34S 115E	170	Tibest Mountains	20N 20E	166
Sweden (country)	62N 16E	161	Tien Shan	40N 80E	163
Switzerland (country)	46N 8E	161	Tierra del Fuego (island)	54S 68W	157
Sydney, N.S.Wales (city, st. cap., Aust.)	34S 151E	170	Tierra del Fuego (st., Argentina)	54S 68W	158
Syr Darya (riv., Asia)	36N 65E	163	Tigris (riv., Asia)	37N 40E	163
Syria (country)	37N 36E	164	Timor (island)	7S 126E	169
Tabasco (st., Mex.)	16N 90W	155	Timor Sea	11S 125E	169
Tabriz, Iran (city)	38N 46E	164	Timor-Leste (country)	8S 125E	164 inset
Tagus (riv., Europe)	40N 6W	160	Tirane, Albania (city, nat. cap.)	41N 20E	161
Taipei, Taiwan (city, nat. cap.)	25N 121E	164	Tisza (riv., Europe)	49N 21E	160
Taiwan (country)	25N 122E	164	Titicaca, Lake (lake, S.Am.)	15S 70W	157
Taiwan Strait	25N 120E	163	Tlaxcala (st., Mex.)	20N 96W	155
Tajikistan (country)	35N 75E	164	Tlaxcala, Tlaxcala (city, st. cap., Mex.)	19N 98W	155
Taklimakan Desert	37N 90E	163	Toamasino, Madagascar (city)	18S 49E	167
Tallahassee, Florida (city, st. cap., US)	30N 84W	155	Tocantins (st., Brazil)	12S 50W	158
Tallinn, Estonia (city, nat. cap.)	59N 25E	161	Tocantins, Rio (riv., S.Am.)	5S 50W	157
Tamaulipas (st., Mex.)	25N 95W	155	Togo (country)	8N 1E	167
Tampico, Mexico (city)	22N 98W	155	Tokyo, Japan (city, nat. cap.)	36N 140E	164
Tanganyika, Lake	5S 30E	166	Toliara, Madagascar (city)	23S 44E	167
Tanggula Shan	33N 91E	163	Toluca, Mexico (city, st. cap., Mex.)	19N 100W	155
Tanimbar Islands	8S 135E	163 inset	Tombouctou, Mali (city)	24N 3W	167
Tanzania (country)	8S 35E	167	Tomsk, Russia (city)	56N 85E	164
Tapajos, Rio (riv., S.Am.)	5S 55W	157	Tonkin, Gulf of	20N 108E	163
Tarim Basin	37N 85E	163	Topeka, Kansas (city, st. cap., US)	39N 96W	155
Tashkent, Uzbekistan (city, nat. cap.)	41N 69E	164	Toronto, Ontario (city, prov. cap., Can.)	44N 79W	155
Tasman Sea	38S 160E	169	Toros Mountains	37N 45E	163
Tasmania (island)	42S 145E	169	Torrens, Lake	33S 136W	170
Tasmania (st., Aust.)	42S 145E	170	Torres Strait	10S 142E	170
Tatar Strait	50N 142E	163	Townsville, Aust. (city)	19S 146E	170
Tbilisi, Georgia (city, nat. cap.)	42N 45E	161	Transantarctic Mountains	85S 150E	173
Teguicigalpa, Honduras (city, nat. cap.)	14N 87W	155	Trenton, New Jersey (city, st. cap., US)	40N 75W	155
Tehran, Iran (city, nat. cap.)	36N 51E	164	Trinidad and Tobago (country)	9N 60W	158
Tel Aviv, Israel (city)	32N 35E	161	Tripoli, Libya (city, nat. cap.)	33N 13E	167
Ténéré	17N 11E	166	Tristan Da Cunha (island)	37S 12W	172

GEOGRAPHIC INDEX

NAME/DESCRIPTION	LATITUDE & LONGITUDE	PAGE	NAME/DESCRIPTION	LATITUDE & LONGITUDE	PAGE
Trujillo, Peru (city)	8S 79W	158	Vattern, Lake	56N 12E	160
Tucson, AZ (city)	32N 111W	155	Venezuela (country)	5N 65W	158
Tucuman (st., Argentina)	25S 65W	158	Venice, Italy (city)	45N 12E	161
Tucuman, Tucuman (city, st. cap., Argen.)	27S 65W	158	Veracruz (st., Mex.)	20N 97W	155
Tunis, Tunisia (city, nat. cap.)	37N 10E	167	Veracruz, Mexico (city)	19N 96W	155
Tunisia (country)	34N 9E	167	Verkhoyansk Range	65N 126E	163
Turin, Italy (city)	45N 8E	161	Verkhoyanskiy Range	65N 130E	163
Turkana, Lake	3N 34E	166	Vermont (st., US)	45N 73W	155
Turkey (country)	39N 32E	161	Vert, Cape	15N 17W	167
Turkmenistan (country)	39N 56E	164	Viangchan, Laos (city, nat. cap.)	18N 103E	164
Turku, Finland (city)	60N 22E	161	Victoria (riv., Australasia)	15S 130E	170
Tuxtla Gutierrez, Chiapas (city, st. cap., Mex.)	17N 93W	155	Victoria (st., Aust.)	37S 145W	170
Tyrrhenian Sea	40N 12E	160	Victoria Falls	18S 26E	166
Ubangi (riv., Africa)	0 20E	166	Victoria Island	71N 110W	154
Ucayali, Rio (riv., S.Am.)	7S 75W	157	Victoria Riv. Downs, Aust. (city)	17S 131E	170
Uele (riv., Africa)	3N 25E	166	Victoria, B.C. (city, prov. cap., Can.)	48N 123W	155
Uganda (country)	3N 30E	167	Victoria, Lake	3S 35E	166
Ukraine (country)	53N 32E	161	Viedma, Rio Negro (city, st. cap., Argen.)	41S 63W	158
Ulan Bator, Mongolia (city, nat. cap.)	47N 107E	164	Vienna, Austria (city, nat. cap.)	48N 16E	161
Uliastay, Mongolia (city)	48N 97E	164	Vietnam (country)	10N 110E	164
Ungava Peninsula	60N 72W	154	Villahermosa, Tabasco (city, st. cap., Mex.)	18N 93W	155
Ungava Peninsula	59N 72W	154	Vilnius, Lithuania (city, nat. cap.)	55N 25E	161
United Arab Emirates (country)	25N 55E	164	Vilyuy (riv., Asia)	63N 115E	163
United Kingdom (country)	54N 4W	161	Vinson Massif 16,864	78S 85W	173
United States (country)	40N 100W	155	Virginia (st., US)	35N 78W	155
Uppsala, Sweden (city)	60N 18E	161	Vistula (riv., Europe)	50N 22E	160
Ural (riv., Asia)	45N 55E	163	Viti Levu (island)	17S 178E	169
Ural Mountains	50N 60E	163	Vitoria, Espiritu Santo (city, st. cap., Braz.)	20S 40W	158
Uruguay (country)	37S 67W	158	Vladivostok, Russia (city)	43N 132E	164
Uruguay, Rio (riv., S.Am.)	30S 57W	157	Volga (riv., Russia)	46N 46E	160
Ürümqi, China (city)	44N 88E	164	Volgograd, Russia (city)	54N 44E	161
Utah (st., US)	38N 110W	155	Volta (riv., Africa)	10N 15E	167
Uzbekistan (country)	42N 58E	164	Volta, Lake	8N 2W	166
Vaal (riv., Africa)	27S 27E	167	Vosges Mountains	48N 7E	160
Vaduz, Lietch. (city, nat. cap.)	47N 9E	161	Walgreen Coast	75S 107W	173
Valdivia, Chile (city)	40S 73W	158	Walvis Bay, Namibia (city)	23S 14E	167
Valencia, Spain (city)	39N 0	161	Warsaw, Poland (city, nat. cap.)	52N 21E	161
Valencia, Venezuela (city)	10N 68W	158	Warta (riv., Europe)	52N 16E	160
Valladolid, Spain (city)	41N 4W	161	Washington (st., US)	48N 122W	155
Valparaiso, Chile (city)	33S 72W	158	Washington, D.C., United States (city, nat. cap.)	39N 77W	155
van Diemen, Cape	11S 130E	170	Wellington, New Zealand (city, nat. cap.)	41S 175E	170
van Rees Mountains	4S 140E	170	West Cape Howe	36S 115E	170
Vancouver Island	50N 130W	154	West Siberian Lowland	60N 80E	163
Vancouver, Canada (city)	49N 123W	155	West Virginia (st., US)	38N 80W	155
Vanern, Lake	60N 12E	160	Western Australia (st., Aust.)	25S 122W	170
Vanua Levu (island)	16S 179E	169	Western Dvina (riv., Europe)	64N 42E	160
Vanuatu (country)	15S 167E	170	Western Ghats	15N 72E	163
Vatican City (country)	41N 12E	161	Western Sahara (country)	25N 13W	167

GEOGRAPHIC INDEX

NAME/DESCRIPTION	LATITUDE & LONGITUDE	PAGE	NAME/DESCRIPTION	LATITUDE & LONGITUDE	PAGE
White Nile (riv., Africa)	13N 30E	166	Yekaterinburg, Russia (city)	57N 61E	161
White Sea	64N 36E	160	Yellow Sea	35N 122E	163
Whitney, Mt. 14,494	33N 118W	154	Yellowknife, N.W.T. (city, terr. cap., Can.)	62N 115W	155
Wichita, KS (city)	38N 97W	155	Yellowstone (riv., N.Am.)	46N 110W	154
Wilkes Land	71S 120E	173	Yemen (country)	15N 50E	164
Windhoek, Namibia (city, nat. cap.)	22S 17E	167	Yenisey (riv., Asia)	68N 85E	163
Winnipeg, Lake (lake, N.Am.)	50N 100W	154	Yerevan, Armenia (city, nat. cap.)	40N 44E	161
Winnipeg, Manitoba (city, prov. cap., Can.)	53N 98W	155	Yokohama, Japan (city)	36N 140E	164
Wisconsin (st., US)	50N 90W	155	Yucatan (st., Mex.)	20N 88W	155
Wollongong, Aust. (city)	34S 151E	170	Yucatan Peninsula	20N 88W	154
Woomera, Aust. (city)	32S 137E	170	Yukon (riv., N.Am.)	63N 150W	154
Wuhan, China (city)	30N 114E	164	Zacatecas (st., Mex.)	23N 103W	155
Wyndham, Australia (city)	16S 129E	170	Zacatecas, Zacatecas (city, st. cap., Mex.)	23N 103W	155
Wyoming (st., US)	45N 110W	155	Zagreb, Croatia (city, nat. cap.)	46N 16E	161
Xaafuun, Cape of	11N 51E	166	Zagros Mountains	27N 52E	163
Xalapa, Vera Cruz (city, st. cap., Mex.)	20N 97W	155	Zambezi (riv., Africa)	18S 30E	166
Xingu, Rio (riv., S.Am.)	5S 54W	157	Zambia (country)	15S 25E	167
Yablonovyy Range	50N 100E	163	Zanzibar (island)	5S 39E	166
Yakutsk, Russia (city)	62N 130E	164	Zimbabwe (country)	20S 30E	167
Yamoussoukro , Côte d'Ivoire (city)	7N 4W	167			
Yangtze (Chang Jiang) (riv., Asia)	30N 108W	163			
Yaoundé, Cameroon (city, nat. cap.)	4N 12E	167			

Sources

Amnesty International. Online access at www.amnesty.org.

Asia-Pacific Economic Organization (APEC). Online access at www.apecsec.org.

Bercovitch, J., and R. Jackson. (1997). *International conflict: A chronological encyclopedia of conflicts and their management 1945–1995.* Washington, DC: Congressional Quarterly.

Boden, Tom, Gregg Marland, and Robert J. Andrew (2009) *National CO2 emissions from fossil-fuel burning, cement manufacture, and gas flaring: 1751–2006.* Carbon Dioxide Information Analysis Center. Oak Ridge National Laboratory. Online access at http://cdiac .ornl.gov.

BP Statistical Review of World Energy. Online access at: http://www.bp.com/bpstats.

Canadian Forces College, Information Resources Centre. Online access at: http://www.cfcsc.dnd. ca/links/wars/index.html.

Central Intelligence Agency. *The world factbook, 2009.* https://www.cia.gov/library/publications/ the-world-factbook/.

Cohen, Saul. (2002). *Geopolitics of the world system.* Lanham, MD: Rowman & Littlefield.

Commonwealth of Independent States (CIS). Online access at: www.cis.minsk.by/english.

Crabb, C. (1993, January). Soiling the planet. *Discover, 14* (1), 74–75.

de Blij, H.J. and Peter O Muller. *Geography: realms, regions, and concepts, 12th edition.* Hoboken, NJ: John Wiley & Sons, Inc.

Domke, K. (1988). *War and the changing global system.* New Haven, CT: Yale University Press.

Economic Community of West African States (ECOWAS). Online access at: www.state.gov.

European Free Trade Association (EFTA). Online access at www.efta.int.

The European Union (EU). Online access at: www.europa.eu.int.

Food and Agricultural Organization of the United Nations (FAO). Online access at www.fao.org.

Freedom House. Online access at www.freedomhouse.org.

Goode's world atlas. (1995, 19th ed.). New York: Rand McNally.

The Greater Caribbean Community (CARICOM). Online access at: www.caricom.org.

Gunnemark, Erik V., *Countries, peoples and their languages.* Gothenburg, Sweden: The Geolinguistic Handbook (n.d., early 1990s).

Hammond atlas of the world. (1993). Maplewood, NJ: Hammond.

Information please almanac, atlas, and yearbook 2002. (2002). Boston & New York: Houghton Mifflin.

International Energy Agency. (2001). *Key world energy statistics 2000.* Paris. Online access: http:// www.iea.org/statist/keyword/keystats.htm.

Johnson, D. (1977). *Population, society, and desertification.* New York: United Nations Conference on Desertification, United Nations Environment Programme.

Köppen, W., & Geiger, R. (1954). *Klima der erde* [Climate of the earth]. Darmstadt, Germany: Justus Perthes.

Lindeman, M. (1990). *The United States and the Soviet Union: Choices for the 21st century.* Guilford, CT: Dushkin Publishing Group.

Murphy, R. E. (1968). Landforms of the world [Map supplement No. 9]. *Annals of the Association of American Geographers, 58* (1), 198–200.

National Oceanic and Atmospheric Administration. (1990–1992). Unpublished data. Washington, DC: NOAA.

North Atlantic Treaty Organization (NATO). Online access at: www.nato.int.

The *New York Times.* Online access at: http://archives.nytimes.com/archives/.

The Peace Corps. Online access at www.peacecorps.gov.

Population Reference Bureau (2001). *World population data sheet.* New York: Population Reference Bureau.

Rourke, J. T. (2003). *International politics on the world stage* (9th ed.). Guilford, CT: McGraw-Hill/Dushkin.

Southern African Development Community (SADC). Online access at www.sadc.int.

Southern Cone Common Market (Mercosur). Online access at http://www.infoplease.com/ce6/ history/A0846059.html.

Spector, L. S., & Smith, J. R. (1990). *Nuclear ambitions: The spread of nuclear weapons.* Boulder, CO: Westview Press.

Time atlas of world history. (1978). London.

United Nations Development Programme (UNDP, 2001). *Human development indicators, human development report 2001.* New York: Oxford University Press. Online access at: http://www.undp.org/hdr2001/back.pdf.

United Nations Food and Agriculture Organization. *FAOSTAT database.* Online access at: http://apps.fao.org/page/collections?subset=agriculture.

United Nations High Commissioner for Refugees, Population Data Unit, Population and Geographic Data Section. (2009) Online access at http://www.unhcr.org/.

United Nations Population Division. *World population prospects: The 2002 revision.* Online access at: http://www.un.org/esa/population/unpop.htm.

United Nations Population Fund. (2000). *The state of the world's population.* New York: United Nations Population Fund.

United Nations Statistics Division, Department of Economic and Social Affairs. (2001). *Social indicators.* Online access at: http://www.un.org/depts/unsd/social/index.htm.

Uranium Institute. Online access at: http://www.uilondon.org/safetab.htm.

U.S. Arms Control and Disarmament Agency. (1993). *World military expenditures and arms transfers.* Washington, DC: U.S. Government Printing Office.

U.S. Census Bureau. (2000). *International database, United States Census Bureau.* Online access at: http://www.census.gov/ipc/www/idbnew.html.

U.S. Central Intelligence Agency, Office of Public Affairs. 2001. *The world factbook.* Washington, DC. Online access at: http://www.odci.gov/cia/publications/factbook/.

U.S. Department of State, (1999) Undersecretary for Arms Control and International Security. *World military expenditures and arms transfers.* Online access at: http://www.state.gov/www/global/arms/bureau_ac/wmeat98/wmeat98.html.

USDA Forest Service. (1989). *Ecoregions of the continents.* Washington, DC: U.S. Government Printing Office.

Watts, Ronald K. (1999). *Comparing federal systems*, 2nd ed. Queens University Press, Kingston, Ont.

The world almanac and book of facts 2001. (2000). Mahwah, NJ: World Almanac Books.

World Bank. *World development indicators, 2003.* Washington, DC.

World Bank. *World development indicators 2001.* Washington, DC. World Bank. Online access at: http://www.worldbank.org/data/.

World Bank. (2001). *World development report 2000/2001: Attacking poverty.* New York: Oxford University Press.

World Health Organization. (1998). *World health statistics annual.* Geneva: World Health Organization.

World Resources Institute. (2000). *World resources 2000–2001. People and ecosystems: The fraying web of life.* Washington, DC: World Resources Institute: Online access at: http://www.wri.org.

World Trade Organization (WTO). Online access at: www.wto.org.

Wright, John W., ed. 2003. *The New York Times almanac 2003.* New York: Penguin Reference.